American University Studies

Series IX
History

Vol. 197

PETER LANG
New York • Washington, D.C./Baltimore • Bern
Frankfurt am Main • Berlin • Brussels • Vienna • Oxford

The King's Towns

Lorraine Attreed

The King's Towns

Identity and Survival in Late Medieval English Boroughs

PETER LANG
New York • Washington, D.C./Baltimore • Bern
Frankfurt am Main • Berlin • Brussels • Vienna • Oxford

Library of Congress Cataloging-in-Publication Data

Attreed, Lorraine Christine.
The king's towns: identity and survival
in late medieval English boroughs / Lorraine Attreed.
p. cm. — (American university studies. Series IX, History; vol. 197)
Includes bibliographical references and index.
1. Cities and towns, Medieval—England—History. 2. England—Social life
and customs—1066—1485. 3. England—Economic conditions—
1066—1485. 4. Civilization, Medieval. I. Title. II. Series.
HT115 .A76   307.76'0942'0902—dc21   00-056406
ISBN 0-8204-5163-0
ISSN 0740-0462

Die Deutsche Bibliothek-CIP-Einheitsaufnahme

Attreed, Lorraine:
The king's towns: identity and survival
in late medieval English boroughs / Lorraine Attreed.
–New York; Washington, D.C./Baltimore; Bern;
Frankfurt am Main; Berlin; Brussels; Vienna; Oxford: Lang.
(American university studies: Ser. 9, History; Vol. 197)
ISBN 0-8204-5163-0

Cover design by Lisa Dillon

The paper in this book meets the guidelines for permanence and durability
of the Committee on Production Guidelines for Book Longevity
of the Council of Library Resources.

Printed in the United States of America

For
Charles Julian Bishko

and in memory of
Lucretia Ramsay Bishko

TABLE OF CONTENTS

TABLES

ACKNOWLEDGMENTS

I am grateful to the following archives and record offices for allowing me access to the documents and for providing help and advice during my visits: British Library, London; Dean and Chapter Archives, Exeter; Devon Record Office, Exeter; Norfolk Record Office, Norwich; Nottinghamshire Record Office, Nottingham; Public Record Office, London; Record Office, House of Lords, London; York City Archives, York.

I have been fortunate to receive financial support for this project from a number of agencies. In 1992, a National Endowment for the Humanities Travel to Collections grant allowed me to check various references in York and Exeter. Between 1991 and 1993, the College of the Holy Cross provided several Research and Publication grants for help with manuscript preparation and travel to archives. During the Fall 1997 semester, a Faculty Fellowship research leave allowed me time off from teaching for final revisions on the manuscript.

Parts of this work were previously published in other forms, although all have been rewritten and reconceptualized. Part of Chapter Three was published as "The Politics of Welcome—Ceremonies and Constitutional Development in Later Medieval English Towns," in *City and Spectacle in Medieval Europe*, ed. Barbara Hanawalt (Minneapolis, University of Minnesota Press, 1994), pp. 208–31. A version of Chapter Five appeared as "Poverty, Payments, and Fiscal Policies in English Provincial Towns," in *Portraits of Medieval Living: Essays in Memory of David Herlihy*, edited by Samuel K. Cohn Jr. and Steven A. Epstein (Ann Arbor: University of Michigan Press, 1996), pp. 325–48. Elements of Chapter Eight were published in "Arbitration and the Growth of Urban Liberties in Late Medieval England," *Journal of British Studies*, 31 (1992), 205–35. I am grateful to the two presses and to the *Journal*'s editor for permitting me to use this material.

The photograph on the front cover is my own work, taken during the summer of 2000, depicting part of the fourteenth-century décor of the west front of the cathedral of St.-Étienne, Auxerre, France.   The idealized cityscape decorating the arcading could be Auxerre itself, but is more likely to be a view of Jerusalem or the heavenly city, a model for urban development that all town governors tried to attain.

Many scholars provided advice and encouragement along the way, although I take full responsibility for my errors of fact and judgment. Assistance came from Anne Crawford, Charles Donahue, David Dunlop, Christian Liddy, W. Mark Ormrod, and Susan Reynolds. In addition, Maryanne Kowaleski gave me valuable critiques of my writing at various stages. David Palliser offered encouragement and opportunities for me to share my work with other scholars. Steven Ozment contributed unsentimental support at a critical time. No one has been more generous than R. B. Dobson, both when I was his student and in the years that followed. Peter and Carolyn Hammond have provided valued friendship and incisive criticism for over twenty years. Juanita Knapp furnished me with numerous articles I could not obtain in my own country, and always had confidence in my achievements. But most important, James F. Powers is the heart and soul of all my work, and slays all the dragons that threaten production. He knows better than anyone else the reason for the dedication of this book. Unlike my husband, I did not have the privilege of being taught by Julian Bishko. Nevertheless, I believe I have learned from him a great deal about the highest standards of scholarship he and his work embody. Julian and Lucretia welcomed me with warmth and friendship from our first meeting, and it is with gratitude that I dedicate this volume to them.

ABBREVIATIONS

B.L.   British Library

C.   Chancery

CChR   *Calendar of Charter Rolls preserved in the Public Record Office, Vols. 3–6.* London: HMSO, 1908–27.

CCR   *Calendar of Close Rolls, etc., 1377–1509.* London: HMSO, 1914–63.

CFR   *Calendar of Fine Rolls, etc., 1377–1509.* London: HMSO, 1926–62.

CPR   *Calendar of Patent Rolls, etc., 1377–1509.* London: HMSO, 1895–1916.

Complete Peerage   Cokayne, G. E., *et al.*, eds. *The Complete Peerage of England, Scotland, Ireland, and the United Kingdom.* 12 vols. in 13. London: St. Catherine Press, 1910–59. Vol. 14, Addenda and Corrigenda. Peter W. Hammond, ed. Stroud: Sutton Publishing, 1998.

CP.   Common Pleas

D.C.A.   Dean and Chapter Archives, Exeter

Dobson, *Chamberlains' Accounts*   Dobson, R. B., ed. *York City Chamberlains' Account Rolls 1396–1500.* Surtees Society, vol. 192. Gateshead, 1980.

D.N.B. — Stephen, Leslie, *et al.*, eds. *Dictionary of National Biography*. 22 vols. 1917; reprint, London: Oxford University Press, 1921–22.

D.R.O. — Devon Record Office, Exeter

E. — Exchequer

Hoker, *Description of the Citie* — Hoker, John (alias Vowell). *The Description of the Citie of Excester*. 3 vols. Edited by W. J. Harte, J. W. Schopp, H. Tapley-Soper. Devon and Cornwall Record Society. Exeter, 1919, 1947.

JI. — Justices Itinerant

KB. — King's Bench

Miller, *VCH* — Miller, E. "Medieval York." In *The Victoria History of the Counties of England: A History of Yorkshire: The City of York*, ed. P. M. Tillott, 25–116. London: Oxford University Press, 1961.

Norwich Records — Hudson, William, and John C. Tingey, eds. *The Records of the City of Norwich*. 2 vols. London and Norwich: Jarrold and Sons Ltd., 1906, 1910.

Nott. Records — Stevenson, W. H., ed. *Records of the Borough of Nottingham*. 5 vols. London: Bernard Quaritch, 1882–1900.

N.R.O. — Norfolk Record Office, Norwich

n.s. — new series

Nt.R.O. — Nottinghamshire Record Office, Nottingham

o.s. — old series

P.R.O.	Public Record Office, London
PSO.	Privy Seal Office
Rot. Parl.	Strachey, John, ed. *Rotuli Parliamentorum.* 6 vols. London, 1767–77.
Rymer, *Foedera*	Rymer, Thomas, ed. *Foedera, Conventiones, Letterae....* 10 vols. 3d ed. The Hague: John Neaulme, 1739–45.
SC.	Special Collections
STAC.	Star Chamber
Statutes of the Realm	Luders, A., *et al.*, eds. *Statutes of the Realm.* 11 vols. London: Dawsons of Pall Mall for the Record Commission, 1810–28.
Y.C.A.	York City Archives, York
York Civic Records	Raine, Angelo, ed. *York Civic Records, Volumes 2–5.* Yorkshire Archaeological Society Record Series, vols. 103, 106, 108, 110. Leeds, 1941, 1942. 1945, 1946.
York House Books	Attreed, Lorraine C., ed. *The York House Books, 1461–1490.* 2 vols. Gloucester, England, and Wolfeboro, N.H.: Alan Sutton Publishing, for the Yorkist History Trust, 1991.
York Mem. Bk.	Sellers, Maud, ed. *York Memorandum Book: Part I (1376–1419), Part II (1388–1493).* Surtees Society, vols. 120, 125. London and Durham, 1912, 1915.

PART ONE
INTRODUCTION

The vitality of medieval town life is a challenging concept to communicate to modern readers. In an age when urban is inevitably associated with decay, the idea of towns as centers of wealth, intellectual activity, international contacts and economic opportunity is as foreign as the concept of medieval itself. It is also true that English towns outside of London contained only a small portion of the population, in centers holding several thousand souls in even the largest boroughs, and thus cannot account for the most common experiences of medieval subjects. Yet for all their failures of hygiene, pleas of poverty, and outbreaks of violence from both internal and external causes, medieval towns embodied political philosophies of self-determination as well as ideals of social and economic advancement which remain recognizable today.

The present work studies royal boroughs, no anomaly during the Middle Ages. Almost half of all English towns, and nearly all of the largest and most prosperous urban centers, were royal towns which owed their privileges to the Crown. Sheltering nearly a fifth of the island's total population and a more considerable portion of its wealth, these towns acted as centers of authority delegated to them by the royal government in order to contribute to the realm's peace. Monarchs made them responsible for a significant share of the realm's peacekeeping, defense, judicial process, and financial services. How they behaved and developed under such a directive during the challenging economic climate following the first bouts of plague is the theme of this book.

What follows is a comparative study, tracking the development of four towns through the reigns of eight kings, from whom came most of the boroughs' liberties and privileges. Many fine studies have been written about single English towns, or restricted time periods within regional society, and these works have contributed valuable insights to the following study. But this project has a much broader scope, not only geographically and chronologically. No other study has looked so closely at the royal government's relations with the towns it brought into existence and constitutionally nurtured, focusing on the late medieval and early modern period as English society struggled to recover from the effects of the Black Death. The work expands our knowledge of political development, legal structures, and social relations of medieval England.

This is also the study of the formation of identity, as civic officials and townspeople learned to live with and exercise the liberties they had achieved in previous centuries and continued to acquire. It examines the delicate balance between relying upon the royal government, the source of one's privileges, and making independent decisions based on self-defined needs. At no time did England suffer the extreme violence and hostilities that marked European towns' relations with their overlords, secular or ecclesiastical. Nevertheless, English towns, their officers, and their residents faced considerable challenges, made harsher by the economic environment of the period. They sought and created an identity separate from the Crown, from rural society, and from ecclesiastical and other corporate bodies neighboring them. As basic liberties of self-government were achieved, the boroughs gained confidence to work for the enlargement and strengthening of both physical size and constitutional privileges.

The four towns have been carefully chosen to maximize in-depth comparisons. York, Norwich, Exeter and Nottingham allow for comparisons in geographic setting, population size, industrial specialization, levels of wealth, and direction of economic forces. York, almost two hundred miles north of London, was considered by contemporaries to be of cultural and economic importance second only to the capital. Its hold on this status was precarious, however, as its post-plague population of c.10,000 declined during the fifteenth century, and its golden age as a major textile and distribution center and international trading port ended by 1450. By the late fifteenth century, Norwich had assumed York's elevated position with a population of over 12,000 and wealth based on profitable cloth manufacture and export. The East Anglian provincial capital is also interesting for the ferocity of its internal politics in the mid-fifteenth century, characterized by citizens' social conflicts exacerbated by the interference of local nobles acting more in their own interests than on behalf of the Crown. Like Norwich, Exeter's brightest economic prospects lay in the near future. The southwestern port's population did not top eight thousand before the sixteenth century, when cloth manufacture and export boomed. In the years of our study, it was a quiet port and county town on the brink of prosperity. Untroubled by financial worries, it nonetheless suffered an uneasy relationship with a local nobleman and his family which forced civic officials into creative responses designed to chart a safe course through the political turbulence of the times. The town of Nottingham completes the picture, a small borough of little over two thousand souls whose central location nevertheless gave it a strategic military and mercantile importance beyond its size. Its legal privileges grew slowly, the result of royal and noble interest unprovoked by violence or crisis, and thus representative of the more typical experience of the king's towns. London was omitted from the study because too much of its experience presents unique situations and because provincial towns allow for a better examination of how royal directives were understood outside of the capital. The early history of the four boroughs chosen is the subject of Chapter One, which describes their political and economic identities when the present study begins.

The time period chosen encompasses the reigns of kings from Richard II (1377–99) to Henry VII (1485–1509). English society during this time still experienced bouts of the plague, but attempts at social and economic recovery were more characteristic and certainly provided the most challenges for towns. National resources continued to be mustered for some time for the French wars, and the second half of the period presented all English subjects with the harrowing experience of civil unrest and royal dynastic disputes. Towns in particular had problems to surmount when the very choice of monarch was in doubt, and their struggles formed important milestones in their development of independent identities. The time span also challenges the assumptions of those historians of the sixteenth century who remain convinced that advances in self-government and autonomous behavior date only from the post-Reformation period.[1] Moreover, the method of study in this time period allows for questions to be raised about the reality of the "new monarchy" and any noticeable transition to early modern forms of government discernibly different from medieval. Historians increasingly characterize late medieval monarchs such as Edward IV and Henry VII as authoritarian and interventionist; tracking their behavior towards the towns that actively sought intervention but resisted appropriation of their rights should contribute uniquely to the argument.[2]

Two advantages of a study spanning these years involve language and records. By the late fourteenth century, there are few disputes over the vocabulary of urban studies. "Borough" had come to mean a privileged place in a legal and constitutional sense, "a place enjoying privileges of local government and representation."[3] "Town" indicates that permanent center of concentrated population living off a variety of non-agricultural occupations and maintaining an identity distinct from the surrounding countryside and other institutions. All four places of this study can be called boroughs or towns; "city," from the Latin *civitas*, is reserved for towns of high status, not necessarily of Roman origin, but often graced by a cathedral.[4] The second advantage permitted this study to be undertaken in the first place. All four towns possess local archives rich in political, social, and economic documents, most of which are unpublished. Not only are financial accounts extant in this period, but more self-conscious narratives of urban experience began to be kept by town councils and their chief officers, taking the form of assembly rolls and house books. The conclusions drawn from such documents are complemented by use of the extensive (and also largely unpublished) royal archives of London's Public Record Office. There are numerous occasions in this study when a problem, such as financial obligation, has been more fully illuminated because both royal and local sources have been consulted and compared.

The study falls into four major parts, the first of which deals with the choice of theme and boroughs, and the early histories of the towns. Part Two focuses on local administration and begins with an examination of those legal and constitutional privileges granted by royal charter and implemented by urban officers. Such privileges often took the form of gifts from the Crown, and they raise the question of whether local or royal individuals determined their nature. The gifts placed urban subjects in a difficult position, one in which they needed to acknowledge their gratitude without impairing their freedom to determine and exercise their own governing abilities. Nowhere is this better seen than in the acquisition of charters. Issued by the Crown and describing behavior from its viewpoint, the documents nonetheless required urban subjects to live under their terms and apply them to unique local conditions. They involved urban officers in a continual process of application of abstract law to concrete problems.

Even as late as the fifteenth century, towns still desired important concessions, particularly those relating to trade and commerce, the limits of their legal jurisdiction, and the number and power of their elected officers. These documents granted what a town had not seized or evolved on its own. The comparative aspect of this study allows us to analyze why some towns were better able than others to implement new chartered policies, and why certain urban subjects needed explicit royal guidance. The comparisons also help to determine the existence and nature of Crown policy towards towns: although Tudor historians perusing the statute books argue that Crown intervention in administration, economy and military organization began only in the 1530s,[5] the present study will illuminate the deeper roots of the relationship.

The officers granted by the charters and charged with governing by them served two masters. Their oaths bound them to act honorably and fairly, and it is not naïve for modern historians to believe that such promises held significant meaning in medieval society, however imperfectly humans could live by them. Evidence of selfish and corrupt behavior of mayors and sheriffs is not hard to come by, but it is worth noting that their fellow citizens did not tolerate such actions or suppress complaints about them, involving the Crown itself if justice proved impossible at home. All of the towns relied upon their wealthier individuals for service within local government, bringing with them the philosophies and experiences of the mercantile world that granted them their wealth and expertise. But as will be seen, that is not the same thing as establishing an oligarchy blind to its moral role in government: neither the king nor the citizens would have tolerated such behavior.

Having granted the means of self-government, the monarch expected his urban subjects to use the opportunity to keep his peace. Disagreements over election procedure and participation prompted royal interference if violence threatened that peace. Once more the comparative approach becomes useful to determine why some towns experienced more disturbance than others. But it is also true that the existence of offices to be filled attracted the attention of monarchs eager to use local positions as sources of patronage. Urban officers defended their right to choose their own men, just as they carefully chose and remunerated their representatives to parliament, where local issues could receive national attention.

Peacekeeping and judicial process make an unexpected appearance during royal visits to town and the spectacles planned by way of welcome. Royal visits provided opportunities for towns to display how well they had earned royal trust in peacekeeping, and for monarchs to advertise themselves as the embodiment of order and power. Towns were no strangers to public pageantry: civic processions and ceremonies formed essential components in the internal life of a medieval town, honoring its officers and confirming its sense of honor and dignity. When involving visiting nobility and royalty, such ceremonies provided occasions for influential outsiders to become acquainted with urban needs and problems. They also served as opportunities to convey civic ideals of cohesion and social unity, while simultaneously clarifying basic divisions and boundaries within urban society. The planning and financing of spectacles provoked challenges to urban budgets already stretched tight, while the dynastic problems of the mid-fifteenth century made offers of hospitality as essential to contenders as to crowned kings. Themes and images included in local ceremonies found lasting place in royal imagery and propaganda, indicating the important role such entertainment played in the manipulation of local and national self-concepts.

Part Two concludes with an analysis of the patterns of patronage that strengthened and clarified towns' relations with the central government. Magnates, gentry, and members of the legal profession effectively influenced town destinies, extending "good lordship" that could be translated into concrete benefits such as charters and legal assistance. These men and women enjoyed urban patronage in the form of gifts and annuities that purchased influence and a devoted relationship as often as direct action. This chapter examines town patronage patterns through each reign to determine how royal and national policies influenced the selection and retention of urban patrons. Each of the four towns pursued a different strategy, depending upon the nature and political success of neighboring magnates, and the gentry and lawyers within their orbit. Dynastic upheaval throughout the fifteenth century made the selection of such civic friends critical, as towns sought patrons to help ease them through changes in monarchs. The study also takes a prosopographical approach to the individuals involved in urban patronage, better to understand the assets they brought to towns and the links they offered to the inner circles of royal power.

Part Three studies borough wealth, expressed as monetary payments, military supplies, and commercial resources. The fiction or reality of town pleas of poverty has exercised historians for over two decades. The comparative approach of this work again allows for a more balanced assessment to be made of the extent to which urban wealth contributed to national finances. Through a study of local budgets as well as payments due the Crown, we can offer some guidelines to determine financial health within town walls. Regarding money owed the Crown, a major financial obligation was a town's annual fee farm, a debt whose payment to or waiver by the king involved boroughs in complex negotiations with royal bureaucracy. Towns also contributed to the realm's lay subsidies, although urban wealth tended to be underestimated by its collectors. Finally, the loan requirements made by late medieval kings were modest and tended to concentrate on wealthy individuals, although urban corporate lending provided opportunities to identify with royal imperatives and campaigns. Total financial demands may be difficult to determine and impossible to quantify, but it is clear that urban officers met their royal debts in full and on time in most cases, yet fear of poverty and concern over raising money fueled pleas of decay and destitution.

Dying for one's king in battle constituted the utmost expression of loyalty to the Crown. Towns' participation in national and international military projects provided the monarchy with a way to connect local concerns to wider issues, a broadening of outlook from which both could benefit. Boroughs provided royal campaigns with troops, supplies and transport, sometimes made a condition of the granting or confirming of a royal charter. Towns even experimented with ordnance, but more typically they looked to the Crown for help in maintaining walls and defenses. The troops they raised were few in number and rarely had adequate training or equipment, but were nonetheless considered essential by monarchs who called for their participation. So frequently, in fact, were they called upon to serve that musters of the late fifteenth century exhausted town populations and budgets. Northern boroughs felt the keenest obligation to muster troops against Scotland, and York's preparations for battle and payment of troops confirm the reality of the financial difficulties that constituted its pleas of poverty. Although the Wars of the Roses consisted of small and scattered skirmishes, urban militias played their part, requiring the utmost shrewdness on officers' parts sometimes merely to determine who was the rightful king deserving of a muster. In all theaters of war, mustering against a common enemy provided cohesion within urban society, and forced citizens to think beyond local preoccupations to the realm's broader policies.

Those royal policies dominated boroughs' trade relations and affected the ways in which urban commercial relations are studied here.

Trade and commerce provided a major component of the urban prosperity upon which the royal government relied, so the focus of the study is on the ways in which townspeople and the Crown interacted to preserve and extend profits. Town residents rarely hesitated to point out to kings the ways in which timely charters and grants could advantage their markets and tame the physical elements that impeded trade. They sought chartered liberties and utilized the Crown's legal venues to assure those conditions that contributed to profit. Cleaning rivers, repairing bridges, and initiating new fairs all prompted petitions to the king or to urban patrons, requests that reflect the four boroughs' varying degrees of growth and economic crisis. Townspeople pursued complex litigation in royal courts to protect their privileges even against guilds and groups in their own midst. Their commercial pursuits took them to foreign lands and into contact with foreign traders, not always in situations that preserved either their investments or their personal safety. The royal government was hard pressed to balance urban desires with policies of international trade, and the former sometimes went unfulfilled in order to serve broader ends. Nevertheless, the king's urban subjects and their trading activities made small but significant contributions to local, national, and international patterns of commerce.

The final section studies the specific ways in which urban subjects succeeded or failed in keeping the king's peace. It begins with an examination of their pursuit of justice, not merely in local courts granted by royal charter, but in a variety of venues provided by the Crown. The desire to avoid unfair judgments at home, to pressure and harass opponents at Westminster, or to seek equity jurisdiction all influenced transfer of cases from urban courts. Common to all royal subjects were high expectations of a royal judicial system that had grown in scope and purview over three centuries, but promised more order and fairness than it could deliver. Nevertheless, royal courts heard numerous urban complaints, although the king's officials took every opportunity to direct cases back to the local venue where more informed decisions could be made and disputing parties learn how to live together in peace. Cases brought before the courts of Common Pleas and Chancery, and the councils of Star Chamber and Requests are examined in detail, as is the role played in York's history of the Council of the North. Complementary to the formal judicial process was dispute settlement achieved through recourse to negotiation, mediation, and arbitration. All four towns turned to combinations of judicial process and arbitration to solve, among other problems, disputes over land claims. Boroughs desperately needed territory to augment annual revenue, extend law enforcement, or to provide pasture. Arbitration was considered the natural starting point for the resolution of disputes and the beginning of the healing process necessary when combatants such as citizens and religious lived in close proximity. The lessons civic officials learned from their pursuit of justice contributed to the process of self-analysis vital to towns' maturity and definition of their urban character.

The nature and magnitude of societal violence has intrigued medieval historians as much as issues of late medieval economic recovery. Recent studies that downplay the existence of violence in medieval society fail to comprehend the full impact of disorder and unrest within towns and especially upon their relations with the royal government. Whatever their true magnitude, such disturbances threatened the basis of the relationship between monarch and urban subjects, mocking the king's role as guarantor of peace and harmony while disturbing the fiscal prosperity essential to town dwellers and monarchy. The unrest resulted from complex combinations of many of the themes previously addressed in this study: internal administrative privileges extended to only part of the urban populace, the pressures of the post-plague economy, noble patrons' abuse of their urban relationships, and the national events of royal dynastic change after 1460. The final chapter presents five case studies by which to measure the impact of unrest upon Crown-town relations: the Great Revolt of 1381, Archbishop Scrope's rebellion in 1405, Norwich 1433–50, the Wars of the Roses, and the first Tudor king's problems with pretenders to his throne. It explores the limits of royal justice, unable in these circumstances to trust delegation of its peacekeeping tasks, but overtaxed and ineffectual in its direct intervention. Within the gap, civic officials fostered the growth of borough power and an expansion of urban means of self-government.

NOTES

[1]   See, for example, Robert Tittler, *Architecture and Power: The Town Hall and the English Urban Community c.1500–1640* (Oxford: Clarendon Press, 1991), esp. ch. 4, "The Civic Hall and the Autonomous Community." Although Tittler examines towns smaller than the ones I have studied and argues that developments common to large cities did not appear in small ones until the late sixteenth century, he nevertheless gives medieval achievements little recognition. For a different

approach, see Marjorie K. McIntosh, "Local Change and Community Control in England, 1465–1500," *Huntington Library Quarterly* 49 (1986): 219–42.

2   Some recent explorations of the "new monarchy" theme can be found in Anthony Goodman, *The New Monarchy: England, 1471–1534* (Oxford: Basil Blackwell, 1988); Christine Carpenter, *Locality and Polity: A Study of Warwickshire Landed Society, 1401–1499* (Cambridge: Cambridge University Press, 1992), esp. chapters 16 and 17; S. J. Gunn, *Early Tudor Government, 1485–1558* (New York: St. Martin's Press, 1995), esp. chapter 1; John Watts, "'A New Ffundacion of is Crowne': Monarchy in the Age of Henry VII," *The Reign of Henry VII: Proceedings of the 1993 Harlaxton Symposium*, ed. Benjamin Thompson (Stamford: Paul Watkins, 1995), pp. 31–53; Christine Carpenter, *The Wars of the Roses: Politics and the Constitution in England, c.1437–1509* (Cambridge: Cambridge University Press, 1997), chapters 11 and 12.

3   Susan Reynolds, *An Introduction to the History of English Medieval Towns* (Oxford: Oxford University Press, 1977), pp. 34 (quotation), 100, 112.

4   *Ibid.*, pp. ix–x, 97, 195. See also David Palliser, "Urban Society" in *Fifteenth-Century Attitudes: Perceptions of Society in Late Medieval England*, ed. Rosemary Horrox (Cambridge: Cambridge University Press, 1994), pp. 132–49. Nottingham, lacking either Roman roots or a cathedral, will not be referred to as a city in this study.

5   Robert Tittler, "The Emergence of Urban Policy, 1536–58," *The Mid-Tudor Polity c.1540–1560*, ed. Jennifer Loach and Robert Tittler (London: Macmillan Press Ltd., 1980), pp. 74–93. Tittler's examples of the ways in which Tudor monarchs intervened by rebating taxes, controlling local elections and mustering, and protecting trade all have medieval precedents.

CHAPTER 1
THE ORIGINS OF PRIVILEGE

B efore any study of late medieval urban government can be attempted, the foundation and early histories of the towns need to be made clear. Most particularly, we must trace first steps towards governmental independence, to determine the foundations upon which later privileges and ruling structures were built. What follows is a brief historical sketch of each of the four towns: their foundations, re-organization following the Conquest, population growth, economic activities, and governmental development. Such sketches provide a context for understanding how the towns handled both the mundane and extraordinary challenges of post-plague society.

York

The self-described second city of the realm after London, York was a natural center of communications and trade.[1] About 1500, an Italian visitor to England commented that "there are scarcely any towns of importance in the kingdom excepting these two: Bristol, a seaport to the West, and Boraco, otherwise York, which is on the borders of Scotland, besides London to the south," almost two hundred miles away.[2] In terms of the cloth trade and overseas commerce, such a high ranking was true of the late fourteenth century. By the mid-fifteenth century, however, competition from London and alien traders, extended economic depression, and mortality crises cut York's population and its fortunes. Assessed for the 1523–27 subsidy, the city dropped to a ranking of ninth in tax yield.[3]

From its foundation, York attained a reputation for military, spiritual, and cultural leadership. Roman troops resided in the city, then called Eboracum, for over three hundred years, and in the fourth century, it was one of the centers of Romano-British Christianity. A darker period followed the withdrawal of Roman troops, until York emerged in the early seventh century as one of Gregory the Great's two chosen sees. In picking York, Gregory may have been relying more upon tradition and historical memory of York's greatness than upon contemporary descriptions, but his optimism was vindicated in 627 when King Edwin built a church there, perhaps because York was already a royal center of some importance.[4] Edwin died shortly afterwards in battle, and the church and city decayed, but both rose again in the eighth century to join Lindesfarne and Jarrow as centers of learning. It was from York, after all, that Alcuin was recruited by Charlemagne's court to renew Christian culture.

Nevertheless, Scandinavian attacks changed both York's orientation and its government. In the 860s, the city was occupied and the region ravaged, but not without positive change as well. Through trade, York acquired active and prosperous relations with northern Europe and beyond, relations which further encouraged the native leather industries so well preserved for modern archaeologists. Viking and English kings alike kept a mint there, and the Scandinavian legacy lasted long after rulers like Eric Bloodaxe had been expelled. By Edward the Confessor's death, population stood at nearly 9000, ruled by a body of twelve Danish *judices* or lawmen.[5]

Thereafter, York became part of the Northumbrian earldom, yet to a large extent a separate unit of government even after the Norman Conquest. In 1067, a town rising against King William grew smaller the nearer the king approached, until the citizens sent the man they finally accepted as their new ruler the keys of their city plus hostages. That act of capitulation, if not loyalty, persuaded William to limit his vengeance in York to building a castle and setting five hundred knights to guard it. The men of York's subsequent attack on those Normans precipitated William's violent punishment of the city and the building of a second castle. So effective were his techniques of devastation that the population was probably halved, and the Domesday survey shows little appreciable recovery by 1086. As further punishment, William raised the farm or geld from £53 to £100, where it remained for over a century, rendered by the sheriff of Yorkshire.[6]

Strikingly, though, in the relative peace that followed the 1060s, York consolidated its traditional role as administrative center for the North. The city was the ecclesiastical capital of northern England, the headquarters of the sheriff of Yorkshire, and the site of Crown assizes and archiepiscopal and royal mints. A gild merchant can be traced back as far as the Conqueror's reign and seems to have served as the foundation for an abortive attempt at commune creation in the 1170s.[7] William Rufus himself laid the foundation stone for the new minster in 1089, while king's men kept the castle, its jail and gate, and the fishpond whose creation robbed York of acres of arable land. The city yielded to the king over £3000 each year in tallages, amercements, and profits of justice.[8]

Royal charters assured York basic territorial and financial privileges and laid the foundations for self-government. Like other towns, York claimed a grant by Henry I of burgage tenure and freedom from toll; although no copy survives, neighboring Beverley referred to these privileges in its own charter. Henry II's grant, dated to the late 1150s, confirmed the gild merchant to manage internal commerce, and allowed citizens freedom from shire tolls. Only in 1212 did the citizens finally gain the right to pay the Exchequer themselves, agreeing to increase their farm to £160 for this privilege. Within a year, certainly as a reward, a mayor headed local government and the actions of its officials gained confidence and solidarity. Since the beginning of the thirteenth century, they had employed a seal and acted in a corporate capacity in testimony and purchases, not waiting for a royal charter to permit them to enjoy such liberties.[9]

Constitutional progress lasted through the thirteenth century, during which York increased its control over justice and administration. The mayor and bailiffs heard pleas of land and trespass, exercising their right to judge local matters in local courts by charter of 1256. The royal sheriff lost effective control as the powers of the citizens' representatives expanded. In 1229, York gained its first coroners, joined at the end of the century by three chamberlains who acted as chief financial officers. The mayor and bailiffs continued to pay the fee farm, a heavy burden that grew so great Edward I seized the city because of its debts. York profits increased only marginally after the city claimed the neighboring wapentake of Ainsty in 1212. When the royal government attempted to re-take control of it in 1280, the citizens resisted, suffering seizure of their liberties for three years in demonstration of the true source of their privileges.[10]

Until late in Richard II's reign, fourteenth-century royal charters were unremarkable, exempting citizens from jury service outside the city and from the interference of certain royal officers within its walls.[11] They contain few clues as to the process of elections, but the heavy burdens of local and royal responsibilities exempted all but the most wealthy and powerful from holding the higher offices. These *probi homines* were willing to suffer frequent re-election to office: only fifteen different men held the office of mayor between 1322 and 1372. By the end of the century, the three-tiered system of government prevailed, with a mayor and inner council of twelve aldermen mostly representing the mercantile class, a council of twenty-four more widely and modestly chosen from urban trades, and a group of forty-eight which met more rarely and represented the commonalty of the city. Newer families with wealth based on trade contested for office, without necessarily changing the process by which money and social prominence provided the experience and leisure necessary for public service. Uprisings were surprisingly few in number, not least because the king was quick to intervene, designate candidates, and threaten the free exercise of the chartered liberties.[12] Only the more intense disturbances of the mid-fifteenth century prompted the royal government to impose radical changes on the electoral process itself.

On several occasions during the thirteenth and fourteenth centuries, York's officials and citizens received unusually close scrutiny by the royal government. Edward I's campaigns against Scotland resulted in unique conditions for the city. In the summer of 1298, the government of England moved to the northern city so that the king could be closer to the enemy. Exchequer, Chancery, and Common Pleas moved into the castle, occasionally joined by the still peripatetic King's Bench. Councils and parliament met in York, as did armies and commissions of array.[13] Local merchants happily anticipated the increase in customers, so much so that a new code of civic ordinances had to be created to ordain fair dealing.[14] For six years, York served as the heart of the nation, and long after government offices had returned to Westminster, it continued to maintain a prominent role in national affairs. Offices migrated to York again in 1392, when Richard II sought to punish Londoners by depriving them of the increased business such offices contributed to the economy.

Even without the boost of wartime occupation, York's prosperity grew throughout the thirteenth and fourteenth centuries. Like Norwich, it acted as a market for county foodstuffs, to such an extent that its defenses could be built with the aid of tolls levied on incoming sheep and cattle. The archbishop held a fair each year, and the city controlled two more of its own: the emphasis of all three on raw materials and distribution emphasized York's character as a regional entrepôt. The most profitable export was wool, but those fleeces that did not leave the city were put to good use by its textile industry. After a slump at the start of the thirteenth century, the industry re-established itself, helped by the needs of war and the presence of government offices, and recovering even from the ravages of plague.[15] Although weavers and others in the cloth industry began to complain of hard times late in the fourteenth century, other fields, such as leather crafts and metalwork remained prosperous at least for a couple of decades. Widespread distress did not take hold until the early fifteenth century, when overseas trade investments dried up and the textile industry departed for the countryside. Until then, York's population continued to rise, from c.7000 at the start of the fourteenth century, to 12–14,000 at the end of Edward III's reign.[16] Regrettably, the quality of life did not increase proportionately: sanitary conditions so deteriorated that Edward III himself complained about York's abominable odors.[17]

Norwich

The city of Norwich rose in the center of an excellent network of communications by both land and water. Over one hundred miles northeast of London, the most formal settlement on the site of the modern town occurred in the ninth century, but the area had long been a nodal point for important Roman roads. The Anglo-Saxon settlement, a collection of small emporia, straddled the banks of the River Wensum at a low crossing point on this navigable river, near the head of a great estuary. The rapid nature of both Viking conquest and English recapture implied that the area contained few burhs or other deliberately-created centers, allowing the site to dominate most of East Anglia administratively and economically. By the tenth century, the settlement was known as Norwich, a single borough born of three or four Anglian settlements whose individual names—Westwick or Wymer, Conesford, and Coslany—remained in use to define leets or wards until the Municipal Reform Act of 1835.[18]

The population grew rapidly between the ninth and eleventh centuries. Under Danish rule, Norwich became the governmental center for East Anglia and acted as a port or market town with international contacts. So prosperous were the city's fortunes that the Domesday survey reported 1320 burgesses resident in 1066, implying a total population of about 5000. These pre-Conquest residents were divided among the lordships of the king and the earl of East Anglia, of Stigand archbishop of Canterbury, and of Harold Godwinson. Extensive agricultural lands, water mills, and grazing rights augmented urban wealth, although the location of many of these assets in areas outside the town or built over by religious houses caused Norwich extensive jurisdictional disputes in later centuries.[19]

As in other towns, the Conquest wrought great physical and administrative changes. A new quarter of Norman settlers, called Mancroft, developed west of a newly-erected castle, the only major royal fortification in East Anglia until late in the twelfth century. Resistance to Norman rule and resentment over the destruction of homes for the erection of the castle brought harsh punishment that slowed recovery. More positive for city fortunes was the move of the diocesan see of East Anglia from Thetford to Norwich about 1095 which contributed ecclesiastical activities to the secular ones already two centuries old.[20]

Typical of other towns throughout the Middle Ages, Norwich developed as a result of royal visits and royal gifts. In 1122, Henry I kept Christmas there and rewarded the citizens with a charter in return for their hospitality. The document took the first steps towards separating town government from that of the royal castle and its constable, but it continued to affirm the leadership of a serjeant or portreeve nominated by the king.[21] A husting or borough court could be summoned for administrative and judicial business, with a royal officer judging the burgesses by local custom. Henry's charter does not survive, but the earliest one in the city archives, dated c.1158, confirmed its basic tenets. The more important charter of 1194 acknowledged previous constitutional acquisitions and consolidated all payments due the king into the fee farm of £113 8s. The now united *civitas Norwici* gained the right to select its own reeve to head the government, although the fee farm remained payable through the royal sheriff. In later centuries, the citizens affirmed this document of Richard I as the foundation of their municipal liberties.[22] It exempted them from tolls, confined local pleas to local courts, and secured the tenure of their property, all basic grants intended to promote the stability conducive to local and national peace.

By the end of the twelfth century, Norwich's population of c.7000 placed it fifth among the realm's towns, but its wealth ranked the borough even higher. Norwich was the marketing and manufacturing center for all East Anglia; the town's administrative and ecclesiastical functions contributed wealth as well. The East Anglian countryside naturally provisioned the town, which supplied in return the textiles, metal goods and fish for rural estates.[23]

A rich community of Jews added to town wealth in this early period, but its real prosperity came from the burgeoning textile industry. A chronicler attributed the easy capture of Norwich in 1174 to the fact that the town was full of weavers with no experience of defense. Still, the conquering force of Flemings probably brought with them the secrets of worsted weaving which assured the town's medieval prosperity. Norwich was one of the first dozen towns whose leaders recognized debts between merchants, according to the 1283 statute of Acton Burnell. The city even acted as a wool staple for part of the fourteenth century, an arrangement that added to its wealth and national stature.[24] Its population at the start of the fourteenth century has been estimated at 17,000, growing to 25,000 by 1333 before falling back to 7500 in 1377.[25] Throughout the fourteenth and fifteenth centuries, Norwich became the kind of county town frequented by wealthy country gentry like the Pastons for winter shopping and entertainment; by the early sixteenth century, it had become the realm's largest provincial town in both wealth and numbers.[26]

Throughout the thirteenth century, Norwich acquired charters and grants that increased its privileges and autonomy. The privileges of this period continued to provide both king and citizens with the means, financial as well as administrative, to encourage peace and prosperity among urban subjects. Sometime during the 1220s, four bailiffs replaced the reeve, exercising both administrative and police functions within the city and increasing their civil and criminal jurisdiction at the expense of royal officials. The documents do not specify whether the bailiffs were elected by all of the freemen or by a more restricted and select group. The four wards—Conesford, Mancroft, Wymer, and Over the Water (formerly Coslany)—supported leet courts, empowered to deal with such varied community offences as breaches of the peace and of bread and ale assizes, forestalling of foodstuffs, and dumping refuse in the river. Granted return of writs by 1256, the citizens soon answered to the Exchequer directly for most demands and debts: the royal sheriff or king's bailiff no longer could enter the city and interfere in local matters. The predominance of the bailiffs' government was secured by a ban on private guilds of craftsmen, a separate and thus dangerous focus for fundraising and loyalty. As a physical manifestation of its newly privileged feelings, Norwich began to enclose itself in 1253 with a bank and ditch designed to control entrances and the tolls that could be levied on them.[27]

The defenses did not please everyone, however, and they may even be directly blamed for the first of many violent confrontations between townsmen and members of Norwich's alternate liberties. The monks of the cathedral priory complained that the city enclosed areas that had hitherto belonged to other lords in other hundreds. The quarrel grew in size and variety of differences, resulting in 1272 in the townspeople's violent attack on the cathedral. Henry III's rushed visit to Norwich and his subsequent seizure of its liberties were two of the last acts of the king's life. For three thousand marks (£2000), the liberties were restored four years later, only to be seized again within a decade for a summary execution of justice displeasing to the king.[28] These events repeated themselves over the following two centuries: quarrels over civic jurisdiction could not be settled by peaceful means or recourse to the Crown, so acts of violence precipitated loss of liberties, heavy fines, and unwanted intervention by the central government. Such actions reminded urban subjects that although their chartered liberties were almost a century old, the king remained the ultimate overlord and could interfere in local issues whenever the realm's safekeeping seemed in danger.

At the end of the thirteenth century, Norwich entered a short period of peace during which it defined and consolidated its restored franchises. Part of the process included a division among the commonalty by the creation of a small and more influential subset, the annually elected body of twenty-four citizens. Although chosen by all those in possession of chartered liberties, this body's very existence resulted from an important and basic recognition: that not all the citizens were able or willing to give local administration the time it needed, and that as a result some would be excluded from active policymaking and relations with the Crown. Mentioned first in the city's own early-fourteenth-century custumal, this division rose from the citizens themselves and was not imposed by the king. Thereafter, local records increase their references to *probi homines*, particularly in regard to the bailiffs and leading citizens most likely to be blamed and seized by the king in time of violence.[29] These are the origins of what has been so misleadingly termed oligarchy, but before we equate it with the selfish rule of wealthy citizens, it must be noted that its roots lie with the unpleasant labor and responsibilities that few other urban subjects wished to bear. Distinguished by their rates of taxation and even the weapons and mounts they could afford to bring to a view of arms (required under the assize of arms), the "great ones" of a city possessed the qualities most likely to attract added responsibilities. In recompense they would be offered prestige, power, and perquisites.

Throughout the fourteenth century, the citizens grew increasingly conscious of their rights and obligations as a royal borough. Royal visits to the town provided the opportunities for charters and grants which increased the physical area under the direct control of the freemen. They had learned to make the winning argument that unless they got what they asked for, the royal government would lose money and control over lawless subjects.[30] By the accession of Richard II, the citizens had distinguished by themselves a group of men who exceeded others of the commonalty in responsibilities, power, influence, experience, and the wealth that brought them leisure to serve others. Although not dictated expressly by the king, this change resulted at least in part from the increasing complexity of royal administration, distribution of wealth, and the example of London's government structure.[31] For both Crown and city, it became desirable to choose a manageable, limited and experienced body with specialized knowledge of government to deal with the outside world and represent to it the borough. The present study of Norwich begins at that point.

Exeter

Almost 175 miles southwest of London, Exeter lies ten miles from the sea on the River Exe. As described by John Vowell alias Hoker, the city's sixteenth-century chamberlain and antiquary, "the situation of [Exeter] is very plesaunte...being sett or situated upon a little hill emongs many hills, the countrie rounde about being montanos and hillye."[32] Its origins belong to the period of Roman occupation. From A.D. 50, a Romano-British settlement flourished, enclosed by walls that survive in part to this day. Known as Isca Dumnoniorum and graced with a forum, basilica and public baths, the city probably resulted from Emperor Claudius's policy to transform southern Britain into a civil province. Certainly it acted as the administrative center for all of present-day Devon, Cornwall, and parts of Somerset.[33] Native Britons, the

Dumnonii, continued to use the site after the Romans withdrew, but by the end of the fourth century the site had declined to the point that rubbish pits were dug in the forum, although some residents continued to import goods from the Mediterranean for another hundred years. Early English occupation remains a mystery, although a Saxon minster flourished there in the late seventh century. Exeter became one of the last burghal hidage centers, to which Alfred granted a mint at the end of the ninth century.[34]

Royal interest in Exeter continued into the eleventh century. Ethelred the Unready's queen received the revenue of the city (£18 *per annum*) as a morning gift upon her marriage, but under the rule of her Norman reeve the city fell to the Danes in 1003.[35] By the time the bishop's see moved there from Crediton in 1050, the city enjoyed a high status, low financial demands, and international trade links.[36] Its central location in a regional road network enhanced its commercial links. In 1066, Exeter had a population of about 2500, who paid the £18 p.a. shared by the queen and the local earl. The inhabitants did not pay geld except when London, York, and Winchester did, although in terms of military service Exeter ranked with smaller towns such as Totnes and Barnstaple.[37]

William the Conqueror was particularly harsh with the city. Its inhabitants refused to swear an oath of fealty to him, prompting a royal siege lasting eighteen days before William relented and agreed to preserve the city's ancient customs and the £18 annual payment. He ordered the immediate construction of Rougemont Castle in the northeast corner of the city, "at the higher ende of it," but "in ruyn and decay" when Hoker wrote his description of the fortress.[38] Its fortunes, however, were not impaired, so that by the twelfth century, contemporaries thought of Exeter as the fourth city of the realm (sixth or seventh is probably closer to the truth).[39] Although the pace of its growth slowed during the thirteenth century, it remained an important administrative, ecclesiastical, commercial and social center for the southwest. Its eminence as a regional capital attracted to it royal interest and the gifts that followed. During the 1150s, Henry II confirmed the privileges granted during Henry I's reign, based on those of London. Freedom from various tolls and charges throughout England received further confirmation not just from Richard I but from John, who had earlier deprived his brother's queen Berengaria of her traditional share of the city farm.[40] Long before Exeter dreamed of a charter of incorporation, its citizens acted in corporate capacity, making and receiving gifts and grants as a united body.[41]

The period between 1259 and 1324 witnessed crucial developments in the city's methods of government. The royal government took particular interest in Exeter's level of prosperity and its debts to the Crown, and intervened actively to assure its payments. Since the mid-thirteenth century, Exeter had had a special relationship with the earls of Cornwall, and in 1259 had received from Earl Richard King of the Romans, previously a guardian of the city, the grant of a fee farm. A lengthy dispute over the earl's ability to make such a concession resulted in the establishment of the farm at the new (and higher) rate of £20 *per annum*.[42] Further privileges came from Edward I, who gave the seal of Statute Merchant to the mayor; within the national system of port customs, the city became the headport for all of Devon and Cornwall.[43] There were sound financial reasons behind Edward II's charter of 1320 as well, which specified that citizens could not plead or be impleaded outside city walls on matters concerning town lands or local problems. All such cases became the province of the mayor and bailiffs unless they concerned the king or his ministers. Foreigners were forbidden to convict natives and could not mix with them on juries. Neighboring Barnstaple found this charter and all that it confirmed so enviable that in the fifteenth century its officers copied Exeter's grants and passed them off to Chancery as their own.[44]

The royal government showed much less interest in the process by which Exeter selected its officers and empowered them to keep order within its walls. Local records refer to a mayor soon after 1200, and court rolls and witness lists indicate the frequent participation of a small group of wealthy and powerful merchants derived from a merchant guild active in the previous century. Only men free of the city could take an active part in urban government, and over the course of the next few centuries Exeter's freemen remained a smaller and more exclusive group than was found in other cities.[45] There is little evidence to support the theory of early democratic principles being overridden by aristocratic and oligarchic tendencies. Democracy was not a hallmark of medieval governments, and if anything Exeter's mayor had to share more of his power in the later Middle Ages than at the birth of the office.

The process of selection for civic office was indirect: from the 1260s, local records speak of thirty-six electors who chose the chief officials of the city and who were themselves selected by a group of four.[46] By the early years of the fourteenth century, the electors also chose a council, sometimes set at twelve and sometimes at twenty-four or more, to help the mayor govern the city, preserve the liberties of the city, observe its statutes and maintain the king's peace. That they had little effect on curbing the mayor's will and avoiding misgovernment can be seen in the changes effected in 1345, when the assent of the council of twelve men was needed for the mayor to condone fines and amercements, elect men to the freedom of the city, and seal letters. This body of twelve experienced frequent change during the early fifteenth century, when it expanded to twenty-four and contracted again, but until the end of the century its development reflected internal factors and occurred without direct royal intervention or interference. All of the most exalted officers, men of political power and wealth, made up less than 6% of Exeter's total householders, and they helped themselves to royal offices and judicial and commercial advantages further to augment their clout. Nevertheless, a further 6% of the householders voted and held more modest offices, participation that may have reduced political tensions in the city.

All of the skills of these mayors and councils were required in dealings with bodies external to the urban liberties. The Courtenay earls of Devon interested themselves in Exeter's affairs, often to the detriment of the city. As early as the 1230s, the Courtenays angered the city by building weirs in the Exe, restricting the flow of water and of trade, and rendering nearly useless the municipal mills. Although Courtenays were lords of Topsham, Exeter's outport at the head of the Exe estuary, the city carefully preserved its link to the sea and its attendant revenues.[47] As the leading family of the county, the Courtenays received the kind of attention most cities paid to influential nobles who might be able to show them assistance or favor, but the ancient dispute over the weirs left a permanent chill on future relations. Nor was Exeter's intercourse much friendlier with the dean and chapter. Exeter's jurisdictional arguments with the cathedral over suburban liberties rivaled those of Norwich in intensity, although parliament was partially effective in maintaining order through a settlement in 1436, and arbitration eased the worst tensions.[48]

As early as the twelfth century, foreign trade and cloth manufacture brought prosperity to Exeter. William of Malmesbury noted that the area's barren soil was more than compensated for by the foreigners who sailed up the still-tidal Exe as yet unimpeded by Courtenay weirs. Even after the river was blocked, sufficient power remained in the water to run mills and support the cloth trade. The results were sophisticated enough to catch the eye of Henry III, who demanded supplies.[49] Even when cloth manufacture moved to the countryside in the fifteenth century, Exeter remained a center of cloth finishing and fulling because of its mills on the Exe and its ability to serve the needs of clothmakers in smaller towns of Devon and Somerset. The power of its guilds of tailors and weavers attests to the prosperity it achieved from these activities. Migrants flowed in from a radius of about twenty miles, and entries to the freedom of the city peaked in the half-century before the Black Death.[50]

Despite population losses in the Black Death, the bright promise of the high Middle Ages turned into steady growth. In the late fourteenth century, Exeter remained a modest provincial town, its population of c.3000 making it one-quarter the size of Norwich or York.[51] Although the Hundred Years' War curtailed the wine trade and Courtenay blockages in the Exe remained in place, ships continued to visit Exeter's port, in growing numbers after 1390, and revenues from the fairs increased.[52] Exports grew substantially after the 1440s when the Devon specialty of light, brightly-dyed kerseys attracted increased foreign and domestic markets. French and Spanish merchants visited again, using Exeter as an entrepôt for many of their goods, in the same way that its hinterland treated the city as a distribution center. The population had almost tripled between the 1380s and the 1550s when John Hoker attributed Exeter's success to the high quality of its cloth, export of which was channeled through the city.[53] But it is more accurate to attest the city's prosperity to the variety and balance of its economic endeavors, and to its shrewd exercise of governmental powers. Although still modest in size, Exeter faced post-plague society with greater confidence than most urban centers.

Nottingham

Geographic centrality and a strong military role influenced the growth and development of Nottingham. Located almost 125 miles north of London, the town developed at a ford across the River Trent, navigable to that point. From prehistoric times, north-south traffic crossed there and the center received even greater impetus from Viking travel to and from the north. A bridge appeared as early as 920, and

Domesday Book noted the town as a major point on the Great North Road from London to York. Lying within easy reach of the Fosse Way, the Humber, and the port of Kingston-upon-Hull, Nottingham provided a focus for commercial activity and defense of the realm.[54]

The town's pre-Conquest history was one of modest development. Paleolithic and Mesolithic communities hunted in the area and made use of the natural caves that honeycomb the local sandstone. In 1639, the poor were still being advised to shelter in them, although during the Middle Ages they had had a more industrial purpose as hide-tanning centers and storehouses for ale. Bronze and Iron Age settlements showed considerable growth, although the area was later generally bypassed by the Romans.[55] Alfred the Great's biographer called the town Tigguocobauc or House of Caves, but we can assume that the Danish borough of Asser's period possessed more sophisticated housing.[56] Settled by kinsmen of the Dane Snot (hence the early form of its name, Snottingham), the town was captured by Edward the Elder in 920 and soon after received a mint. As a frontier settlement, Nottingham played a key role in the tenth century as Saxon and Scandinavian rulers fought for domination in the Five Boroughs area, making the town a main center of royal and comital power in the Trent Valley.[57] In 1066, Nottingham consisted of the English borough clustered on St. Mary's hill and housing 173 burghers, and a total population of about one thousand, a figure that nearly doubled by the start of this study in 1377.[58]

Nottingham gained a castle soon after the Conquest and with it significant royal attention. News of its erection frightened the rebels of York into capitulating to William, and the needs of the garrison dominated economic growth thereafter. As in Norwich, a Norman or "French" borough developed between the castle and the old Saxon center, chiefly for the followers of the new governor, William Peverel. Two sheriffs and two bailiffs accommodated the divided settlement, whose annual payment to the royal government (one usually enjoyed by the reigning queen) increased from £18 to £30.[59] Henry II, his sons and grandson all strengthened the castle's fortifications, and Edward I used it to incarcerate Scottish and Welsh prisoners. Isabella and Mortimer were holding a parliament there in 1330 when they were overpowered by the young Edward III who had made his way from the town via the underground caves and passages. In the period of this study, Nottingham and its castle provided Richard II with a center to rival London when the city angered him. It was to Nottingham that Edward IV called to him "the nobility and gentlemen of the district to render him their honour and support," and the town hosted Richard III in his last days before entering battle with Henry Tudor.[60]

Shared economic interests joined the two boroughs, developing the town as a general trading center and source of manufactured goods for its hinterland. As early as the eleventh century, residents guarded the waters of the Trent and the road towards York to prevent the hindering of ships or carts.[61] Cattle and barley entered Nottingham to supply the tanning and brewing industries. Derbyshire lead and Sherwood Forest charcoal also found profitable markets there. Contact with the Low Countries encouraged some Nottingham men to reside in Brabant, and colonists from the duchy to set up trade in the town.[62] Nottingham also shared in the wool trade, serving as an outlet for Midlands fleeces. The guild of weavers was the first to be established (1155), and the earliest royal charter supported the working of dyed cloth in the borough.[63] Jews resided peacefully in Nottingham until their national expulsion in 1290, indicating the business and lending opportunities the town had to offer.[64] Nevertheless, the early fourteenth century witnessed pleas of poverty and economic distress. In 1330, residents could not find men in sufficient numbers or wealth to serve as bailiffs. The weavers complained of reduced membership, the burgesses of decayed or vacant houses. During the fifteenth century, town officers attempted unsuccessfully to convince the king to establish Nottingham as a wool staple to renew its role as entrepôt for Midlands wool. Local records preserved the conviction that poverty was widespread, although other evidence indicates that licenses to trade increased, wholesale business rose, and there were always enough wealthy burgesses able to be tapped for loans to the Crown.[65]

By the start of our study in 1377, the population stood between 1400 and 2000 inhabitants, rising to four thousand by the early sixteenth century when it ranked 38th among provincial boroughs.[66] Such an important county town, a military and commercial center of strategic importance, received its share of constitutional privileges. The first written record of the town is Henry II's charter dating from the 1150s. Beginning as a confirmation of an earlier grant of Henry I, the charter gave townsmen the right to levy tolls on traders who crossed the Trent and entered the town. The weavers' guild received a monopoly of working dyed cloth within a ten-mile radius, while the citizens as a body gained jurisdictional rights like infangetheof within the borough and directions on how to extend their liberties to newcomers.[67]

Royal interest increased during the thirteenth century with charters that recognized town financial and administrative needs. As earl of Mortain and later as king, John's interest in the town was more positive than the Robin Hood legends claim. His most important gift was that of a reeve, chosen by the burgesses from among their own numbers (although subject to John's approval) by which to answer more efficiently to royal financial demands. John also granted freedom from all the realm's tolls, and awarded a gild merchant.[68] In 1272, Henry III granted return of writs, an essential privilege in urban relations with the Crown.[69] Restoration of liberties in 1284 after a royal seizure for insubordination included the grant of a mayor, a single officer to be chosen by the burgesses of both Norman and English quarters. A direct gift of the king, "ad relevationem status Burgensium et aliorum hominum eiusdem villae," the mayor dominated the town's governing structure and exceeded the bailiffs in power and dignity.[70] Economic privileges were not forgotten: Edward I concluded his charter with the grant of a second fair, further confirmation of mercantile vitality.[71]

Despite its small size and only modest survival of its medieval records, Nottingham remains a sound choice for study, with more than an adequate number of sources to consult. Largely untroubled by internal riots or the overbearing interest of a local noble family, the town provides many examples of royal interest unprovoked by violence or crisis. The spectacular disputes of a Norwich or the creation of York as a rival capital make us forget that most Crown-town relations developed as a result of natural, sequential growth and change. New officers resulted from charters, often given after royal visits; freedoms stemmed from petitions which were postponed from legal term to legal term over many frustrating years. The Crown rarely acted suddenly or with sweeping changes. Preservation of peace and stability was far more important both to boroughs and the central administration. The study of small towns such as Nottingham and Exeter help us remember that, while the inclusion of Norwich and York forces us to determine whether their exceptions prove a rule.

NOTES

[1]   York ran a distant second to London, of course, but also battled for its place with Bristol in the thirteenth and fourteenth centuries: David Palliser, "The Birth of York's Civic Liberties, c.1200–1354," *The Government of Medieval York: Essays in*

Commemoration of the 1396 Royal Charter, ed. Sarah Rees Jones, Borthwick Studies in History 3 (York, 1997), p. 106, citing Y.C.A., D.1, f.348r.

2   Charlotte A. Sneyd, ed. and trans., *A relation, or rather a true account, of the isle of England, about 1500*, Camden Society, o.s., vol. 37 (London, 1847), p. 41.

3   W. G. Hoskins, "English Provincial Towns in the Early Sixteenth-Century," *Transactions of the Royal Historical Society*, 5th series, 6 (1956): 4–6; P. J. P. Goldberg, "Mortality and Economic Change in the Diocese of York, 1390–1514," *Northern History* 24 (1988): 41–42; A. J. Pollard, *North-eastern England During the Wars of the Roses: Lay Society, War, and Politics 1450–1500* (Oxford: Clarendon Press, 1990), pp. 44–52.

4   Miller, *VCH*, pp. 2–3; Daniel G. Russo, *Town Origins and Development in Early England, c.400–950 A.D.* (Westport and London: Greenwood Press, 1998), pp. 119–22; Bede, *Ecclesiastical History of the English People*, trans. Leo Sherley-Price (1955; Harmondsworth: Penguin Books, 1990), Book II, ch.12–14, pp. 125–32.

5   John F. Benton, ed., *Town Origins: The Evidence from Medieval England* (Boston: D. C. Heath and Co., 1968), p. 73; Miller, *VCH*, p. 21; Richard Hall, *The Viking Dig* (London: Bodley Head, 1986), ch.7.

6   Miller, *VCH*, pp. 17–19, 22.

7   Palliser, "Birth of York's Civic Liberties," p. 91.

8   Miller, *VCH*, p. 31.

9   *Ibid.*, pp. 31–33; Palliser, "Birth of York's Civic Liberties," pp. 92–93.

10   Palliser, "Birth of York's Civic Liberties," p. 97. The Ainsty proved to be of greater service in later centuries when it contributed troops for Scottish campaigns.

11   Martin Weinbaum, ed., *British Borough Charters 1307–1660* (Cambridge: Cambridge University Press, 1943), p. 132; Palliser, "Birth of York's Civic Liberties," p. 103.

12   The twelve became known as aldermen by the late fourteenth century, and were associated with the six wards of the city: Miller, *VCH*, pp. 70, 77–80; Sarah Rees Jones, "York's Civic Administration, 1354–1464," *The Government of Medieval York*, pp. 122–23. Election disturbances between 1357 and 1371 resulted in such intervention by Edward III. His grandfather had not hesitated to seize civic liberties three times between 1280 and 1297.

13   Miller, *VCH*, p. 54; D. M. Broome, "Exchequer Migrations to York in the Thirteenth and Fourteenth Centuries," in *Essays in Medieval History Presented to Thomas Frederick Tout*, ed. F. M. Powicke and A. G. Little (Edinburgh: R. and R. Clarke, 1925), p. 293.

14   Michael Prestwich, ed., *York Civic Ordinances, 1301*, Saint Anthony's Hall Publications, Borthwick Papers no. 49 (York, 1976).

15   Herbert Heaton, *The Yorkshire Woollen and Worsted Industries*, 2d ed. (Oxford: Clarendon Press, 1965), pp. 3–7.

16   Miller, *VCH*, pp. 84–89; J. N. Bartlett, "The Expansion and Decline of York in the Later Middle Ages," *Economic History Review*, 2d ser., 12 (1959): 17–20.

17   *CCR, 1330–33*, p. 610; *1369–74*, p. 438; T. P. Cooper, "The Medieval Highways, Streets, Open Ditches and Sanitary Conditions of the City of York," *Yorkshire Archaeological Journal* 22 (1912–13): 270–86.

18   D. Howard and C. A. Pratt, "The Evolution of Norwich," *Geography* 26 (1941): 125–26; A. Carter, "The Anglo-Saxon Origins of Norwich: The Problems and

Approaches," *Anglo-Saxon England* 7 (1978): 175–203; Bruce H. Allen, "The Administrative and Social Structure of the Norwich Merchant Class 1485–1660," (Ph.D. dissertation, Harvard University, 1951), pp. 3–5; Susan Reynolds, *An Introduction to the History of English Medieval Towns* (Oxford: Oxford University Press, 1977), p. 41.

19   James Campbell, "Norwich," *Historic Towns Atlas, Volume II*, gen. ed. Mary D. Lobel (London: The Scolar Press, 1975), p. 3; *Norwich Records*, 1:iii–iv. See below, pp. 260–64.

20   W. H. Hudson, "Traces of Early Development of Municipal Organization in the City of Norwich," *Archaeological Journal* 46 (1889): 294–95; Barbara Dodwell, "Herbert de Losinga and the Foundation," in Ian Atherton, *et al.*, eds., *Norwich Cathedral: Church, City and Diocese, 1096–1996* (London and Rio Grande: The Hambledon Press, 1996), p. 39; *The Victoria History of the County of Norfolk*, ed. W. Page, 2 vols. (London: Archibald Constable and Co., Ltd., 1901, 1906), 2:35–36.

21   *Norwich Records*, 1:xiii; *History of the City and County of Norwich, from the Earliest Accounts to the Present Times* (Norwich: John Crouse, 1768), p. 22.

22   *Norwich Records*, 1:xviii–xx, 12–14 (for an extension of these terms by Edward I in 1305, see pages 18–20); Campbell, "Norwich," p. 9; Benton, *Town Origins*, p. 101.

23   Norwich's position at the head of the estuary allowed it to be listed in the Pipe Roll of 1204 as a seaport, a designation that helps explain its annual render to the king of twenty-five herring pies, a service last performed in 1816: Francis Blomefield, *A Topographical History of the County of Norfolk*, 11 vols., 2d ed. (London: William Miller, 1805–10), 3:375. Domesday Book records that the city was required to furnish the king yearly with a bear: Campbell, "Norwich," p. 6.

24   *Norwich Records*, 2:xii, lx–lxii.

25   Elizabeth Rutledge, "Immigration and Population Growth in Early Fourteenth-Century Norwich: Evidence from the Tithing Roll," *Urban History Yearbook 1988*, 27; A. Dyer, *Decline and Growth in English Towns, 1400–1640* (Cambridge: Cambridge University Press, 1995), p. 6; Richard Britnell, "The Black Death in English Towns," *Urban History* 21 (1994): 200–201.

26   H. S. Bennett, *The Pastons and Their England*, 2d ed. (Cambridge: Cambridge University Press, 1979), pp. 57, 67; Hoskins, "English Provincial Towns in the Early Sixteenth-Century," 5–6; Dyer, *Decline and Growth*, pp. 62–64.

27   W. H. Hudson, *Wards of the City of Norwich* (London: Jarrold and Sons, 1891), pp. 15–21; Hudson, *Leet Jurisdiction in the City of Norwich*, Selden Society, vol. 5 (London, 1892), pp. 3–4; *Norwich Records*, 1:xxvii–xxx, 16–18. The walls were not finished until the 1340s.

28   *Norwich Records*, 1:xxx–xxxii; *History of the City and County of Norwich*, pp. 52–54.

29   *Norwich Records*, 1:xxxvi–xxxvii.

30   *Ibid.*, 1:xli–xlii, 23–26 (charter of 1345).

31   *Ibid.*, 1:l–liv; 2:cxxii; Campbell, "Norwich," p. 16. In 1378, Norwich citizens obtained a copy of the young king's most recent charter to London and learned much about desirable privileges from its perusal: see below, p. 40.

32   D.R.O., Book 55, f.131b (1559); Wallace T. MacCaffrey, *Exeter 1540–1640: The Growth of an English County Town*, 2d ed. (Cambridge, Mass.: Harvard University Press, 1975), p. 6.

33   Aileen Fox, *Roman Exeter*, History of Exeter Research Group, Monograph 8 (Manchester: Manchester University Press, 1952), pp. 7, 16. See also P. T. Bidwell, *Roman Exeter: Fortress and Town* (Exeter: Exeter Museum Service, 1980); and Christopher Henderson, "Exeter (*Isca Dumnoniorum*)," in *Fortress into City*, ed. Graham Webster (London: Batsford, 1988), pp. 91–119.

34   Reynolds, *English Medieval Towns*, p. 11; J. R. Maddicott, "Trade, industry and the wealth of King Alfred," *Past and Present* 123 (1989): 23–35 (see also Maddicott's reply to criticism in *Past and Present* 135 [1992]: 164–88).

35   E. A. Freeman, *Exeter* (London: Longmans, Green and Co., 1890), pp. 26–32; J. J. Alexander, "The Early Boroughs of Devon," *Transactions of the Devonshire Association* 58 (1926): 279.

36   Frank Barlow, "Leofric and his times," in *Leofric of Exeter: Essays in Commemoration of the Foundation of Exeter Cathedral Library in AD 1072*, ed. F. Barlow (Exeter: University of Exeter Press, 1972), pp. 1–16; Benton, *Town Origins*, p. 59; William of Malmesbury, *De Gesta Pontificum Anglorum*, ed. N. E. S. A. Hamilton, Rolls Series, vol. 52 (London, 1870), pp. 200–201.

37   R. Welldon Finn, "Devonshire," in *The Domesday Geography of South-West England*, ed. H. C. Darby and R. Welldon Finn (Cambridge, 1967), pp. 280–82; Thomas Madox, *Firma Burgi* (London: W. Bowyer, 1726), p. 7; W. G. Hoskins, *Two Thousand Years in Exeter* (Exeter: James Townsend and Sons, 1960), p. 21.

38   William of Malmesbury, *De Gestis Regum Anglorum*, ed. William Stubbs, 2 vols., Rolls Series, vol. 90 (London, 1887, 1889), 2:307; D.R.O., Book 55, f.132 (quotation).

39   K. R. Potter, ed. and trans., *Gesta Stephani*, rev. ed. (Oxford: Clarendon Press, 1976), pp. 32–35; Maryanne Kowaleski, *Local Markets and Regional Trade in Medieval Exeter* (Cambridge: Cambridge University Press, 1995), p. 83.

40   Freeman, *Exeter*, pp. 56–57; D.R.O., Charters I–VIII; Adolphus Ballard, ed., *British Borough Charters 1042–1216* (Cambridge: Cambridge University Press, 1913), pp. cxl, 6, 13–14, 186.

41   Bertie Wilkinson, *The Mediaeval Council of Exeter*, History of Exeter Research Group, Monograph 4 (Manchester: Manchester University Press, 1931), pp. xvi–xvii.

42   D.R.O., Charters XII, XVI, XX; *CChR*, 4:260.

43   Henry S. Cobb, "Local Port Customs Accounts prior to 1550," *Journal of the Society of Archivists* 1 (1958): 219; E. M. Carus-Wilson, and Olive Coleman, *England's Export Trade 1275–1547* (Oxford: Clarendon Press, 1963), pp. 7–8, 36ff.

44   Susan Reynolds, "The Forged Charters of Barnstaple," *English Historical Review* 84 (1969): 699; D.R.O., Charter XVIIIA.

45   Kowaleski, *Local Markets and Regional Trade*, p. 96.

46   In addition to the mayor, early officers included four stewards and a recorder or town lawyer. Discussion of the evolution of Exeter's council is based on Wilkinson, *Mediaeval Council*, pp. xxiv–xxxiii, and upon analysis found in Kowaleski, *Local Markets and Regional Trade*, pp. 100–108.

47   Joyce Youings, *Early Tudor Exeter: The Founders of the County of the City* (Exeter: University of Exeter, 1974), p. 7; Hoskins, *Two Thousand Years*, pp. 24–25; A. M. Jackson, "Medieval Exeter, the Exe, and the Earldom of Devon," *Transactions of the Devonshire Association* 104 (1972): 57–79.

[48]   Youings, *ibid.* Many original sources and an overview of the problem can be found in Muriel E. Curtis, *Some Disputes between the City and Cathedral Authorities of Exeter,* History of Exeter Research Group, Monograph 5 (Manchester: Manchester University Press, 1932). See below, pp. 264–68.

[49]   P.R.O., SC.1/2/99; Hoskins, *Two Thousand Years,* pp. 23–25; Joyce Youings, "The Economic History of Devon 1300–1700," *Exeter and Its Region,* ed. Frank Barlow (Exeter: University of Exeter Press, 1969), p. 164.

[50]   Kowaleski, *Local Markets and Regional Trade,* pp. 86–87.

[51]   Population grew to about 7000 in the 1520s. For ways of calculating population, see Kowaleski, *Local Markets and Regional Trade,* pp. 371–75.

[52]   *Ibid.,* pp. 89, 91–92 (Table 3.2); E. M. Carus-Wilson, *The Expansion of Exeter at the Close of the Middle Ages* (Exeter: The University of Exeter, 1963), pp. 5–7; Joyce Youings, *Tuckers Hall, Exeter* (Exeter: University of Exeter Press, 1968), pp. 2–3. For further analysis of Exeter's fairs, see below, p. 221.

[53]   D.R.O., Book 55, f.133; Carus-Wilson, *ibid.,* pp. 16 n.20, 22–31; G. D. Ramsay, *English Overseas Trade during the Centuries of Emergence* (London: Macmillan and Co. Ltd., 1957), pp. 133–34.

[54]   *Victoria History of the Counties of England: Nottinghamshire,* ed. William Page, 2 vols. (London: Archibald Constable and Co., Ltd., 1906), 1:248.

[55]   Emrys Bryson, *Portrait of Nottingham,* 2d ed. (London: Robert Hale, 1978), p. 26; Charles Deering, *Nottinghamia Vetus et Nova* (Nottingham: G. Ayscough and T. Willington, 1751), p. 15; Philip Dixon, David Knight, and Ron Firman, "The Origins of Nottingham," *A Centenary History of Nottingham,* ed. John Beckett (Manchester and New York: Manchester University Press, 1997), pp. 9, 13, 20.

[56]   Bryson, *Portrait of Nottingham,* p. 26; David Roffe, "The Anglo-Saxon Town and the Norman Conquest," *Centenary History of Nottingham,* p. 25.

[57]   M. W. Barley and F. I. Straw, "Nottingham," in *Historic Towns, Volume I,* gen. ed. Mary D. Lobel (London: Lovell Johns, 1969), pp. 1–2; Roffe, "Anglo-Saxon Town," pp. 29–31.

[58]   Roffe, "Anglo-Saxon Town," p. 35.

[59]   Barley and Straw, "Nottingham," pp. 3–5; Pamela Marshall and Trevor Foulds, "The Royal Castle," *Centenary History of Nottingham,* pp. 46–47; F. M. Stenton, *Anglo-Saxon England,* 3rd ed. (Oxford and New York: Oxford University Press, 1989), pp. 601, 604. The farm rose to over £54 in the fifteenth century.

[60]   *Victoria County History Nottinghamshire,* 1:329–31.

[61]   *Ibid.,* 1:238.

[62]   Trevor Foulds, "Trade and Manufacture," *Centenary History of Nottingham,* p. 75.

[63]   K. C. Edwards, "The Geographical Development of Nottingham," *Nottingham and Its Region* (Nottingham: Nottingham Local Executive Committee of the British Association, 1966), pp. 367–68.

[64]   Trevor Foulds, "The Medieval Town," *Centenary History of Nottingham,* p. 65. Twenty household heads were recorded at the time of the expulsion.

[65]   Barley and Straw, "Nottingham," p. 4; *Rot. Parl.* 6:164; Foulds, "Trade and Manufacture," *Centenary History of Nottingham,* p. 76; David Marcombe, "The Late Medieval Town, 1149–1560," *Centenary History of Nottingham,* p. 85.

[66]   Norwich then led the list of provincial towns, followed by Bristol and York, with Exeter in fifth place: Charles Phythian-Adams, *Desolation of a City: Coventry and*

the Urban Crisis of the Late Middle Ages (Cambridge: Cambridge University Press, 1979), p. 12; Josiah Cox Russell, *British Medieval Population* (Albuquerque: University of New Mexico Press, 1948), p. 142. Dyer, *Decline and Growth*, pp. 58–59, has a slightly different ranking, placing Norwich first, followed by Bristol, Exeter, Salisbury and York, with Nottingham dropping from twentieth-eighth place (its 1377 rank) to forty-first.

[67]   W. H. Stevenson, ed., *Royal Charters Granted to the Burgesses of Nottingham* (London and Nottingham: Bernard Quaritch, 1890), pp. 2–5; Duncan Gray, *Nottingham through 500 Years* (Nottingham: Derry and Sons, 1960), p. 4.

[68]   Stevenson, ed., *Royal Charters*, pp. 5–13.

[69]   *Ibid.*, pp. 13–19; M. T. Clanchy, "The Franchise of Return of Writs," *Transactions of the Royal Historical Society*, 5th series, 17 (1967): 59, 65.

[70]   Stevenson, ed., *Royal Charters*, pp. 19–21. Stevenson translates the clause "for the alleviation of the estate of the burgesses," but an elevation of dignity is implied as well. Citizens continued to elect one bailiff from each of the Norman and English "boroughs" until 1330, when Edward III allowed them to fill the offices with any two men they could find: *ibid.*, pp. 33–35. For the legal differences between the two "boroughs," see Foulds, "The Medieval Town," *Centenary History of Nottingham*, p. 66.

[71]   Stevenson, ed., *Royal Charters*, p. 21. A fifteen-day fair starting 20 November joined their eight-day fair of 21 September until 1378, when Richard II replaced the former with a five-day fair starting 22 February: *CChR*, 5:240.

PART TWO, CHAPTER 2
THE PRIVILEGES OF POWER

Charters, the privileges they conferred, and the local officers they empowered to exercise them, formed the foundation of a town's relations with the royal government. Although no English charter rivals the length and complexity of the Iberian *fueros*, neither the Crown nor its urban subjects took the possession of such privileges for granted. A charter was the most valuable gift a king could make to a borough, and one that towns pursued with considerable investment of money and patronage. In authorizing elections of officers to act on both local and national levels, the documents encouraged boroughs to choose the ways and means by which they represented themselves to society at large. Charters not only enumerated financial and administrative rights, but made considerable contributions to the characterization of a town's identity. Sometimes out of ignorance, they also changed the terms upon which various constituencies within a town related to each other, with disastrous effects.

To historians of the late nineteenth and early twentieth centuries, the study of borough charters and officers revealed the building blocks of clear constitutional development. Today, these same elements take their value from the insight they provide about town identity, growth and maturity. They also raise questions about the nature of the grants. When kings gave chartered rights, did this mean they were privileges designed primarily to make life easier for the royal administration without regard for borough needs? Which party articulated needs and suggested solutions to problems? Can we discern a royal policy towards towns expressed in charters and the duties of their officers? If such a policy existed, did it tend to favor wealthy officeholders at the expense of other segments of the urban population? Some historians have determined to their own satisfaction that charters themselves perpetuated oligarchic rule in towns as the kind of government most easily dealt with by the central administration.[1] The four towns of our study provide opportunities for testing this theory and determining the nature of the input civic officials had on the charters they sought. The duties and responsibilities of the officers themselves also bear scrutiny to avoid facile characterization as selfish oligarchs. Equally illuminating are the actions of their parliamentary representatives both at home and in their meetings with the king. Throughout the fourteenth and fifteenth centuries, all four town governments had to relate to an exalted figure from whom came all enrolled privileges. In doing so, the determination and exercise of their own abilities became a matter of the highest importance.

We must be careful not to imbue charters with too much power. The four towns received different charters at different moments in their history, and the documents alone are not the only influences on their development. Although the charters described terms of governance and expectations of behavior from the royal government's point of view, living under those terms allowed towns to recognize their own capacities for self-government. The immunities and liberties they granted were rarely so unambiguous or complete that urban subjects did not have to cultivate powers of interpretation to apply them. The offices they created had to be filled by urban subjects of some talent whose very choice forced towns to face issues of social and economic division. Serving both a local and a royal master required keen judgment by civic officials, whose oaths of office stressed the possession of virtue as much as governing ability. In addition, prevailing upon the great men and women of the day to exercise "good lordship" and convey town needs to the monarch prompted urban subjects to develop useful skills of diplomacy and negotiation. Obtaining a royal charter was not an end, the fulfillment of every need, but the start of a process.

But most important, the need for self-respect required towns to move beyond the dependent relationship inherent in merely being given one's privileges. Many towns chose to achieve this by placing a high value on their chartered ability to deal directly with the central administration, unencumbered by royal servants and equal in dignity to the other estates of the realm. The charters and the officers who enacted their rights provided the basic means by which towns could make this claim a reality. They also courted social unrest when they failed to respect local custom, saved the greatest new privileges for a select few, and moved too quickly and insensitively to change the nature of borough identity.

Charters in the Later Middle Ages

English towns of the later Middle Ages had a long acquaintance with charters and the process of acquiring them. Since the twelfth century, charters had granted them fee farms, freedom from tolls and the interference of royal servants, local courts for the investigation of petty crimes, and some of the municipal officers needed to direct borough government. The financial clauses provided both revenue and independence from the Crown; the legal and administrative grants gave citizens added responsibilities for peacekeeping within their jurisdiction. But as late as the fifteenth century, many privileges remained to be won, ranging from the great gifts of county status and the official sanctioning of corporate behavior, to the humbler but no less valuable acquisitions of new fairs and markets. Such charters augmented what contemporaries called the dignity and worship of a town, defining its nature as it interacted with other bodies.

To that end, between the 1370s and the 1520s, our four towns sought new charters for three essential reasons: to create opportunities for trade and commerce in the troubled post-plague economy; to define the limits of the borough's legal and administrative jurisdiction, often after bitter disputes with other corporate bodies; and to increase the number and power of local officers who were both directly responsible to the Crown and selected by a restricted group of citizens. While the last goal suggests the intensification of oligarchic behavior, the first two reveal a broader concern for the financial and legal security of the entire population.

However, simple confirmation of previously achieved liberties took high priority. Most of the charters granted during this period confirmed older documents, occasionally repeating in some detail and thus assuring specifically cherished privileges. By the fifteenth century, towns customarily renewed earlier grants at the start of each reign, despite the expense, inconvenience, and the unwelcome acknowledgment that delegated powers were revocable.[2] Rapid changes in dynasty during that century increased the costs and anxieties of civic officials, but they also multiplied the occasions on which privileges could be assured and loyalty rewarded. As an undated petition in York's archives specifies, such renewals could be occasions on which to praise the new king, remind him of the generosity of his "tresnobles progenitours et predecessours Roys Dengleterre," and cast the fulfillment of their desires as an act of charity and sound rule.[3]

Richard II's accession provided a typical occasion for confirmations. Fully one-quarter of English boroughs had their charters confirmed during the first three years of the young king's reign.[4] All four of the towns in this study received such a grant in 1378, partially in reward for contributing barges to Edward III's royal navy for the war with France.[5] Confirmations required little labor and less deliberation, but they were not without cost. Norwich also received a confirmation because it had contributed a balinger, but not before two citizens traveled to London and expended over £4 in rewards to clerks and administrators. Dissatisfied with the terms of the grant, Norwich soon after began to petition for a new charter with broader financial and jurisdictional powers.[6]

The financial and military assistance that turned a usurper into a crowned king could also result in special privileges for a borough. York citizens' timely loan of five hundred marks to Henry of Bolingbroke on his march south "in his necessity, before he undertook the governance of the realm" helped assure them rapid confirmation of city liberties in 1399.[7] Edward IV's preamble to the second of his two 1462 confirmations of Norwich's liberties stated that the grant was made "in consideration of the good conduct and great costs and expenses of the Citizens of the said City and moreover of the free services many times borne by them for us against our adversaries and rebels" encountered in the process of taking the throne.[8] More specifically, Edward was responding to a petition drawn up by the city mentioning the "importable charges and costs" borne by a number of towns, and requesting confirmation of liberties granted by the Lancastrian monarchs, nervously described as "late in dede and not of right kinges of England."[9] The French *bonnes villes* exhibited similar concerns throughout the fifteenth century in their frequent requests to the Valois kings for confirmation of charters.[10] By way of contrast, English requests tapered off after Henry V's reign. Uncertainty about the longevity of a Yorkist or Tudor reign dissuaded some towns from the cost, but a more compelling factor was the danger of reminding new kings of the gifts of disgraced predecessors.[11]

Although borough liberties had been expanding for over two centuries, civic officials continued to find reasons for requesting new charters. Pressing reasons were often financial, resulting in some of the towns' most straightforward grants. York's charter of 1393 took particular advantage of royal gratitude for extraordinary services rendered: granted one year after the transfer to the north of the major offices of royal government and the expensive hospitality shown the king, the charter allowed the city to acquire lands to the value of £100 *per annum* to finance bridge repairs and religious services. Its administrative and judicial clauses, naming the mayor and eight aldermen *ex officio* justices of the peace, also had financial ramifications.[12] Norwich's charter of 1380, the second granted by Richard II, reiterated the contents of a recent statute confining the activities of foreign merchants within a city to sales to freemen only and compelling non-citizens to join trade fraternities and submit to the authority of city government.[13] The Composition of 1415 and the royal charter that accepted its tenets two years later addressed the issue of competition from merchants within the city who had not taken up the franchise but expected commercial benefits such as the right to have apprentices and shops.[14] During the 1440s, persistent pleas of poverty also gained York two important charters. A 1442 grant restricted the mercantile activity of non-citizens, while seven years later, the city gained a fair and the formal annexation of a neighboring wapentake, the Ainsty.[15]

Citizens relied on documents other than charters to settle disputes between towns and rival corporate bodies, but the tenets of the formal documents reveal citizens' understanding of exactly what was at stake. Exeter's dispute with the bishop over jurisdiction had been settled by arbitration in 1448, but Edward IV addressed the citizens' lasting needs in a charter fifteen years later. The king gave them a fair, plus all fines and confiscations of felons, in an attempt to augment their financial resources, provided they made no further claim to jurisdiction within the bishop's fee.[16] Norwich citizens sought no fewer than three chartered confirmations of an arbitration presented by Cardinal Wolsey in 1524 to defuse hostilities between the city and prior.[17] Charters could not only recompense citizens for financial losses in these disputes, but they were essential to confirm royal recognition of informal means of conflict settlement.

Charters that addressed administrative privileges and their changes were the most complex. Although it can be argued that such documents added no privileges that the boroughs were not already exercising, it is undeniable that medieval officers themselves initiated the requests, journeyed personally to Westminster to make them, and distributed considerable gifts of money and comestibles for their gain.[18] Their efforts indicate a confidence that the written assurances of the royal government constituted the highest degree of guarantee for the liberties they sought to claim and exercise. Time-honored custom and the historic memory of such privileges were no longer enough, especially when the Crown itself needed reminding of the grants it had made.

The most detailed charters of the fourteenth and fifteenth centuries articulated corporate behavior or raised a town to county status, or combined the two. Martin Weinbaum insisted that "the real innovation of the period 1307–1660 is the incorporation of boroughs," listing five definitive concessions: perpetual succession of offices, the power to sue and be sued as a whole and in the name of the corporation, the ability to hold lands, use of a common seal, and the authority to issue bylaws.[19] As we have seen from their earlier histories, towns exercised some or all of those rights before the fourteenth century, with or without specific royal permission. Weinbaum himself admits that the formal grant was made infrequently, and certainly the first two boroughs to receive charters of incorporation, Coventry (1345) and Hedon (1348), were not leading towns of the realm but boroughs in need of administrative help for commercial growth or extrication from rival jurisdictions.[20] Of the four boroughs in this study, only Nottingham received a charter specifically mentioning incorporation.[21] Anxious to decrease royal interference in local matters, York and Norwich more eagerly sought county corporate status, following Bristol's grant of 1373. Exeter had to wait until 1537 for the attainment, just preceding a second wave of chartered incorporations beginning in the 1540s and peaking in Mary's reign.[22]

All of these charters had a long history, but York's experience was the most straightforward. Its important charter of 1396 extending internal self-government resulted from Richard II's bitter altercations with London, his desire to punish the old capital by favoring what could become the new regional government center, his own visits to York, and the city's desire to keep up with competitors like Bristol.[23] The formulaic language refers to the king's affection for the city and its good deeds and services before separating York from the surrounding county and its royal sheriff. As a consequence, the mayor of the new entity, the county of the city of York, acquired additional responsibilities towards the Crown, the chief of them being royal escheator. Two sheriffs, chosen by the citizens and community, replaced the three bailiffs particularly to execute those financial duties once monopolized by the royal sheriff. These men also inherited the judicial duties of the bailiffs, and no liberty exercised by the latter was to be lost or denied. Neither the charter of 1393 nor the new one specifically mentioned the existence of the separate ecclesiastical liberties, requiring the dean and chapter of York Minster to sue for their own charter to protect their precincts from such an extension of civic jurisdiction. Most particularly, royal officers, of the county or the royal household, no longer could interfere in local matters or represent the city to the offices of the central administration, including the Exchequer. However, if the local officers became negligent in their relations with the government, the chancellor or his appointee could investigate and punish them on behalf of the king.

The nature of their duties elevated the mayor and sheriffs far above the rest of the populace, but ceremony and symbolism were not forgotten. The mayor won the right to have his sword (in York's case, given by the king) carried before him in public processions with the point erect, in front of all magnates and lords of the realm, excepting only the king himself. The mayor's and sheriffs' serjeants could carry their maces, bearing the royal arms, at any time, "as the king's serjeants at arms do, without question."

Except for the distinction drawn between citizens and community (*cives et communitas*), the king did not directly address election procedure in this charter or dictate the maintenance of an elite ruling body. The citizens themselves had long before evolved such an attitude towards governance and did not need a royal charter to choreograph their exercise of power. The new charter was most useful in giving the city what it could not take or evolve by itself, namely the rights and duties of a county corporate able to deal directly with the royal administration. In doing so, it shifted the focus and source of municipal power from the community of all freemen to a restricted group of officers working directly and closely with the Crown.

Charters that raised the other boroughs to the status of counties offer some comparisons. Nottingham's 1449 document opened with the admission that the town had been incorporated for a long time, and would now only change the name by which it characterized its legal identity.[24] Henceforth, it would be a perpetual incorporated community by the name of the Mayor and Burgesses of the Town of Nottingham, continuing to be able to exercise perpetual succession, land ownership, and judicial duties as before. After three months, it could act as a county

separate from the royal shire. As at York, burgesses replaced the bailiffs
with two elected sheriffs, although only Nottingham's document
specified election dates. Moreover, the king also directed Nottingham's
burgesses to elect seven aldermen for life, one of whom was to be mayor.
He did not specify the details of election or the breadth of the franchise,
but gave all seven the right to be justices of the peace within the town
with all fines and forfeits due the office. York had already evolved for
itself a select group of mayoral advisor-candidates; Henry VI had to
create such a body in Nottingham in order for the privileges of his grant
to be properly executed. Although the tenets of the charter reflected royal
concern over the men sitting as royal justices, this document did not go
as far as a 1438 letter patent to Lincoln, in which Henry VI ordered the
elections of only worthy and wealthy men to avoid damage to city and
realm alike.[25] The king did, however, further set apart Nottingham's
aldermen from the rest of the burgesses and broadcast their higher rank
by their right to wear gowns, hoods and cloaks of the style and materials
used by London's officers.

Norwich's 1404 charter raising it to county status was as important
for what it omitted as for what it articulated. Its failure to specify the
exact geographic range of the city's liberties caused decades of
frustration in Norwich's disputes with rival jurisdictions.[26] But its
vagueness on the distribution of power among various groups within the
city created the most immediate difficulties. The complex history of the
grant and the effects it had upon internal policies provide an illuminating
study of the interplay between town and Crown. Most particularly, the
case shows the extent to which the royal government was ignorant about
local conditions and established customs, and the freedom which urban
subjects enjoyed to shape their own policies.

When Richard II ascended the throne, Norwich officers had dutifully
confirmed their older grants but hoped to augment their liberties before
too long. The citizens, through two representatives sent to London,
petitioned the king and council soon after, requesting the ability to
change and remedy borough customs by act of the four bailiffs and
twenty-four citizens, or the greater part of them, without the assent of the
commonalty. London's privileges had influenced their request, but they
credited the need for it to threatening local conditions, "because many of
the commune of their town have of late been very greatly contrarious and
perchance will still be [?] so unless there be there better remedies and
ordinances for the good government of the town and of victuals."[27] The

royal government understood the implied threat to the realm's peace well enough to grant Norwich what it requested in a charter of 1380.[28]

The citizens wanted more, but Richard turned a deaf ear. Even their expensive patronage of John of Gaunt, thought to be an influence on his royal nephew, produced no help.[29] Gaunt did, however, influence the city's support of Henry Bolingbroke, who actively encouraged the citizens to frame their own charter and approach the throne again once he himself was settled on it. Norwich's new charter was cast in familiar terms that nonetheless reflected the development of serious internal divisions.[30] It stressed that the ascent to county status and the change of name to "the county of the city of Norwich" abolished or restricted no previously-exercised privilege. It empowered the citizens and commonalty (deliberately distinguished but acting together) to choose a mayor and two sheriffs annually, the former to act as king's escheator and the latter to replace the bailiffs while dealing with the Exchequer as the royal sheriff once had. Details of mayoral and shrieval elections were omitted, and thus left to city custom. In addition, the citizens and commonalty relied upon the mayor and four *probi homines* chosen only by him to hear pleas belonging to the chief magistrate's new position as justice of the peace. As in York, the symbolism of the sword and maces further augmented the dignity and importance of the small group of officers serving the citizens at large and the king more directly than ever before. The ceremony, the extension of jurisdiction over places and pleas, and the more intimate relations with the royal government were gifts only the king could grant, and he chose to grant them not to the commonalty but to a more restricted group.

Conflict arose when the 1404 charter began to co-exist with the restrictions of the 1380 document, all within the context of older custom that divided actual choice from initial nomination of officers. Within a few years, a body of eighty citizens was assembled from the commonalty, representing the four leets. They nominated men for mayor and for sheriff, but the final decision rested with the incumbent mayor and sheriffs and a select body of twenty-four, which constituted the "court." This was a critical period in which the commonalty at large lost direct influence over elections and policymaking, and royal charters had not ameliorated the situation.[31]

A series of complaints and a later arbitration award clarify some of the issues and reveal the background to the 1404 grant. In 1415, the commonalty complained that the 1380 charter empowering the bailiffs and twenty-four alone to make changes in custom, had been obtained secretly without the assent of their group. Indeed, the exercise of that assent, hallowed by custom and by charter (including the 1404 grant), had been ignored for some years. Beginning in 1406, they had tried to exercise their right to elect the mayor directly, but their choice had been deposed by the "prudeshomes who are called the people of estate." The greater part of the city thus felt "sorely aggrieved" and believed the city's reputation to be damaged.[32] The sheriffs and body of twenty-four replied, arguing that when changes for the better had to be made, no one should have to wait until the commonalty made up its mind. By the commonalty, the complainants meant the poorer and more humble as well as those of authority and power, and these "prudeshommes" could not countenance the participation of such people in the government. The commonalty had never directly elected a mayor nor had it ever had the right to do so. The situation touched the royal government when the sheriffs and twenty-four pleaded with an interested local noble, Sir Thomas Erpingham, to persuade the king to remove all references to the commonalty from the 1404 charter, better to keep administration in the hands of those able to execute it.[33]

Erpingham arbitrated the dispute, persuading both sides from their more extreme positions. He did not excise the commonalty completely from the government, but neither did he affirm the freemen's elevated view of their powers. The eighty leet representatives of the freemen were reduced to a common council of sixty. They joined the retiring mayor and twenty-four each May Day when the commons at large were welcomed to the guildhall and allowed to nominate candidates for mayor (confining their choices to men who had previously served as mayor or sheriff). The final choice rested with the mayor and twenty-four, who in September also chose one sheriff while the commonalty selected the second. Where previously the eighty had annually chosen the twenty-four, restricted to men who had previously served in the city's highest offices, now the small inner circle would stand perpetually as in London. Nevertheless, the body of twenty-four was to enact nothing binding on the city without the consent of the commonalty. This arbitration, known as the Composition of St. Valentine's Day 1415, became the basis of Henry V's 1417 confirmation and alteration of his father's charter.[34]

That Norwich needed the Composition and the 1417 charter that followed suggests that the 1404 royal document was somehow inadequate. The more influential men of Norwich did not intend to lose status by any granting of new offices and duties. Indeed, they had been encouraged by the favor shown them in numerous royal documents such as the grant of 1380. They had honed their skills in convincing the king and his government that internal restrictions on "contrarious" elements of the citizenry profited not just his urban subjects but assured the realm's peace and prosperity. Although the civic officials did not attempt to cut the commonalty from the most important charter they had ever sought, they obviously believed that the trust the Crown showed in them allowed them to interpret the document as they saw fit. Wisely, however, they valued internal harmony more and accepted peacemaking efforts sealed appropriately enough on the feast day of a saint dedicated to love and goodwill.

It is also true that the king and his ministers do not seem to have investigated local conditions very closely to see whether the connection between restrictions and peace was reasonable. If there existed a conscious royal policy towards towns, it was largely uninformed of how Crown grants affected local conditions and meshed with existing privileges. Even the intervention of influential friends did not help. As the following chapters will show, towns dedicated no small amount of money and effort to identifying, rewarding, and directing the "good lordship" of interested nobles and gentry, and even of the king himself. Although they hoped that friends in high places would more easily gain them the privileges they desired, such investments did not usually result in a more knowledgeable central administration.

However clear the language of a charter or well-defined the duties of civic officials, total compliance with its tenets remained impossible. Royal officers refused to recognize chartered rights, as in York in 1408 when only the presentation of their most recent confirmation excused the citizens from having to answer to the steward and marshal of Henry IV's household.[35] Occasionally, citizens themselves refused to acknowledge chartered rights, particularly those involving litigation. They interpreted the privileges as infringements upon their own liberty, and pursued their right to have their cases heard at common law or in equity courts. Urban subjects of means showed the greatest ingenuity in their resistance, appealing to justices at Westminster for the right to remove the cases from the local venue to the royal. Walter Ingham caused Norwich extensive aggravation to this end throughout the 1470s and 1480s regarding actions of debt he did not want heard at home. His cases were eventually remitted to Norwich, but not before the city charters themselves were transported to London, and numerous gifts of food, wine, and money had been lavished on Westminster officials as well as local legal counsel.[36]

Strenuously sought and carefully confirmed, charters solved some problems but also raised new difficulties. The privileges they described did not always accurately reflect urban subjects' understanding of their role in the realm. Some elements in towns deliberately tested the limits of the delegated rights, and called upon the royal government to take sides. Yet charters provided unsurpassed occasions for urban subjects to learn how to interpret and apply their new privileges themselves, equitably and maturely. The best solutions were those that developed from the community itself, involving as many of the franchised members as practicable. Royal charters allowed towns to find for themselves a viable balance between elitist dominance and broad-based participation, and to maintain conditions of peace and profit that benefited all subjects of the realm. To fail was to invite unrest and intervention welcomed by neither Crown nor town.

Officers and Their Duties

The urban officers sanctioned by royal charter and responsible to both townspeople and the king fulfilled sensitive roles in medieval society. Sworn to serve two masters, they are too often dismissed today as supporters of oligarchic rule, using their access to the Crown solely to restrict local power to a select and selfish few. As Susan Reynolds has often reminded us, this use of the Aristotelian concept in a narrow pejorative sense inadequately describes English towns in the later Middle Ages.[37] It may accurately delineate economic divisions of the period, but it fails to consider urban subjects' own principles and their acceptance of basic concepts of order and hierarchy. Very real ideological and political constraints prevented magistrates from governing selfishly or with prejudice. The principles that underlay those constraints placed a high value on civic harmony in the face of inevitable inequality. As Norwich's Composition of 1415 stated, the object of civic government was the establishment of peace, unity and accord, making poor and rich of one heart in love and charity, without division or dissolution that attracted unwanted royal attention.[38] The restricted numbers who became mayors, sheriffs and stewards were held to high expectations by both the royal government and the larger pool of citizens who delegated to them authority based on local custom, civic consensus, and local bylaws.

Civic officials' oaths reveal the assumptions against which their behavior was measured. Medieval society regarded oaths as solemn promises affirming one's loyalty and responsibility as one passed to a new stage of life. Honor and virtue were frequently stressed, for as Hoker affirmed, a city could flourish and the commonwealth prosper only "where the magistrate is wise, virtuous, and goodly."[39] Only residents of means and influence were thought best able to grasp this concept and secure the peace and order valued by all subjects. The oaths that Norwich's mayor took during the fifteenth century assert that the chief magistrate represented the entire community to the outside world, by the sober execution of his internal duties as well as by his contacts with the king and the central administration. In the first of two oaths that he swore, the chief magistrate promised to maintain the laws and liberties, good customs and franchises of the city. He carried out regulations pertaining to food for the good of the community, while correcting and redressing defaults in general, bringing justice and equal right to the poor as well as to the rich. The mayor's own courts provided an appropriate venue for such activities, while the early fifteenth-century royal charters granted him the powers of a justice of the peace also able to try pleas concerning apprentices and laborers.[40]

Duties owed the royal government found mention in a separate oath pertaining to the mayor's charge as escheator.[41] This oath gave highest priority to service to the king and the keeping of the city for his profit. Mayors vowed to be especially careful of the king's prerogative, usually manifested in the property that fell to the Crown each year by treason or for lack of an heir.[42] Norwich's oath concluded by admonishing him to treat justly citizen and stranger, rich and poor, and to avoid acting out of hate or favor, or the desire for wealth and power. Even in duties owed only to the king, the officer could not forget his broader responsibilities and constituency.

Sheriffs' oaths resembled those of mayoral escheators. Duties to the king received primary mention, but these officers also swore to treat all people they contacted "buxumly and rightfully," doing right to the poor as well as to the rich and acting without hate or favor. Serving royal writs, accounting at the Exchequer, and defending the king's rights within the liberty received less detailed attention in the oath than instructions regarding the holding of local courts and safekeeping of prisoners. Such duties made it necessary for their names to be returned (with those of their shire counterparts) to Chancery upon their appointment, and for the Chancellor to approve of mid-year elections to replace deceased sheriffs.[43] All of Norwich's oaths ended with the admonition, "so help you God at the [day of] holy doom," reminding officers that negligence might go unpunished on earth but not in the afterlife.

The oaths can be supplemented by royal correspondence that gives a more detailed sense of the variety of duties expected of local officers. Mayors also received orders from Chancery to act on the king's behalf. They could be directed, as were Exeter's mayor and bailiffs, to protect an episcopal election, or restore an abbot's temporalities.[44] Other orders directed the arrests of merchants, citizens, and even of mayors of other towns, to be transported to Chancery for interrogation.[45] On happier occasions, the mayor with the greatest of his fellow officers greeted exalted visitors and conducted them personally into the liberties of the borough he represented.

Local and national documents express concern over the financial requirements of public office. The post of sheriff particularly burdened the men who held it with heavy financial and judicial responsibilities and required them to have access to wealth. Nottingham's sheriffs, for example, were forced to post a £100 bond to assure satisfactory performance of both their local and national tasks.[46] Financial inadequacy imperiled the reputation of the entire community. In 1500, a York sheriff was fined for dereliction of his duties, for he did not travel with a proper entourage or with his mace carried before him, nor had he invited the chamberlains and other officers to an annual feast. He had even neglected to provide the proper cloths and towels at the dinner he did manage to host. York had earlier exempted a young man from election as sheriff for eight years, unless in the meantime "he grew in goods and riches."[47] The commons of these towns recognized that any office with financial responsibilities should be held by men of property. In 1475, the self-described "poor commonalty" of York, far from upholding democratic principles, petitioned the mayor and his brethren to choose only "the most able men in goodes and discretion" as chamberlains and bridgemasters, best endowed to cover civic expenses and keep the city out of debt.[48]

The remuneration some officers earned on the job did not go far to recompense them. In 1372, York's council decided that the mayoral stipend should be established at £20 *per annum*. Raised to £50 in 1388, it was returned to its earlier rate under Henry VII in conjunction with pleas of urban poverty and a decision to audit mayoral expenses.[49] Nottingham paid its mayor a comparable rate, while the lower figures expended in Exeter and Norwich were supplemented with gifts of wine and bread.[50] These stipend ranges put mayors on a level more with a man-at-arms, earning about £18 *per annum*, than with an average baron of the day, although something close to a princely level of hospitality was expected of the urban official during his term. To make up the shortfall, a mayor could draw on his own wealth, and most high-ranking officials also expected preferential financial treatment in local affairs, putting themselves first in line for rents, gifts, and pardons of their amercements and fines.[51]

The job descriptions themselves dwelt as much on the wealth of the candidate as on his past experience in government, but the former almost automatically assured participation in the latter. After the mid-fourteenth century, Exeter's government ordered that no one should be elected mayor unless he had previously served as bailiff or steward, in order to be experienced in judicial matters. The candidate had to have respect for the law and for God, to be prudent and diligent, and to care for the city's profit, a term used in more than just its economic sense. He had to be a man of discretion, sober and serious, able to act with decorum. Royal progresses, entertainment of the nobility and visiting officials, and journeys to Westminster required a mayor and officers able to afford the time and money needed to execute the office properly for the honor of both city and Crown. Not only had the officers to neglect their own callings to some extent, but they had to be wealthy enough to resist bribery and to contribute generously to local and royal causes. An ordinance of 1340 declared that an Exeter mayor had to have lands and rents worth one hundred shillings *per annum*, but by Hoker's time the requirement was less specific: "reasonable wealth, better to support the burden and charge of his office."[52] In representing the entire town and its history to the outside world, the chief magistrate needed all the influence that virtue and wealth could grant him.

The fourteenth century saw critical changes in the sources of urban officials' wealth. By the end of the century, the men who reached the highest levels of local political office possessed great wealth gained more often from trade and commerce than landholding or artisanal activities. The transition contributed its own tensions to the inner circles of local

government, as the "new men" only gradually recognized their
responsibilities to the commonalty at large and imbued urban society
with the philosophies and methodologies of investment and commerce.
Exeter in the late fourteenth century was not unique in finding its most
important rulers (mayor, stewards, recorder, councilors) from the top 6%
of its householders, whose wealth came overwhelmingly from overseas
trade. York's bailiffs, sheriffs, and mayors also came predominantly
from the mercantile class. [53]

The mayor's dual role in society, particularly in the context of social
tensions, demanded protection and respect. The officer chiefly
responsible for presiding over local courts and formal arbitration needed
the regard and esteem of all residents or his decisions would be
worthless. York and Bristol were two cities among many which imposed
heavy fines on those who defamed the mayor's personal or professional
life.[54] Fellow officers could be as insulting as the commonalty, and as
harshly punished, the better to impose internal order.[55] The disputes
illuminate lasting tensions between the most important magistrates and
the lesser merchants and artisans who filled the slighter posts. York
citizen John Sponer suffered imprisonment for three days in 1477 as
much for speaking harshly to Mayor John Tong and for hoping to have a
better lord after the next election, as for neglecting to account for money
he received the year before as the city's common serjeant.[56] In 1463,
Miles Greenbank, several times a sheriff of York, called Mayor John
Newton "fals harlett and odyr unsittyng langage," suffering punishment
of a fine of five marks. At the same council meeting, measures were
taken to protect civic officers from slander. Any franchised man who
slandered the mayor, an alderman, or one of the council, or who revealed
their business, was to pay £10 to the commonalty, the same amount
levied for the drawing of an officer's blood.[57]

Those truly dissatisfied with justice dispensed by civic officials
could complain to the royal government. Mayors were most often the
subject of pleas to the Chancellor, probably because of the breadth of
their duties and powers. If we are to believe some of the pleas before
Chancery, mayors changed the venues of cases illegally and renewed
actions in their towns which were already being heard at Westminster.
They were accused of ignoring Chancery writs "out of spite and malice,"
and of forcing Londoners to buy the freedom of their towns.[58] More
seriously, the conditions under which they imprisoned suitors could be
fatal. The widow of a Norwich fuller demanded an investigation after her

husband's death in city prison, while Edmund Force blamed "his utter undoing" on thirty weeks of Norwich imprisonment.[59] During Henry VII's reign, Devonshire resident Alice Tapton sued the widow of Exeter's mayor whom she claimed had imprisoned her cruelly and illegally. According to the records of the Council in Star Chamber, where the case was heard, Mayor John Colshill ordered his officials to arrest Alice in June 1494. The men he chose were violent and armed ("arrayed for war"), and the order was brutally executed. Dragged to the city prison, she was fettered with irons weighing thirty pounds and left for six months. Three times brought before commissions of jail delivery but never tried, Alice was released but soon rearrested when she could not find sureties. Claims of riot may have brought the case to the attention of the council, but the real issue was the property (lands, livestock, and furnishings) seized by the late mayor and retained by his executrix, who claimed that she was not responsible for her late husband's actions.[60]

How much justice the defendants-turned-plaintiffs received is unclear; harassment of the ruling circle and revelation of their abuse of power may have been more the point of their actions. Certainly they did not feel constrained to silence by the cognizance of internal pleas promised in charters and oaths. Townspeople unhappy with the way their officers behaved did not believe their search for justice was confined within city walls. They acted on their belief that if civic officers misused their dual responsibility and ruled unfairly, the royal government had a vested interest in investigating the problem and calling their urban servants to account. Far from sanctioning selfish behavior, the Crown and its charters provided yet another means by which to achieve the good government that "pleases God, brings rest and tranquillity, nourishes and increases love, and causes plenty and abundance."[61]

Elections, Appointment, and Evasion

Urban elections and the appointments of new officers created opportunities for the monarch to interfere in town government and insert men loyal to him alone, thus posing a potential threat to civic liberties. Election violence most frequently provided the king with an excuse to intervene, but despite the vivid and memorable terms used in the records to describe it, such upheaval was rare. Exeter and Nottingham generally experienced peaceful elections; Norwich calmed its tendency towards dissension by moderate changes in the process after suffering royal seizure of its liberties. York knew the worst and longest-lasting election violence in the period, requiring royal intervention to enforce solutions. It is no coincidence that York suffered from a contracting economy at the same time, making access to political office and its privileges so disputative.

Conflicts over elections generally resulted from restrictions on the number and status of citizens empowered to participate. When the king intervened in such cases, he tended to restrict participation even further, in fear of the lawlessness and disorder such conflicts engendered. Well-known are the examples of Leicester and Northampton, where in 1489 the popular elements of election were replaced by restricted councils.[62] In none of these boroughs were residents at large given a role in elections; women and the poor were never considered. Not even all the male franchised citizens (a third of the householders in fourteenth-century Exeter; roughly half in York) participated in the multi-layered procedure of choosing local leaders.[63] All of the towns in this study relied upon either a small group of experienced men to make the final decision or let it rest with the incumbents alone, sometimes choosing from a pool of appropriate candidates (i.e., ones with previous experience) nominated by a larger gathering of the citizenry. Nomination, and the power to give or withhold assent to the actions of the mayor and aldermen or *probi homines*, were all the commonalty of these towns possessed and all that was likely to be sanctioned by either the king or his local representatives.

York's long history of election disturbance deserves special mention. Three times in office during the 1370s, Mayor John Gisburne represented the new mercantile wealth and profited from royal court contacts as well. Accused of scandals and malpractice, Gisburne was literally chased from town in 1380 by commons and craftsmen disgusted by his abuse of power. His enemies proclaimed Simon Quixley mayor after breaking into the Guildhall, forcing the *bones gentz* to confirm their decision, and urging the commons to rise. Quixley objected to the deed, but they were intoxicated by their overturning of city ordinances and perceived injustices. The royal government slowly investigated the insurgents and Quixley himself, compelling the rich men of the city to enter into bonds of £40 to keep the peace (one of the drawbacks of being wealthy and involved in civic government). Calm might have been restored had not the events of the Great Revolt the following summer proved inspiring. Smoldering resentments over access to office were linked to national dissatisfactions by the mayoralty itself and its dual relations. The year 1381 was a bad time to remind "a remarkably self-confident and articulate commons" of the links between local and national powers.[64] By the following year, fruitless investigations had persuaded the king to offer York a general pardon for one thousand marks.[65]

York had not seen the end of royal intervention. In 1462, an obstructed election prompted Edward IV to investigate, naming John Thrisk as mayor to break the deadlock. Thrisk agreed to the appointment despite feebleness of age and reluctance to serve a second term (he had first been mayor in 1442). Edward rewarded him and pardoned him from holding office again, while cautioning the citizens to be obedient to the new mayor, "whom we had commanded to do everything needful to keep the peace."[66] But continued disruptions forced the king to broaden the groups empowered to choose civic leaders. Two weeks before the elections of 3 February 1464, the incumbent mayor summoned the searchers of the city's crafts (in effect, the council of forty-eight) to call all their workers to the Guildhall. The crafts then nominated two aldermen, neither of whom had been twice mayor or had held the office in the past five years. The names of the two aldermen were then submitted to the mayor and council, and each man declared his choice to the recorder, the senior sheriff, and the common clerk.[67] In effect, the same civic officials still elected their own kind to succeed them, but it was impossible to ignore the king's intervention and his insistence that the crafts and not the ruling circle had an initial role in the elections.

Royal involvement in York was not at an end. Henry VI faced the same problems with the city during his brief return to power 1470–71. One of his last duties as king was the appointment of a new mayor and the threat of a £100 fine if opposition continued.[68] Edward IV continued to intervene throughout the rest of his reign whenever contested elections threatened the realm's peace, making some effort to acknowledge the commons' trenchant observation that "forasmuch as we be all one body incorporate, we think that we be all alike privileged [including any] of the commonalty which has borne no office in the city."[69]

The city did not passively wait for trouble to happen. Before the elections of 1489, York's council ordained that no man was to walk about armed, and that strangers should not carry weapons or otherwise incite violence. The mayor reminded the searchers that the crafts had the responsibility of choosing the candidates and that the process should be carried out peaceably.[70] Despite the precautions, the elections were disturbed so violently that an investigative commission intervened, headed by the archbishop of York and the earl of Northumberland. For the election of 1490, the crafts were asked to nominate three aldermen as candidates, one of whom was later selected by the mayor, aldermen, and council. The crafts were forbidden to conduct the nominations in the Guildhall, the scene of too much violence over the years.[71]

York election violence was fiercer than most because it was often tied to economic problems arising from jurisdiction rivalries with the Minster's vicars choral and St. Mary's Abbey. In 1501, the citizens became so angry about the abbot's enclosures that had robbed them of common lands that they tried to pressure civic officials by refusing even to hold an election unless the obstructions were pulled down.[72] Jurisdiction issues formed at least part of the petition the commons submitted in 1504 to the council in Star Chamber, refusing to proceed with the coming election until it was granted.[73] Contemporary records estimated a crowd of three thousand people gathered outside the Guildhall, imprisoning the mayor and council until after dark. Henry VII ordered sixteen of the offenders to appear before his council and receive punishment, "as may bee to the ferefull example of all other semblably toffende hereafter." Others were punished by the mayor himself, who tried to insist that the seminal charter of Richard II gave the commons no role at all in elections.[74] Such an extreme view was not tenable, and in 1517 Henry VIII tried his hand at peacemaking. To the mayor, sheriffs, and aldermen was added a common council of forty-one, chosen from both great and small crafts and empowered to nominate three of the aldermen to serve as mayor.[75] The indirect method of electing the chief officers remained unchanged and largely unchallenged; far more disturbing was the identification of local disagreement as breaches of the king's peace, an equation that encouraged the monarch to interfere in local matters.[76]

In addition to changing the process of local elections, monarchs exercised their right to impose their own nominees on a variety of urban positions. Nevertheless, there is nothing in England's history during this time to compare with the royal imposition of Iberian *corregidores* or French provincial governors, even when the very existence of mayors, sheriffs, or swordbearers derived from royal *fiat* or the offices themselves could be suspended along with franchises and liberties.[77] Kings replaced mayors only in times of dire need and destructive violence, but lesser offices presented themselves as appropriate rewards for royal servants. Henry VII was particularly adept at inserting men of his own choosing in local offices, to act as agents and representatives of the king in towns and shires.[78]

It was more serious when the king expressed an interest in one of the most important of offices in a town, that of the recorder or chief legal officer of a town. Usually recruited from the ranks of those already retained by a town as *legisperiti* and not required to be resident, the recorder was often a member of the county gentry and might spend as much time in Westminster as in the city that hired him.

The appointment of one of York's recorders involved the city in decades of political tension. When the incumbent resigned in 1477, Edward IV recommended lawyer Miles Metcalf for the office. The younger son of a gentry family of Nappa, Metcalf was unanimously chosen by a compliant council and enjoyed a successful career, but neither his Yorkist nor his Yorkshire associations recommended him to Henry VII. In October 1485, the king accused Metcalf of working against him and nominated Richard Green for his place. The council apparently accepted Green, but later correspondence from Henry and the earl of Northumberland revealed that Green was not given full power or trust.[79] York officers delayed their promise to remedy the situation on the grounds that the city's representatives should return from parliament before the matter was decided. The town finally took action in February 1486 when Green was accepted not as recorder but as a counselor whose appointment could take place only when the office was vacated.

The decision was a clever compromise, but the city had not counted on incumbent Metcalf's death within two weeks.[80] Further excuses delayed an appointment until March, when Henry abandoned Green as a candidate and nominated Thomas Middleton as recorder. The king's promise "to have you in the more tendre remembraunce of our good grace in tyme to come" did not sway the council from rejecting Middleton and unanimously electing serjeant-at-law John Vavasour instead.[81] The selection was a statement of York's right, both ancient and more recently declared in charters, to control internal city affairs. Despite the inconvenience to the king and the offense he might take against the city's independence, the monarch could not deny the truth of York's reminder that

hertofore it pleased the King to shew unto [the civic officials] how his mynde, wol, and pleasur was and shuld be that thei shuld enjoy the auncheunt liberties and costomes with free eleccion . . . notwithstanding any writing to be maide fro his grace in favour of eny persone herafter.[82]

For reasons related more to ceremony and symbolism than administrative power, the office of swordbearer was the subject of the most strife between cities and the Crown. Although the position brought honor to the town and its officials, the job was chiefly valuable for its stipend (£2 *per annum* in Norwich and Exeter, £3 13s. 4d. in York), and for its ability to make its incumbent the king's local agent. In 1411, Henry IV granted the position at Norwich to a man of his own choosing, who was pressured to renounce the post after the city hired William Paston to defend its right to a free election.[83] Norwich only accepted a royal nominee in 1464 when the council discovered the man would be liveried as a king's esquire, granting added dignity to the post.[84] When age and illness forced York's incumbent swordbearer to retire in 1486, Henry VII nominated his own choice for the office. The mayor and aldermen dryly observed that at one time monarchs had been willing to support York's "auncheunt liberties and costomes with free eleccion of all maner ther officers for the tyme." The officers themselves recalled (or invented) a local custom that those who had sought royal aid were deliberately passed over for the office they desired. Henry's candidate suffered the same fate.[85]

Offended officeholders could call upon the king to intervene for them, to return them to office or to help them retain their positions. One of the strangest examples of this kind of petition concerns York's swordbearer John Eglisfield.[86] Removed from office in 1481 and imprisoned for various offenses, Eglisfield petitioned the king for assistance. Edward's letter to the city repeated in particular the swordbearer's charges against "the malice and evill wille of one Wrangwyssh," the former lord mayor and parliamentary representative. Within a month, Edward IV wrote again to admit that the council's removal of Eglisfield had been correct, accepting that the man was "[one] of them that do ayanest your laudable usags and custumes."

The nature of the council's complaint against Eglisfield was only made clear the following spring, when the city again refused to reinstate him, this time on the grounds that he had formerly purchased the office and misused public funds. By October 1485, Eglisfield's crimes had been augmented by charges of counterfeiting and adultery. Incensed by the charges, Eglisfield called the officials traitors "and therupon he departed out of the Citie toward the King as it is said." Civic officials asked the archbishop of York to intervene for them, and admitted that the belief that Eglisfield was the king's servant had prevented them from punishing him earlier. Henry VII's response showed how successful Eglisfield had been with the king, who stated that the swordbearer had legally bought his office and deserved to be compensated for his dismissal. The council postponed discussion of the matter until its next meeting, but the topic does not appear on the records again. The obstreperous Eglisfield made one of his last appearances in the civic records when he attacked the earl of Northumberland's bailiff in 1486. The swordbearer's case, nevertheless, had broader implications. When Henry VII chided the civic officials with failing to keep his peace, he threatened, "I must and woll put in other rewlers that woll rewle and govern the Citie accordyng to my lawez."[87] He was clearly acting on a long tradition of royal interest and intervention in the quality and character of officeholding. But even the first of the Tudors quailed before the solidarity of urban self-confidence and the tradition of autonomy guaranteed by his predecessors' charters.

Equally disturbing to civic officers were the exemptions kings granted to citizens who refused to take office. Like the *curiales* of Roman imperial cities, many citizens sought freedom from holding those offices that made heavy demands on their purses or their schedules. The Crown made sure it would benefit most from their reluctance: for a few marks paid into the hanaper, a citizen could purchase a letter patent granting exemption, often for life, from being made mayor, sheriff, escheator, juror, or subsidy collector against his will. Purchase of an exemption meant that the citizens with enough wealth to hold office were also the men with the means to excuse themselves from the duty.

York's troubled economy prompted a disturbing number of exemptions. In 1419, its council dealt with the problems that arose when aldermen not wishing to be chosen mayor left town on election day, without bothering to excuse themselves. The council unanimously passed an ordinance permitting the offending alderman to be fined one hundred marks, "sixty [marks] to go to the newly elected mayor to help defray his expenses of office, forty to go to the sheriffs for the use of the city."[88] But Crown generosity with letters patent remained a problem despite local measures. The parliamentary representatives of 1450–51 submitted a petition requesting that all such royal letters be canceled and that future petitioners be fined £40.[89] Henry VI agreed, but his successors had shorter memories; although some petitioners pleaded age and illness, others simply purchased their freedom for the best price available.[90] In such ways, the wealthy could influence local politics by avoiding as well as dominating office.

Parliamentary Representation

Attendance at parliaments provided townsmen with their most direct experience of the royal government. All four of the towns studied had sent representatives regularly since the 1280s, although the loss of many returns robs us of complete data and reliable statistics. Local records are often disappointing as well: although representatives undoubtedly reported back to civic officials, council records and assembly rolls rarely recorded the burgesses' impressions of their participation in national policymaking. Their profile in the records reflected their treatment in the House of Commons in general: the knights of the shire, though outnumbered by the potential number of burgesses seven to three, dominated commissions, committees, and legislation by and about representatives. However, there is no compelling evidence for arguing that burgesses' importance declined during the course of the fifteenth century. Although some towns turned increasingly to county gentlemen of the legal profession for representation in place of resident merchants and civic officeholders, full presentation of borough concerns and problems remained a top priority. [91]

The four towns studied here considered service in parliament an honor to which they sent their wealthiest and most experienced men, and reimbursed them as well as they could. Before the mid-fifteenth century, representatives were franchised and resident in the boroughs they served, merchants often with international trade experience and sometimes members of the Calais Staple, able to conduct business of their own on the side particularly when parliament met at Westminster. A growing number possessed legal training, and city recorders could be valuably sent to Westminster when a borough sought a charter or judicial assistance. [92] Apart from the recorders and town clerks, few members represented a town without first having served in an entry-level office such as bailiff or sheriff; many went on to become mayors, and in addition won royal appointment to local commissions. The four towns suffered little interference in their selection process by local magnates, although some of the representatives chosen (particularly men of law) accepted the livery of neighboring nobles or provided them with legal advice on a retainer's fee.[93]

How representatives were selected by their boroughs remains something of a mystery. Unless and until a town had county status, the royal sheriff often handled the writs ordering and reporting elections, although it must not be assumed that the county servant chose the burgesses. Local records from Norwich, Nottingham, and York indicate that a small group, usually composed of the mayor, bailiff or sheriff, and some of the councilmen, met informally or as part of a council meeting, and made their choice of two burgesses. On rare occasions, larger and less wealthy groups of freemen complained that their voices should be heard: Nottingham experienced such agitation in 1412 when a gathering of one hundred preferred their choice to that of a select band of forty-nine, who tended to tap men who had already served as bailiff and mayor.[94] Norwich records speak of two elections, a preliminary one by the assembly of freemen later confirmed formally by the mayor, sheriffs, and council of twenty-four.[95] Town governors then returned the writs to Chancery, stating that the representatives had been legally and freely elected by the entire responsible community, that they were resident and "of sufficiency and discretion," invested by their community with full power (*plena potestas*) and authority to act on the borough's behalf.[96]

But no matter how many or how few made the ultimate decision, the time and expense involved in parliamentary service meant that only the wealthy could endure it. Rates of payment varied from borough to borough, and the central administration showed no concern about a uniform salary or the ways in which it was raised. Many towns, like Exeter and Nottingham, paid each burgess two shillings *per diem*, although the former town occasionally paid less.[97] Norwich paid more, up to 3s. 4d. a day until 1422 when the rate stabilized at 2s. per day.[98] York was most generous, treating burgesses like knights of the shire with a payment of 4s. *per diem*.[99] Occasionally, representatives had trouble collecting their fee. After serving over six weeks in the parliament of January-February 1478, Norwich member Henry Wilton had accumulated unpaid wages of £4 16s. He agreed to accept this situation in return for perpetual exemption from the city's offices of coroner, sheriff, and constable. The same assembly that sent him to Westminster, taking into consideration his good service, agreed that the trade was a fair one.[100]

For the town's maximum profit, it helped to send men with experience or who had valuable connections. Incomplete records notwithstanding, over half of the borough representatives had served before in another parliament. Re-election to consecutive sittings was not typical, but each of our four towns sponsored three or four such trusted representatives over the course of a half-century.[101] York's member Thomas Graa provides an example of such behavior, sitting in twelve parliaments between 1377 and 1399, four of them consecutively. One of the leading wool merchants of his day, Graa participated fully in local and shire politics, served on judicial and financial commissions under royal appointment, and represented his fellow merchants' overseas interests in a diplomatic journey to Prussia.[102]

The mercantile interests of the majority of the burgesses influenced the occasions on which they spoke and petitioned. Early in Richard II's reign, Norwich officers had read London's charter and coveted its clause prohibiting strangers to their franchises from selling any merchandise at retail within the city. They petitioned successfully for a similar clause, expressed in a 1380 charter of confirmation.[103] Complaints about attacks on shipping by pirates could spark sympathy from the king if the burgesses were crafty enough to relate their personal injuries to attacks on the royal tax base.[104] Commercial losses nearer to home also dominated parliamentary business. In planning for the January 1483 parliament, York's council not only replaced an ailing alderman with its experienced recorder, but carefully dictated the topics it wished its representatives to discuss. Heading the list was the request that certain towns pay tolls on goods they brought to York to trade. If the towns' exemptions were not overturned, the king would have to decrease York's fee farm by the amount of the missing tolls, for the king's progenitors had made the city "a hole bodey and corporet," with a mayor and a fee farm that was becoming increasingly difficult to pay.[105]

Problems of local administration also occupied the burgesses. In 1482, Exeter's members assured Edward IV that they could not maintain the king's peace within their borough if the tailors' guild, the wealthiest and most powerful craft group, continued to ignore the mayor and council with its own charter of incorporation. The connection between local problems and national peacekeeping had the desired effect, and the king promised to annul the incorporation.[106] For York, no less threatening to peace and good government were the many exemptions from officeholding granted by the king. York's citizens proposed in parliament that all such letters be voided, and that those who received them in future be fined £40. Henry VI agreed, perhaps influenced by the promise of one-half of the fines.[107] Burgesses also brought to parliament problems with local mills, river obstructions and shoddy bridges that hurt trade, and local streets in need of paving.[108] York burgesses were particularly interested in the use Henry VII intended to make of their fee farm. Promised complete discharge of the £160 farm (with the exception of £18 5s. diverted to compose the mayor's annuity), they were understandably upset and confused to find that Henry VII's first parliament had claimed over £112 *per annum* of the same farm. Their feelings were at first expressed in a letter to the king, and later within parliament itself, where Henry agreed to look elsewhere for household support.[109]

From the town's point of view, a representative's most important duties, however, did not always lie within parliament itself. Many helped to get charters confirmed, sought help with other petitions, and undertook private business for constituents in or near London. While in Westminster, members could scrutinize Exchequer and Chancery documents for information pertaining to suits over jurisdiction. Some, like Norwich's members in 1423, might remain in London for days after the dissolution of parliament to discuss a problem like tolls and customs with London's mayor and council.[110]

A Norwich source attests to the variety of work undertaken by a representative.[111] An action brought by Thomas Ingham's heirs in 1453 noted that as a member of parliament eight years earlier he had made good use of the many prorogations the meeting suffered. He distributed gifts of money and wine in the Exchequer and law courts for legal documents needed at home. Thomas and his fellow representative Robert Toppes "contynued [at Westminster] to seke upon the good lordship of the Lord of Suffolk and other lordes...." Riding to the earl of Suffolk at his home cost over four shillings, eight times the price of the boat hire and wine expended when the men "labored by water to Lord Cromwell." The charges for the issuance of a privy seal letter are carefully listed as well. In all, Ingham's heirs claimed that he had never been paid for over two hundred days of service in parliament, including the three days going to and coming back from Westminster. A partial total of expenses, including those incurred during the five days spent with "Lord of Suffolk and other lordes for to sue to their grace and to know their will," came to over £10, for which the heirs brought suit in Westminster.[112]

Service in parliament brought with it a few privileges. Knights and burgesses alike excused themselves from personally collecting the general subsidies they approved at their meetings, and reserved to themselves the right to nominate others to the task, taking a few bribes along the way.[113] All members expected protection traveling to and attending parliament, but an Exeter burgess discovered how far such a privilege could be extended. In 1478, merchant John Tayllour sued representative John Atwyll in the Exchequer and obtained judgment by default. Atwyll remained ignorant of the suit because of his Westminster duties, and thus was condemned to pay £160. His fellow burgesses brought the matter to the king's attention for the benefit of them all, arguing that Atwyll hesitated to start for home for fear of being arrested and his horses and possessions attached. While on the king's business, they argued, members deserved the privilege of postponement of legal actions against them until they could give them their full attention. The protection thus included the period dedicated to return home, a privilege they assumed had been ratified along with the other liberties at the beginning of parliament. They successfully won a merciful verdict for Atwyll on the grounds that such harassment of members could impair parliamentary proceedings and deny the king the fulfillment of his urgent needs.[114] Such arguments had been made since early in the century, and as usual, the king could be moved by appeals to his own advantage.

Charters and the officers who represented their granted privileges provided the most basic opportunities for urban growth and the formation of identity. Unlike contemporary Continental examples or English seventeenth-century evidence of royal impositions, the late medieval towns under study here experienced little Crown intervention that failed to respect or at least acknowledge their own needs. Towns sought and achieved privileges that eased financial and jurisdictional problems, and which allowed urban subjects to deal directly and independently with the central administration. Their officers acted under solemn oaths intended to remind them that their exalted position in urban society carried with it responsibility both to its humblest members and to the monarch himself. Mayors, recorders, and parliamentary representatives took seriously their tasks of integrating new grants into networks of local custom, of mastering the challenges of equitable self-rule, and of learning from their failures as well as from their triumphs.

Although examples exist of Crown ignorance of local matters, or the selfish rule of officers benefiting only themselves and their friends, they do not characterize the spirit in which these documents were sought or issued. While royal policy is rarely clear or overtly articulated, the Crown consistently employed instruments like charters to delegate power to the most trusted elements of the urban populace, to achieve a balance whereby the king's peace and profit were maintained without undue dependence of the town upon the Crown. Urban policy balanced a desire for legal independence with the reassurance of a strong monarchy willing to support the town in times of conflict. Medieval townspeople were blissfully unaware of modern historians eager to dismiss their petitions as unnecessary: urban subjects of royal towns understood, perhaps better than we, the rare combination of security and freedom that characterized their chartered spaces of action and identity.

NOTES

[1] Peter Clark and Paul Slack, eds., "Introduction," in *Crisis and Order in English Towns 1500–1700* (Toronto: University of Toronto Press, 1972), pp. 22, 49 n.69.

[2] Wallace T. MacCaffrey, *Exeter 1540–1640: The Growth of an English County Town*, 2d ed. (London and Cambridge, Mass.: Harvard University Press, 1975), p. 26. Monarchs could choose to ignore a predecessor's grants, as Henry VII ignored the generous chartered privileges given to Scarborough by Richard III: Jean W. Rowntree, "The borough, 1163–1500," in *The History of Scarborough*, ed. Arthur Rowntree (London and Toronto: J. M. Dent and Sons, 1931), p. 134. I am grateful to Professor David Palliser of the University of Leeds for this reference.

[3] *York Mem. Bk.*, 1:177–78.

[4] Martin Weinbaum, ed., *British Borough Charters 1307–1660* (Cambridge: Cambridge University Press, 1943), lists 235 English towns; 59 of which, or 25%, had their charters confirmed during this period.

[5] Nottingham received one charter of confirmation and a second document changing the date and length of one of its fairs: Duncan Gray, *Nottingham Through 500 Years*, 2d ed. (Nottingham: Derry and Sons, 1960), p. 10; *CChR*, 5:240; *CPR, 1377–81*, p. 173; *Nott. Records*, 1:197. York built three vessels rather than the usual two, and asked that its confirmation be awarded without further cash payments: P.R.O., SC.8/216/10758.

[6] N.R.O., 7a-b, Treasurers' Roll, 2–3 Richard II; P.R.O., SC.8/129/6443; *Rot. Parl.*, 3:42; *Norwich Records*, 1:271; 2:xxxv, 45.

[7] *CPR, 1396–99*, p. 354.

[8] *Norwich Records*, 1:40–41; *CPR, 1461–67*, p. 171.

[9] N.R.O., 8-c, number 8. Number 9 of this series may be an abstract of the lost charter dated 12 February 1462 and printed in *Norwich Records*, 1:40–41. Norwich paid ten

marks for the first charter of 1462 and £2 for the second, and spent over £60 to send two citizens to London to arrange the confirmation: N.R.O., 21-f, 9-58, Kirkpatrick Notes, *sub anno.*

[10] B. Chevalier, "The *bonnes villes* and the King's Council in Fifteenth-Century France," in *The Crown and Local Communities in England and France in the Fifteenth Century*, ed. J. R. L. Highfield and Robin Jeffs (Gloucester: Alan Sutton, 1981), p. 113.

[11] Of the 235 towns listed in Weinbaum's *British Borough Charters*, 24% confirmed charters early in Henry V's reign, 14.5% in the first few years of Henry VI's reign, 15.7% in the early 1460s, 8.5% upon Richard III's accession, and 6.4% during the early years of Henry VII's reign.

[12] *York Mem. Bk.*, 1:143–46; *CChR*, 5:333–34, 336–37; Sarah Rees Jones, "York's Civic Administration, 1354–1464," *The Government of Medieval York: Essays in Commemoration of the 1396 Royal Charter*, ed. Sarah Rees Jones, Borthwick Studies in History 3 (York, 1997), p. 116. See below, p. 76. The petition for this charter specifies the importance of the justices of the peace: P.R.O., SC8/103/5147. I am grateful to Dr. Christian Liddy for confirming this reference for me. W. M. Ormrod, "York and the Crown Under the First Three Edwards," *ibid.*, pp. 32–33, argues that the charter redressed the political balance between York and Bristol after the latter's 1373 elevation to county status.

[13] *Norwich Records*, 1:29–30, citing 2 Richard II, c.1; Ben R. McRee, "Peacemaking and its Limits in Late Medieval Norwich," *English Historical Review* 109 (1994): 842.

[14] *Norwich Records*, 1:36–37, 105–6.

[15] The Ainsty brought added revenue, contributed soldiers to urban musters, and extended York officials' jurisdiction further into the county: *CChR*, 6:30; *CPR, 1446–52*, p. 221. See also *CChR*, 6:102 for a new fair given in 1502.

[16] *CPR, 1461–67*, p. 275; D.C.A., no.2361.

[17] *Norwich Records*, 1:43–44. The first confirmation stated that the citizens had relinquished land in the suburbs; the second, that the citizens had released jurisdiction within priory walls. The third charter, sealed in 1539, acknowledged the creation of the dean and chapter, and transferred the priory (i.e., cathedral) precinct from the shire to the city. For details of Wolsey's 1524 arbitration and the jurisdictional dispute, see below, pp. 260–64.

[18] For the argument about the lack of need for such charters, see Susan Reynolds, "Medieval Urban History and the History of Political Thought," *Urban History Yearbook 1982*, p. 16, and Reynolds, *An Introduction to the History of English Medieval Towns* (Oxford: Clarendon Press, 1977), pp. 113–14. For arguments particularly against the need for charters of incorporation, see Stephen Rigby, "Urban 'Oligarchy' in Late Medieval England," in *Towns and Townspeople in the Fifteenth Century*, ed. John A. F. Thomson (Gloucester: Alan Sutton, 1988), pp. 78–79; and "Discourse of Corporations," c.1587–89, printed in R. H. Tawney and Eileen Power, eds., *Tudor Economic Documents*, 3 vols. (New York: Longmans, Green and Company, 1924), 3:273–74. Susan Reynolds has argued that the laws of corporation could limit the actions of the groups which conformed to them, and that collective behavior was recognized by law but not created solely by it: "The history of the idea of incorporation or legal personality: a case of fallacious teleology," in

Ideas and Solidarities of the Medieval Laity: England and Western Europe (Aldershot: Variorum Press, 1995), p. 17.

19 Martin Weinbaum, *The Incorporation of Boroughs* (Manchester: Manchester University Press, 1937), p. 18, and Weinbaum, ed., *British Borough Charters*, pp. xxiii–xxviii.

20 Of 278 English and Welsh boroughs, forty-three or 15.5% achieved incorporation before the end of Henry VII's reign, and only six of the forty-three were raised as counties at the same time: Weinbaum, *British Borough Charters*, pp. xxiii–xxiv, xxx–liv. Four of the forty-three were made counties in separate charters before 1509. Calculations for county status may be too low, for Norwich's rise is omitted in his charts. See also Weinbaum, *Incorporation of Boroughs*, Appendix pp. 126–31, whose entries differ slightly from the charts in his later work. For Coventry, see P. R. Coss, "Coventry before incorporation: a reinterpretation," *Midland History* 2 (1974): 137–51.

21 *CPR, 1446–52*, p. 265; Henry Stevenson, ed., *Royal Charters Granted to the Burgesses of Nottingham* (London and Nottingham: Bernard Quaritch, 1890), pp. 48–71; Weinbaum, *Incorporation of Boroughs*, p. 78. After 1468, all towns held at fee farm were henceforth considered incorporate.

22 Rigby, "Urban 'Oligarchy' in Late Medieval England," p. 79, citing Weinbaum, *Incorporation of Boroughs*, p. 88; Robert Tittler, "The Incorporation of Boroughs, 1540–1558," *History* 62 (1977): 24–42. Ironically, Exeter's incorporation proved inadequate when the city desired to purchase lands, and civic officials had to petition for a second and fuller incorporation in 1550: Robert Tittler, *The Reformation and the Towns in England: Politics and Political Culture, c.1540–1640* (Oxford: Clarendon Press, 1998), p. 79.

23 For what follows, see *CChR*, 5:358–60; *York Mem. Bk.*, 1:157–63; W. M. Ormrod, "York and the Crown under the first three Edwards," p. 33. Nigel Saul casts doubt on Richard's contemplation of York as an alternate capital: "Richard II and the City of York," *The Government of Medieval York*, pp. 2–3, 9. See below, p. 76.

24 For what follows, see *CPR, 1446–52*, p. 265; Henry Stevenson, ed., *Royal Charters Granted to the Burgesses of Nottingham* (London and Nottingham: Bernard Quaritch, 1890), pp. 48–71.

25 J. W. Francis Hill, *Medieval Lincoln* (Cambridge: Cambridge University Press, 1948), pp. 276–78. Henry VI, aged sixteen, had taken personal power the year before, and Lincoln's admonition may be an example of youthful exuberance and overreach. It does, however, illustrate that Tudor monarchs were not the only ones tempted to intervene in local politics.

26 See below, p. 261.

27 *Norwich Records*, 1:64–66.

28 *CChR*, 5:264; for London's charter of 1341, see *ibid.*, 5:5.

29 Simon Walker, *The Lancastrian Affinity 1361–1399* (Oxford: Clarendon Press, 1990), pp. 184–87; Francis Blomefield, *A Topographical History of the County of Norfolk*, 2d ed., 11 vols. (London: William Miller, 1805–10), 3:103, 113–15; N.R.O., 7a-b, Treasurers' Rolls 2–3, 9–10, 16–17 Richard II. See below, p. 112.

30 *CChR*, 5:421–23; *Norwich Records*, 1:31–36.

31 *Norwich Records*, 1:lix, citing Blomefield, *History of Norfolk*, 3:114–20. The system may only be a reiteration of an earlier procedure: Blomefield, 3:123–25.

[32]   *Norwich Records*, 1:66–77; McRee, "Peacemaking and its Limits," 847–48, 850–51.
[33]   *Norwich Records*, 1:77–93. For Erpingham's relations with the city, see below, pp. 113–14.
[34]   *Ibid.*, 1:36–37, 93–108.
[35]   *York Mem. Bk.*, 1:175–76.
[36]   N.R.O., 16-d, Assembly Book I, ff. 98, 113b; 18-a, Chamberlains' Account Book III (1479–88), ff.32r–32v; 17-a, *Liber Albus*, ff.56r–56v; 18-a, Chamberlains' Account Book II (1470–90), f.117v. A Westminster advisor was paid to petition the king on behalf of the city, which tried to help itself by electing a local committee to discuss prevention of future infringements of its chartered liberties. Since 1424, Norwich officers, at least, were prohibited from taking cases out of the city to sue at common law without having first approached the mayor for mediation: *Norwich Records*, 1:110–11. A statute of 1504, however, prohibited municipal corporations from obstructing suits to royal courts: *Statutes of the Realm*, 2:652–53; see below, p. 243.
[37]   Susan Reynolds, "Medieval Urban History and the History of Political Thought," *Urban History Yearbook 1982*, pp. 14–23. Important syntheses include Stephen Rigby, "Urban 'Oligarchy' in Late Medieval England," pp. 62–86, and Jennifer I. Kermode, "Obvious Observations on the Formation of Oligarchies in Late Medieval English Towns," pp. 87–106, both in *Towns and Townspeople in the Fifteenth Century*, ed. John A. F. Thomson (Gloucester: Alan Sutton, 1988). For individual towns, see Maryanne Kowaleski, *Local Markets and Regional Trade in Medieval Exeter* (Cambridge: Cambridge University Press, 1995), pp. 95–119; Gervase Rosser, *Medieval Westminster 1200–1540* (Oxford: Clarendon Press, 1989), p. 236; and David Gary Shaw, *The Creation of a Community: The City of Wells in the Middle Ages* (Oxford: Clarendon Press, 1993), pp. 167–76, 178–97. The sixteenth-century view is concisely summarized in Robert Tittler, *Architecture and Power: The Town Hall and the English Urban Community c.1500–1640* (Oxford: Clarendon Press, 1991), pp. 98–100.
[38]   *Norwich Records*, 1:94. A similar statement of civic principles forms the preambles of the 1478 Nuremberg and 1498 Worms codifications of urban law (*Stadtrechtsreformation*): Hans-Christoph Rublack, "Political and Social Norms in Urban Communities in the Holy Roman Empire," in *Religion, Politics and Social Protest: Three Studies on Early Modern Germany*, ed. Kaspar von Greyerz (London: George Allen & Unwin, 1984), p. 26. A broader European context is offered by Christopher R. Friedrichs, "Urban Politics and Urban Social Structure in Seventeenth-Century Germany," *European History Quarterly* 22 (1992): 187–216, esp. 194.
[39]   Hoker, *Description of the Citie*, pp. 801–3. For discussion of the social and unifying role of oaths, see Tittler, *Reformation and the Towns*, pp. 29, 142, 202–4.
[40]   *Norwich Records*, 1:123; William L. Sachse, ed., *Minutes of the Norwich Court of Mayoralty*, Norfolk Record Society, vol. 15 (Norwich, 1942), pp. 14–17.
[41]   *Norwich Records*, 1:123.
[42]   Throughout the fifteenth century, York's mayors took responsibility for the townhouses and local properties of several generations of attainted Percy earls of Northumberland until the fourth earl gained custody in 1470. For example, see York's accounts for 1406–7 when the escheator administered the attainted earl of Northumberland's goods: P.R.O., E.357/18, mem.8. During the early years of

Edward IV's reign, York's escheator complained at the Exchequer about the local Percy properties: P.R.O., E.357/44, mem.84; E.357/45, mm. 7, 80; Dobson, *Chamberlains' Accounts*, pp. 117–18. During the 1420s, York's mayor was also authorized by Chancery to account fully for city lands to the heir of Henry Lord Scrope of Masham, executed for his treasonous attack on Henry V: *CPR, 1422–29*, p. 277.

43   P.R.O., E.159/219, Brevia directa, Michaelmas 21 Henry VI, rot. 23; N.R.O., 16-d, Assembly Book I, ff.59–59v. Norwich's sheriffs' oath is printed in *Norwich Records*, 1:125–26.

44   Rymer, *Foedera*, 7:792; *CPR, 1408–13*, p. 463.

45   *CPR, 1401–1405*, p. 188; *1405–1408*, p. 359; *1436–41*, p. 87; *1429–36*, p. 474.

46   Gray, *Nottingham*, pp. 24–25; N.R.O., 16-d, f.4; 21-f, 9-58, Kirkpatrick Notes, *sub* 1485; Nt.R.O., CA380A, sheriffs' bond 1488.

47   *York Civic Records*, 2:162 (16 December 1500 reprimand for unsatisfactory linens); *York House Books*, p. 137. David Palliser estimated that a man had to be worth £80–£100 per annum to be elected sheriff: "Some Aspects of the Social and Economic History of York in the Sixteenth Century," (D.Phil thesis, University of Oxford, 1968), p. 166.

48   *York Mem. Bk.*, 2:246. Candidates for chamberlain should have previously held the financially-responsible post of bridgemaster.

49   *York Mem. Bk.*, 1:lxvii, 116; *York House Books*, p. 674.

50   *Nott. Records*, 3:62–71. Exeter's yearly stipend of £5 rose to twenty marks in 1460–61, supplemented by bread given at Christmas and Easter: D.R.O., Receivers' Rolls, 39 Henry VI–1 Edward IV; 2–3, 10–11 Edward IV. Norwich's sum fluctuated throughout the fifteenth century, from fifty marks to £20 *per annum* after 1469: N.R.O., 7-d, 7–8, 36–37 Henry VI; 18-a, Chamberlains' Account Book, 1470–90, ff.1–15 (1469), 54–64 (1473–74), 98b–107b (1477–78), 121–99 (1488–89).

51   For men-at-arms earnings, see below, p. 208 note 59. Kowaleski, *Local Markets and Regional Trade*, pp. 104–5, lists the ways in which magistrates c.1377 profited from office; while S. Bhanji, "The Involvement of Exeter and the Exe Estuary in Piracy," *Transactions of the Devonshire Association* 130 (1998): 23–29, tracks some extra-legal ways of making a profit. Cf. Tittler, *Architecture and Power*, pp. 106, for late sixteenth-century rates of mayoral pay.

52   D.R.O., Miscellaneous Roll 2, no. 54, part 4 (affirmed 1379); Hoker, *Description of the Citie*, pp. 802–803. Norwich ordinances forbade its higher officers from keeping a hostelry and forced an alderman-elect to renounce his butcher's trade: Blomefield, *History of Norfolk*, 3:129; *Norwich Records*, 2:107.

53   Kowaleski, *Local Markets and Regional Trade*, pp. 100–108; see also Jennifer I. Kermode, *Medieval Merchants: York, Beverley and Hull in the Later Middle Ages* (Cambridge: Cambridge University Press, 1998), p. 2 for comments on mercantile influences of civic officials, and p. 39 for statistics on mercantile officeholding.

54   *York Mem. Bk.*, 2:viii; F. B. Bickley, ed., *The Little Red Book of Bristol*, 2 vols. (London: W. C. Hemmons, 1900–1901), 1:149–53. Bristol's mayor was required to make himself available for arbitration nearly every day, while the York records are filled with bonds and agreements overseen by the mayor: Toulmin Smith, ed., *English Gilds*, Early English Text Society, o.s., vol. 40 (London, 1870), 426; *York House Books*, pp. 77, 80–82, 84, 89.

55   See Kowaleski, *Local Markets and Regional Trade*, p. 117, for similar cases of insulting officers in Exeter, which she believes was caused by jealousies felt by lower-ranking oligarchs.

56   *York House Books*, pp. 122–23.

57   *Ibid.*, pp. 305, 511–12. See also Tittler, *Architecture and Power*, pp. 103–7, and Reynolds, *An Introduction to the History of English Medieval Towns*, pp. 179–80, for discussion of towns' protective developments of dignity and ceremony.

58   P.R.O., C.1/31/78; C.1/46/209; C.1/131/32; C.1/47/84.

59   P.R.O., C.1/16/57; C.1/31/429. See also C.1/12/112 for a case in Nottingham in 1433.

60   C. G. Bayne and W. H. Dunham, eds., *Select Cases in the Council of Henry VII*, Selden Society, vol. 75 (1956), p. clix; I. S. Leadam, ed., *Select Cases before the King's Council in the Star Chamber, Volume I, 1477–1509*, Selden Society, vol. 16 (1903 for 1902), pp. cxxxvi–cxxxvii, 51–54. See Ralph B. Pugh, *Imprisonment in Medieval England* (Cambridge: Cambridge University Press, 1968), pp. 177–79, for the use of "ironing" prisoners with chains, fetters, manacles, etc. By law, such weights should not have exceeded twelve ounces.

61   Rigby, "Urban 'Oligarchy,'" p. 64, citing Northampton's *Liber Custumarum*.

62   *Rot. Parl.*, 6:431–33.

63   For Exeter, see Kowaleski, *Local Markets and Regional Trade*, p. 96; for York, Jennifer I. Leggett, "The 1377 Poll Tax Return for the City of York," *Yorkshire Archaeological Journal* 43 (1971): 130.

64   R. B. Dobson, "The Risings in York, Beverley and Scarborough, 1380–1381," in *The English Rising of 1381*, ed. R. H. Hilton and T. H. Aston (Cambridge: Cambridge University Press, 1984), pp. 119–23, 138–41. See below, pp. 284–86.

65   Miller, *VCH*, pp. 80–82; *York Mem. Bk.*, 2:69–70; *Rot. Parl.*, 3:96–97.

66   P.R.O., E.28/90.

67   *CPR, 1461–67*, p. 366; Rymer, *Foedera*, 11:529–31; Thomas Madox, *Firma Burgi* (London: W. Bowyer, 1726), p. 33; Rees Jones, "York's Civic Administration, 1354–1464," *The Government of Medieval York*, pp. 135–36.

68   *CPR, 1467–77*, 239; Rymer, *Foedera*, 11:700.

69   *CPR, 1467–77*, p. 416; *York House Books*, pp. 284–49, 701–2; *York Mem. Bk.*, 2:245–47 (quote translated in Reynolds, *An Introduction*, p. 185). In 1473, the crafts chose one alderman to serve as mayor. In 1489, the council petitioned the king to restore the 1464 procedure.

70   *York House Books*, pp. 630–31.

71   *CPR, 1485–94*, p. 297. The letters patent of 1473, nominating one alderman for election, were surrendered at that time.

72   *York Civic Records*, 2:163 (15 January 1501).

73   *Ibid.*, pp. 191–93 (15 January 1504).

74   *Ibid.*, 3:1–8; Bayne and Dunham, *Council of Henry VII*, pp. clxii–clxiii; Maud Sellers, "The City of York in the Sixteenth Century," *English Historical Review* 9 (1894): 276, 279.

75   Herbert Heaton, *The Yorkshire Woollen and Worsted Industries*, 2d ed. (Oxford: Oxford University Press, 1965), pp. 52–53; Sellers, "City of York," 279.

76   Although usually associated with the Tudor monarchs (as in R. Harold Garrett-Goodyear, "Revival of Quo Warranto and Early Tudor Policy towards Local

Governors, 1485–1540," (Ph.D. dissertation, Harvard University, 1973), pp. 134–35), such an argument could have been used by any medieval king anxious about his delegated powers. After 1517, York's election committee was composed of craft representatives and senior searchers of the crafts: Miller, *VCH*, p. 137.

[77] For analysis of the *corregidores* and their limitations (which could negate many of their powers), see John Edwards, *Christian Córdoba: The City and Its Region in the Late Middle Ages* (Cambridge: Cambridge University Press, 1982), esp. pp. 27–45; and Marvin Lunenfeld, *Keepers of the City: The Corregidores of Isabella I of Castile (1474–1504)* (Cambridge: Cambridge University Press, 1987), esp. ch.9. Bernard Chevalier discusses the limited role of governors sent by the French king in "The *bonnes villes* and the King's Council," *Crown and Local Communities*, ed. Highfield and Jeffs, pp. 110–13, 124, and in his *Les Bonnes Villes de France du XIVe au XVIe siècle* (Paris: Aubier Montaigne, 1982), esp. pp. 94–106. Medieval England also bears no resemblance to the seventeenth century, when the later Stuart monarchs manipulated the composition of local government and of parliamentary representation through the repeal and reissuance of urban charters: John Miller, "The Crown and the Borough Charters in the Reign of Charles II," *English Historical Review* 100 (1985): 53–84; M. J. Short, "The Corporation of Hull and the Government of James II, 1687–8," *Historical Research* 71 (1998): 172–95.

[78] For Henry VII's strategy and its relation to changes in the royal household, see Dominic Luckett, "Crown Office and Licensed Retinues in the Reign of Henry VII," in *Rulers and the Ruled in Late Medieval England: Essays Presented to Gerald Harriss*, ed. Rowena E. Archer and Simon Walker (London and Rio Grande: Hambledon Press, 1995), pp. 223–38.

[79] *York House Books*, pp. 114, 370–71, 378, 383–84; Davies, *York Records*, pp. 58–59; Y.C.A., Robert H. Skaife, *Civic Officials of York*, 2:498; Michael Van Cleave Alexander, *The First of the Tudors* (Totowa, N.J.: Rowman and Littlefield, 1980), p. 49; A. J. Pollard, *Northeastern England During the Wars of the Roses* (Oxford: Clarendon Press, 1990), pp. 103, 111–12, 370.

[80] *York House Books*, pp. 398, 466–67.

[81] *Ibid.*, pp. 472–73, 475–76, 478–79.

[82] *Ibid.*, pp. 487–88.

[83] *CPR, 1408–13*, p. 293; *Norwich Records*, 1:76–77, 2:58–59.

[84] N.R.O., 16-d, Assembly Book I, f.62v. The man in question received the liberty of the city shortly after his appointment, in reward for good service: *ibid.*, f.68v.

[85] *York House Books*, pp. 487–88.

[86] For what follows, see *ibid.*, pp. 252, 377–78, 393, 395, 700–701.

[87] *York Civic Records*, 2:115.

[88] *York Mem. Bk.*, 2:xv.

[89] *Rot. Parl.*, 5:225. But that was not the end of the story: see above, at p. 58–59.

[90] If exemptions had to exist, boroughs preferred to control their issue. Shortly after York's complaint in parliament, its council sold several discharges for £10 each (Norwich freemen paid over £13). For examples of Crown-issued exemptions, see P.R.O., E.28/90; *CPR, 1476–85*, p. 484; *1485–94*, p. 461. For town-based fines, see N.R.O., 16-d, Assembly Book I, ff.17v, 18, 33, 38v, 48, 66v, 89; *Norwich Records*, 1:286; *York House Books*, pp. 302, 305; *York Civic Records*, 2:121–22. Monetary payments alone were not always required: in 1461, Norwich excused a former

mayor from holding office for three years after he gave the chamberlains a dozen jackets for soldiers or archers.

[91] *The History of Parliament: The House of Commons, 1386–1421*, ed. J. S. Roskell *et al.*, 4 vols. (Stroud: Alan Sutton Publishing for the History of Parliament Trust, 1992), 1:41–48, 51–53. For opposing views of borough representation, see Rosemary Horrox, "The Urban Gentry in the Fifteenth Century," in *Towns and Townspeople in the Fifteenth Century*, edited by John A. F. Thomson (Gloucester: Alan Sutton Publishing, 1988), pp. 158–59; and Patricia Jalland, "The 'Revolution' in Northern Borough Representation in Mid-Fifteenth-Century England," *Northern History* 11 (1976 for 1975): 27–51.

[92] The Crown only once tried to dictate the profession of the men returned to parliament, when in 1404 Henry IV forbade men with legal training from being elected. Only six of the ninety-nine representatives fell into this category, including town clerk John Lake of Exeter: *House of Commons 1386–1421*, 1:57.

[93] None of the four towns experienced the interference Grimsby suffered when the second earl of Westmorland pledged his good will and favor only if town officials accepted his councilors as representatives: Carole Rawcliffe and Susan Flower, "English Noblemen and Their Advisers: Consultation and Collaboration in the Later Middle Ages," *Journal of British Studies* 25 (1986): 174. This paragraph does not present the evidence in statistical form because of the loss of so many returns. The History of Parliament Trust has studied the period from 1386 to 1421 intensively, and although figures can be calculated from its findings, even that material is not perfect. For that period, see *House of Commons 1386–1421*, pp. 348–53 (Exeter), 524–28 (Norwich), 555–59 (Nottingham), and 742–50 (York). Conclusions about the remainder of the fifteenth century are drawn from the evidence cited in the following paragraphs.

[94] *Nott. Records*, 1:7–8, 23, 41, 47, 109; 2:3.

[95] *Norwich Records*, 1:107.

[96] *Statutes of the Realm*, 2:341–43; K. N. Houghton, "Theory and Practice in Borough Elections to Parliament during the Later Fifteenth Century," *Bulletin of the Institute of Historical Research* 39 (1966): 131. According to the statute, sheriffs ignoring these orders were to be fined £100, and if mayors sent any but those chosen by the citizens, the guilty had to pay £40 to the king and £40 to the aggrieved party.

[97] *House of Commons 1386–1421*, 1:351; *CCR, 1377–81*, pp. 252–54, 498; *1389–92*, p. 180; *1399–1402*, p. 331; *1405–1409*, p. 283; *1413–19*, p. 185; D.R.O., Receivers' Roll, 19–20 Henry VII; *Nott. Records*, 3:62–71. Both the Close Rolls and the Chamberlains' Accounts of Nottingham contradict antiquary William Gregory's assertion that burgesses earned 16d. *per diem*: *Nott. Records*, 2:421.

[98] May McKisack, *The Parliamentary Representation of the English Boroughs during the Middle Ages* (Oxford: Oxford University Press, 1932), p. 87; N.R.O., 16-d, f.66b; 7a-b, Treasurers' Roll, 4–5 Henry IV; 7-c, 7–8 Henry V; 7-d, 1–2 Henry VI.

[99] Dobson, *Chamberlains' Accounts*, pp. 25, 34; *York House Books*, p. 667; *York Civic Records*, 2:56.

[100] McKisack, *Representation*, pp. 88–89.

[101] The diagrams demonstrating members' previous experience of parliaments are helpful for the period they examine: *House of Commons 1386–1421*, 1:770–836. See McKisack, *Representation*, pp. 41–42 for analysis of the fourteenth century.

[102] *House of Commons 1386–1421*, 3:218–20. See below, p. 232. Equally well-connected were York officers Miles Metcalfe and Thomas Wrangwish, both in Richard of Gloucester's affinity and sitting in the parliaments of 1483 and 1484: Miller, *VCH*, pp. 62–63.

[103] *Norwich Records*, 1:29–30, 2:xxxv; *Rot. Parl.*, 3:41.

[104] *Rot. Parl.*, 4:88, 402–403. See below, p. 230.

[105] *York House Books*, p. 271. York's council also hoped something could be done about the Hansa merchants whose freedom to buy and sell in England could not be matched abroad by English traders in general and York merchants in particular.

[106] *Rot. Parl.*, 6:219–20; McKisack, *Representation*, p. 134; P.R.O., SC.8/30/1462; D.R.O., Receivers' Roll, 22–23 Edward IV. See below, pp. 224–25. *CPR, 1461–67*, p. 543, prints the original grant of incorporation of the guild in honor of St. John the Baptist.

[107] *Rot. Parl.*, 5:225.

[108] *Ibid.*, 3:298, 5:43–44 (mills and bridge); D.R.O., Book 51, f.315; Book 55, ff.137–38 (paving). For a survey of topics from a variety of boroughs, see A. R. Bridbury, "English Provincial Towns in the Later Middle Ages," *Economic History Review*, 2d ser., 34 (1981): 2; and Miriam Rose, "Petitions in Parliament under the Lancastrians, from, or relating to, Towns," (MA thesis summary), *Bulletin of the Institute of Historical Research* 15 (1927): 174–76.

[109] *Rot. Parl.*, 6:390; *York House Books*, pp. 507–10, 603–604; Lorraine C. Attreed, "The King's Interest: York's Fee Farm and the Central Government, 1482–1492," *Northern History* 17 (1981): 40–41. See below, pp. 148–49.

[110] McKisack, *Representation*, pp. 120, 137–38.

[111] For what follows, see N.R.O., 7-d, Ingham bill; 17-d, Apprenticeship Indentures, 35–36 Henry VI, f.32v.

[112] At 2s. *per diem*, Ingham deserved over £20 for representation alone. Ingham served as mayor of Norwich in 1425 and 1431, as well as city treasurer and sheriff: B. Cozens-Hardy and Ernest A. Kent, eds., *The Mayors of Norwich* (Norwich: Jarrold and Sons, 1938), pp. 19–20.

[113] *House of Commons 1386–1421*, 1:147.

[114] *Rot. Parl.*, 6:191–92; *House of Commons 1386–1421*, 1:151, 154–55. This request received royal assent as did similar appeals in 1460 and 1472.

CHAPTER 3
VISITS AND SPECTACLE

The presence of the king physically within a borough constitutes the most immediate expression of Crown-town relations. Whatever the reason for a visit, local conditions inevitably impressed themselves upon the monarch. The initial welcome provided occasions for the spectacle of triumphant entry, pageantry expressive of a unique art form and vital to the legitimating of royal rule. But monarchs' presence and cognizance during the visit interested urban subjects more. When the pageantry ended, townspeople took pains to acquaint them with local needs and the ways in which the Crown could help. Much of that help came later in the form of charters and concessions that extended civic liberties and boosted the economy. Although the costs of such entertainment were burdensome, royal visits could result in indirect benefits. Here, the remarks of Henry VI are salutary. In 1449, in granting the city of York various privileges and monetary concessions, the king concluded that the borough's poverty was caused directly by the fact that "[it] has not been relieved for [a] long time by the king's presence, courts, councils or parliaments."[1] Rather than urging civic officials to avoid such costly outlay, Henry understood that the initial expense of hospitality and spectacle could reap long-term financial as well as constitutional benefits.

Town policy towards visiting royalty was self-interested but far from simple. Civic officials believed that kings and their entourages should be entertained by pageantry and spectacle when possible, and rewarded with a valuable gift. They should also be advised of the town's problems, and the ways in which the king could help, even if cries of urban poverty seemed at odds with the presents and processions they offered. Moreover, especially during the most difficult periods of the Wars of the Roses, monarchs in possession of the throne should be recognized and respected, while worthy contenders should not be so rebuffed that they would be inclined to seek revenge if by a change in fortune they gained the crown. The power of the monarchy would be enhanced and borough privileges displayed, but each party tried to avoid falling too far into the other's debt. If the king were unable to visit in person, hospitality should be extended to those close to him, as when the papal legate visited York in 1486, enjoyed a ceremonious welcome, and promised in return to "report ther demenaunce and humanitee in this partie unto the kinges highnesse, that his grace shuld be rather inclined graciously to here there peticions to be ministred unto hyme herafter."[2]

On a deeper level, these ceremonies were also influential in the way medieval citizens and town officers understood themselves and wished to be understood by the outside world. These were public ceremonies, with significant sensory impact, "designed to impress events on collective memory."[3] They entertained a visiting monarch, but also involved him in a ritual supportive of both royal and urban power while symbolic of an internal spiritual reality. As public events, they boasted of cohesion and civic unity, but tended to celebrate the male leaders of a town, leaving women, artisans and servants on the sidelines or confined to private and parochial rituals. By demonstrating who was included and excluded, the events and ceremonies illustrated the basic divisions of society, reinforced boundaries, and validated respect for them.[4] They could celebrate the status quo, or mask disruptive forces. The line between merrymaking and public disorder was a fine one, as Norwich argued when its officials tried to pass off a riot as a Shrovetide festival.[5] Although steeped in spirituality and respectful of tradition, these ceremonies were not unchanging rituals from which deviation meant flaw. Their contents were in fact tailored to each situation, with traditions and pedigrees invented without a blush. What remained constant, however, was their assertion of royal power, its symbolic link to divinity, and the rectitude of a king's town welcoming its sovereign lord with rituals imitative of the pious receiving Christ Himself.

Internal Parallels

Towns' own ceremonies provide important parallels, as kings and nobles were not the only individuals welcomed by pageants and processions. Newcomers to civic office were greeted with ceremonies that initiated them into positions of influence and responsibility in the town. Incumbents cherished the ceremonies that accompanied many of their public duties, and enjoyed the deference all citizens were supposed to show them. Religious obligations and holy days such as the feast of Corpus Christi inspired elaborate arrangements meant to strengthen both the unity of urban subjects and the precious liberties which gave them a privileged identity in medieval society.[6] Inclusion in such ceremonies, the position one physically took in them, and the garments one wore were all matters of the utmost importance to the individuals who participated and to the society that measured rank and precedence with exceptional care. They bore witness to the prestige of the community, expressed the power relationships of its members, and visualized the ordered and unified structure composed by all the parts of the urban social body. Such ceremonies and the participants who brought them to life celebrated a town's very right to exist and to act in the medieval world with dignity, power, and autonomy. Most importantly, they were occasions upon which members of the urban community could present and define themselves in relation to society at large.[7]

What civic spectacle really meant to medieval citizens can be seen most immediately in their comments about the ceremonies performed by and for town governors. Officials such as mayors and aldermen may have been elected in many towns by a small group of wealthy merchants, but they were ultimately responsible to the citizenry at large. Expected to be just, honorable, and industrious, urban officials represented the town to the rest of society and upheld its honor and dignity. To do so properly, they themselves had to convey a sense of that honor and dignity, and they relied heavily upon the use of powerful symbols. Language itself was an influential tool: the chief officers of London and York had acquired the title "lord mayor" by the early fifteenth century, and even small towns imposed heavy fines upon those who attacked by words or blows the personal or professional lives of the officers.[8] Sheer numbers could also be powerful: the major officers of towns, copying the royal and noble entourages of the time, preferred to go about even mundane chores surrounded by servants and assistants in an informal procession.[9] The ceremonies that expressed urban unity nevertheless delineated the superior and inferior parts of that whole.

These displays gained added power when graced by a town's regalia, another expressive symbol of urban dignity and influence. Swords, maces, and caps of maintenance were often given by monarchs in recognition of a town's status, along with the right and obligation to bear these objects in processions and during visits. Serjeants and servants of the mayor and other officers bore the regalia in public ceremonies that emphasized the town's wealth and privilege.[10] So strong were these symbols, not every officer had the right to be in their company. Anxious to fill offices, York's city council nevertheless excused promising candidates if they did not have the wealth or dignity with which to grace their positions.[11] During Richard III's reign, York citizen Thomas Wrangwish was elected mayor while in Westminster attending Parliament. Upon his return, the council ordered the swordbearer with his sword and mace, and all the serjeants with their maces, to escort him into the city's liberties with sword and mace before him. Wrangwish, sensitive that he had not yet taken his oath of office, accepted the escort but "he wald not let [the regalia] be born to fore [him] in so myche as he was unsworn" and thus undeserving of the honor.[12]

Wrangwish's reluctance illustrates the belief that ceremonies and spectacles could become meaningless if they were enacted too often or wasted upon individuals who did not take them seriously. City records contain numerous entries about the importance of public processions and displays: officers were reminded to attend, to bear the regalia, to quell arguments about precedence, and to remember that these ceremonies preserved ancient custom.[13] Although small in expense and modest in display compared to spectacles arranged for kings and princes, these ceremonies were no less expressive of urban identity. When they were performed with respect by a town's citizens, they increased the honor and dignity not just of the participants, but of the city itself. As the town records of Beverley expressed it, officers and citizens participated in the ceremonies "for the praise and honour of God and the Body of Christ, and for the peaceful union of the worthier and lesser commons of the town."[14] However impossible solidarity was to achieve, such unity remained an ideal and a guiding principle.

Preparations and Expectations

A town's ideas about its own identity and its relationship with the Crown were magnified when its officers were called upon to welcome the monarch and his entourage. The reasons for such visits could vary. Between 1377 and 1509, monarchs made fifty-nine trips to the four boroughs, excluding only those of the briefest duration.[15] Almost half of them occurred during a royal progress or for purposes of pleasure. Military preparations accounted for about 15% of the visits, particularly to Nottingham and York, strategic bases with access to the Scottish enemy. On nearly half as many occasions, town disputes with bishops and monasteries over conflicting liberties drew kings as arbitrators of the quarrels. Kings and queens occasionally visited towns on their way to religious shrines like Walsingham and Beverley. Richard II affected local administration and economy drastically when he transferred the central offices of the government to York in 1392. Treason, real or suspected, prompted about 10% of these royal visits, in order to quell violence and discourage further rebellion. But the most challenging visits occurred during the years of dynastic conflict for the throne, forcing boroughs to treat Yorkist and Lancastrian claimants with almost equal reverence or risk backing the losing candidate.

Advance preparation smoothed the way for a king's arrival no matter what the cause. Members of the royal household announced the king's impending arrival and ascertained that prospective hosts were ready to meet the challenge of entertaining royalty. In 1483, the king's secretary advised civic officials of York to give their new monarch an appropriate welcome, a true civic triumph, urging them to present pageants and hang the streets with tapestries to impress the southern lords and other nobles traveling with the monarch.[16] In the autumn of 1461, the mere rumor of Edward IV's coming set the mayor of Norwich to order the collection of a gift assessed on all trades and crafts.[17] Edward did not arrive until the following year, when, arrayed in new clothes, Norwich's aldermen and council rode to welcome him to a city whose residents had been warned not to carry a weapon for the duration of the visit.[18] In 1486, nervous members of Nottingham's council voted to send a rider to determine whether Henry VII would visit on his way to York, and whether he would punish the town for letting a prisoner escape.[19] Towns also had to know as early as possible from what direction a visitor would come, especially if officers were gathered or pageants erected at the physical limits of the borough.[20]

The royal entourage presented problems and expenses on its own. Unless exempt by charter or other royal grant, a town had to endure the presence of the king's clerk of the market. This officer interfered with local economy and local custom while the monarch was in town, setting prices, testing weights and measures, and fining dishonest merchants. Money payments, to the point of bribery, often encouraged the clerk to

hold his interference to a minimum.[21] Exempt since 1345, Norwich still
paid the clerk a nominal sum during royal visits in 1448 and 1474. In
1452, the clerk received £1 and some wine for giving the city his favor
and agreeing not to hold his sessions within its liberty: such an action
violated their privileges, but Norwich could not find the relevant writs to
fight his presumption.[22] Likewise, town finances stretched to reward both
royal messengers bringing news, and those royal and noble minstrels
who expected payment in return for entertainment.[23]

Royalty expected monetary gifts when they arrived, even if they
sometimes displayed generosity (or made a bid for support) in refusing to
accept them. Henry VI's queen, even traveling on her own in 1453, not
only received a welcoming gift of cash from Norwich but also gained for
her husband a loan of one hundred marks.[24] Different financial
arrangements were in order for Edward IV's first visit, when an
assessment tapped the crafts for the necessary funds. In September 1461,
masters received orders to divide the assessment among their members,
but four months later nothing had been accomplished and the city wards
had to bear the payment.[25] The royal visit in the spring of 1469 caused
even more problems. Assessors were advised to fine all those who did
not ride to greet the king in their livery. The most recalcitrant found
themselves in prison. The city's usual gift was £160, and orders came for
a general tallage to be levied. Lack of success saw the scheme abandoned
in favor of a benevolence, most unkindly enforced by further threats of
imprisonment. The money did not appear, and even during Henry VI's
return to power Norwich continued to try to raise the money for its gift to
"Lord Edward formerly king."[26]

Rewards for civic hospitality could come in tangible forms during
the visit itself or in its immediate wake, or take the form of "good
lordship" and influence exercised in later years by the monarch with fond
memories of his stay. Richard II's 1392 transfer of government offices to
York illustrates both forms. He ameliorated the imposition by presenting
a gilt mace and cap of maintenance for the mayor's swordbearer to
increase civic dignity.[27] Important charters followed in 1393 and 1396;
they did not necessarily have to result from York's hospitality alone, as
the former at least responded to a petition which moved the city's
particular needs to the forefront of Richard's mind.[28] This give-and-take
relationship operated when five wealthy citizens were coerced into
acceding to Richard's infamous blank charters agreeing to future loans—
loans that remained largely unpaid and may have persuaded the city to

back Henry of Lancaster the following year.[29] Exeter also knew immediate benefits when it received a sword and cap of maintenance from Henry VII following his 1497 visit, while Norwich received a trade fair in 1482 after several occasions of hospitality shown Edward IV and his family.[30] There is no foolproof way to determine whether a city's actual expenses of hospitality balanced out by the profitable acquisition of privileges and trade opportunities. True reward lay as well in the dignity of being chosen a royal stopover, and in the opportunities granted for displays of honor, status, and unity.

Pageantry, Punishment, and Spectacle

Successful and impressive pageants did not just happen: not only were they the result of careful preparation, but they often involved the participation of "professional" planners. Although civic records are often silent on the identity and experience of such men, their expertise was clearly valuable enough to convince larger town governments to invest in their skills. Queen Elizabeth Woodville's visit to Norwich in 1469 received such professional attention. Edward IV had visited in the spring of that year, and according to the Paston correspondents had such "good cheer and great gifts" that he planned to return and bring his queen.[31] Messengers sought early to ascertain the time and direction of the July arrival. Eager to make a good impression, the Corporation contacted their recorder in London for advice and called in a man named Pernall from Ipswich, experienced in the planning of pageants. He was rewarded with 6s. for devising scaffolds, while newly-repaired leather-covered giant figures greeted the visitors, perhaps inspired by London's Gog and Magog creatures. These were surrounded on the scaffolds by representations of angels and patriarchs. Singers led the party into the city, and at some point two bachelors of theology earned their 6s. 8d. by providing an exposition on a learned theme. Civic officials wore new cloth, which along with the sets and costumes were damaged when a rainstorm interrupted the proceedings and chased the royal party out of public view. Expenses for the pageantry topped £18, but the mayor and brethren may have considered it a good investment when they later petitioned the king to pardon their loyal city from sending him troops.[32]

We know a little more about the consultant the city of York used during the 1480s. Planning for the visit of Richard III and his family began soon after the king's coronation in early July 1483. Parish priest Henry Hudson was at first one of seven clergymen called upon to devise a "sight" for the royal progress; at the end of the year, however, only his stipend of 40s. gains mention in the council records.[33] The king's pleasure with the pageant and resultant generosity to the city encouraged York officials to call on Hudson again in 1486 to plan a spectacle for Henry VII. By then parish priest of Spofforth (N. Yorks.), Hudson presided over an elaborate pageant mixing pagan and Biblical figures joined in praise of the first Tudor.[34] His reward (five marks in payment plus expenses) found record among the city archives, but not his sources of inspiration, whether they were of his own devising or dictated by the royal court itself.

The royal visitor received his or her first impressions of urban hospitality by the ceremonies of greeting and escort into town. The greater the distance from town where one was met, the greater the honor conferred. Visiting Devonshire in 1452 as part of a commission of oyer and terminer, Henry VI was met about four miles east of Exeter "by the most part of the knights and gentlemen, the Mayor and Commonalty…being above thre hundred persones, and everye one apparolled yn the livory of the citie…." Franciscans and Dominicans waited half a mile out of town, "then came the prior of St. Nycholas and the prior of St. Johns and all the curates, preestes, and chaplyns of the citie being ravished and clothed yn their copes and vestymentes and too crosses before theym, and mett hym at the cross without of the Southgate…." The mayor then led the procession through town, riding bareheaded and carrying the mace of office.[35] York's officers, eager to convince Henry VII of their loyalty, agreed to meet the new king much further from the city boundaries than was customary during his first visit in 1486. Sheriffs and two of the aldermen went as far as Tadcaster, about eight miles away, to give the first welcome, while the mayor and his attendants waited five miles from town rather than the usual two.[36] None of this, however, compares with the situation in 1398, when York's major officers escorted Richard II all the way from Nottingham, no doubt in gratitude for the major charters he had granted since his last visit.[37]

An element of ceremony not to be neglected concerns the public spectacle of judicial process and punishment. The early modern period is better served than the medieval by studies of public aspects of the penal process, many of them inspired by Foucault's definition as both a judicial and a political ritual, but the earlier period provides fascinating examples useful in this context.[38] The active intervention of the monarch in a borough, exercising royal justice while superseding the officers' privileges, could threaten urban rights but also ally a town population with the peacekeeping duties of royal power. Judicial rituals sanctioned violence and punishment in the lord's name, and royal visits to towns also provided overt opportunities for peacekeeping and displays of judicial power.

One of the most unusual judicial visits occurred in Nottingham when Henry IV presided over a trial by battle. One Bordeaux merchant had accused another of using treasonous language against the English. In the summer of 1407, Henry, his sons, and the captive king of Scotland witnessed the trial on specially constructed scaffolding. The monarchs stopped the duel before the combatants hurt themselves, and Henry later wrote to Bordeaux affirming that both men had acted honorably. Nottingham received from the visit the usual increased business sparked by the presence of royalty and the gathering of crowds.[39] The effect of such a public and violent form of justice is harder to measure; certainly the monarchs displayed their power over life and limb by intervening and choosing to show mercy only they could mete out.

Visiting monarchs involved themselves in both process and punishment. Several royal visits to towns coincided with commissions of oyer and terminer or actions of arbitration often involving urban religious institutions.[40] The more dramatic spectacles included the public executions that provided additional and sobering spectacle to the welcoming ceremonies, as in York in 1405 after Archbishop Scrope's revolt. Later in the century, Henry VII's second visit to the northern capital included the beheading of a citizen who had admitted pretender Lambert Simnel into the city. Eager to please the monarch, the officials made sure the council records noted York's alliance with right and truth on that occasion.[41] Buffeted by the violence of neighboring lords and petitioned by rebels protesting Edward IV, Exeter strove to prove its loyalty to the Crown not just by welcoming ceremonies but also by judicial process. Richard III's visit after Buckingham's rebellion included the execution of one of the latter's adherents.[42] Henry VII added a form of judicial tableau to his visit to Exeter after Perkin Warbeck's revolt by witnessing spectacles of justice. Installed in the cathedral treasurer's house, the king daily viewed the rounded-up rebels, who begged for mercy beneath his window with halters around their necks. Many, though not all, were pardoned, and the city itself was not blamed for permitting the rebellion to go so far. Once more, the monarch displayed his full control over life, limb, and disgrace, affirming his unique powers and sharing others with favored subjects.[43]

As these examples begin to indicate, England's dynastic upheaval informs us of the unique challenges faced by towns planning royal welcomes after the mid-fifteenth century. An early hint of the stresses emerged in Henry VI's 1453 visit to Norwich, only a few months before the king's first bout with mental illness. The journey was taken at least in part to rival the duke of York's efforts at peacekeeping in East Anglia earlier in the decade, when the duke made it clear Henry had failed to keep order in his towns and provinces.[44] But true problems began in the spring of 1461, when Edward of York's forces defeated at Towton an impressive and numerically superior royal Lancastrian army, prompting Henry VI to flee to Scottish exile. If the city of York, only twelve miles away, had any doubts about how to receive the young victor, they were assuaged by the intercession of the Yorkist Lords Montagu and Berners. The noblemen gained from Edward a pardon for the city's previous loyalty to the Lancastrians, and directed civic officials to accept the new situation by greeting Edward "with great solemnity and processions."[45] The ceremonies served as a backdrop for Edward's personal mission at York, namely the removal of his father's severed head from Micklegate Bar, displayed there since the battle of Wakefield three months earlier.[46] York's welcome and Edward's filial gesture confirmed the installation of a new dynasty as strongly as any of the coronation ceremonies held months later in London.[47]

York's attendance upon Edward varied with his hold on the throne. The king's capture and subsequent imprisonment after the battle of Edgecote in July 1469 was apparently not interpreted by his urban subjects as a full loss of power. Edward was free in York by September, and upon regaining power passed through the city several times during 1470 to quell Lancastrian sympathizers in the north. A more difficult moment took place in March 1471 soon after his return from exile in the Low Countries. The Yorkist-slanted *Historie of the Arrivall of Edward IV in England* recounts the king's decision "not to goo agayne to the water, but to holde the right waye to his City of Yorke."[48] Edward was met three miles outside of the city by the recorder, who advised him that he was not welcome. Edward ignored the warning and gave his pledge that he had come only to seek his inheritance, his father's title of duke of York. Wearing the ostrich feather of the Prince of Wales and cheering for the continued reign of Henry VI, Edward was permitted to enter with only a few companions to rest one night. Welcoming ceremonies were not extended to this figure of dubious rank, but neither did the city actively reject him in case the wheel of fortune rotated him to power once more. As it happened, Edward regained the throne, and York survived to honor him with spectacle and illuminations on his 1478 visit.[49] Not until the accession of Henry VII did York or any other town face such a dilemma about the kind of welcome a contender for the throne deserved.

York's eloquent records provide the clearest example of the problems visits could cause during the Wars of the Roses, but its difficulties were not unique. During their 1470 revolt against Edward IV, the duke of Clarence and the earl of Warwick retreated to Exeter hoping to gather some of the duke's western retainers. Both the magnates and the town soon found themselves in the middle of a siege led by local knight Sir Hugh Courtenay. Realizing that Hugh's private grievance could not be turned to their advantage, Clarence and Warwick embarked for the Continent from nearby Dartmouth. Within a week, Edward IV arrived in Exeter, whose officers were quick to extend a ceremonious welcome to convince the king of their sincere loyalty.[50] The city had far less to be embarrassed about when Richard III arrived after Buckingham's rebellion in 1483. Exeter had neither supported the rebel duke nor neglected its duty to the king with extravagant displays, among which should be included the public execution of Richard's brother-in-law and Buckingham adherent Thomas St. Leger.[51] Henry VII's 1497 visit to Exeter has already been mentioned, an occasion when the welcome combined with spectacles of capital punishment. Before his departure and as a sign of his affection, Henry presented the city with the honor of a civic sword and a cap of maintenance.[52]

Special Relationships

Although a fuller discussion of towns' patronage of the nobility can be found in the following chapter, the special relationship that prevailed between one aristocrat and a city deserves analysis here. To the city of York, Richard duke of Gloucester was a local noble confidently petitioned for help by civic officers in the 1470s and greeted with delighted anticipation when he became King Richard III in 1483.

Although far from universally liked by the citizens, Richard took the kind of active, personal interest in York's fortunes that made its significant investment in gifts and greetings worthwhile. Records of Richard's visits to York before 1475 are lost, but surviving documents inform us of a city willing to invest in spectacle to influence a leading nobleman.[53] On his first recorded visit in 1476, for example, Richard was met by all the civic officials in their ceremonial gowns. Accompanied by local noble Henry Percy earl of Northumberland, and an armed force of five thousand men, Gloucester delivered a royal proclamation against unlawful violence.[54]

Thereafter, York's officials wasted no time in providing Richard with opportunities to display his interest in civic welfare. Frequent letters advised the duke of river blockages, criminal officials, civic poverty, and the problems encountered in mustering soldiers for the Scottish campaigns Richard personally led.[55] The duke's visits were treated as state occasions which officials and guild members attended in their best array or risked incurring a monetary fine. Wine, bread, fish and game were showered upon Richard and his wife, particularly after he had persuaded the king not to suspend York's liberties following election riots. Responding with positive action to nearly every civic request, Richard earned from York on each visit "a lawde and a thank of his greit labours, gude and benevolent lordship don tofore tyme for the honour and common wele of this cite." Although one citizen complained that Richard did nothing for the city "but grin [at] us," and another that he unfairly influenced city elections, most residents took pride in Richard's interest in York and the many ways he accurately depicted its problems to the king.[56]

York remained on Richard's mind even during the hectic weeks of his usurpation of the throne in the spring of 1483. Preoccupying the civic officials at that time was the matter of their declining prosperity. In June 1483, Richard wrote to York that he had no time to consider such matters at the moment, but the city could oblige him by sending troops to defend their good lord against the threats of the widowed queen and her adherents.[57] The soldiers who responded to the call played a considerable role in transforming Duke Richard into King Richard, providing him with the force necessary to secure the throne. The city's hopes for maintaining its relationship with him can best be seen in the ceremonial procession made to Middleham shortly after his coronation, to deliver to the king's small son an impressive array of wine and foodstuffs.[58]

The royal progress Richard and his queen embarked upon in July 1483 included York as a significant stop. The spectacle planned for their visit was to be the culmination of the couple's relationship with the city. Arrangements to meet the royal party in proper array began weeks before the king's secretary worriedly addressed a letter to the officials. John Kendal wrote that although he was certain they had everything in hand, he hoped York like the other towns on the route would greet the couple with pageants and speeches, and decorate the streets appropriately. Further to inspire them to new heights of celebration, Kendal reminded the officials of the king's gratitude to York, and how he planned to grant them privileges greater than any monarch ever had before.[59]

York's elaborate arrangements fulfilled the highest expectations. The "sights" or entertainments planned for the visit cost the city chamberlains so much money, their numbers had to be increased in order to bear the charges.[60] By no coincidence, the royal procession trod the same path as the city's annual Corpus Christi play cycle. Although he had missed their performance three months earlier, Richard had timed his visit to a day particularly hallowed within the city. He arrived on 29 August, the feast of the Decollation of John the Baptist, a symbol the citizens understood to be analogous to the Body of Christ worshipped so visibly by their leading guild and the ceremonies it sponsored.[61]

Religious symbolism mounted as high as the costs of all this spectacle. Most of the officials contributed generously to the gifts of money presented to the king and queen, while "the most honest men of every parish" underwrote the performance of the Creed Play for the royal entourage.[62] The mayor and council members accompanied King Richard to the performance, while the dean and chapter viewed the procession of scenes from the Minster gates.[63] But even this was not the highlight of the royal visit. Richard planned to honor the city even more by holding in it his son's investiture as Prince of Wales, a move calculated to consolidate support for his line.[64] The investiture ceremony was so lavish, one chronicler believed the royal couple had undergone a second coronation. On September 8, the feast of the Nativity of the Blessed Virgin Mary, the king and queen donned their crowns and processed through the streets to the Minster with their young son. After Mass, the royal family presided over a sumptuous feast in the archbishop's palace, a four-hour event enjoyed by the Minster staff, five bishops, a score of nobles, and the Castilian ambassador.[65]

In a bid for support, Richard had shown generosity to his hosts along the progress, most notably giving the city of Gloucester significant financial and legal privileges.[66] Likewise, York did not have to wait very long for Richard to show his gratitude. On September 17, the king gathered the civic officials together in the Minster's Chapter House and praised them for the generous musters they had provided for recent Scottish campaigns and for his own accession. For these acts, and because of "the dekey and the grete povert[y] of the said cite, of hys most speciall good grace, withowt ony petecion of askyng of any thyng by the said mair or of ony odyr," Richard released all toll charges paid by non-resident merchants in order to promote increased trade in the city. The city and the mayor himself also received annuities.[67] The civic officials were rightfully jubilant; their good lord and former neighbor had not only reached a position in which he could help his friends, but he had not forgotten them or their specific requests. The cost of dazzling the king with spectacles had produced an appropriate response that would bolster their faltering economy. Only after the king had left town did civic officials begin to question the implications of the grant. Doubt turned to frustration when the officials discovered the bureaucracy of the central administration did not or would not act upon the king's grant. The king's generous gift was to provide the city of York with over fifty years of aggravation with the royal Exchequer, as neither Richard nor the Tudor kings could coordinate royal generosity with bureaucratic expectations.[68]

The Symbols of Legitimacy

Despite the financial confusion, York remained loyal to Richard throughout his short reign, fidelity that caused its officials distress upon the accession of Henry Tudor in 1485. No sooner had the city received word that Richard had been killed in battle, than its officials wrote to the Percy earl of Northumberland, expressing the wish that he be their new "good lord" and that he advise them how to act "at this woofull season."[69] As a neighboring lord, Percy was a reasonable choice, but he was at that moment under Tudor's arrest and he never fully gained the new king's trust. Before he could reply with advice, York's officials were forced to cope with Tudor's messenger, who demanded admittance to the city. Far from sending out a welcoming party in ceremonial gowns, much less planning processions and greetings, the city could not even guarantee the messenger's safety in a borough still recalling "the moost famous prince of blissed memory King Richard late decesid."[70] Although Henry assured the city that its privileges were secure, he only earned the officials' annoyance by spending the first year of his reign imposing on them his own candidates for town offices.[71] But once more ceremony and spectacle would play a part in reconciling a monarch to his urban subjects, who continued to seek expansion of their rights and privileges.

Sensitive to the task ahead of him, Henry Tudor quickly began to emphasize by ceremonial means the justice of his victory and his claim to the throne. In particular, he presented himself as the most recent fulfillment of a long line of heroes from the distant, almost entirely mythic, past of Britain. He stressed his Welsh descent and bore the red dragon device and heraldic arms of Cadwallader, the last British king who had prophesied his race's ultimate triumph over the Saxon (English) invaders. Although Edward I and Edward IV before him also claimed British roots, Henry dedicated far more energy in publicizing his ancestry, especially his claimed descent from King Arthur, naming his first son after the renowned king. So strongly associated was the British monarch with the entire regime that Arthurian symbolism far outlasted the frail prince destined to predecease his father.[72] Henry's use of British myth was tremendously important in its influence on the concept and writing of history under the Tudors. Historians such as Polydore Vergil, John Leland, William Camden, and Edward Hall all interpreted the Middle Ages and the Wars of the Roses in ways complementary to Henry's vision of himself as savior of a battered nation.[73] The resulting histories continue to influence our view of the medieval world even today, but for the multitudes who never accessed the literature, the public acts of spectacle and ceremony made identical points.

The first year of Henry VII's reign was a critical one of establishment and justification. Assisted by joyous events such as his marriage to Yorkist Princess Elizabeth and the birth of their son nine months later, Henry was able to face enemies and doubters with evidence that Divine Providence was on his side. Unlike previous kings, he did not embark upon a royal progress through his kingdom immediately after the coronation. An epidemic of the sweating sickness, the November 1485 parliament, the arrangements for his January wedding, and his bride's pregnancy produced sufficient grounds for delay, but what was really keeping Henry at home was rumor of armed discontent in the realm and the survival of many Yorkist supporters.[74]

Henry set off on his first royal progress early in March 1486. Informed that Yorkist supporters were gathering in the north at Richard's Middleham Castle, Henry added several thousand men to his escort from the retinues of his uncle and the earl of Northumberland, and proceeded to York. The northern capital had prepared for the visit since mid-March: officers wrote to the archbishop of York for advice on how to receive the king, hired veteran spectacle arranger Henry Hudson, and wondered in the pages of their council records whether the king would think they were as glad of his visit as the arrivals of previous monarchs.[75] Late in Henry's first year, York officials sent a long letter to the king, describing the history of their loyalty to the Lancastrian house, and blaming their poverty on Edward IV's vindictiveness over that fidelity. The poverty of the city, so the civic officials claimed, was such that a monetary gift could not be given.[76] Originally to be greeted by the ceremonially-gowned officials at the southern limit of York's franchises, this part of the welcome was changed closer to the time of arrival when it was determined that Henry had better be shown greater honor by twice the usual number of horsemen, greeting him five miles away from York instead of two. Nothing was left to chance: even the children who formed part of the welcoming committee were prompted to cry "King Henry" on cue. The city had reason to be nervous about the visit, not least because the Yorkist rebels gathering to the west might expect Richard III's special borough to assist them.

Here we enter the realm of theory, for York's records of the ceremonies were all written in the future tense, delineating what was supposed to happen but failing to comment at all on how the spectacle really turned out.[77] As in the pageants performed at Hereford and Bristol, and planned but not given at Worcester, York's ceremonies intended to stress Henry's suitability for the throne and celebrate his year-old military triumph. The characters chosen to perform, and the speeches they made, argued that Henry was king by hereditary right, divine election, providential victory in battle, personal virtue, and popular assent. Three kings and the Virgin Mary recalled the Epiphany complete with symbolic gift-giving, perhaps the greatest of which was the acknowledgment of Henry as Christ's own knight and the city's rightful king.

At York, Henry was to be greeted just inside the first gate by a pageant depicting heaven. Under the celestial roof was planned a desolate world of trees and flowers springing to life as the king neared. On his approach, the blooms bowed down to an entwined red rose (symbolizing Henry and his Lancastrian ancestry) and a white rose (the badge of the house of York and symbolic of the queen). The two flowers united, as Henry and Elizabeth had been in marriage, to be covered with a crown that descended from heaven. The happy union brought life into the world, as the garden set was then filled with people and turned into the city of York itself. Ebrauk, the legendary founder of York, then came on stage to greet the king and in feudal homage give him the keys of the city, his title, and his crown. He recited a poem, which not only flattered Henry but reminded him to be compassionate to the city that derived so much joy from his visit. Henry was then to pass through the streets hung solidly with cloth and tapestries. If the weather were fair that day, the city planned to run devices raining rose water and candy hailstones upon the crowd, concluding with a snow of heavenly wafers.

Closer to the center of the city, Henry would encounter the heart of the spectacle, a royal throne bearing six kings, specifically the monarchs who had shared his name. In a second act of feudal homage, the six Henries were directed to give a "septour of sapience" to the actor playing King Solomon, who offered it to Tudor as a symbol of wisdom and justice. Solomon's speech revealed that the six previous Henries had been looking forward to the seventh of their name, and all of them were fully approving of what he had done since the start of his reign. They urged him to keep up the good work, and concluded with a stanza requesting the king to show the city a little of his "bountevous Benevolence."[78] In front of the Guildhall, the center of York's civic government, was planned a show starring the third of the three mighty kings of this epiphany, namely King David atop a castle and accompanied by citizens clad in the Tudor colors green and white. David compared Henry favorably to Charlemagne (a fellow member of the Nine Worthies), gave him a sword of victory, and surrendered the castle in a gesture of military submission. David then reminded the king that York had always been loyal to his family and often suffered for it. After a shower of fake snow, the royal entourage would have come to the last pageant, the culmination of the show, presided over by the figure of the Virgin Mary descending directly from heaven to York's streets by the miracle of stagecraft. Her speech was York's most self-serving, telling

Henry outright that Christ believed the city to be trustworthy and that she would always intercede on behalf of the king, Christ's own knight, for her son's grace.

York's pageants craftily ignored the city's relationship with Richard III and other Yorkists, and concentrated instead on those elements of antiquity and religion that flattered both the town and the monarch. If the speeches and performances went off as planned, Henry would have had every reason to believe that York delighted in his rule, rejoiced in his marriage, recognized the role Divine Providence had played in his accession, and looked forward to continuing a long and happy relationship with the Lancastrian-Tudor dynasty. As Keith Thomas has noted, "the most common reason for invoking the past was to legitimize the prevailing distribution of power," a sentiment fueling the nature of the pageant and the hopes of York's civic authorities.[79] How close the reality conformed to the plan is something we will never know, but it is true that unlike Richard, Henry gave the city no grants or privileges after the visit.

Henry left York with the good news that the Middleham rebels had dispersed, but he was forced to head for another center of treason in Worcester. This town had also prepared pageants and displays with Henry VI as the leading character, but never performed them, perhaps because of the threat of Yorkist insurrection. From Worcester, Henry traveled to Hereford, whose pageants introduced the characters of Saint George, King Ethelbert of East Anglia (whose relics were in the town's cathedral), and the Virgin Mary. At Gloucester, Henry had some respite from pageants, but Bristol performed five of them, presided over by the figure of the mythical British king Brennius said to be Bristol's founder. Some stanzas about the city's decline from greatness had the desired effect: later in the visit, Henry questioned the civic officials about their poverty and urged them to develop their shipping.[80]

Henry's second visit to York was recorded after the fact, so we have a more accurate idea of what actually occurred. This visit followed closely upon the king's victory over pretender Lambert Simnel and the Yorkist adherents who promoted him.[81] Set for late July and early August 1487, the spectacles included performances of the Corpus Christi plays, postponed from earlier in the summer by royal command. These joyous ceremonies were far outnumbered, at least in the records, by public proclamations to keep the peace, directives for the fair pricing of food, and nervous warnings to maintain the watch against invaders. The lineage themes of the first visit were abandoned in favor of a stress on law and order, culminating in the vivid spectacle of the public beheading of a citizen who had admitted some of the king's rebels through York's gates. The visit concluded with the knighting of the lord mayor and an alderman for their services against the rebels in June. This unsurpassed boon to two leading governors of the city increased the honor of York, but did not begin to solve some of its basic problems. During this visit as at other times, the civic officials begged for a clarification of their financial difficulties, but to no avail.[82]

There is no surviving evidence that the court dictated the content of the urban pageants, but it is interesting to observe how rapidly civic officials caught on to the more flattering elements of royal propaganda. Although it was natural for them to include characterizations of their ancient, often mythical founders, in doing so they had tapped into a source of vital importance to the first Tudor. That so many of these founders were of British descent only reinforced Henry's own claims of descent from Cadwallader and Arthur, and gave the towns a unique relationship with the Tudor dynasty. On the other hand, the rose symbols were new elements in the royal propaganda and still in flux: the hybrid we recognize as the Tudor rose slowly developed out of the images of white and red roses, often depicted as growing from the same plant.[83] At first only a symbol of Henry's marriage to the heiress of York, the rose came to be associated with the entire dynasty and the success it had had in ending internecine strife. York's use of the flower as a centerpiece of a pageant confirmed the importance and popularity of the symbol. Likewise, the town of Worcester was particularly shrewd in discerning the important role Henry VI played in the Tudor world view. Often called his uncle, the sixth Henry was a half-cousin of the first Tudor, considered to be a saint and mourned as a victim of Yorkist ambition.[84]

Few of the pageants gained more for their towns than the kind of supportive advice Henry freely gave to Bristol. In York's case, Henry turned a deaf ear to pleas of poverty, fee farm difficulties, and tradition of self-government.[85] The fairs, swords, and charters acquired after other royal visits and spectacles are nowhere in evidence in the first Tudor's progress. But most civic officials probably breathed a sigh of relief that Henry at least had not taken retaliatory action against them. They may have been unaware of the most important results of Henry's first visits, namely the influence their pageants and spectacles had upon the formation of royal propaganda and the concept of the divinely-blessed

Tudor dynasty.[86] Their acceptance of symbols and themes Henry was just trying out confirmed their popular and persuasive power and helped him overcome his shaky start in politics.

This overview of the role of spectacle in urban development reveals a key aspect of the reciprocal nature of town relations with the royal government. Those English towns which were royal creations could not survive or mature without the cooperation of the monarch and the privileges of self-government only he could grant. When the king or a noble close to him visited a town, civic officials spared no expense in expressing their loyalty and delight by devising spectacles and pageants of welcome. By displays of a form of ritualized communal drama which anthropologist Clifford Geertz has called "theatre state," king and citizens reinforced their understanding of their linked identities and celebrated an urban manifestation of Christian polity.[87] Even if no gift or grant was immediately forthcoming after a visit, a town usually relied upon such ceremonies to give it a good reputation with national leaders and to make clear the social unity and autonomy of the borough.

But it is also true that the monarch needed alliances with his urban subjects, and depended heavily upon the general tone their loyal, unified expressions set. Throughout the Middle Ages, kings had delegated many responsibilities to towns, the chief one being the need to uphold the king's peace among urban subjects. Such visits provided opportunities for towns to display how well they had earned royal trust in peacekeeping, and for monarchs to advertise themselves as the embodiment of order and power, imitative of Christ's own majesty. Moreover, for all their financial problems, towns remained important sources of wealth, power, and culture in medieval society. To have them on one's side gave a king significant influence. Richard III's urgent need for support during his short reign explains much of his generosity to York after his accession. Henry VII survived early threats to his rule largely because of his own confident demeanor, supported in great part by royal propaganda and towns like York which accepted its tenets and broadcast its claims. The welcoming spectacles that town leaders devised and national leaders watched bound all of them together in a sharing of status, honor, and unity, which with any luck would last longer than the show.

NOTES

1   *CPR, 1446–52*, p. 221; Francis Drake, *Eboracum* (London: W. Bowyer, 1736), p. 105.

2   *York House Books*, pp. 470–71.

3   Barbara A. Hanawalt and Kathryn L. Reyerson, eds., *City and Spectacle in Medieval Europe* (Minneapolis and London: University of Minnesota Press, 1994), p. ix. The introduction to this volume contains some important comments on the usefulness and applicability of anthropological analysis to this topic, and includes a helpful bibliography of recent writings. See also *Civic Ritual and Drama*, ed. Alexandra Johnston and Wim Hüsken (Amsterdam and Atlanta, Ga.: Rodopi, 1997). Gordon Kipling, *Enter the King: Theatre, Liturgy, and Ritual in the Medieval Civic Triumph* (Oxford: Clarendon Press, 1998), confines his valuable and detailed study to "the art of the medieval royal entry," a specialized form of monarchical visit celebrated for a king no more than once in a given city, and not the only kind of visit studied in this chapter.

4   Robert Darnton, "A Bourgeois Puts His World in Order: The City as a Text," *The Great Cat Massacre and Other Episodes in French Cultural History* (New York: Basic Books, 1984), p. 124; Charles Phythian-Adams, "Ceremony and the Citizen: The Communal Year at Coventry 1450–1550," in *Crisis and Order in English Towns 1500–1700*, eds. Peter Clark and Paul Sack (Toronto: University of Toronto Press, 1972), p. 63. See also Richard Trexler, *Public Life in Renaissance Florence* (New York: Academic Press, 1980), pp. 249–63, *passim*.

5   The argument proved unconvincing as the riot occurred five weeks before the festival: Philippa C. Maddern, *Violence and Social Order: East Anglia 1422–1442* (Oxford: Clarendon Press, 1992), pp. 109, 197. Carnival and inversion ceremonies such as the boy bishop celebrations had some role in medieval society, but such disruptive forces have been better studied in later periods: see Mikhail Bakhtin, *Rabelais and His World*, trans. Helene Iswolsky (Bloomington: Indiana University Press, 1984), and E. Le Roy Ladurie, *Carnival in Romans*, trans. M. Feeney (Harmondsworth: Penguin Publishing, 1981), chapter 7.

6   Phythian-Adams, "Ceremony and the Citizen," pp. 58–64. The focus of this study is not the Corpus Christi cycle of plays dramatized by many of the towns mentioned here. The plays will be referred to only when their performance coincided with a royal or noble visit. For further comment, see Miri Rubin, *Corpus Christi: The Eucharist in Late Medieval Culture* (Cambridge: Cambridge University Press, 1991).

7   Mervyn James, "Ritual, Drama, and Social Body in the Late Medieval English Town," *Past and Present* 98 (1983): 12. Darnton calls such occasions "a social order representing itself to itself": *Great Cat Massacre*, p. 124. See Jennifer I. Kermode, *Medieval Merchants: York, Beverley and Hull in the Later Middle Ages* (Cambridge: Cambridge University Press, 1998), p. 12 n.50 for further references on this topic.

8   F. B. Bickley, ed., *The Little Red Book of Bristol*, 2 vols. (Bristol: W. C. Hemmons, 1900–1901), 1:149–53; *York Mem. Bk.*, 2:viii; *York House Books*, pp. 122–23, 305, 511; Susan Reynolds, *An Introduction to the History of English Medieval Towns* (Oxford: Oxford University Press, 1977), pp. 179–80. Local tradition claims York's mayor received the title from Richard II in 1387: J. H. Harvey, "Richard II and

York," in *The Reign of Richard II: Essays in Honour of May McKisack*, ed. F. R. H. Du Boulay and Caroline Barron (London: The Athlone Press of the University of London, 1971), p. 205. See above, p. 48.

9   For example, beating the bounds of a city's liberties required the mayor to be accompanied by council members and representatives from the craft guilds, not just to act as witnesses but to confirm the dignity in which the officers were held: *York House Books*, pp. 281, 355–56.

10   Exeter acquired four maces as early as 1385, but did not achieve the right to a sword and cap until Henry VII's visit in 1497: D.R.O., Receivers' Rolls, 9–10 Richard II, 13–14 Henry VII; Book 51, f.329v; H. Lloyd Parry, "The Exeter Swords and Hat of Maintenance," *Transactions of the Devonshire Association* 64 (1932): 421–28. In 1404, Henry IV gave Norwich the right to have both a mayor and a sword to be borne before him in procession: *Norwich Records*, 1:lxi, 32, 77, 103; N.R.O., 7-c, Treasurers' Rolls, 8–9, 9–10, 11–12 Henry IV. For the meaning of regalia in sixteenth-century society, see Robert Tittler, *Architecture and Power: The Town Hall and the English Urban Community c.1500–1640* (Oxford: Clarendon Press, 1991), pp. 107–9.

11   *York House Books*, pp. 137, 573–74. See above, p. 46.

12   *Ibid.*, pp. 301–2, 426.

13   *Ibid.*, pp. 4–5, 40, 135–36, 257, 388.

14   A. F. Leach, ed., *Beverley Town Documents*, Selden Society, vol. 14 (London: 1900), p. 34.

15   Of the 59 visits, 26 (44%) were made during a royal progress or for purposes of pleasure; 9 (15%) for purely military reasons; 9 (15%) during the Wars of the Roses (mixing pageantry with military reasons); 6 (10.3%) to provide justice and 4 (7%) for matters of arbitration; 4 (7%) for religious pilgrimages; and 1 (1.7%) when the government moved to York in this period.

16   *York House Books*, p. 713.

17   N.R.O., 21-f, 9-58, Kirkpatrick Notes, *sub* 8 September 1461; 16-d, Assembly Book I, f.48.

18   N.R.O., 16-d, ff.50v–51v. Visits of queens excited similar anxieties, as the preparations for Edward's consort eight years later indicate. Anxious officials wrote to the recorder in London for advice on how to welcome Queen Elizabeth: James Gairdner, ed., *The Paston Letters*, 6 vols. (London: Chatto and Windus, 1904): 5:34.

19   *Nott. Records*, 3:263–64.

20   In 1503, York officials sent a messenger to the south to inquire how Princess Margaret had been received at Northampton and whether she was on schedule, during her progress north to join her Scottish bridegroom: *York Civic Records*, 2:184–85.

21   During the royal visit of 1396, York officers paid him and other royal ministers over £12: Dobson, *Chamberlains' Accounts*, p. 5. For the clerk's duties, and his reliance upon "the better and more discreet men" of the city to execute their chartered rights of exemption from his overview, see *York Mem. Bk.*, 1:141–42.

22   N.R.O., 17-d, Apprenticeship Indenture Book, ff.8–8v, 19v–20; 18-a, Chamberlains' Account Book, 1470–90, f.74v.

23   Rosemary Horrox, "Urban Patronage and Patrons in the Fifteenth Century," in *Patronage, the Crown, and the Provinces in Later Medieval England*, ed. Ralph Griffiths (Gloucester: Alan Sutton Publishing, 1981), p. 149.

24   The former was covered by the aldermen, the latter raised by the commons in assembly: N.R.O., 16-d, Assembly Book I, ff.18v–19; Francis Blomefield, *A Topographical History of the County of Norfolk*, 2d ed., 11 vols. (London: William Miller, 1805–10), 3:158. The queen's visit prompted Margaret Paston to borrow jewelry from her cousin so that she would look well among the crowd, "for I durst not for shame go with my beads among so many fresh gentlewomen as were here at that time": Norman Davis, ed., *Paston Letters and Papers of the Fifteenth Century*, 2 vols. (Oxford: Clarendon Press, 1971, 1976), 1:248–50 (20 April 1453).

25   N.R.O., 16-d, Assembly Book I, ff.50v–51. The following wards contributed to the 1462 gift: Mancroft, £43 11s. 8d.; Wymer, £63 5s. 8d.; Ultra Aquam, £31 11s. 7d.; Conesford (with suburb of Trous) £22.

26   *Ibid.*, ff.78, 80–81, 86v. Nor did it help town finances when royal entourages neglected to return horses supplied by their hosts to move them to their next venue. Henry IV and his queen caused Exeter such expense during their 1403 visit: D.R.O., Receivers' Roll, 1402–1403; Cecily Radford, "An Unrecorded Royal Visit to Exeter," *Transactions of the Devonshire Association* 63 (1931): 255–62. Likewise, after Henry VII's visit in 1497, city mounts disappeared with departing dignitaries: D.R.O., Receivers' Rolls, 1496–97.

27   *CPR, 1388–92*, pp. 65, 69.

28   *CChR*, 5:333–36, 358–60; *York Mem. Bk.*, 1:143–46, 157–63; Nigel Saul, "Richard II and the City of York," *The Government of Medieval York: Essays in Commemoration of the 1396 Royal Charter*, ed. Sarah Rees Jones, Borthwick Studies in History 3 (York, 1997), pp. 3–7; Barrie Dobson, "The Crown, the Charter, and the City, 1396–1461," *ibid.*, p. 39. See above, pp. 37 and 38. Richard's 1396 visit incurred entertainment costs of over £224: Dobson, *Chamberlains' Accounts*, pp. 5–8.

29   Miller, *VCH*, p. 57; cf. Saul, "Richard II and the City of York," p. 7.

30   D.R.O., Book 51, f.329v; Receivers' Roll, 1496–97; P.R.O., E.101/414/16, ff.1–4; N.R.O., 16-d, Assembly Book I, f.118; 17-b, Liber Albus, f.54v; *Norwich Records*, 1:42–43.

31   Davis, ed., *Paston Letters and Papers*, 1:338–39, 400–401, 540–41 (April and June 1469). During his visit, members of Edward's entourage were besieged with petitions from the Paston family to show them favor in their property disputes with the duke of Norfolk: *ibid.*, 543–45.

32   Gairdner, *Paston Letters*, 5:34; N.R.O., 18-a, Chamberlains' Account Book, 1470–90, ff.10–13; Henry Harrod, "Queen Elizabeth Woodville's Visit to Norwich in 1469," *Norfolk Archaeology* 5 (1859): 32–36; and see below, p. 199. Kipling's argument (*Enter the King*, p. 315) that this queen's *adventus* foreshadowed a princely nativity includes the false assumption that Elizabeth was pregnant with her second daughter in July 1469. She had, in fact, given birth to her third daughter, Cecily, on 20 March 1469 and her first son was born 2 November 1470: Cora Scofield, *The Life and Reign of Edward the Fourth*, 2 vols. (London, 1923), 1:482, 546.

33   *York House Books*, pp. 288, 298. In March 1484, Hudson received additional payment for charges he had incurred in producing the play: *ibid.*, p. 304. In comparison, the man who designed Margaret of Anjou's 1456 entry into Coventry earned 25s.: Mary D. Harris, ed., *The Coventry Leet Book*, 2 vols., Early English Text Society, o.s., vols. 134–35, 138 & 146 (1907, 1913; reprint, Millwood New York: Kraus, 1971), 1:292. Hudson's expertise may have been confined to the staging of the Creed Play. Neither as long nor as elaborate as the Corpus Christi cycle, the performance was still impressive with its use of pageant wagons to bear the costumed actors and sets in twelve scenes enacting the major points of the Creed: Alexandra F. Johnston, "The Plays of the Religious Guilds of York: The Creed Play and the Pater Noster Play," *Speculum* 50 (1975): 68–69.

34   *York House Books*, p. 474–75, 479, 481–85.

35   D.R.O., Receivers' Roll, 1451–52; Book 51, ff.309v–310.

36   *York House Books*, p. 482 (undated; spring 1486). The Tadcaster greeting also prevailed when Henry's daughter Margaret passed through York in 1503 on her way to join her Scottish husband. York's officers sent anxiously to Northampton to find out how the queen had been received there and whether she was expected to arrive on time. They wanted her memory of civic hospitality to be "tender and gracious": *York Civic Records*, 2:184–85.

37   Miller, *VCH*, p. 57.

38   Michel Foucault, *Discipline and Punish: The Birth of the Prison*, trans. Alan Sheridan (New York: Vintage Books, 1979). Recent studies focusing on capital punishment include Peter Linebaugh, *The London Hanged: Crime and Civil Society in the Eighteenth Century* (Cambridge and New York: Cambridge University Press, 1992), and V. A. C. Gatrell, *The Hanging Tree: Execution and the English People 1770–1868* (Oxford and New York: Oxford University Press, 1994).

39   P.R.O., C.61/112, mem.14; E.404/23/140; *Nott. Records*, 2:42–47; J. L. Kirby, *Calendar of Signet Letters of Henry IV and Henry V*, (London: Her Majesty's Stationery Office, 1978), p. 194 (2 September 1408, to the mayor, jurats and commonalty of Bordeaux). The serjeant of the royal household paid the construction costs for the scaffolding.

40   D.R.O., Receivers' Roll, 1451–52; Book 51, ff.309v–310 (Henry VI in Exeter, 1452); E. F. Jacob, *The Fifteenth Century* (Oxford: Oxford University Press, 1961), p. 53 (Henry IV in York, 1403).

41   See below, pp. 287–89 and 300–301.

42   D.R.O., Receivers' Roll, 1483–84. Expenses for the beheading included payments to witnesses, necessities like bread and candles, scaffold construction, and refreshment for commissioner Lord Scrope.

43   D.R.O., Book 51, f.329v; Receivers' Roll, 1496–97; P.R.O., E.101/414/16, ff.1–4.

44   Ralph A. Griffiths, *The Reign of Henry VI* (Berkeley and Los Angeles: University of California Press, 1981), pp. 589–92, 597; Bertram Wolffe, *Henry VI* (London: Eyre Methuen, 1980), pp. 261–62; P.R.O., C.81/1371/33. Queen Margaret visited the city on her own two months later: see above p. 76.

45   Charles Ross, *Edward IV* (London: Eyre Methuen, 1974), pp. 36–37. The phrase comes from a 4 April 1461 letter of William Paston II describing York's welcome five days earlier: Davis, ed., *Paston Letters and Papers*, 1:165–66 (no.90).

[46]   J. H. Ramsay, *Lancaster and York*, 2 vols. (Oxford: Clarendon Press, 1892), 2:237–38. Legend, reinforced by a near-contemporary chronicle, insists that York's head was adorned with a paper crown to mock his failed pretensions to the throne: Ross, *Edward IV*, 30, n.3. Shakespeare expands on the scene in *Henry VI, Part 3*, Act I, Scene 4, lines 179–80.

[47]   A more traditional welcome waited until November 1462, when the city provided a body of men-at-arms to oppose Margaret of Anjou's campaign and lay siege to three Northumbrian castles still in Lancastrian hands: Scofield, *Edward the Fourth*, 1:262–64; Ross, *Edward IV*, p. 51.

[48]   J. Bruce, ed., *Historie of the Arrivall of Edward IV in England*, Camden Society, o.s., vol. 1 (London: John Bowyer Nichols and Son, 1838), pp. 4–7; Scofield, *Edward the Fourth*, 1:570–71. Polydore Vergil, writing in the early sixteenth century, recounted that the citizens threatened violence against Edward if he forced his way into York. They gave way after Edward made numerous promises to benefit them once he regained the throne, but "the whole day almost was spent in this parley": Henry Ellis, ed., *Three Books of Polydore Vergil's English History*, Camden Society, o.s., vol. 29 (London: John Bowyer Nichols and Son, 1844), pp. 138–39.

[49]   Dobson, *Chamberlains' Accounts*, pp. 165, 169–70. The city spent 16d. on illuminations for Edward's visit, and £36 3s. 7d. for wine, cloth, and bread given the king and other important lords who accompanied him.

[50]   Hoker, *Description of the Citie*, pp. 51–55; Michael Hicks, *False, Fleeting, Perjur'd Clarence* (Gloucester: Alan Sutton Publishing, 1980), pp. 71–72. See below, p. 110 for Exeter's treatment of Clarence and his duchess.

[51]   D.R.O., Book 51, f.322; Richard Polwhele, *The History of Devonshire*, 3 vols. (London, 1793–1806; rpt., Dorking, 1977), 1:253. Shakespeare recorded the king's legendary reaction to Exeter castle in *Richard III*, Act IV, Scene 2, lines 102–106.

[52]   D.R.O., Book 51, f.329v; Receivers' Roll, 1496–97; P.R.O., E.101/414/16, ff.1–4.

[53]   City chamberlains' rolls record gifts of wine in 1468 and 1470, almost certain proof that Richard visited the city in those years: Dobson, *Chamberlains' Accounts*, pp. 126, 137.

[54]   *York House Books*, pp. 8–9. The number is, of course, suspect.

[55]   *Ibid.*, pp. 9–10, 128–30 (fishgarths in the River Ouse); 46–48 (former common clerk dismissed for embezzlement and immoral acts); 696–97, 703 (reduced number of soldiers because of the city's poverty).

[56]   *Ibid.*, pp. 78, 233–34, 248–50, 254, 259, 279, 696, 707. In the years before 1483, Gloucester and his duchess spent most of their time at her late father's castle at Middleham, about forty miles from York, where in 1477 they became members of York's Corpus Christi Guild: R. H. Skaife, ed., *The Register of the Guild of Corpus Christi in the City of York*, Surtees Society, vol. 57 (Durham, 1872 for 1871), pp. xii, 101; Y.C.A., C.99:5.

[57]   *York House Books*, pp. 282, 284–86, 712–14. See below, p. 200. The troops arrived too late to deal with this crisis; any anticipated problems at Edward V's parliament became moot when Richard himself took the throne. As it turned out, they arrived in time to witness Richard make this claim: P. W. Hammond and Anne F. Sutton, *Richard III: The Road to Bosworth Field* (London: Constable and Company, 1985), p. 103.

58 *York House Books*, pp. 286–87.

59 *Ibid.*, pp. 287–89, 713.

60 *Ibid.*, pp. 289, 300. The number increased from three to four in 1484, "to bere soch great chargez as is to be born in thys cite." Between 1484 and 1500, the number varied between four and six. See below, p. 144.

61 Pamela Tudor-Craig, "Richard III's Triumphant Entry into York, August 20th (*sic*), 1483," in *Richard III and the North*, ed. Rosemary Horrox (Hull: University of Hull Centre for Regional and Local History, 1986), pp. 111, 113; James, "Ritual, Drama, and Social Body," 10. Events had kept Richard in London during the May feast of Corpus Christi, but the August date was second in importance on York's religious calendar. Miri Rubin, "Corpus Christi Fraternities and Late Medieval Piety," in *Voluntary Religion*, ed. W. J. Sheils and Diana Wood, Studies in Church History vol. 23 (Oxford: Basil Blackwell, 1986), pp. 97–109, provides the background of the personal meaning of the cult.

62 *York House Books*, pp. 290–92. The king was to have 500 marks in a pair of silver-gilt basins, and his consort £100 of gold in a piece of plate.

63 Johnston, "The Plays of the Religious Guilds of York," 58, 64; Eileen White, *The York Mystery Play* (York: Ebor Press, 1984), p. 29; *York House Books*, pp. 289–93. The Creed Play was performed every twelve years, except in the case of special visits such as Richard's, until 1568. The Corpus Christi cycle was performed annually until 1569.

64 Richard announced his intention to create his son Edward Prince of Wales in letters to the archbishops dated 24 August from Nottingham. The letters do not choose a site for the ceremony, but on 31 August Richard sent to London for cloth and banners (including 13,000 [*sic*] livery badges bearing the device of Richard's white boar) to be sent him in York (thus sparing civic officials some expense): Rosemary Horrox and P. W. Hammond, eds., *British Library Harleian Manuscript 433*, 4 vols. (Upminster and London: Alan Sutton Publishing, 1979–83), 1:81–83; 2:42; Hammond and Sutton, *Richard III*, pp. 137–38.

65 Hammond and Sutton, *Richard III*, pp. 140–41, citing the Bedern College Statute Book held in the York Minster Library. It was the Croyland Chronicle that believed Richard and Anne had had a second coronation: Nicholas Pronay and John Cox, eds., *The Crowland Chronicle Continuations 1459–1486* (London: Alan Sutton Publishing, 1986), p. 161.

66 Hammond and Sutton, *Richard III*, pp. 125–28. The charter remitted part of Gloucester's fee farm, allowed for an elected mayor, and incorporated the town.

67 *York House Books*, p. 729.

68 See below, pp. 146–49. For a full discussion of York's problems with the fee farm, see my two articles, "The King's Interest—York's Fee Farm and the Central Government," *Northern History* 17 (1981): 24–43, and "Medieval Bureaucracy in Fifteenth-Century York," *York Historian* 6 (1985): 24–31. A. J. Pollard of the University of Teesside has wondered whether Richard had any intention at all of acting on his promise to York, and never told the Exchequer to excuse the city. Without doubting that any medieval king was capable of such duplicity, I would argue that Richard probably intended the gift sincerely. Before leaving York, he arranged for a change in the annuity of Sir John Savage, an important supporter in the Welsh marches. Savage had previously derived his annuity from York's fee

farm, but now the money was to come from another source. As Richard explained in a new grant, "it is soo that now of late at oure being in oure said Citee for gret causes us specialy moving, We have disposed the said Fee ferme aswelle to the Releeff and socouring of the said Citee as otherwise, so that the saide annuite ne may be paiable there...": Horrox and Hammond, *Harleian MS. 433*, 2:18. York was no less important a source of support than Savage, and it is unlikely that Richard intended to confuse or offend either one.

[69] *York House Books*, pp. 368–69, 734–38.

[70] *Ibid.*, pp. 373–74, 734–36. The mayor and his brethren had to meet the messenger at an inn called The Sign of the Boar (an ironic reminder that they still respected the king who carried the badge of the white boar?). He assured them that Henry VII would be as generous a king to York as any of his predecessors.

[71] See above, p. 54.

[72] B.L., Additional MS. 46354, f.72v (p. 144), Sir Thomas Wriothesley's Book of Arms; Sydney Anglo, "The 'British History' in Early Tudor Propaganda," *Bulletin of the John Rylands Library* 44 (1961): 18, 35 n.4, 38; Roger Loomis, "Edward I, Arthurian Enthusiast," *Speculum* 28 (1953): 114, 126; J. S. P. Tatlock, "The Dragons of Wessex and Wales," *Speculum* 8 (1933): 223–35; A. H. Thomas and I. D. Thornley, eds., *The Great Chronicle of London* (1938; reprint, Gloucester: Alan Sutton Publishing, 1983), pp. 238–39. For the uses of Arthurian symbols in the reigns of Henry VIII and Elizabeth, see Hugh A. MacDougall, *Racial Myth in English History* (Hanover, New Hampshire: University of New England Press, 1982), pp. 17–26; *Calendar of State Papers, Spanish, Vol. IV, Part 2, 1531–1533*, ed. Pascual de Gayangos (London: Her Majesty's Stationery Office, 1882; rpt., Nendeln: Kraus Reprint, 1969), pp. 22–28.

[73] For a detailed analysis of Tudor historiographical concepts of medieval society, see my article "England's Official Rose: Tudor Concepts of the Middle Ages," in *Hermeneutics and Medieval Culture*, ed. Patrick J. Gallacher and Helen Damico (Albany: State University of New York Press, 1989), pp. 85–95.

[74] Henry did not begin to plan a progress in earnest until he received word of the death of York's recorder, Miles Metcalf, a supporter of Richard III considered so dangerous he had been especially exempted from the general pardon granted the late king's other supporters: John C. Meagher, "The First Progress of Henry VII," *Renaissance Drama*, n.s., 1 (1968): 46; *York House Books*, pp. 372, 466–67.

[75] *York House Books*, pp. 474–79, *passim*.

[76] *Ibid.*, pp. 390–91. In various pieces of correspondence, York and the king agreed to remember that the city had been loyal to the Lancastrians and had assisted them militarily and financially: C. E. McGee, "Politics and Platitudes: Sources of Civic Pageantry, 1486," *Renaissance Studies* 3 (1989): 31. See Kipling, *Enter the King*, pp. 117–20 for comment on the necessity of a monetary gift and its role in an epiphany motif.

[77] The account of Henry's visit can be found in *York House Books*, pp. 481–85. A slightly confused but eyewitness account is also found in B.L. MS Cotton Julius B. XII, discussed by Kipling, *Enter the King*, pp. 134–39, esp. note 46.

[78] The last stanza is not included in the city council records, but was written by a herald who recorded the scene: Sydney Anglo, *Spectacle, Pageantry, and Early Tudor Policy* (Oxford: The Clarendon Press, 1969), p. 26. The herald's account is

found in John Leland, ed., *De rebus Britannicis Collectanea*, ed. Thomas Hearne, 6 vols. (London: Gvl. and J. Richardson, 1770), 4:187–90. For the parallels between the pageant speeches and scenes from various Corpus Christi plays, see Meagher, "First Progress," 53–55, and Lucy Toulmin Smith, ed., *York Plays* (Oxford: Oxford University Press, 1885; rpt., London: Russell and Russell, 1963), pp. 10–11, 18, 20.

[79]   Keith Thomas, *The Perception of the Past in Early Modern England*, The Creighton Trust Lecture (London: University of London, 1983), p. 2.

[80]   Anglo, *Spectacle*, p. 34. Bristol's pageant master seemed heavily influenced by the *Secreta Secretorum* as expressed in the works of poets such as Lydgate: McGee, "Politics and Platitudes," 32–33.

[81]   Michael Bennett, *Lambert Simnel and the Battle of Stoke* (New York: St. Martin's Press, 1987), pp. 89–103. For York's official interpretation of Stoke, see *York House Books*, pp. 571–73.

[82]   *York House Books*, pp. 584–89. The two citizens themselves, however, were granted annuities from the Hull customs to ease the burden of knighthood: Kermode, *Medieval Merchants*, p. 17, where the date of the knighthoods is incorrect.

[83]   Illustrations of roses accompany the poetry of court writers Pietro Carmeliano (B.L., Additional MS. 33736, ff.1 and 2) and Giovanni de Gigli (B.L., Harleian MS. 336, f.70). Their poems celebrated Henry's victories in battle and in the bedchamber, the birth of Prince Arthur described as the major blessing Henry brought to the land by his accession, an act fully in accord with God's plan: Henry A. Kelly, *Divine Providence in the England of Shakespeare's Histories* (Cambridge, Mass.: Harvard University Press, 1970), chapter 3, *passim*.

[84]   For years following the Worcester pageant, court poets depicted Henry VI as spokesman for the convocation of saints in heaven, a visionary who prophesied that young Tudor would take up the crown and bring peace to England. Henry VII urged his cousin's canonization, an act he believed would bring increased renown to his line, but for complex reasons he failed and his son was not interested in pursuing the task: Anglo, *Spectacle*, p. 43, n.1.

[85]   After returning to Westminster, he continued to promote his own candidates for local office: *York House Books*, pp. 487–88.

[86]   Influences of earlier, provincial pageants should be searched for in Henry VII's Household Ordinances of 1494, which dictated how royalty ought to be received in London: Kipling, *Enter the King*, p. 36.

[87]   Geertz's ideas are best expressed in "Centers, Kings, and Charisma: Reflections on the Symbolics of Power," in *Local Knowledge: Further Essays in Interpretive Anthropology* (New York: Basic Books, 1983), pp. 121–46; see also Kipling, *Enter the King*, p. 47.

CHAPTER 4
THE PATTERNS OF PATRONAGE

oyal visits and the direct nature of borough petitions to a king present within town walls were important components of urban relations with the Crown. But they should not overshadow the role played by magnates, gentry, and members of the legal profession.[1] Such individuals received from civic officials quantities of wine, bread, stipends, and warm welcomes, even when their visits to towns did not coincide with the royal presence. A few of these individuals never left Westminster, yet they were frequently reminded of the existence of generous towns by gift-laden messengers sent by urban councils. Their interest was particularly important to boroughs that were not seigneurial towns, for the exercise of choice reveals much about urban strategies and self-concepts.

An analysis of how the recipients of urban bounty were chosen, what connections they had to the Crown, and what towns hoped to gain from the relationship concludes this section of the study of local borough administration and the central government. This look at patronage patterns differs from the preceding chapters in its ventures into prosopography and its inclusion of the role of women, more important here than in more purely political aspects of urban history. But political factors remain important, to chart the influence of national events on local choices, the intersection of local and national concerns, and the efficacy of Crown rule in the provinces.

For this study, patronage refers to that voluntary, reciprocal, intimate, but asymmetrical relationship between parties of unequal status exchanging goods and services in expectation of advantage.[2] Most specifically, medieval towns gave gifts and cash rewards, to peers of the realm and significant gentry, with every hope and expectation of reciprocity. Their object was to gain from the powerful what they could not obtain or influence by themselves.

Towns concentrated their gifts on three groups of people. These individuals were not always the most powerful men in government, although court connections were essential. Boroughs preferred to contact those with established influence rather than rising figures or those on the political margins. Foremost in town officers' thoughts were individuals of local influence: the nobles, their retainers, and the gentry who held land and offices in or near the cities that rewarded them. Gifts also went more generally to magnates from England's armigerous families: those within the king's immediate family, those who served the Crown, or who visited the region occasionally on judicial or military commissions. Less exalted civil servants, ranging from justices to Exchequer clerks, received isolated gifts, as did gentry with legal careers, although men-at-law could be more formally retained by towns with yearly stipends to guarantee permanent service. Towns' relations with the last group paralleled those of magnates and clerics who had retained justices and attorneys since the late twelfth century, assuring themselves expert legal advice with gifts, fees and robes. Although king and parliament suppressed the worst abuses of this patronage during the late fourteenth century, medieval society generally tolerated such *quid pro quo* relationships. No town expected a charter to be copied or a petition to be processed without a gift made to the clerk who recorded or the judge who deliberated. These occasional gifts differed from the more formal and regular fees annually budgeted, which carried specific expectations of service and attention.

The influence of these individuals helped towns in three different ways: by assisting boroughs to gain from the Crown the liberties, privileges and properties thought necessary to urban autonomy; by providing guidance during complicated law suits brought to the central courts or by arbitrating such cases in the town; and by helping boroughs preserve their liberties during the difficult changes in dynasty that occurred in fifteenth-century England. Outsiders were deliberately chosen for their contacts within the royal government and their facility in navigating its bureaucracy.

But most of the time, such expressions of direct benefit were rarely articulated. Except on those occasions when towns asked a nobleman outright to persuade the king to grant a charter or restore lost liberties, even civic officials probably had no specific aim in mind when they sent food and money to highly-placed friends. They did not intend to join a lord's affinity in any official or binding sense. Many simply hoped such people would become "good lords" to their town, extending the benefits of their local rule to the urban populace. In extremely troubled times, the gifts take on the appearance of protection money, extended to prevent a powerful individual from becoming a "heavy lord."[3] But often it was enough to establish a relationship, to remind men and women of influence of the respect extended by certain towns, in the hope that the patronized would remember such demonstrations of esteem and act upon them when urban needs arose. Nobility who received occasional gifts scarcely depended on urban fish or cash for survival, though the attention of an important town added to their sense of distinction. The gifts contributed to and confirmed their own high status without placing them in a subordinate position, although "'good lordship' needed to be demonstrated in order to be maintained."[4] They were not obliged to respond in any way, although boroughs certainly hoped feelings of responsibility might grow.

With rare exceptions, urban budgets easily managed these occasional gifts and modest regular fees. Tables 1–3 show the proportion of annual urban receipts and expenses that the officials of Exeter, Norwich, and York were willing to spend on patronage.[5] Gift-giving usually consumed between 6 and 8% of all receipts and 5 to 10% of expenses, except on those occasions (as in York in 1396–97 and 1478–79) when royal visits considerably added to borough costs. Law suits also increased the amount of patronage believed necessary or desirable, as in Exeter during the late 1440s when city officials in the pursuit of justice sought the favor of government servants. Most of these presents purchased influence rather than direct action. The expenditure is best interpreted as an investment, for even the smallest towns were willing to stretch their budgets for the opportunity of a well-placed word or the helpful action of a gracious patron with a convenient memory.

Exeter

Exeter's patronage took complex forms, given the nature of the local families involved and changes in royal policy regarding the local ascendancy of traditional leaders. Dominating urban patronage were the earls of Devon and their Courtenay relatives. As the largest landholders in Devonshire and the most powerful lords of the west country, an earl and his brothers or uncles received civic gifts almost every year

Table 1: Exeter Municipal Gifts & Patronage Expenses, 1377–1509

	Average gift expenses per account	Gifts as percentage of receipts	Gifts as percentage of expenses
Richard II 1377–1399	£ 5 13s.	4.3%	5.7%
Henry IV 1399–1413	£10 13s.	7.3%	8.3%
Henry V 1413–1422	£12 7s.	8.4%	9.8%
Henry VI 1422–1461	£10 5s.	7.8%	10.4%
Edward IV 1461– 1483	£10 8s.	7.3%	8.7%
Richard III 1483–1484	£16 12s.	10.5%	10.8%
1484–1485	£27 11s.	11.1%	10.9%
Henry VII 1485–1509	£ 7 17s.	4.2%	4.6%

Source: D.R.O., Receivers' Rolls

Table 2: Norwich Municipal Gifts & Patronage Expenses, 1378–1509

	Average gift expenses per account	Gifts as percentage of receipts	Gifts as percentage of expenses
Richard II 1377–1399	£15 5s.	7.6%	10.3%
Henry IV 1399-1413	£15 11s.	8.3%	10.3%

Continued next page

Table 2—*Continued*

Henry V **1413-1422**	£11 17s.	6.7%	8.5%
Henry VI **1422-1461**	£ 8 13s.	4.0%	5.3%
Edward IV **1461–1483**	£11 13s.	7.9%	8.7%
Henry VII **1485–1509**	£ 6 1s.	3.7%	5.2%

Sources: N.R.O., Treasurers' and Chamberlains' Rolls. Gift and patronage expenses for the reign of Richard III average £1 per annum. The accounts are fragmentary.

Table 3: York Municipal Gifts and Patronage Expenses, 1396–1500

		Gifts and fees	**Gifts and fees as percent- age of receipts**	**Gifts and fees as percent- age of expenses**
1396-97[1,2]	**gift:**	£224 9s. 1d.		54.9%
	minstrels:	£ 7 7s. 4d.		1.8%
	legal:	£ 10 16s. 9d.		2.6%
1433–34[3]	**gift:**	£ 1 4s. 1d.	0.5%	
	minstrels:	£ 4 7s. 0d.	1.8%	
	legal:	£ 23 3s. 4d.	9.8%	
1442–43	**gift:**	£ 1 4s. 7d.	0.5%	0.7%
	minstrels:	£ 5 19s. 4d.	2.6%	3.3%
	legal:	£ 10 6s. 8d.	4.5%	5.8%
1445–46	**gift:**	£ 2 14s. 6d.	1.1%	1.2%
	minstrels:	£ 5 9s. 10d.	2.3%	2.4%
	legal:	£ 13 6s. 8d.	5.6%	5.9%
1449–50[3]	**gift:**	£ 1 4s. 8d.	0.6%	
	minstrels:	£ 6 3s. 5d.	3.0%	
	legal:	£ 13 6s. 8d.	6.6%	

Continued on next page

Table 3—*Continued*

1453–54	gift:	£	6	4s.	7d.	3.0%	2.8%
	minstrels:	£	2	8s.	4d.	1.2%	1.1%
	legal:	£	12	16s.	8d.	6.3%	5.7%
1454–55	gift:	£	7	12s.	3d.	3.7%	3.4%
	minstrels:	£	1	8s.	4d.	0.7%	0.6%
	legal:	£	14	6s.	8d.	7.0%	6.5%
1462–63	gift:	£	5	16s.	1d.	2.9%	2.9%
	minstrels:	£	3	3s.	4d.	1.6%	1.6%
	legal:	£	11	6s.	8d.	5.8%	5.8%
1468–69	gift:	£	1	10s.	6d.	0.6%	0.8%
	minstrels:	£	1	12s.	2d.	0.6%	0.8%
	legal:	£	11	6s.	8d.	4.4%	5.7%
1470–71[4]	gift:	£	1	2s.	0d.	0.3%	0.5%
	legal:	£	12	6s.	8d.	3.6%	5.2%
1475–76	gift:	£	1	14s.	1d.	0.9%	0.7%
	minstrels:	£		16s.	0d.	0.4%	0.3%
	legal:	£	12	6s.	8d.	6.7%	4.9%
1478–79[1]	gift:	£	36	3s.	7d.	15.2%	14.5%
	minstrels:	£	1	19s.	4d.	0.8%	0.7%
	legal:	£	12	6s.	8d.	5.2%	4.9%
1486–87[1]	gift:	£	70	10s.	3d.	32.1%	22.7%
	minstrels:	£	5	17s.	0d.	2.7%	1.9%
	legal:	£	12	6s.	8d.	5.6%	3.9%
1499–1500[4]	minstrels:	£	1	1s.	8d.	0.5%	0.6%
	legal:	£	4	6s.	8d.	1.9%	2.4%

Source: Dobson, *Chamberlains' Accounts*

[1] Years of royal visits to the city.

[2] Receipts not provided on this account.

[3] Expenses not provided on this account.

[4] Incomplete figures on account roll.

throughout the fourteenth and fifteenth centuries. The family may have been "the least well endowed and least powerful comital family in the fourteenth century," but they were undoubtedly the wealthiest family resident in Devonshire.[6] Courtenay retainers also benefited from urban largess: attorneys, stewards, and gentlemen liveried of the earl received gifts from Exeter in return for legal advice.

Edward the third earl inherited from his grandfather in 1377 and shared Exeter patronage with several young uncles who founded rival Courtenay lines of their own. Although blind for part of his career, Edward retained a tight hold over Devon society and Exeter government. During the 1380s, he headed commissions of array and of the peace in Devon, and served as a justice of the peace. Admiral of the western fleet between 1383 and 1385, Edward was soon after appointed by John of Gaunt as lieutenant of the duchy of Lancaster in Devonshire, and was as active and well-liked in court circles as his uncles Philip and Peter.[7] Any interest that such a man expressed in Exeter carried special weight.

Yet relations between the city and the earls had been uneasy since the thirteenth century. Courtenays controlled manors along the River Exe below the city, and the weirs they erected stopped shipping from reaching Exeter. As lords of the manor of Topsham, four miles down the Exe, they controlled cranage at the port and affected all trade on the river.[8] The need to overcome this constrictive influence, as well as the desire to become a county in its own right, drove Exeter to patronize a wider variety of nobles than did other boroughs, despite its more restricted resources.

The opportunity for broader patronage arose in the 1380s, when Richard II began to shower favors upon his half-brother, John Holand. Admiral of the western fleet (Courtenay's old position) and chamberlain of the royal household, Holand held substantial west country estates, established his home near Totnes with his wife Elizabeth, Gaunt's daughter, and had been created duke of Exeter.[9] The city could not afford to ignore this aggressive newcomer with strong ties to court circles: without neglecting the Courtenays, civic officials sent Holand and his wife gifts of wine and requests for advice and friendship. Exeter balanced Holand's ties to Richard and Gaunt not only with support of the Courtenays, but with modest gifts to the duke of Gloucester during his period of domination over the king, and to former Appellant the earl of Warwick.[10] Civic officials also favored Gaunt's son, Henry earl of Derby, in the decade before his usurpation of the throne. Such a balanced approach to the influential of the day allowed the city to survive unscathed Holand's execution in 1400 at the hands of Henry IV, and the earl of Devon's political inefficacy resulting from his blindness and the minority of his heir.

Under the first Lancastrians, Exeter officials continued to seek a wider variety of friends for the city. As expected in a coastal city contributing men, ships, and supplies to the war effort, the admiral (since 1412, Gaunt's son Thomas Beaufort) received gifts in return for favor.[11] Patronage of the Holands was negligible until Henry V's reign, during which John junior served diligently under Admiral Beaufort and at Harfleur and Agincourt, and regained some of his ancestral titles and lands.[12] The Courtenays were not so fortunate. The blind third earl of Devon literally moved into his twilight years (he died in 1419), with the power of the line eclipsed first by the early death of the fourth earl followed by the inheritance of Thomas the fifth earl, a minor until 1433. Men, including those of city government, looked elsewhere for leadership: to Sir Philip Courtenay of the Powderham branch of the family, and to William Bonville, a local knight whom Exeter began rewarding with gifts in 1408 and who became a considerable rival to Courtenay influence during the 1440s.[13] Nevertheless, for a brief period during the reign of Henry V many of these men worked together under the leadership of the realm's greatest nobles, guarding the Channel and providing men-at-arms and archers for service in France. Exeter officials honored these individuals with gifts and trust, and reached out not only to the nobles they lived with but to others with connections to the households of Henry V and his infant heir, thus assuring the city of a wide variety of contacts.[14]

Courtenay influence, however, was not confined to individual earls but was extended more broadly to administrators and men-at-law. By the end of the fourteenth century, not only did the city patronize the third earl's liveried servants, but several civic officials themselves were retained by the Courtenays. From his household records we know that in 1384–85, Earl Edward gave livery to 135 people for their counsel, to maintain his own prestige, and to extend and consolidate his influence in the west.[15] Exeter itself benefited from the earl's trained and loyal retainers. Citizen John Hille, for example, received many gifts from the city during Richard II's reign. A king's serjeant-at-law from 1382 and a judge of King's Bench in 1388, Hille also served as a councilor and burgess for Exeter in 1380 while liveried of Earl Edward Courtenay.

Hille received occasional reward from the city, regard which increased to a regular pension of £2 *per annum* in 1387–88. Another Courtenay retainer was John Grey, a prominent Exeter goldsmith who served as mayor, councilor and parliamentary representative many times during Richard's reign and collected the town's customs and subsidies.[16]

Throughout the fourteenth and fifteenth centuries, contact with the Courtenays also introduced Exeter to important civil servants able to influence the central government, local magnates, and the city itself. Walter Clopton, one of the city's legal advisors, was not only Sir Philip Courtenay's liveried attorney and the earl's retainer, but also a king's serjeant-at-law since 1378 and Chief Justice of King's Bench from 1389.[17] Barons of the Exchequer received attention from both the earl and the city: Chief Baron John Cary's civic pension was prompted not only by his national office but by his marriage to a Devon woman, his position as warden of Devon's ports, and his father's reputation as a knight of the shire during the 1360s.[18]

Despite personal tragedies of blindness and minority at the start of the fifteenth century, the Courtenay family did not totally relinquish control over administrators useful to the city. Exeter's gifts went to John Copleston, steward for both Earl Edward and his son Hugh, and receiver for Hugh's minor heir. One of the most influential men in Devon, Copleston advised Exeter on its chartered liberties as early as 1414–15. He was instrumental in dealing with royal jewels left with the city by Henry V as collateral for loans, and he intervened at the city's request in the long-standing quarrel between Exeter and cathedral authorities during the 1430s and 1440s.[19] Alexander Hody was another who served both earl and city: a lawyer for Earl Edward and his brother Sir Hugh of Haccombe, Hody was destined to become Exeter's recorder and the object of much civic patronage during the reigns of Henry V and Henry VI.[20] While examples can be found of recipients of city gifts with no connection to these families, Exeter never strained itself to maintain an independent attitude. The same training and connections that recommended these men to the major county families attracted the interest and support of a town eager not just to survive the early years of the fifteenth century, but eventually to thrive.

Henry VI's long reign and the many shifts of power it witnessed offered special challenges to urban patronage. During the king's minority, Exeter rewards went to the restored Holand earl of Huntingdon and to the Courtenay family. The earl of Devon himself received gifts even before he reached his majority, as did his wife Margaret Beaufort, one of Gaunt's granddaughters and sister of the earl of Somerset. Margaret's uncle, Thomas Beaufort, continued to receive gifts from both Exeter and Norwich, as did Humphrey of Gloucester, considered to be a figure of influence even with curtailed powers on the royal council.[21]

The decade following Henry VI's declaration of majority presented stressful challenges to urban development, and towns sought the help of old and new friends to survive local and national threats. In Exeter, Sir William Bonville's increasing power began to be marked in the city's financial records by gifts that kept pace with those of the Courtenays. Bonville's military career, judicial service, and prosperous marriages marked him for favor with the king. Unfortunately, Henry's grasp of who deserved which office was notoriously weak. When he appointed Bonville royal steward in Cornwall for life, traditionally a Courtenay office, jealousy drove the earl of Devon first to protest the appointment with armed bands of retainers, then to petition the king that Devon himself be made steward of the duchy of Cornwall. Henry VI thoughtlessly agreed, and disorder swept Devonshire and the west until 1444 when Bonville left the country to take up duties as seneschal of Gascony.[22]

Not only did this physical violence threaten Exeter's liberties, but the city was simultaneously involved in a complex legal case with the cathedral.[23] Under ordinary circumstances, town officials could expect the local nobility to exercise their good lordship and dedicate their own and their counselors' judicial wisdom to the dispute. The Bonville-Courtenay feud disturbed those expectations, and gave the city little hope for favor when in 1448 the case moved from Westminster to the arbitration of Earl Thomas and the recently-returned Sir William. But the sea of wine and schools of fish that had made their way to noble and knight, chancellor and humble clerk, floated the citizens to a decision not entirely to their detriment. Particularly identified, and rewarded, for his help was Chief Justice John Fortescue, who had been personally counseling Exeter since the 1430s.[24]

The final decade of Henry VI's reign revealed whether town alliances had been wise or foolish. How would they balance loyalty to the Lancastrian monarch with interest in the Yorkist power that promised greater rewards and more effective peacekeeping? Exeter found the answer in the native Bonville-Courtenay rivalry that persisted into the 1450s. The earl of Devon adopted the duke of York as a friend and advisor, although this cramped his style when the duke ordered him to stop besieging Bonville in Taunton Castle and to maintain peace in the west country.[25] When York attained the protectorate in 1454, Devon felt his own local and national influence increase. A member of the royal council for a few months, Courtenay soon returned to Devonshire where his men embarked on a series of attacks against rivals and tenants, including the notorious murder of Bonville legal advisor and city recorder Nicholas Radford. In his absence, Bonville had become constable of Exeter castle and conservator of the Exe, influential enough for the city to turn to him when it wished to be excused from provisioning ships for an invasion of France.[26] But he was unable to spare the city from the earl's attack or to prevent Devon's henchmen from leading armed men into Exeter, where they seized the gates, attacked the mayor, and assaulted the citizens for two days.[27] Nevertheless, generous gifts to Bonville and his friend Lord FitzWarin, a loyal Lancastrian, balanced attention paid to Courtenay while he remained allied to York. When the earl tired of York's peacekeeping demands and his own heir married the queen's kinswoman, Devon drifted back to the royalist fold.[28] Exeter patronage at the end of the decade consequently reached out to include Yorkist adherent Sir John Dynham and the duchess of Exeter, Richard of York's daughter Anne.[29] Bonville himself, and friends FitzWarin and Philip Courtenay, eventually made peace with the Yorkists as well, with tragic personal results: Bonville's son and grandson were both killed with York at Wakefield, and Bonville himself was executed early in 1461, leaving as heir a young great-granddaughter. The earl of Devon had died in 1458; his heir, the sixth earl, was executed after Edward IV's victory at Towton and when attainted all his honors were forfeit.[30] The city would need new friends for the new reign.

With the exception of the Readeption period 1470–71, the four towns should have enjoyed straightforward relationships with Yorkist relatives and adherents throughout the reigns of Edward IV and Richard III. In general, this is true, although certain stresses appear beneath the surface, particularly at times when boroughs pursued complex legal cases or became involved in personal suits and attacks. To make matters worse, the people best connected to the Yorkist court and most able to convey a town's needs did not always have its best interests at heart.

With both the Courtenay and Bonville families decimated by the events of 1460–61, Exeter needed new patterns of patronage. The

officials quickly settled upon Humphrey Stafford, favored by Edward IV
for his military service and raised as earl of Devon in 1469 in the wake
of Courtenay rebellion.[31] Stafford received gifts from the city throughout
the 1460s, as did former Bonville associate William Bourchier Lord
FitzWarin and, in the next decade, his son Fulk. Fulk Bourchier married
the sister and co-heir of Sir John Dynham, a faithful Yorkist since 1459
and long-patronized by Exeter.[32] Anne duchess of Exeter, the king's
sister, continued to receive gifts, as did her second husband Sir Thomas
St. Leger.[33] Relations with the cathedral had lost most of their
antagonism, and even the bishop of Exeter appeared more regularly on
the financial accounts as the recipient of wine in hopes of his favor.[34]
None of these friends, however, proved particularly useful to help the
city weather the transition to Richard III. St. Leger was beheaded for his
part in Buckingham's rebellion and several members of the Courtenay
family fled the country to join Henry Tudor abroad. Civic patronage for
the rest of Richard's reign went primarily to John Lord Scrope of Bolton,
a northerner whom the king had sent to the west country after the rising
to counter rebellion and indict traitors.[35]

    With Henry VI's brief return to power, Exeter accounts show a sense
of anxiety to keep up with political events. Civic attention returned to
Lancastrian sympathizer Sir Hugh Courtenay of Boconnoc, whom the
officers asked to approach Readeption chamberlain Sir Richard Tunstall
with a problem about their charter's confirmation.[36] The duke and
duchess of Clarence received wine and fish during a quick visit to the
city in April 1470. Wine also cheered Lancastrian chancellor-in-exile and
former city counselor Sir John Fortescue when he accompanied Queen
Margaret and her entourage to the city at Easter the following year.[37] But
by March 1471, as Yorkist fortunes ameliorated, civic officials
approached Clarence, then assessing his chances of rejoining Edward's
party. No doubt his decision, and the king's victory, influenced the return
of their own loyalties and gifts to Yorkist adherent Lord FitzWarin.[38]

    The destruction of the Yorkist cause in August 1485 and the
accession of the Tudor king revived hopes among those of the realm's
nobles barred so long from power and influence. Civic officials were
forced to reassess their networks of contacts and renew relationships,
some of which had been neglected for a quarter of a century. When the
king created Edward Courtenay, son of Sir Hugh of Boconnoc, earl of
Devonshire within weeks of his accession, the city wasted no time
extending to him the gifts and compliments given his ancestors. Edward

was one of a small group of favored men, close to Henry in his household and military activities, their bonds forged in the years of exile prior to 1485.[39] Another of the group, Robert Lord Willoughby de Broke, joint steward of the royal household and admiral of the fleet, also received gifts from Exeter.[40] Political survivors continued to earn attention, trust, and civic gifts: Lord Dynham, once rescuer of Yorkist fortunes, became Lord Treasurer in 1486 and raised sizeable funds for the king's needs. The young Lord FitzWarin, son of Fulk Bourchier and Dynham's sister, also offered potential links to the Tudor court in place of memories of his family's Yorkist past.[41] And although the Bonville family had been nearly blasted out of existence, the heiress Cecily remained, her second husband Lord Harry Stafford welcomed to town with wine during a break from his attendance upon Henry VII's court.[42]

In general, however, the financial accounts of these years are narrower in scope, more reticent in description, and more conservative in patronage than in any previous reign. The frequent turns of fortune impressed greater caution on towns. Henry VII may have appeared to them as a king not likely to grant favors even to close friends and relatives, for as one historian has noticed he treated the landholders likely to act as urban patrons as "enemies to be reduced to servitude rather than natural allies."[43] Moreover, town needs themselves had changed. In terms of charters alone, the rush to acquire new ones and confirm old ones had definitely diminished. A more focused approach to patronage thus emerged as the new regime took hold, a shift not necessarily resulting from the emergence of a more authoritarian "new monarchy." Exeter's accounts certainly exemplify these trends, recording gifts fewer in number but focused on Henry's most trusted followers.

Norwich

More secure than Exeter in its legal privileges and economic prosperity, Norwich nonetheless faced problems in its choice of urban patrons. Local nobles provided considerably less assistance and more opposition to civic needs than in Devonshire, forcing Norwich to turn to patrons of lower social class but greater legal and administrative abilities. Stronger than in other cities, civic patronage of noblewomen provided the alliances shirked by their male relatives.

During the reign of Richard II, the delicate diplomacy of balancing political favorites and royal relatives is well-illustrated in Norwich's fourteen surviving accounts. The natural focus of civic gifts and petitions was the Mowbray family, frequent visitors to Norwich and possessed of wide holdings in East Anglia. On Richard's accession, the family was headed by Margaret, *suo jure* countess of Norfolk, and recognized as a person of influence by the city's gift of a tun of wine. Her heirs, grandsons John (d.1383) and his younger brother Thomas earl of Nottingham as minors failed to attract civic patronage, and thanks to Margaret's longevity and generous dower, never enjoyed the full extent of their inheritance.[44] When old enough to attract patronage himself, Thomas courted controversy by his Appellant leanings and suffered banishment in 1398. But dangerous politics alone did not impede civic gift-giving: Thomas's Appellant father-in-law the earl of Arundel received abundant food and wine from Norwich even when in opposition to the king, as did his compatriot the earl of Warwick.[45] The other major local figure was Michael de la Pole. When created earl of Suffolk in 1385 and while serving as Lord Chancellor, he attracted gifts from Norwich, but he died four years later with all honors forfeit and a young son bereft for a decade of title and influence.[46] Clearly, Norwich did not discriminate against Appellant activists, but its patronage policies were influenced far more by local issues and the presence or absence of adult figures with court connections able to pursue urban interests.

Consistently honored by the city was John of Gaunt, a figure of international stature with local holdings and significant influence over his royal nephew. Gaunt may have helped the city gain two charters early in the reign, although he either could not or would not attain for them the broader financial and jurisdictional liberties they craved. Civic officials treated his visits like royal entries, imposing fines on those who failed to don livery or ride out to meet him. Although he did not have many retainers on his East Anglian lands, he earned significant attention from the city and helped to establish a relationship with the Lancastrians that eased Norwich's transition to the new regime in 1399.[47]

Norwich sought the best legal counsel it could afford, and Gaunt's influence is apparent in this sphere as well. Civic attorneys included stewards of Lancastrian lands and influential members of Gaunt's affinity.[48] Prominent among city counsel during the reigns of Richard II and Henry IV was John Winter, steward and receiver of Gaunt's lands in the region, escheator for the county, local agent for the Staffords as well as man-at-law for Norwich, and possessed of the lands required of gentry status. By the early fifteenth century, Winter was established in the Prince of Wales's service, assuring for his borough clients connections to the future leader and his circle.[49] Norwich may have failed to attain all the chartered privileges its officers thought it deserved, but it had identified important friends able to carry the city into a new century and a new regime.

Throughout the reigns of Henry IV and Henry V, the local nobility of East Anglia continued to play a minor role in the borough. The De la Pole heir was restored to the earldom of Suffolk by Henry IV, but concentrated on a military career rather than local affairs and died in 1415.[50] Thomas Mowbray duke of Norfolk had died in exile in 1399, his elder son was executed in the Archbishop Scrope conspiracy before he reached majority, and his younger son only won restoration of the dukedom in 1425 by military service under Henry V and participation in Henry VI's council of regency; he received no acknowledgment from the city before 1427.[51] Norwich took some slight notice of the king's immediate family and his Beaufort relatives, but those gentlemen along with Henry IV's younger sons spent too little time in England and its boroughs to attend to urban petitions.

Of far greater use to the city was the interest of two local knights. Sir Simon Felbrigg and Sir Thomas Erpingham assisted the city several times and helped it make the transition to the Lancastrian regime. Erpingham was a member of the prosperous Norfolk gentry, who inherited his father's house in Norwich and used it when consulting on various civic matters. An annuitant and member of the retinues of both John of Gaunt and his son Henry Bolingbroke, he traveled with the latter to Prussia and the Holy Land in 1390, having already served on various Norfolk commissions for the king. After sharing Henry's exile in 1399, he accompanied him back to England that year, to play a major role in Richard's deposition.[52]

Norwich quickly identified Erpingham as a man whose friendship was worth cultivating, particularly in the search for a new charter. Beginning in 1399, Norwich lavished gifts upon Erpingham and his wife for bearing his good word to Henry IV and for his own counsel.[53] Sealing the relationship between knight and town was Henry's grant in 1400 which gave Erpingham an annuity of £40 from Norwich's fee farm.[54] Grateful as he may have been to Henry and attentive to Norwich, Erpingham was never unrealistic. He turned his attention to the Prince of

Wales from 1409 to 1411 when the king was ill and the younger man held power. During this period, he was able to obtain a grant of cloth aulnage for Norwich, as well as the survey of worsteds in the city and county, both calculated to increase urban revenue; he received a gift of ten marks for his concern. He may also have convinced Norwich of the wisdom of rewarding Chancellor Thomas Beaufort in 1410–11, another of the Prince's faction. A noted soldier in Henry V's French campaigns, Erpingham acted as arbitrator for Norwich during the city's constitutional struggles and received quantities of wine for his counsel before his death in 1428.[55]

Erpingham's friend Sir Simon Felbrigg also enjoyed Norwich's patronage. Felbrigg was Richard II's standard bearer, a Knight of the Garter whose Bohemian wife was Queen Anne's cousin and maid of honor. As a royal annuitant from 1393, the source of fifty marks of his pension was Norwich's fee farm. With the assent of the council of twenty-four, Norwich gave him £10 in 1398 for the counsel and friendship he showed in planning for a future royal visit.[56] Felbrigg appears to have lost some influence after Henry IV's accession, but his friendship with Erpingham and the memory of his relations with Gaunt eased him through the early years of the new regime. Norwich patronized him throughout his life, albeit on a smaller scale than Erpingham, paying his bills at inns in London and Norwich as an expression of gratitude for his attention and advice.[57]

As one historian has noted, "[a] lawyer with local knowledge and connections was a powerful and dangerous man, an ally well worth the gaining."[58] Accordingly, Norwich sought the legal advice of two quite remarkable men. Beginning in Henry IV's reign, William Paston (1378–1444) emerged as an advisor worth retaining on a permanent basis. The son of a modest husbandman, William studied law at the Inns of Court, became a trusted steward and executor of properties, and by 1429 a justice of the common bench. He took fees from the burgesses of Great Yarmouth and Lynn as well as Norwich, from a variety of East Anglian religious houses, and from noble families such as the Mowbrays.[59] Paston used his money and connections to acquire lands and prosperous marriages for his own family, whose litigation found record in their extensive correspondence. Most of the nobles, gentry, and men-at-law given gifts by Norwich were known to the Pastons as either friend or foe and mentioned in their letters, suggesting the complexity of county society networks. Judge Paston received mention and rewards in the

Norwich records, from 1414 when he acted as arbitrator in election disputes, through the 1430s, perhaps most interestingly on two occasions for quashing royal writs that thwarted citizens' interests.[60]

Late in Henry V's reign, Norwich also focused attention to William Babington, Chief Baron of the Exchequer. Babington advised the city of York as well, during Henry VI's reign when he had risen to become Chief Justice of the Common Bench. A man of property in Nottinghamshire, he had benefited from a wealthy marriage and a meteoric rise in law.[61] Learned in law, active in royal courts, conversant with county gentry and nobility, Babington and Paston were exactly the kind of friends towns sought with retaining fees, gifts, and dinners. Combined with the attention of well-connected and able knights like Erpingham and Felbrigg, these "good lords and well-wishers" helped to augment Norwich's liberties and navigate the confusing waters of the central courts.

As in Exeter, the reign of Henry VI posed new challenges to town patronage policies. Local noblemen failed to provide a strong focus for urban gifts, taking little or hostile interest in town affairs. John Mowbray, for example, had been restored to the dukedom of Norfolk in 1425, but he and his Beaufort wife received little civic attention considering that he was a member of the regency council. Upon his death in 1432, his heir was an inexperienced minor who shortly after inheriting began a military career that took him out of the county.[62] Far more apparent on the records were William de la Pole earl of Suffolk and his countess Alice Chaucer (another Beaufort relation). Although a privy councilor by 1432 and steward of the king's personal household the following year, Suffolk's career had so far concentrated on the French war, and his importance to Norwich at this stage is chiefly as a local landholder and retainer of influence.[63]

More money and attention were directed towards men of the legal profession. Norwich's advisor William Paston was joined by other administrators whose careers can be tracked through Paston and Fastolf correspondence. William Yelverton became counsel for Norwich in 1430 to help with confirmation of charters, disputes over suburban land, and negotiations with other boroughs, becoming Norwich's recorder three years later. Norwich officers also appreciated his protection of their rights against the attacks made by Suffolk's retainers, John Heydon and Sir Thomas Tuddenham.[64] Like Yelverton, Sir Henry Inglose also had a long career serving the city. With extensive Norfolk properties, blood ties to local gentry, and an impressive military career serving Bedford, Clarence, and Suffolk, he brought considerable legal experience and a vast network of contacts to his employers.[65] East Anglia has been described as being settled and ruled by a "military community" between 1415 and 1455,[66] composed of men whose careers and characters were shaped by their service on the battlefield. Norwich showed shrewd judgment by tapping the talents of a number of nobles and gentry who composed that society.

Norwich in the 1430s and 1440s was torn by internal electoral disputes and external threats to suburban lands and properties. The city needed sound advice from skilled individuals who shared its officers' beliefs that civic privileges should grow in direct proportion to civic wealth and dignity. Norwich was not that fortunate during this period. Preoccupied with appointments in Scotland and France, the duke of Norfolk maintained a distant relationship with the city.[67] The mayor's 1443 petition to the politically marginal Humphrey duke of Gloucester for restoration of city liberties reflects a history of gift-giving to a royal uncle and a public perception of his importance as a royal counselor. In reality, the royal government showed Gloucester little trust after 1441, and the city's appeal shows more desperation than any awareness of political realities.[68] It is surprising that the city's legal advisors did not offer wiser counsel. William Yelverton, from 1443 a justice of King's Bench, continued to serve the city. He was joined by John Jenney and later by Jenney's brother William, favored as borough representatives and advisors well into Henry VII's reign "for they kun seye well," as John Paston remarked. Sir John Clifton was also well-paid for his advice: made governor of the city by the duke of Norfolk when its liberties were suspended in 1443, Clifton was one of Suffolk's retainers and a member of the East Anglian military community that included men such as Sir John Fastolf.[69]

It was William de la Pole, earl (soon to be marquis in 1444, and duke in 1448) of Suffolk, who filled political vacuums both in East Anglia and Westminster. The younger officers of Norwich considered him a baleful influence and so feared his intervention and that of his retainers that the gifts directed to this local magnate look as much like protection money as invitations for his good lordship. His associates, lawyer John Heydon and Sir Thomas Tuddenham, may have derived their influence from the Lancastrian affinity of Erpingham's and Henry V's day, but the city regarded them with disdain, an opinion magnified in the Paston correspondence.[70] Between 1435 and 1442, Suffolk intervened in a disputed election and in problems with the prior and the abbot of St. Benet's in Holm, each time making awards and obligations upsetting to one faction in the city.[71] Distress over his intervention resulted in unrest so severe the king twice seized Norwich's liberties (1437–38, 1443–47). When petitions to the discredited Gloucester did not restore them, Suffolk was again asked to act as good lord and intercede with the king. Civic officials tried to shape the nobleman into their image of a helpful friend, but he proved unmalleable. Reflecting years later on the events of 1438, citizens recalled that Tuddenham and Heydon "threatened to make William late Duke of Suffolk the heavy lord ("gravem dominum") of the Mayor and Commonalty," a frightening inversion of the normal relations towns expected to enjoy.[72]

Suffolk's murder in 1450 had rid Norwich of a troublesome figure, but not of the need to read the political environment carefully. The duke of Norfolk emerged as a dominant force in the region, the man to whom civic officials and Paston correspondents alike looked for peace, leadership, and favor. Although married to the duke of York's niece, he did not join the Yorkist camp until early 1461, preferring to work with the loyal royalist John de Vere earl of Oxford to impose order in the area.[73] Unfortunately, in suppressing the excesses of the Suffolk clique, he adopted some of their extra-legal methods, although the Pastons more than the city had cause for complaint. The duke of York himself toured the region during the weeks prior to the opening of the 1450 parliament, collecting a substantial following to bring to London and winning a reputation as a nobleman powerful enough to suppress the misdeeds of Suffolk's retinue. His appearance gave East Anglia, and Norwich in particular, hope that oppression did not have to be permanent. The city's faith in him lasted through York's changes in status and exile in Ireland, when it continued to be expressed in gifts to his wife, also a local landholder.[74]

Under the Yorkist kings, Norwich records are dominated by local nobles, often women, with family ties to England's new rulers. For almost two decades, the widowed duchess of York was ceremoniously greeted by city officials and given gifts, her opinion on their conflict with the priory welcomed.[75] The third duke of Norfolk spent the last months of his life providing the military and ceremonial basis of the new king's reign. His heir inherited the title late in 1461 at the age of seventeen; his youth and his absence abroad on diplomatic missions may explain why his duchess received so many more gifts than her husband. He did, however, prove useful in 1469 to plead with the king to pardon Norwich from supplying troops.[76] One presumes the duchess mentioned on the records is the fourth duke's wife Elizabeth; his mother Eleanor died only in 1474, and his grandmother Katherine lived until 1483, both of them draining the estate so badly with their dower lands that the young duke was forced to borrow money from relatives and his own legal counsel. Such an individual, even when not preoccupied with besieging Paston property, may not have been Norwich's idea of a powerful friend.[77]

The new duke of Suffolk was only slightly older and more experienced, although in 1465 he quickly showed whose son he was when he imperiously ordered Norwich officials to arrest his personal enemies in the wards. Although trusted by the king, he was never active in court circles, and his local activities indicate an overbearing and violent nature that may have made him unattractive to civic patrons. Certainly his profile in the financial records is lower than that of his wife, Elizabeth, sister to Edward IV.[78] Far more favored by the city was the queen's brother, Anthony Woodville, who had married the daughter of local landholder and ardent Lancastrian Thomas Lord Scales. Woodville was deeply involved in city matters, arbitrating disputes with the prior of St. Benet's, discussing grain supplies, and attempting to influence Norfolk parliamentary elections.[79] When the king appointed Woodville governor to the prince of Wales in 1473, the city must have thought they had found an interested and influential friend to promote their interests well into the next reign.

Edward IV's unexpected death, the usurpation of his brother Richard, the execution of Woodville and the disappearance of Edward V, all occurring between April and September 1483, disabused them of that trust. In response, the city increased their attentions to the duke and duchess of Suffolk, the latter once again sister of a king. The couple's influence increased from 1484 when their son John de la Pole earl of Lincoln took on the position and duties left vacant by the death of Richard's son, and when the king offered their daughter Anne as a bride to the future James IV of Scotland.[80] As for the Mowbrays, the duke of Norfolk had died suddenly in 1476, and Richard raised John Lord Howard to the title in June 1483. Fortunately for Norwich, Howard had been an active and respected figure in East Anglia for some time, and already the recipient of civic gifts along with his son the earl of Surrey.[81] As Richard's reign began, the city also retained as counsel James Hobart, steward of Howard's lands and those of the fourth duke of Norfolk. "One of the foremost men of law of the day," he survived into Henry VII's reign to become the first Tudor's attorney general and privy councilor as well as recorder of Norwich.[82] The transition from the Lancastrian regime had been jarring for the city, but their chosen friends saw to their needs in both the short and the long run.

As in Exeter, the Norwich accounts of Henry VII's reign list far fewer gifts than for any of the previous monarchs. John Howard duke of Norfolk had died at Bosworth defending his king; his son the earl of Surrey had been wounded in the fray, taken prisoner, and attainted. Although he worked his way back into Henry VII's favor, his duties kept him in the north and York paid him far more attention than Norwich. City gifts went instead to local nobles such as the duchess of Norfolk.[83] Continuing to receive attention were the duke and duchess of Suffolk, whose influence depended upon the latter's blood ties to her niece, Henry's queen. Although their eldest son died in revolt against Henry, the king showed no diminution of trust in the couple. Upon the duke's death in 1492, his second son Edmund made peace with the king, suffered demotion to an earldom, and initiated relations with Norwich.[84] The most curious omission from the records is that of John de Vere earl of Oxford, the recipient of urban attention only on the 1487–88 account. Oxford has been described as "a mainstay of the Tudor crown," active in local government and administration, arbitrating disputes, advising commissioners, leading the county's military forces, and holding some of the realm's most influential offices.[85] The city invested far more gifts in their continuing relationship with James Hobart, now the king's attorney as well as city recorder, and in what today would be termed "power breakfasts" with visiting justices.[86] Such figures of the legal profession, possessing land and influence in county society, had proved to be effective patrons and political survivors, a valuable combination for ambitious cities.

York and Nottingham

The fragmentary survival of financial records for York and Nottingham facilitate a joint analysis of their patronage patterns. Both boroughs favored leading figures of the North, with special concern for military contributions and defense measures. The earls of

Northumberland expected to dominate local politics, but comparative newcomers like the Neville family also played a significant role in the two centers, traceable in York's records from the early 1430s.[87] Early gifts went to Gaunt's daughter Joan Beaufort, married to Ralph Neville earl of Westmorland and with him the progenitors of a large family whose influence over local and national politics demanded civic recognition. Joan's nephew, Edmund count of Mortain, also received wine from York, perhaps during a stopover while serving as ambassador to the Scottish king.[88]

Like Norwich and Exeter, York conflicted with local religious houses over property and jurisdiction rights. The northern city's dispute with St. Mary's abbey focused on fishgarths, traps placed in waterways to catch large numbers of fish but which impeded navigation and trade. Local records indicate the payments and actions required by the city to pursue the case at law: accounts dating from 1444–45 and 1445–46 reveal a reliance upon local magnate the earl of Northumberland and also John Lord Beaumont, a distinguished soldier and royal councilor serving at that time as Constable of England.[89] Beaumont received carriage-loads of bread, wine, wax, spices, and meat sent from the city, while a number of serjeants-at-law and clerks were also rewarded "pro consilio et favore." Beaumont had married a daughter of Ralph Neville earl of Westmorland and Joan Beaufort, and increasingly the offspring of that fertile match found mention in York records. The countess of Northumberland, née Eleanor Neville, received gifts separately from her husband Henry Percy; William Neville Lord Fauconberg was honored by gifts of wine; and his brother Richard Neville earl of Salisbury was handsomely rewarded while acting as warden of the west march towards Scotland. The city of York tried carefully to balance interest in traditional rivals Neville and Percy, following a policy in fact initiated by John of Gaunt the previous century, but the former were rapidly outnumbering the latter.[90]

The city of York was not immune to factional struggles as the reign of Henry VI drew to a close. Located between the major holdings of the Nevilles and the Percy earl of Northumberland, the city tried to appease both powers while steering clear of their violence. That had not been easy when Thomas Percy Lord Egremont recruited from the urban populace for his attacks on his Neville enemies and his mutinous uprising in behalf of the duke of Exeter. The chamberlains' accounts for 1453–54 record the costs of arbitration attempts and embassies to the families involved. The disturbances increased the number of gifts given to city counselors, and to the duke of York himself, who made a visit the following year to discourage such behavior.[91] Had council records for the period survived, the earl of Northumberland might be seen as a greater factor in city affairs, but his involvement in the duke of Exeter's rising probably discouraged interest in him. The surviving accounts indicate that patronage of the Nevilles was civic officials' preferred course of action. In addition to the earl of Salisbury (appointed chancellor 1454–55), his wife Alice, his brother William Lord Fauconberg, his sons Richard earl of Warwick and John, and his brother-in-law the duke of York, the city also sent gifts to Salisbury's retainers such as Ralph Lord Greystock.[92] Although the duke of York's severed head decorated town walls after Wakefield and city officials had to beg pardon of the new king for their loyalty to the Lancastrians, York's history of patronage made them more than ready to greet the new regime of Edward IV.

Financial accounts begin to survive for Nottingham in 1460, allowing for more direct comparisons with York. Both boroughs sought the attention and influence of William Lord Hastings, chamberlain and life-long friend to Edward IV, and married to one of the earl of Salisbury's daughters.[93] A major power in the north midlands, Hastings received many gifts from Nottingham, especially after deciding in favor of the town in a dispute over mills and weirs. Borough loyalty to him lasted beyond his execution in 1483, after which his widow and son received gifts from civic officials.[94] York patronage of the Nevilles continued, as individuals close to the king and especially to his brother Richard. This favoritism paid off in 1464 when the earl of Salisbury's third son, John Neville Lord Montagu, became earl of Northumberland as a result of the Percy earl's death at Towton and subsequent attainder.[95] Nottingham also considered the Nevilles forces worthy of investment, rewarding the earl of Warwick when he returned from northern campaigns as well as his brothers George the lord chancellor and John while earl of Northumberland.[96]

Both boroughs also looked to the king's brother for assistance. York had more success in maintaining this relationship than Nottingham, although Richard was expected to help the latter with a jurisdiction suit while on his way south after Edward IV's death.[97] Yet it is Richard's relationship with the northern capital that comes closest to the ideal of "good lordship" that benefited all concerned. The chamberlains' accounts, supplemented after 1476 by the council records, describe the myriad of legal and social matters on which civic officials consulted with the duke, and the quantities of food and wine sent to his household. A few citizens openly grumbled about Richard's influence, but most appreciated his willingness to inform the king of the city's needs and loyalty.[98]

Henry VII's reign saw a narrowing of patronage in Nottingham as in other boroughs, focusing primarily upon the king's closest associates and most trusted members of nobility and gentry. Fringing the north midlands, the town had irregular contact with figures more active, often in a quasi-legal sense, in Warwickshire and points west. Gifts went to Sir John Savage, related to the Stanleys and commander of Tudor's left wing at Bosworth, and to Henry Willoughby whose position as commissioner of the peace in his home county of Nottinghamshire inadequately describes the considerable power he wielded in the north midlands.[99] Until the late 1490s when Henry's suspicions led to more direct control, such men had every hope of ruling the area unchecked, and Nottingham showed foresight in attracting their attention. Ignored by Norwich, Thomas Howard Lord Surrey enjoyed gifts of wine from the town, as did George Talbot earl of Shrewsbury, active in the north suppressing rebellion.[100] Nottingham officials did not forget totally past friends who had supported them. They rewarded political survivors such as Lord Hastings's son Edward, and also Sir Gervase Clifton, whose career had moved from Lord Hastings to Richard III to Henry VII.[101] Moreover, their choice of legal advisors settled on men whose careers had begun over a decade earlier under Hastings's leadership or in Richard of Gloucester's council. But their intent was always practical, as they noted when rewarding esquire of the king's body Sir Richard Nanfan, "[so] that he shuld owe his gode wyll to the town in suche maters as they had to do afore the Kynges grace...."[102]

Of the four towns, York found it most difficult to accept the new regime, its close relationship with Richard III providing only one of the reasons. Upon hearing news of Richard's death in battle, civic officials turned to Henry Percy earl of Northumberland for advice and good lordship. The new king, however, kept the earl under arrest until early the next year, when he restored him as warden of the east and middle marches and as an influential noble of use to the city. York's officials frequently consulted him on matters of city justice although he was permitted no influence on local elections and fell victim to murder in 1489 when he imposed an unpopular tax for his king.[103] Henry Lord

Clifford expected to become York's good lord thereafter, but civic officials refused to accept his arrogant claims that his ancestors had had a long and noble relationship with them.[104]

By 1490, they had turned instead to Thomas Howard, earl of Surrey, who spent most of his time only ten miles from York in Sheriff Hutton. Surrey presided over the Council of the North, shaped by Richard III but losing much of its independence by the end of the century. Assisted by Sir Richard Tunstall and the abbot of St. Mary's, both of whom received gifts from York, Surrey examined petitions and witnesses and offered arbitration as an extension of the king's peace. Until his departure from the north in 1499, Surrey and the abbot worked diligently to arbitrate jurisdiction and property disputes between the city and the cathedral chapter.[105] Acting more directly on the king was his mother Margaret Beaufort, who promised to be the city's good lady when as lieutenant and high commissioner in the north she exercised power on behalf of her son.[106]

York's bitter and protracted conflict with neighboring religious institutions prompted its officials to offer clerical leaders opportunities to extend friendship and good will in exchange for gifts. The surviving financial accounts indicate many gifts given to the bishop of Durham, the abbot of St. Mary's, and the archbishop of York (not least because the holder of the office often acted as chancellor as well).[107] The overtures resulted in frequent arbitration, but the disputes were too deeply rooted to be easily resolved by the fragile ties of good lordship. Civic officials also had great hopes of their friendships with a variety of royal secretaries and chaplains, and compromised their own claims to suburban lands in order to please highly-placed clergy. There was, however, little return on their investments.[108] York thus witnessed the end of the first Tudor's rule without the strong and trusted support of an interested, influential friend.

Although this survey of patronage patterns during seven reigns is necessarily cursory, none of it could have been attempted had not town clerks kept such detailed records. The care that they took should persuade us that there is more than one dimension to the choice of a borough advisor. Political power and the wielding of influence mattered a great deal, but so also did ties of marriage, family, and friendship. The scrupulous recording of every fish, bread loaf, and wine barrel given as a gift is more than evidence of financial efficiency. It is also a record of a town's friends, the people upon whom its officers and citizens could rely, individuals whose power and position reflected directly upon the borough's own status and shaped its identity.

Even for boroughs that owed their autonomy and liberties to the king, local lords and their retainers wielded particular influence. Noble families who lived close to or within a town, or visited it with any frequency were expected to take an interest along with the gifts and greetings offered. Civic officials may have refrained from striking up relationships with the very young and the very old or infirm, but Norwich's persistent belief that even the earl of Suffolk could be turned into a "good lord" indicates the level of loyalty and dedication boroughs extended to their powerful neighbors. The financial accounts could have had a very different profile had towns decided to involve in their affairs only the most powerful men in government. Although urban lists of "must have" privileges could be very long, such an entirely practical and mercenary approach did not define town policy. In many cases, civic officials did not always know what they wanted or needed, or at least could not articulate it in precise terms. And as the fifteenth century progressed, and economic stresses combined with royal dynastic upheaval, such precision could be detrimental to a borough's legal existence as well as to its financial health. Far better, and far more flexible, to have the friendship of the powerful, developed over many years and sometimes over several generations.

None of the four towns possessed unbroken records of successful patronage. All of them scrambled at times, particularly during the second half of the fifteenth century, to fit their local relationships into the context of national political developments. Changes in monarchs meant changes in royal relatives and household officers, the level at which most towns sought contact. Much more continuity was found in borough patronage of justices and men-at-law, relationships in which professional expertise counted more than royal social or familial connections. Civic officials placed great trust in the legal retainers of their local noble families, but nothing stopped them from initiating and cultivating relationships on their own when judicial matters required expert, and perhaps extra-legal, care. Urban budgets stretched to include regular fees as well as the more serendipitous presentations to visitors of social standing.

Of the four towns examined here, Exeter's gift-giving reached the widest variety of individuals. Even as the sixteenth century began, the borough still believed it had substantial chartered privileges to gain. Its local nobility contributed more upheaval to its existence than outright assistance, prompting a broad distribution of gifts and goodwill. Exeter's position on the southwest coast also brought to its shores a wide spectrum of visitors, ranging from royal siblings in rebellion to the rulers of Castile washed ashore by a storm. Blessed with the survival of most of its financial accounts for the period, the city also possessed an articulate spokesman of urban patronage in Mayor John Shillingford. His letters from London to his civic brethren at home during 1447 and 1448 are uniquely revealing of the expectations boroughs placed on their gifts and the people who accepted them.

While representing the city in its jurisdiction battles with the cathedral, Shillingford "prosecuted his suit through the stomach as well as through the ears of his judges."[109] Overhearing that Chancellor John Stafford and Chief Justice Fortescue expected to dine together that day and craved some salt fish, Shillingford took the initiative and provided them with their main course. He later discovered the meal was attended also by such powerful magnates as the marquis of Suffolk and the duke of Buckingham, so that Exeter problems and Exeter bounty reached a wide and powerful audience. Shillingford took particular care to interest Fortescue in the case: "Y fynde hym a gode man and well willed yn oure right, and like to have the grete rule of the mater...," not surprising given Fortescue's history of interest in the city. But it was the chancellor who determined the fate of the case, a dispute he clearly wanted settled at home with the assistance of neighboring nobles Courtenay and Bonville. Shillingford acknowledged Stafford's central role, "knellyng and salutyng hym yn the moste godely wyse that y cowde and recommended yn to his gode and gracious lordship my feloship and all the comminalte, his awne peeple and bedmen of the Cite of Exeter."[110] Although not every potential patron could be buttonholed so directly by the boroughs of England, these sentiments of respect, hope, and gratitude sum up the delicate balance between the debt that was incurred and the desserts medieval towns justly expected.

NOTES

[1]   With rare exceptions, members of the clergy are not studied here. In general, towns sent gifts to the local bishop or abbot, and consulted with such figures on judicial as well as religious matters. Some of these relations are discussed below, p. 257, and will be the subject of a separate study I am preparing.

2   Edward Powell, "After 'After McFarlane': The Poverty of Patronage and the Case
     for Constitutional History," *Trade, Devotion and Governance: Papers in Later
     Medieval History*, ed. Dorothy J. Clayton, Richard G. Davies, and Peter McNiven
     (Stroud: Alan Sutton Publishing Ltd., 1994), p. 5, citing the work of R. P. Saller,
     Personal Patronage under the Early Empire (Cambridge: Cambridge University
     Press, 1982), p. 1. Study of patronage in the anthropological literature is most
     clearly discussed by Eric R. Wolf, "Kinship, Friendship, and Patron-Client
     Relations," *The Social Anthropology of Complex Societies*, ed. Michael Banton
     (London: Tavistock Publications, 1966), pp. 16–18. For anthropological analysis of
     the meaning of gift-giving and the obligation to receive as well as to give, see
     Marcel Mauss, *The Gift: The Form and Reason for Exchange in Archaic Societies*,
     trans. W. D. Halls (New York and London: W. W. Norton, 1990), pp. 11–14.

3   For use of the phrase regarding the earl of Suffolk in the 1430s, see *CCR, 1454–61*,
     p. 77, and above at p. 117.

4   Ralph A. Griffiths, *The Reign of Henry VI* (Berkeley and Los Angeles: University of
     California Press, 1981), p. 570.

5   Nottingham is omitted from the tables because its financial accounts are
     fragmentary, although the *dona* entries regarding gifts contain useful information for
     this study. Only the York records list *feoda legisperitorum* separately from *dona et
     exennia*; legal fees in Exeter and Norwich accounts are mixed in with wages to the
     mayor and other civic officials and can be included in their *dona* sections. For
     similar financial analysis, see Rosemary Horrox, "Urban Patronage and Patrons in
     the Fifteenth Century," in *Patronage, the Crown, and the Provinces in Later
     Medieval England*, ed. Ralph A. Griffiths (Gloucester: Alan Sutton Publishing,
     1981), p. 154, based on a wider selection of towns than is attempted in this chapter.
     Seventeenth-century towns channeled only about 3 or 4% of annual expenses to
     patronage, but the figures are based on a very small sample: Catherine Patterson,
     *Urban Patronage in Early Modern England: Corporate Boroughs, the Landed Elite,
     and the Crown, 1580–1640* (Stanford: Stanford University Press, 1999), pp. 17–18.

6   G. A. Holmes, *The Estates of the Higher Nobility in Fourteenth-Century England*
     (Cambridge: Cambridge University Press, 1957), p. 10. Only the annual income of
     the bishopric of Exeter, said to be slightly under £1100, could compare with theirs of
     about £1500 *per annum*. For a short list of Exeter properties held by the second earl
     and taken into the king's hands because of the nonage of his heir, see *CCR, 1422–
     29*, p. 10. Courtenay wealth came from the local textile industry, harbor dues and
     customs connected to their Topsham port, and the levy of the third penny on wine
     carried from the port to Exeter: Martin Cherry, "The Crown and the Political
     Community in Devonshire 1377–1461," (Ph.D. diss., University College of
     Swansea, University of Wales, 1981), pp. 1–2, 47 (quotation).

7   Cherry, "Crown and Political Community," pp. 126–28; *idem*, "The Courtenay Earls
     of Devon," *Southern History* 1 (1979): 71–72.

8   Hoker blamed many of the city's economic problems and lack of an incorporating
     charter directly upon baleful Courtenay influence: *Description of the Citie*, 3:657.
     For further analysis of Courtenay economic control, see Wallace T. MacCaffrey,
     Exeter 1540–1640: The Growth of an English County Town, 2d ed. (London and
     Cambridge, Mass.: Harvard University Press, 1975), p. 19; A. M. Jackson,
     "Medieval Exeter, the Exe, and the Earldom of Devon," *Transactions of the*

Devonshire Association 104 (1972): 57–72; and W. G. Hoskins, *Two Thousand Years in Exeter* (Exeter: James Townsend and Sons, Ltd., 1960), pp. 49–50.

9   *Complete Peerage*, 5:195–200; Nigel Saul, *Richard II* (New Haven and London: Yale University Press, 1997), pp. 243–44.

10   D.R.O., Receivers' Roll 13–14 Richard II (Gloucester); 16–17 Richard II (Warwick).

11   *Complete Peerage*, 5:200–4; Christopher Allmand, *Henry V* (Berkeley and Los Angeles: University of California Press, 1992), p. 227; D.R.O., Receivers' Roll, 13–14 Henry IV. Beaufort was also duke of Exeter from 1416 to his death in 1426.

12   *Rot. Parl.*, 4:100–1; *Complete Peerage*, 5:205–8, 6:654; Allmand, *Henry V*, p. 227; D.R.O., Receivers' Roll 3–4 Henry V. Holand held the significant posts of admiral and constable of the Tower, indicating "that his status was higher than his often moderate political influence might otherwise suggest": Michael Stansfield, "John Holland, Duke of Exeter and Earl of Huntingdon (d.1447) and the Costs of the Hundred Years' War," in *Profit, Piety and the Professions in Later Medieval England*, ed. Michael Hicks (Gloucester: Alan Sutton, 1990), p. 113.

13   Cherry, "Courtenay Earls of Devon," 95; *idem*, "The Struggle for Power in Mid-Fifteenth-Century Devonshire," in *Patronage, the Crown and the Provinces in Later Medieval England*, ed. Ralph A. Griffiths (Gloucester: Alan Sutton Publishing, 1981), pp. 123–40; *Complete Peerage*, 2:218.

14   Allmand, *Henry V*, pp. 224, 227. For some examples of the breadth of Exeter patronage, see D.R.O., Receivers' Rolls, 2–3 Henry V (Sir John Tiptoft, treasurer of Henry IV's household), 6–7 Henry V (Thomas Lord Camoys, who led the left wing at Agincourt, and whose daughter married the third earl of Devon, by whom he was retained), 8–9 Henry V (Sir Walter Hungerford, close to Henry V and entrusted to care for the infant Henry VI).

15   Of the ten sheriffs of Devon appointed during the 1380s, seven were closely associated with him, as were 19 of the 42 justices of the peace, 12 of the 20 commissioners of array, and 9 of 12 parliamentary representatives for the shire: Cherry, "Crown and Political Community," p. 128; *idem*, "Courtenay Earls," p. 75; *idem*, "The Liveried Personnel of Edward Courtenay, Earl of Devon, 1384–5, Part I," *Devon and Cornwall Notes and Queries* 35.4 (1983), pp. 151–54.

16   Cherry, "Crown and Political Community," p. 353; *idem*, "Courtenay Earls," 85; Edward Foss, *The Judges of England*, 9 vols. (London: Longman, Brown, Green, and Longmans, 1848–64), 4:170–71; D.R.O., Receivers' Rolls, 50 Edward III–1 Richard II, 1–2, 11–12, and 14–22 Richard II. For Hille, see Cherry, "The Liveried Personnel of Edward Courtenay, Earl of Devon, 1384–5, Part IV, *Devon and Cornwall Notes and Queries* 35.7 (1985): 260. For Grey, *ibid.*, Part III," *Devon and Cornwall Notes and Queries* 35.6 (1984): 224.

17   Foss, *Judges*, 4:156–58; Cherry, "Crown and Political Community," pp. 340–41; *idem*, "The Liveried Personnel of Edward Courtenay, Earl of Devon, 1384–5, Part II," *Devon and Cornwall Notes and Queries* 35.5 (1984): 189–90; D.R.O., Receivers' Rolls, 3–10 Richard II.

18   *D.N.B.*, 3:1153; Foss, *Judges*, 4:39–41; D.R.O., Receivers' Rolls, 50 Edward III–1 Richard II, 1–10 Richard II. Also patronized by Exeter while liveried of the earl was Robert Belknap, Chief Justice of Common Pleas from 1374 and active on Earl Edward's judicial bench from 1381: *D.N.B.*, 2:9–10; Foss, *Judges*, 4:31–35; Cherry,

"Crown and Political Community," p. 143; D.R.O., Receivers' Rolls, 4–5, 8–9, 10–11 Richard II.

[19] Cherry, "Crown and Political Community," pp. 176, 217; D.R.O., Receivers' Rolls, 2–3, 4–5 (pension), 7–8 (royal jewels), 9–10 Henry V; 3–5, 10–19, 22–23, 26–27 Henry VI. See below, p. 156.

[20] Cherry, "Crown and Political Community," pp. 176, 199; Foss, *Judges*, 4:329; *D.N.B.*, 9:972.

[21] D.R.O., Receivers' Roll, 1–2, 2–3, 3–4, 4–5 Henry VI; N.R.O., 18-a, Chamberlains' Account Book I, f.145r-v; 7-d, Treasurers' Roll, 5–6 Henry VI; *Norwich Records*, 2:64. For Gloucester's actions in an arbitration at Norwich concerning William Paston, see Edward Powell, *Kingship, Law and Society: Criminal Justice in the Reign of Henry V* (Oxford: Clarendon Press, 1989), pp. 93–94.

[22] R. L. Storey, *The End of the House of Lancaster* (London: Barrie and Rockliff, 1966; rpt., Gloucester: Alan Sutton Publishing, 1986), pp. 85–88; *CCR, 1413–19*, p. 199. See below, p. 296. Bonville had married successively daughters of Lord Grey of Ruthin and the earl of Devon. His second marriage, to Elizabeth Courtenay, daughter of the third earl, required papal dispensation as Elizabeth had stood as sponsor to Bonville's daughter by his first wife: *Complete Peerage* 2:218. Storey, p. 86 speculated that bad feelings over this marriage may have fueled the disputes between Bonville and the earl. But in light of the christening reference, could there have been friendlier relations at some time between these families than the public record argues?

[23] See below, pp. 264–68.

[24] D.R.O., Receivers' Rolls, 9–10 to 12–13 Henry VI, and 16–17 to 17–18 Henry VI. Fortescue became Chief Justice of King's Bench 1442: Foss, *Judges*, 4:308–15. Although their opponent Bishop Edmund Lacy also sought to interest a local noble on his side ("to be brothyr to the Churche of Exeter"), his choice of the duke of Exeter was badly timed to the period of John Holand's final illness and his inexperienced teenage son's succession. Civic officials had a far better outcome with their proven patterns of patronage.

[25] Storey, *House of Lancaster*, pp. 88–92; G. L. and M. A. Harriss, eds., *John Benet's Chronicle*, Camden Miscellany XXIV, 4th ser., 9 (1972), pp. 167–68, 205–206.

[26] D.R.O., Receivers' Roll, 30–31 Henry VI.

[27] Griffiths, *Henry VI*, p. 753; Mrs. G. H. Radford, "The Fight at Clyst in 1455," *Transactions of the Devonshire Association* 44 (1912): 255–56; Cherry, "Crown and Political Community," pp. 291–92; Storey, *House of Lancaster*, p. 166; P.R.O., KB.9/275, mem. 137.

[28] Griffiths, *Henry VI*, pp. 802, 841. The 1457 marriage of Thomas Courtenay to Marie de Maine resulted in luxurious gifts to the young couple by both the king's great wardrobe and the city of Exeter: N.R.O., Receivers' Rolls, 36–37, 37–38 Henry VI (gifts of wine and satin).

[29] D.R.O., Receivers' Rolls, 34–35, 35–36, 36–37, 37–38, 38–39 Henry VI, *passim*. Dynham helped York and his eldest son escape from Devon to Calais late in 1459 when the court turned against them: D.R.O., Book 51, f.313. The duke of Exeter himself, Henry Holand, received gifts during 1456–57, probably while a justice of the peace for Devonshire, and Admiral of England. He was a staunch supporter of Henry VI and accompanied the monarch to exile in Scotland in 1461: *Complete*

Peerage, 5:212; Storey, *House of Lancaster*, p. 145; Cora L. Scofield, *The Life and Reign of Edward the Fourth*, 2 vols. (London: Longmans and Co., 1923), 2:150–51.

[30] Storey, *House of Lancaster*, pp. 174–75; *Complete Peerage*, 2:218, 4:327.

[31] John Warkworth, *A Chronicle of the First Thirteen Years of the Reign of King Edward the Fourth*, ed. James O. Halliwell, Camden Society o.s., vol. 10 (1839), pp. 6–7; D.R.O., Book 51, f.315v; Scofield, *Edward IV*, 1:482, 496–98. Edward executed the sixth earl after his younger brother conspired to return the Lancastrians to the throne. Leading troops provided by Exeter, Stafford marched against the rebellious Robin of Redesdale, but was killed by a mob three months after attaining the title. His will funded sermons in parish churches throughout the west country: Nicholas Harris Nicolas, ed., *Testamenta Vetusta*, 2 vols. (London: Nichols and Son, 1826), 1:301.

[32] D.R.O., Receivers' Roll, 2–3 Edward IV, lists gifts to all three men. Dynham was also distantly related to the Courtenay family.

[33] D.R.O., Receivers' Rolls, 37–38, 38–39 Henry VI; 2–3, 14–15 Edward IV; *CPR, 1461–67*, p. 275; D.C.A., no.2361.

[34] D.R.O., Receivers' Roll, 16–17 Edward IV.

[35] D.R.O., Receivers' Rolls, 1–2 Richard III, 2 Richard III–1 Henry VII. Lord Scrope's son Henry also received gifts during the latter year. Scrope is an example of Richard's imposition of northern loyalists in southern offices: A. J. Pollard, *North-Eastern England During the Wars of the Roses: Lay Society, War, and Politics 1450–1500* (Oxford: Clarendon Press, 1990), pp. 346–53.

[36] Exeter's gifts are listed in D.R.O., Receivers' Roll, 10–11 Edward IV. The city ignored the seventh earl of Devon, whose older brothers had been executed under the Yorkists and who died himself at Tewkesbury seven months after his creation. Sir Hugh also died at Tewkesbury and his son Edward became heir male to the earldom, although the Yorkist kings made no move to restore the family: Rosemary Horrox, *Richard III: A Study of Service* (Cambridge: Cambridge University Press, 1989), pp. 168–69; Michael A. Hicks, *False, Fleeting, Perjur'd Clarence* (Gloucester: Alan Sutton Publishing, 1980), p. 95.

[37] Hicks, *Clarence*, pp. 71–72; Warkworth, *Chronicle of the First Thirteen Years*, p. 17; Thomas (Fortescue) Lord Clermont, ed., *A History of the Family of Fortescue in All Its Branches*, 2d ed. (London: Ellis and White, 1880), p. 84; Griffiths, *Henry VI*, pp. 891–92. See above p. 108 for Fortescue's earlier relations with Exeter.

[38] D.R.O., Receivers' Roll, 10–11 Edward IV; Scofield, *Edward IV*, 1:572–73.

[39] D.R.O., Receivers' Roll, 2–3 Henry VII, is the first to survive from the first Tudor's reign. Edward united two lines of the family by marrying Sir Philip Courteney's daughter Elizabeth: Nicolas, *Testamenta Vetusta*, 2:494–95.

[40] S. B. Chrimes, *Henry VII* (Berkeley and Los Angeles: University of California Press, 1972), pp. 58, 138.

[41] For Dynham, see Michael Van Cleave Alexander, *The First of the Tudors: A Study of Henry VII and His Reign* (Totowa, N.J.: Rowman and Littlefield, 1980), pp. 35, 71, 194; and R. Pearse Chope, "The Last of the Dynhams," *Transactions of the Devonshire Association* 50 (1918): 431–92. For FitzWarin, see *Complete Peerage*, 2:16; 5:510–11.

[42] D.R.O., Receivers' Roll, 21–22 Henry VII; *Complete Peerage*, 12.1:182 and 12.2:738–39. Stafford was a cousin of Henry's queen.

[43] Carpenter, *Locality and Polity*, p. 586; see also M. M. Condon, "Ruling Elites in the Reign of Henry VII," in *Patronage, Pedigree and Power in Late Medieval England*, ed. Charles Ross (Gloucester: Alan Sutton, 1979), p. 121, 123 for the nobility's lack of influence with the king. However, S. J. Gunn, "Courtiers of Henry VII," *English Historical Review* 108 (1993): 29–30, provides details of Giles Daubeny's attendance upon the king and his resultant role as successful conduit of others' requests.

[44] N.R.O., 7a-b, Account Roll 1381–84; Rowena E. Archer, "Rich Old Ladies: The Problem of Late Medieval Dowagers," in *Property and Politics: Essays in Later Medieval English History*, ed. Tony Pollard (New York: St. Martin's Press, 1984), p.28.

[45] N.R.O., 18-a, Chamberlains' Account Book I (1384–1448), f.10v (Arundel); 7a-b, Account Roll 1381–84 (Warwick).

[46] *Complete Peerage*, 12.1:437–41; N.R.O., 7a-b, Treasurers' Roll, 9–10 Richard II.

[47] Simon Walker, *The Lancastrian Affinity 1361–1399* (Oxford: Clarendon Press, 1990), pp. 184–87; Francis Blomefield, *A Topographical History of the County of Norfolk*, 2d ed., 11 vols. (London: William Miller, 1805–10), 3:103, 113–15; N.R.O., 7a-b, Treasurers' Rolls 2–3, 9–10, 16–17 Richard II. For discussion of the charters, see above, p. 41.

[48] Men such as Edmund Gournay, Edmund Clippesby, and Sir Robert Cayley: Walker, *Lancastrian Affinity*, pp. 191–92; *Norwich Records* 2:44; N.R.O., 7a-b, Treasurers' Roll, 2–3 Richard II.

[49] Walker, *Lancastrian Affinity*, pp. 191–95, 200; Colin Richmond, T*he Paston Family in the Fifteenth Century: The First Phase* (Cambridge: Cambridge University Press, 1990), pp. 2, 72, 89; *Norwich Records* 2:41, 53, 58–60.

[50] *Complete Peerage*, 12.1:441–42; he received a gift from Norwich 1410–11: N.R.O., 7c, Treasurer's Roll, 12–13 Henry IV.

[51] *Complete Peerage*, 9:600–5; Rowena E. Archer, "Parliamentary Restoration: John Mowbray and the Dukedom of Norfolk in 1425," in *Rulers and the Ruled in Late Medieval England: Essays Presented to Gerald Harriss*, ed. Rowena E. Archer and Simon Walker (London and Rio Grande: Hambledon Press, 1995), pp. 99–101; N.R.O., 18-a, Chamberlains' Account Book I, f.165v (torches and wine for the arrival of the duke of Norfolk at night).

[52] J. H. Druery, "The Erpingham House, St. Martin's at Palace, Norwich," *Norfolk and Norwich Archaeological Society* (*Norfolk Archaeology*) 6 (1864): 144, 147; Trevor John, "Sir Thomas Erpingham, East Anglian Society and the Dynastic Revolution of 1399," *Norfolk Archaeology* 35 (1970): 96–97; Walker, *Lancastrian Affinity*, pp. 37n, 92n, 188, 200, 269; *CPR, 1381–85*, p. 557.

[53] John, "Sir Thomas," 101; *Norwich Records*, 2:52–53. The city did not seem troubled by Erpingham's reputation for lawlessness: late in Edward III's reign, he had been the subject of an investigative commission: Walker, *Lancastrian Affinity*, p. 208, citing *CPR, 1370–74*, p. 242.

[54] *CPR, 1399–1401*, p. 274. He also received grants from the counties of Norfolk and Suffolk and the fee farm of Cambridge when the Norwich grant was declared invalid: *CPR, 1401–1405*, p. 47.

55 Blomefield, *History of Norfolk*, 3:125; John, "Sir Thomas," 106; Peter McNiven, "Prince Henry and the English Political Crisis of 1412," *History* 65 (1980): 1; *Norwich Records*, 1:lxiv; 2:56, 63; Walker, *Lancastrian Affinity*, p. 194.

56 *Norwich Records*, 2:52; John D. Milner, "Sir Simon Felbrigg, K. G.: The Lancastrian Revolution and Personal Fortune," *Norfolk Archaeology* 37 (1978): 84–85; John, "Sir Thomas," 102; R. W. Ketton-Cremer, *Felbrigg: The Story of a House* (London: The Boydell Press, 1962), pp. 5–6; *CPR, 1391–96*, p. 227.

57 He continued to live on the Ricardian grants, totaling £100 *per annum*, that the first Lancastrian monarch confirmed shortly after taking the throne. In 1441, a year before his death, Felbrigg suffered a 50% cut in the annuities: *CCR, 1399–1402*, p. 143; *CPR, 1436–41*, p. 552; P.R.O., SC.6/1278/9, mm. 5, 6, 12–25; *Norwich Records*, 2:58–59; Blomefield, *History of Norfolk*, 4:74, 87; Ketton-Cremer, *Felbrigg*, p. 7.

58 E. W. Ives, *The Common Lawyers of Pre-Reformation England* (Cambridge: Cambridge University Press, 1983), p. 115.

59 H. S. Bennett, *The Pastons and Their England*, 2d ed. (Cambridge: Cambridge University Press, 1979), pp. 1–3; Philippa C. Maddern, *Violence and Social Order: East Anglia 1422–1442* (Oxford: Clarendon Press, 1992), p. 64.

60 Blomefield, *History of Norfolk*, 3:126 for the arbitration; for the writs, N.R.O., 18-a, Chamberlains' Account Book I, f.145v (1423–24), and 7-d, Treasurers' Roll 1425–26. On the former occasion, he was rewarded (as was the sheriff of Norfolk) "pro imbellisando brevis domino rege versus cives de civitate"; on the latter (with the cellarer of Holy Trinity, Norwich) "pro imbesellace brevis..." etc. Although the verb in the second passage implies mutilation or defacement of a royal writ, it is more likely that his intervention or quashing of the writs is what the clerk meant to record in both cases. I am grateful for the advice of Professor Charles Donahue of the Harvard Law School on this matter. Paston received 20s. on each occasion. The situation invites more investigation than can be attempted here.

61 Foss, *Judges*, 4:283–85; Josiah C. Wedgwood, *History of Parliament: Biographies of the Members of the Commons House 1439–1509* (London: His Majesty's Stationery Office, 1936), p. 32; Simon Payling, *Political Society in Lancastrian England: The Greater Gentry of Nottinghamshire* (Oxford: Clarendon Press, 1991), pp. 36–37.

62 *Complete Peerage*, 9:605–7; Archer, "Parliamentary Restoration," 115.

63 *Complete Peerage*, 12.1:443–50. For analysis of his landholdings in Norfolk and Suffolk, see John Watts, *Henry VI and the Politics of Kingship* (Cambridge: Cambridge University Press, 1996), pp. 158–59. Suffolk collected money in East Anglia in 1431 to help hold France, persuading Norwich to make a timely and generous contribution: Griffiths, *Henry VI*, pp. 59, 119. Alice Chaucer's great-aunt was Katherine Swineford, mother of the Beauforts.

64 Edgar C. Robbins, "The Cursed Norfolk Justice: A Defence of Sir William Yelverton (c.1400–1477)," *Norfolk Archaeology* 26 (1936): 1–5; *Norwich Records* 1:xcvii; Maddern, *Violence and Social Order*, p. 183; Foss, *Judges*, 4:461; Colin Richmond, *The Paston Family in the Fifteenth Century: Fastolf's Will* (Cambridge: Cambridge University Press, 1996), pp. 95–96. See above, pp. 116–17.

65 N.R.O., 7d, Treasurers' Roll, 8–9 Henry VI; Richmond, *Paston Family: The First Phase*, pp. 90, 123n, 207–13, 221, 224n; Maddern, *Violence and Social Order*, pp. 35, 135n.; Wedgwood, *History of Parliament: Biographies*, pp. 492–93.

66 Philip Morgan, *War and Society in Medieval Cheshire 1277–1403*, Chetham Society, 3rd series, vol. 34 (London, 1987), ch. 4, cited in Richmond, *Paston Family: The First Phase*, p. 224 n.75.

67 Letters survive declaring his support of Thomas Wetherby, instigator of some of the city's election disputes in 1433: *Norwich Records*, 1:xcii, 347; James Gairdner, ed., *The Paston Letters*, 6 vols. (London: Chatto and Windus, 1904), 2:49.

68 N.R.O., 18a, Chamberlains' Account Book I, ff. 225r–226r; *Norwich Records*, 1:351. Gloucester took little active role in government after 1441; he was arrested and died in 1447: Ralph A. Griffiths, "The Trial of Eleanor Cobham," *Bulletin of the John Rylands Library* 51 (1968–69), 381–99; Watts, *Henry VI and the Politics of Kingship*, pp. 182–90.

69 N.R.O., 17-d, Apprenticeship Indentures, ff. 4v–7v. For the Jenneys, see Foss, *Judges*, 4:488–90, and Richmond, *Paston Family: Fastolf's Will*, p. 49. For Clifton, see Richmond, *Paston Family: The First Phase*, pp. 90, 92n, 239n, and Maddern, *Violence and Social Order*, p. 197n.

70 Helen Castor, "The Duchy of Lancaster and the Rule of East Anglia, 1399–1440: A Prologue to the Paston Letters," in *Crown, Government and People in the Fifteenth Century*, ed. Rowena Archer (New York: St. Martin's Press 1995), pp. 72–73, 77–78. Tuddenham was Sheriff of Norfolk in 1431 and keeper of the great wardrobe in 1446; Heydon was recorder of Norwich 1431–33. The Pastons' own dark view of Tuddenham and Heydon is echoed by the family's latest biographer: Richmond, *Paston Family: The First Phase*, pp. 84, 155, 171n, following Roger Virgoe, "The Divorce of Sir Thomas Tuddenham," *Norfolk Archaeology* 35 (1969): 406–18. See below, pp. 290–92.

71 N.R.O., Chamberlains' Account Book I, ff.204r–214r, 221v, 223r–224v; *Norwich Records*, 1:117.

72 *Norwich Records*, 1:346. For Margaret Paston's fears that Suffolk would become a heavy lord, or enemy, to her husband, see Norman Davis, ed., *Paston Letters and Papers of the Fifteenth Century*, 2 vols. (Oxford: Clarendon Press, 1971, 1976), 1:236.

73 Griffiths, *Reign of Henry VI*, p. 591; Richmond, *Paston Family: The First Phase*, p. 246. He received wine from Norwich 1451–52: N.R.O., 17-d, Apprenticeship Indentures, ff.16v–19r.

74 Griffiths, *Reign of Henry VI*, pp. 689–90; N.R.O., 21-f, 9–58, Kirkpatrick Notes, *sub* 1459, 1462; 17-d, Apprenticeship Indentures, ff.22v–25r; 7-d, Chamberlains' Roll, 37–38 Henry VI. I am grateful to Peter Hammond for making me aware of the duchess's Norfolk and Suffolk holdings. The duchess also gave advice on the city's continuing problems with jurisdiction.

75 N.R.O., 21-f, 9–58, Kirkpatrick Notes, *sub* 1462; 18-a, Chamberlains' Account Book II (1470–90), f.74v (14–15 Edward IV); Chamberlains' Account Book III (1479–87), ff.5v–7r (19–20 Edward IV). In August 1475, Margaret Paston remarked that "my Lady of Yorke and all her howsold is here at Sent Benetts [at Holm], and purposed to abide there stille, til the Kynge come from be yonde the see [from

France], and lenger if she like the eyre ther": Davis, *Paston Letters and Papers*, 1:376–77.

[76] See below, p. 199. John Lord Wenlock was appointed the young duke's governor until 1465, and that connection may explain why Norwich honored Wenlock with gifts of wine and bread in 1463–64: N.R.O., 7-e, Chamberlains' Roll (fragment).

[77] Colin Richmond, *Paston Family: Fastolf's Will*, p. 119, sketches the duke as henpecked by his wife, the queen, and the widowed duchess of Suffolk.

[78] J. A. F. Thomson, "John de la Pole, Duke of Suffolk," *Speculum* 54 (1979): 532, 537–41. Again, one presumes Elizabeth is the duchess of Suffolk in question, and not her mother-in-law Alice Chaucer, who lived until 1475 trying to carry out her late husband's wishes: Richmond, *Paston Family: The First Phase*, pp. 5n, 236–37, 241. For the duke and the city, see Davis, *Paston Letters and Papers*, 1:323–31, and Bennett, *Pastons and Their England*, pp. 16–17. N.R.O., 7-e, Chamberlains' Roll (fragment) contains examples of their gifts.

[79] *Norwich Records*, 1:353–55 (New Mills); N.R.O., 21-f, 9–58, Kirkpatrick Notes, *sub* 1482 (grain); E. W. Ives, "Andrew Dymmock and the Papers of Antony, Earl Rivers, 1482–3," *Bulletin of the Institute of Historical Research* 41 (1968): 222–23, 227–28 (nominees).

[80] Charles Ross, *Richard III* (London: Eyre Methuen, 1981), pp. 158–59, 182–83, 168, 193.

[81] For Howard's activities in Norwich, see N.R.O., 18-a, Chamberlains' Account Book III, ff. 50v–51r, 60v–67v, *The Household Books of John Howard, Duke of Norfolk, 1462–1471, 1481–1483*, introduction by Anne Crawford (Stroud: Alan Sutton Publishing, 1992), Book 1, pp. 200, 212, 281, 349; Book 2, pp. 438, 447.

[82] Crawford, *Household Books*, p. xvii; Roger Virgoe, "The Recovery of the Howards in East Anglia, 1485–1529," in *Wealth and Power in Tudor England: Essays Presented to S. T. Bindoff*, edited by E. W. Ives, R. J. Knecht, and J. J. Scarisbrick (London: Athlone Press, 1978), pp. 6–7, 14; Richmond, *Paston Family: The First Phase*, pp. 34, 113 (quotation); Wedgwood, *History of Parliament: Biographies*, pp. 458–59.

[83] N.R.O., Chamberlains' Account Book II, f.190v (4–5 Henry VII); 7-e, Chamberlains' Rolls, 6–7 Henry VII; Virgoe, "Recovery of the Howards," pp. 12–16. The duchess in question was presumably Elizabeth, widow of the fourth Mowbray duke, as John Howard's widow would have suffered from his attainder. I am grateful to Dr. Anne Crawford of the Public Record Office for advice on this question.

[84] N.R.O., 18-a, Chamberlains' Account Book III, ff. 96r (2–3 Henry VII); 7-e, Chamberlains' Rolls, 6–7 and 11–12 Henry VII; *Complete Peerage*, 12.1:449–53, and Appendix I pp. 21–25; J. D. Mackie, *The Earlier Tudors, 1485–1558* (Oxford: Clarendon Press, 1952), pp. 167–71, 184–85; Alexander, *First of the Tudors*, pp. 176–77, 197–98, 207–8. The city would have been foolish to count on his continued loyalty to the throne, however, as he adopted his elder brother's cause and with two other siblings asserted his right to rule as the last "White Rose" of the Yorkist plant, a claim leading only to execution. Norwich raised troops against the earl's pretensions in 1501–2: see below, p. 201.

[85] C. E. Moreton, *The Townshends and Their World: Gentry, Law, and Land in Norfolk c.1450–1551* (Oxford: Clarendon Press, 1992), p. 53 (quotation). See also

Virgoe, "Recovery of the Howards," pp. 7–11; *Complete Peerage*, 10:239–44; Nicolas, *Testamenta Vetusta*, 2:526–27.

[86]   For Hobart's gifts, see N.R.O., 7-e, Chamberlains' Roll 1492–93, and 7-f, Chamberlains' Roll 1503–4. For examples of breakfasts, see 7-f, Chamberlains' Roll 1509–10.

[87]   York's sole chamberlains' account from Richard's reign (3 Feb. 1396–3 Feb. 1397) is preoccupied with the expenses consequent upon the king's visit and the labor expended at Westminster to obtain copies of their new charter: Dobson, *Chamberlains' Accounts*, pp. 5–8, and above p. 38. There is also some evidence that several Nottingham residents were in the service of Henry duke of Lancaster just before his usurpation of the throne, but there survive no records of gifts to or contact with him: *Nott. Records*, 1:359–61.

[88]   Dobson, *Chamberlains' Accounts*, p. 15 (account of 1433–34). Joan Beaufort was active in Yorkshire throughout the 1420s and 1430s, holding the lordships of Middleham and Sheriff Hutton in dower until her death in 1440: R. B. Dobson, *Durham Priory 1400–50* (Cambridge: Cambridge University Press, 1973), pp. 185–87. Edmund, son of John Beaufort, had a career in war and diplomacy during the 1420s: *Complete Peerage*, 12.1:49–53.

[89]   Dobson, *Chamberlains' Accounts*, pp. 37–48. Beaumont had served with the duke of York in France in the 1430s. His second wife was Katherine Neville, daughter of the earl of Westmorland and Joan Beaufort, and widow of the duke of Norfolk: Griffiths, *Henry VI*, p. 668; Watts, *Henry VI and the Politics of Kingship*, p. 257; *Complete Peerage*, 2:62. Fishgarths remained a problem: see above, p. 82.

[90]   Dobson, *Chamberlains' Accounts*, pp. 33, 63; Storey, *House of Lancaster*, pp. 111–17; Watts, *Henry VI and the Politics of Kingship*, pp. 258–59.

[91]   Dobson, *Chamberlains' Accounts*, pp. 75, 94. The earl of Salisbury and his son Warwick were prominent members of the royal council 1453–54: Ralph A. Griffiths, "Local Rivalries and National Politics: The Percies, the Nevilles, and the Duke of Exeter, 1452–1455," *Speculum* 43 (1968): 594–99.

[92]   Dobson, *Chamberlains' Accounts*, pp. 74–75, 93–94. Greystock headed numerous commissions to treat for peace with Scotland, and held the office of Master Forester of the nearby forest of Galtres. He also served the earl of Warwick and Richard duke of Gloucester, remaining with the latter after his accession: Pollard, *North-Eastern England*, pp. 124, 253, 276, 355; *Complete Peerage*, 6:197–98.

[93]   Ross, *Richard III*, p. 39; Davies, *York Records*, p. 6. His manors included Bolton Percy near York. Neville dominance of the 1461 parliament ("twelve of the forty-one lay lords...had some kinship by blood or marriage to the House of Neville") is noted by William Huse Dunham, Jr., ed., *The Fane Fragment of the 1461 Lords' Journal* (New Haven: Yale University Press, 1935), pp. 52–53.

[94]   *Nott. Records*, 3:412–19 (1461–62); 2:369–77 (1463–64); 3:239 (1484–85); 3:317 (1503–4); *Complete Peerage*, 6:370–74. For Hastings's power in the north midlands, see Christine Carpenter, *Locality and Polity: A Study of Warwickshire Landed Society, 1401–1499* (Cambridge: Cambridge University Press, 1992), pp. 523–47. Hastings's will directs the friars of Nottingham to distribute £100 to the town's poor: Nicolas, *Testamenta Vetusta*, 1:368–75. His heirs, the earls of Huntingdon, became active civic patrons in later decades: Patterson, *Urban Patronage in Early Modern England*, pp. 196–97.

95 *Complete Peerage*, 9:92, 716–17; Dobson, *Chamberlains' Accounts*, pp. 126, 129 (1468–69).
96 *Nott. Records*, 3:416–17; 2:369–77.
97 *Ibid.*, 3: 394.
98 *York House Books*, pp. 696, 707. His supporters in civic office included recorder Miles Metcalfe (1477–85), and mayors Thomas Wrangwish (1484) and Nicholas Lancaster (1485, 1493). For details of his relationship with York, see above, p. 82.
99 *Nott. Records*, 3:252–66 (Savage), 285–95, 311–21 (Willoughby). For background on their activities in Warwickshire, see Carpenter, *Locality and Polity*, pp. 111–12, 525, 549, 572–94 *passim*. Civic officials may have been afraid not to reward Willoughby, given the violence he inflicted on Nottingham during the sessions while pursuing a private feud with Lord Grey: *Report on the Manuscripts of Lord Middleton*, Historical Manuscripts Commission (London: His Majesty's Stationery Office, 1911), pp. 118–20; C. G. Bayne and W. H. Dunham, eds., *Select Cases in the Council of Henry VII*, Selden Society, vol. 75 (1956), p. 17.
100 *Nott. Records*, 3:276 (1493–94).
101 Nt.R.O., CA7423, Mayors'/Chamberlains' Account c.1500; *Nott. Records*, 3:317 (1503–4, Hastings); Horrox, *Richard III*, pp. 111n, 267 (Clifton). As a receiver of crown lands in Nottinghamshire under Edward IV, Clifton would have been familiar with local needs: *CPR, 1476–85*, p. 19.
102 *Nott. Records*, 3:252–66 (quotation p. 262), 270–81; *D.N.B.*, 14:31–32.
103 Alexander, *First of the Tudors*, pp. 32, 34–35, 92. For gifts and consultations, see Dobson, *Chamberlains' Accounts*, pp. 186–87, and *York House Books*, pp. 369, 393, 469–70, 571, 525–27, 588–89, 616, 635, 646, 734, 736. Percy's heir was only eleven when the fourth earl was murdered, and excluded by Henry VII from the influential northern offices his father had held, to the extent that his biographer calls him "the unemployed magnate": Mervyn James, "A Tudor magnate and the Tudor state: Henry fifth earl of Northumberland," *Society, Politics and Culture: Studies in Early Modern England*, Past and Present Publications (Cambridge: Cambridge University Press, 1986), p. 73. The first reference in York records to the fifth earl (known as Henry the Magnificent) being welcomed with wine and fish occurred when he and his countess entered the city in July 1502: *York Civic Records*, 2:177.
104 *York House Books*, pp. 382, 480. Hope of a congenial relationship with Clifford was dashed when the city refused him entry during the tax riots that had claimed Percy's life: *Complete Peerage*, 3:294–95.
105 *York House Books*, pp. 679; *York Civic Records*, 2:101, 105–7, 112, 113, 115–17, 130; Rachel R. Reid, *King's Council in the North* (London: Longmans, Green and Company, 1921; rpt., Totowa, N.J.: Rowman and Littlefield, 1975), pp. 78–79, 81–82.
106 *York Civic Records*, 2:88–89; Reid, *King's Council*, p. 487. She held the position 1507–9. The city also looked to younger members of the royal family to extend favor: the ten year old duke of York was asked for help when the city fought St. Mary's abbey over suburban land, and a sumptuous welcome was extended to fourteen year old Princess Margaret on her progress to meet her Scottish bridegroom, in the hope that she give her favor to the city: *York Civic Records*, 2:154–55, 166, 173, 184–85.

107   For example, Dobson, *Chamberlains' Accounts*, pp. 75 (gifts to the archbishop of
      York on the occasion of his enthronement, 1453), 152 (prior of St. John of
      Jerusalem, joining with the earl of Northumberland in wardenship of the east and
      middle marches, 1475); *York House Books*, pp. 9 (bishop of Durham concerning
      fishgarths, 1476), 653 (wine to the archbishop of York, also chancellor of England,
      to be a good lord to the city, 1489); *York Civic Records*, 3:1–8 (gifts to archbishop
      of York and president of Council of the North Thomas Savage during time of riots,
      1504).

108   See below, p. 260. In the 1480s, York officials had tried to please the holders of
      Tanghall grazing land when such men were highly-placed servants of the archbishop
      or the king: *York House Books*, pp. 513, 515–16, 519, 522, 655. In 1502, against the
      wishes of many citizens, the city council allowed the land to be held by the nephew
      of Henry VII's councilor and former treasurer Reginald Bray, "as in the lieu of a
      reward unto hym for to have hym good maister unto this Citie": *York Civic Records*,
      2:178–79. M. M. Condon calls Bray "one of the most influential men in England,
      one of the most prominent of all Henry VII's councillors, and one of the few with
      ready access to the person and mind of the King himself": "From Caitiff and Villain
      to *Pater Patriae*: Reynold Bray and the Profits of Office," in *Profit, Piety and the
      Professions in Later Medieval England*, ed. Michael Hicks (Gloucester: Alan
      Sutton, 1990), p. 138; for Bray's influence see also *idem*, "Ruling Elites in the Reign
      of Henry VII," in *Patronage, Pedigree and Power in Late Medieval England*, ed.
      Charles Ross, pp. 123–24; and DeLloyd J. Guth, "Climbing the Civil-Service Pole
      during Civil War: Sir Reynold Bray (c.1440–1503)," in *Estrangement, Enterprise
      and Education in Fifteenth-Century England*, ed. Sharon D. Michalove and A.
      Compton Reeves (Stroud: Sutton Publishing, 1998), pp. 57–61.

109   Stuart A. Moore, ed., *Letters and Papers of John Shillingford, Mayor of Exeter
      1447–50*, Camden Society, n.s., vol. 2 (London, 1871), p. xxi.

110   *Ibid.*, pp. 6–9. For the chancellor's letter to Fortescue, asking him to "induce my
      said Brother [the dean and chapter of Exeter] and all parties to put the matter in
      entreaty at home," see Fortescue (Lord Clermont), *History of the Family of
      Fortescue*, pp. 57–58.

PART THREE, CHAPTER 5
FINANCES AND PAYMENTS

In 1419, the mayor of Exeter ordered a half-gallon of wine while accounting for the money his city owed the Crown.[1] Like all officers of medieval English boroughs, Exeter's chief magistrate needed to fortify himself when calculating the central government's fiscal demands for urban contributions. These demands were particularly heavy during Henry V's reign and remained so for several decades, coinciding with an extended period of both agrarian and urban economic contraction affecting much of post-plague Europe.[2] This was the age in which town complaints about poverty became commonplace, and when kings unstable on their thrones responded to them to bolster both reigns and receivers' rolls. Local revenues remained steady or fell in value throughout the late fourteenth and fifteenth centuries, directions that worried town officials during reigns with heavy lay taxation or petitions for corporate loans.

The royal government was not entirely deaf to urban complaints. After 1433, the Crown remitted portions of lay subsidies, waived ancient fee farm payments, and refrained from asking beleaguered towns for loans. Yet because these three kinds of payment constituted a significant part of Crown income, monarchs had to weigh urban crises against government solvency. Taxes, farms and loans helped pay for military campaigns, royal household expenses, and personal annuities for servants loyal to the Crown. The period under study witnessed significant change in royal accounting methods, as Yorkist monarchs and the first Tudor turned to financial practices centered on the Chamber. Yet those practices did not seriously affect boroughs' relations with the royal government, for whether an Exchequer clerk or a royally-appointed receiver expected payment, civic officials faced identical challenges in raising funds from local sources in a time of economic stress.

Any town's contribution to the central administration formed only a small portion of total Crown revenue, yet raising the payments caused some boroughs considerable grief. Time failed to bring about improvement: the demands of the French campaigns, particularly those of Henry V, burdened towns with debts that lasted for over three generations. The following examination of urban fiscal policies reveals the financial claims made upon borough budgets, shows the strategies of civic officials when under economic stress (real or imagined), assesses urban complaints about poverty, and illuminates larger problems of late medieval monarchs' relations with their urban subjects.

Local Budgets and Records

Any study of urban finances must begin with local records and their accounts of domestic budgets: the receipts and expenses pertaining to internal administration and government.[3] Receipts accrued from trade-related activities such as tolls and market fees, as well as rents, fines, and freemen's entry payments. The listed receipts often possess a slightly fictitious quality, as the amount included both payments already made and those which were expected to be recorded on later accounts. Expenses consisted of wages and payments for civic officials, retainer fees for lawyers and gifts for patrons, and payments for repair of buildings and public works. Local authorities had a good sense of exactly how much needed to be budgeted each year: significant excess remaining in the account was rare, and far more common were deficit entries either carried over to the following fiscal year or personally covered by the receivers or chamberlains unfortunate enough to be in charge that year.[4] Tables 4–7 present the data of the seven reigns studied. Receipts (however fictitious) and expenses are averaged for the time periods indicated, and expenses expressed as a percentage of receipts in order to reveal indebtedness. As valuable as these records are, they tell us little about the nature of wealth in the community, about payments required by the Crown, or about how much additional money could have been raised if assessment methods had changed.

Despite many expressions of concern over poverty, Exeter's finances were in good shape. Fiscal records complement narrative sources that attest to population growth and commercial prosperity commencing after 1350 and continuing into the sixteenth century. A regional entrepôt for

Table 4: Exeter finances, 1377–1509 (domestic budget)

	Average receipt per annum	Average expense per annum	Expense as percentage of receipt
Richard II 1377–1399	£130 17s.	£ 98 10s.	75%
Henry IV 1399–1413	£144 19s.	£128 16s.	89%
Henry V 1413–1422	£146 6s.	£125 14s.	86%
Henry VI 1422–1432 1433–1444 1445–1460	£139 19s. £119 4s. £136 3s.	£110 11s. £ 92 19s. £ 91 17s.	79% 78% 67%
Edward IV[1] 1461–1483	£142 0s.	£119 0s.	84%
Richard III[2] 1483–1484 1484–1485	£157 10s. £249 3s.	£153 8s. £253 3s.	97% 102%
Henry VII 1485–1509	£188 19s.	£170 0s.	90%

Sources: D.R.O., Receivers' Rolls (121 surviving for period)

[1] Uncollectable rents first began to be recorded on the rolls during Edward IV's reign, and ranged from £4 to £6 *per annum*.
[2] Accounts of these two rolls differ widely, thus both are presented here.

Table 5: Norwich finances, 1378–1509 (domestic budget)

	Average receipt per annum	Average expense per annum	Expense as percentage of receipt
Richard II 1377–1399	£199 18s.	£148 15s.	74%

Continued next page

Table 5—*Continued*

Henry IV 1399–1413	£187 7s.	£151 14s.	81%
Henry V **1413–1422**	£176 1s.	£138 15s.	79%
Henry VI **1422–1432**	£194 9s.	£175 17s.	90%
1433–1444	£205 6s.	—[1]	—[1]
1445–1460	£229 16s.	£150 17s.	66%
Edward IV **1461–1483**	£146 2s.	£134 1s.	92%
Henry VII[2] **1485–1509**	£165 1s.	£116 2s.	70%

Sources: N.R.O., Treasurers' and Chamberlains' Rolls (105 surviving for the period, 67 with both receipts and expenses listed)

[1] Insufficient local data
[2] Accounts for the reign of Richard III are fragmentary.

Table 6: Nottingham finances, 1461–1504 (domestic budget)

	Receipts	**Expenses**	**Expenses as percentage of receipts**
1461–1462	£112 0s. 4d.	£124 0s. 0d.	111%
1463–1464[1]	—	£ 38 0s. 7d.	—
1467–1468	£117 16s. 1d.	£102 6s. 10d.	87%
1470–1471	£178 16s. 6d.	£159 10s. 9d.	89%
1484–1485[1]	—	£ 26 18s. 8d.	—[2]
1485–1486[1]	—	£ 22 11s. 3d.	—
1493–1494[1]	£ 37 1s. 0d.	£ 61 14s. 10d.	167%
1495–1496[1]	—	£ 7 6s. 2d.	—
1499–1500[1]	£ 78 8s. 4d.	£ 36 12s. 10d.	47%
1503–1504[1]	—	£ 9 2s. 7d.	—

Continued next page

Table 6—*Continued*

Sources: W. H. Stevenson, ed., *Records of the Borough of Nottingham*, 5 vols. (London: Bernard Quaritch, 1882–1900), 2:369; 3:62–71, 229–41, 252–66, 270–81, 285–95, 311–21, 412–23. Unpublished account rolls in the Nottingham Record Office are too fragmentary for useful inclusion here.

[1] Partial account only
[2] Legal problems concerning John Mapperley and the Corner Wong property consumed £14 15s., or 55% of the expenses

Table 7: York finances, 1396–1509 (domestic budget)

	Total receipts	Net Expenses[1]	Net expenses as percentage of receipts
1396–1397	—	£408 12s. 9.5d.[2]	—
1433–1434	£235 4s. 4 d.	—	—
1442–1443	£230 7s. 1.5d.	£178 19s. 2 d.	78%
1445–1446	£237 1s. 8 d.	£230 2s. 5.5d.	97%
1449–1450	£202 10s. 9 d.	—	—
1453–1454	£204 11s. 4 d.	£224 19s. 9 d.	110%
1454-1455[3]	£203 2s. 5.5d.	£220 12s. 1 d.	109%
1462–1463	£195 2s. 5 d.	£196 3s. 2.5d.	101%
1468–1469	£254 16s. 10.5d.	£198 6s. 7.5d.	78%
1470–1471	£343 4s. 11 d.	£234 17s. 8 d.	68%
1475–1476	£182 18s. 5.5 d.	£247 3s. 7 d.	135%
1478-1479[4]	£237 16s. 3.5 d.	£249 2s. 8 d.[5]	105%
1486–1487	£219 10s. 7 d.	£310 15s. 5 d.	142%
1499–1500	£232 1s. 4 d.	£188 1s. 1 d.	82%
1501–1502	£272 17s. 0 d.	£210 15s. 6 d.	77%
1506–1507	£217 3s. 0 d.	£221 6s. 4.5d.	102%
1508-1509[6]	£199 7s. 4.5 d.	£189 1s. 7.5d.	95%

Sources: Dobson, *Chamberlains' Accounts*, Appendix II (1396–1500); Y.C.A., C5:1, C5:2, C5:3 (1501–1509).

Continued next page

Table 7—*Continued*

[1] Excludes deficits carried over from the previous account (*superplusagium*).   Such deficits ranged from a low of £23 in 1475–76 to over £506 in 1486–87.
[2] Only gross total expenses are included on this account.
[3] For the reign of Henry VI (1422–61) covered by these six accounts, average receipts totaled approximately £219, average net expenses £214, consuming 98% of receipts.
[4] For the reign of Edward IV (1461–83) covered by these five accounts, average receipts totaled approximately £243, average net expenses £225, consuming 93% of receipts.
[5] Account fragmentary, partial expenses only
[6] For the reign of Henry VII (1485–1509) covered by these five accounts, average receipts totaled approximately £228, average net expenses £224, consuming 98% of receipts.

southwestern cloth, Exeter also prospered from wine imports, fishing, and the tin trade.[5] City receipts, derived from rents and charges on trade, rose by 44% between the reigns of Richard II and Henry VII. Although expenses rose even more sharply (by 73%) and receipts were increasingly consumed, officials were able to balance their books in all but seven years.

New ways to spend money kept pace with the growing receipts in a borough eager to join the major leagues. With the exception of Richard III's reign, the years 1403–5 and 1430–31 proved the most trying for Exeter's citizens, with expenses swollen by wall repairs, legal fees, and gifts to city patrons. In 1445, the city became seriously involved in Crown courts over jurisdiction issues with the cathedral, yet expenses for the latter half of Henry VI's reign are the lowest recorded even with gifts and legal fees consuming nearly 8% of receipts. Beginning in Edward IV's reign, the receivers began to note uncollectable ("defective") rents, which composed no more than 4% of receipts but whose very notice on the rolls indicates civic concern over finances during the mid-century slump. The visits of Richard III in 1483 and Henry VII in 1497 caused expenses to soar as the city scrambled to extend sumptuous hospitality, initiate judicial proceedings against rebels, and attend to needed work on the guildhall, roads, and bridges. Although Exeter experienced increasing financial demands over time, those demands did not yet exceed the sources of its wealth.

Norwich records present a mixed picture (Table 5), which may help to explain discrepancies between actual budgets and perceptions of them. Early in Richard II's reign, civic officials bought lands, stalls, and other properties to increase urban income almost three-fold. Rents and increases in admissions to the freedom allowed the city to undertake building and repair during Henry IV's reign and to pursue the acquisition of a new charter, although these activities increased their expenses.[6] After 1400, receipts became less predictable, provoking cries of poverty. Their comparatively high level under Henry VI is remarkable considering that the city spent part of the reign without its privileges and torn by factionalism. The increase was largely the result of the burgeoning cloth manufacture which filled rental properties and swelled the ranks of freemen. The increase did not last, thanks in part to heavy royal fines levied on the unruly citizens but also to a steady decrease in the value of traditional revenues like tolls and the ancient property tax "landgable."[7] Yet another cause of the lowered receipts was lack of attendance at the two annual fairs granted in 1482.[8]

By Henry VII's reign, Norwich officials enjoyed 17% less revenue than had their predecessors a century earlier, although they lowered their expenses 22% as well. Nevertheless, expenses rarely exceeded receipts, at least on parchment.[9] Expenses consumed most of receipts under Edward IV, with almost 8% of the latter diverted to patronage of local Yorkist nobles, royal relations, and to legal advisors, all of whom were expected to help with the city's jurisdiction problems. Such gifts were halved under Henry VII, whose reign saw the lowest level of urban expense. But neither the officers nor the citizens focused only on the bottom line: throughout the fifteenth century, they perceived Norwich as poverty stricken, especially when required to make traditional payments. Whatever their budgeting success, the stress involved in keeping expenses low communicated to them a more dire financial profile than modern statistics reveal.

Generalizations are more dangerous to make in the cases of Nottingham and York. Accounts for the former (Table 6) do not begin until Edward IV's reign, and only four of the ten surviving rolls contain complete and credible figures. It is difficult to calculate even average receipts during the period, although they probably hovered around £120 *per annum*. Nottingham's narrative records contain few complaints of poverty, and there is little on the surviving fiscal accounts to argue for severe financial problems during the second half of the fifteenth century.

York's seventeen surviving accounts reveal that the city enjoyed receipts worth almost twice that of Nottingham, but that they failed to keep its chamberlains out of debt. Over the course of the fifteenth century, admissions to the freedom declined steadily, as did property rents, merchandise tolls, and the farm of the crane, sources that attest to York's depressed commercial state.[10] York's expenses remained at such a high level (on average £216 *per annum*) that receipts did not cover them and a deficit (*superplusagium*) appeared on many accounts. (This deficit has been subtracted in Table 7 to reveal actual and renewable [net] expenses, i.e., for wages, gifts, and repairs. But even without the deficit, the city spent more than it collected nearly half the time.) Royal visits could make even small deficits difficult to recover from: in 1396, two silver dishes presented to Richard II cost the city an extra £200, while a "convenyent shew" organized for Henry VII's first visit in 1486 helped to raise total expenditure to over £300. Contributions to Edward IV's military campaigns against the Scots also taxed York's resources during the 1460s. By 1484, the mayor and council were forced to elect four chamberlains rather than three to share the burdens of that office, and many freemen chose to pay fines of five to ten pounds rather than take up such an arduous task.[11] The most stringent economies, ordered by the mayor and council in 1490, could not reduce the chamberlains' basic commitments to less than £188. Unlike Norwich and Exeter, the city of York lost ground at each successive accounting, and its officers' pleas of poverty expressed true distress, which only deepened during the reigns of Henry VIII and his children.[12]

Fee Farms

Even York might have been able to survive and perhaps prosper if no further demands had been made upon its resources. But no medieval town existed in a vacuum. The Crown expected a variety of payments from its urban subjects, granting in return a complex of privileges which sometimes did little more than assure that townspeople themselves would pay the central government instead of suffering the intrusion of royal officials. Crown demands for direct payments were commonplace elements of the relationship; reductions in taxes and dismissals of farms were extraordinary measures made in response to specific town pleas for royal mercy. The payment of such sums was as much a recognition of a monarch's power and status as was the raising of troops for the defense of the realm, but more costly and more frequent.

The most regular and predictable payment made to the royal

government was a town's fee farm (*firma burgi*). Each year the sheriff of the county or the town's own officers made this fixed payment to the Exchequer, in lieu of a variety of small payments demanded by the Crown in recognition of a town's favored status. Fee farms resulted from proceeds from fairs, rents, and tolls levied on merchandise entering the town and sold in its markets.[13] Nottingham required its bakers to contribute £3 to the king's fee farm, and its bailiffs confiscated a pot worth ten shillings when one baker refused to pay her share. One citizen took zealous officials to court for unjustly detaining his washing-jug and basin as security for a fee farm payment not due until the following day. Nottingham's archives also preserve a rare surviving sheriff's account of 1430–31, revealing the properties, guilds, and even former Jews' properties that contributed to its payment to the Crown.[14] No source of wealth was too mundane for borough sheriffs and bailiffs to tap when the Exchequer demanded satisfaction.

Fee farms provided the royal government with nearly £2500 *per annum*, 90% of which was alienated to royal pensioners, ecclesiastical foundations, or used to repay Crown lenders.[15] Each queen during these centuries enjoyed a small sum "what is due her" derived from borough fee farms. More essential to personal financial survival were the annuities fed by Norwich and Nottingham farms and given to unemployed clerks and yeomen of the crown until they found work paying a comparable wage.[16] Religious establishments benefited from fee farms: Exeter's annual payment of £45 12s. 6d. contributed almost equally to the Crown and Holy Trinity Priory, London; while Nottingham's farm supported an anchorite, a recluse, and a Derby convent whose nuns had been praying for King John since Henry III's reign.[17] Urban farms covered kings' jewelry costs and household expenses, proving to be modest but generally dependable sources of financing for the myriad of debts the royal government could incur.[18]

Fee farm amounts had been set early in the towns' histories, often in the twelfth century, and tied to trade and revenue levels of those years. Many civic officials of the fourteenth and fifteenth centuries bitterly complained that their towns no longer reached such levels of commerce and begged the king to ease their burdens.[19] Trade-based revenues were also difficult to collect and pay to the royal government when the Crown seized borough privileges in punishment for local unrest and violence, Norwich's particular problem during the 1430s and 1440s. Between 1443 and 1447, the city made no fee farm payments and accumulated a debt of over £440, arguing that "by reason of this seizure the citizens from the day their liberties were taken have totally lost all the profits of their courts, of the market and tollhouse, from strangers coming to the city to sell or buy."[20] Norwich's commercial growth during this period should have made its sheriffs immune to financial pressure, had not its loss of liberties decreased the very activities that contributed to the farm.

The story of York's problems with its fee farm during the reigns of Richard III and Henry VII sheds light not only on local economic conditions but also on the changing nature of accounting within the royal government. Taking place at a time when the Chamber was more active in accounting and payment than the more traditional offices of finance, the dilemma reveals the conservative nature of many Exchequer records and casts that office in the worst possible light.[21] Slow to note changes in debts and even slower to act on them, Exchequer clerks in particular and Crown financial machinery in general were ignorant of many urban needs and the ways in which kings tried to help. Even when formal records acknowledged local conditions, contradictory writs and lack of coordination between Westminster offices deterred implementation. In all cases of town pleas for financial assistance, the Crown had to weigh the cost of helping and thereby waiving its claim to revenue, against ignoring the petition. If a king chose the latter course, he could survive a rebuffed town's resentment, but at the same time he ran the risk of losing all the revenues due him if the town fell into irrevocable debt. In York's case, both Richard III and Henry VII chose to help, but their actions plunged the city into fifty years of confusion over the nature of its fiscal relationship with the Crown.

At the time of Domesday Book, York owed the king £100 *per annum* for the fee farm, an amount that rose to £160 in 1212 and remained at that figure for the rest of the medieval period.[22] From 1318, £100 of the farm was alienated each year to the Roos family of Yorkshire in exchange for a strategic castle held by William the second Lord Roos.[23] The pension remained in the family, benefiting even Roos widows, until 1461 when Thomas the ninth lord chose to support Henry VI rather than Edward of March at the battle of Towton. Upon Thomas's attainder in Edward IV's first parliament, forty marks *per annum* of the original parcel were given to the king's brother, George of Clarence.[24] Clarence's own attainder in 1478 benefited one of the king's servants, Sir John Savage, who gained the forty-mark annuity the following year.[25] Other annuitants dependent upon York's farm included Saint Stephen's chapel,

Westminster (£35 14s. 7d. p.a.); civic attorney and baron of the Exchequer Brian Roucliff (£20); royal French secretary Stephen Fryan (£10); and the heirs of the king's lardiner in the nearby forest of Galtres (£7 12s. 1d.).[26] In addition, from 1478 to 1481 Richard of Gloucester received £50 p.a. in partial payment of his salary as warden of the west marches towards Scotland. In 1482, he became keeper of the farm, rendering £50 p.a.[27] Thus, the city's continued payment of the farm assured the Crown of a stable, efficient means by which to reward its dependents.

By the early 1480s, however, the fee farm began to be viewed by civic officials as York's chief financial burden. In 1482, the city noted with distress that various northern towns had gained exemptions from tolls when trading in York. Knowing that tolls composed a large part of the fee farm, civic officials asked Edward IV either to restore the tolls or "els to have a metigacion of the kynges ferm of as moch as the tolles of the said towns amountes."[28] The king did not act on the request, but his successor Richard III responded to the complaint during his visit to the city in September 1483. In a move planned to garner northern support, Richard released all toll charges in order to promote increased trade in the city. This loss of an estimated £58 11s. 2d. *per annum* was eased by a gift of £40 p.a. to the community and of £18 5s. p.a. granted to the mayor as the king's chief serjeant-at-arms. There was no overt recognition that tolls composed part of the fee farm: if the release of toll payments had been meant to bring about a concomitant easing of shrieval responsibilities to the Crown, this was not clearly stated. The ambiguities of the meeting must have occurred to York officials as well, for within a week the council sent three aldermen to Pontefract, Richard's next stop on his royal progress, in order to discuss the terms of the York grants.[29]

Although there is neither Exchequer nor Chancery evidence that autumn for confirmation of full dismissal of the fee farm, Richard's intent was clear. Just before leaving York, the king arranged for John Savage to continue receiving his annuity from a source other than York's farm.[30] Savage's important holdings in South Wales and his family ties to the Stanleys made him a figure Richard hesitated to slight, so the king worked rapidly for the knight to retain his pension. But York was no less important to a king eager for support. In February 1484, letters patent noted that Richard remitted £60 *per annum* of the farm, a payment combining the £40 annuity with £20 remitted "for the relief of the poverty of the city and the repair of the walls." More important, the king released the residue of the farm, freeing the sheriffs even from making an account.[31]

Records of both the Crown and York's council reveal the lasting confusion that arose from the waiver of tolls and the changes in Savage's pension. Pipe and memoranda rolls continue to provide us with records of expected payments and assignments: for the first year of Richard's reign they noted that £60 should be remitted to the city, as well as a prorated sum representing the fee farm debt after the February 1484 letter patent. The roll for the following year, Richard's last, contained much the same information, and both accounts concluded that York sheriffs were quit of all debts.[32] But local records indicate that the officers had trouble collecting what was due them. In September 1484, the city received a writ under Richard's sign manual, containing the release of the farm and authorizing a privy seal document to take effect. However, within two weeks recorder Miles Metcalf met with the king in order to assure that the privy seal would be executed properly. Metcalf failed to get a guarantee, and he spent most of the autumn and winter 1484–85 in London negotiating for confirmation of the king's fee farm release by the barons of the Exchequer, "and also for the purchesing of a newe graunt, for soo moch as the first [of February 1484] was not sufficient for the discharge of the said ffee ferme...."[33] Whatever the pipe rolls declared, clearly the sheriffs were not receiving their due at the Exchequer nor had the original royal grant been fully accepted. It should be noted that however dependent Richard was upon Chamber financing, York's officials dealt with the barons of the Exchequer for fee farm accounting rather than appointed receivers, and the king's own directions always addressed those barons regarding York's problems. It is possible, however, for the fee farm to have fallen between the two offices, creating the confusion over waivers and payments.

Matters worsened upon Henry VII's accession. The pipe roll account for his first year is incomplete, and contains the wildly inaccurate statement that Richard of Gloucester was not only alive but deeply in debt as receiver of York's fee farm. Indeed, the city's total debt for the year came to £376 12s.[34] Unable or unwilling to pay, the officers incurred a debt that was carried over to the account of 1486–87, on which the duke of Gloucester still appeared but which did not mention Henry's own confirmation of Richard's original release.[35] Both the king and York's sheriffs became aware that the Exchequer had not accepted or acknowledged the releases, a refusal that perhaps encouraged Henry to claim over £112 for household expenses from a fee farm that supposedly no longer existed.[36] A new recorder called upon the Exchequer, whose officials were "not very certaine nor stable of ther opinion," despite the gifts he lavished upon them. The recorder achieved little more than confirmation of the grants due the city.[37]

Although Exchequer records for the remainder of Henry VII's reign recognized the releases and declared the sheriffs quit of most debts, civic officials became increasingly uncertain and confused.[38] They were ignorant of how the city was supposed to satisfy the annuitants (apart from Savage) dependent upon the farm, never specified in the records. The Roos family caused the most trouble in this respect, when the young lord claimed the traditional pension by arguing that his father's attainder had been reversed by Henry VII's accession.[39] His heirs continued the claim and sued the city for their annuity. Uncertainty about the extent of York's responsibility to the Crown continued well into Henry VIII's reign, during which the mayor confessed in desperation that if forced to pay the fee farm and the Roos annuity, the citizens would desert the city and surrender the liberties into the king's hands.[40]

Both the problem and the records that describe it indicate the complex nature of fiscal machinery which prevented the king and his urban subjects from fully understanding the processes of government. Fee farm waivers were not unique to York—Chester, Chichester, Gloucester, and Nottingham all received such boons between 1462 and 1488[41]—but none caused the problems experienced by York. Even Norwich had an easier time winning concessions from the Crown than did the northern capital. Part of the difficulty lay with the vague manner in which the original grant was expressed, even if one is not cynical enough to accuse the kings of promising fiscal releases they had no intention of honoring. Financial responsibilities shared by both the Exchequer and the Chamber after 1462 may have contributed to the confusion, although civic authorities always seemed sure they should deal with officials of the former. It is more likely that both Crown and town shared desperation for both revenue and respect. Neither the last Yorkist monarch nor the first Tudor could do without the £160 farm or the support of the city that paid it. In the end, urban subjects suffered most of all, as confused courts and accounts recorded an ever-increasing lien against York's slender revenues.

Direct Taxation

Direct taxation in the form of the lay subsidy assessments (the fifteenths and tenths) burdened urban budgets less regularly than the fee farms. A parliamentary tax usually granted to boost Crown revenue in times of war, the levy was defined as the fifteenth part of the value of movable property belonging to persons outside the royal demesne, and the tenth part of such value within the demesne and in cities and boroughs. Since John's reign, the tax had been assessed anew at each grant, until it was fixed in 1334 on the basis of a composition between royal commissioners and the communities that paid it. The composition did not result from an accurate assessment of local wealth, but the charges certainly reflected the boroughs' relative status in pre-plague England: York's payment slightly exceeded its fee farm, while Exeter's charge of less than £37 per subsidy matched the borough's modest profile. Calculated at just over £37,000, one fifteenth and a tenth was equal to 70–101% of the four boroughs' fee farms, and had to be raised in addition to the farm and the revenues directed solely to local expenses.[42]

The collection of an established and agreed upon sum according to a time-honored system proved easy to accept. Poll taxes and other extraordinary subsidies sometimes provoked hostile reactions, but violence is not generally associated with the fifteenths and tenths. Collectors were appointed by royal commission, and for borough collection they were obliged to choose town inhabitants to oversee the actual levy. Although these residents were in turn to appoint one or two of the "more sufficient" citizens to gather the money or (if wealthy) to advance the total sum, double delegation of power did not always take place. York records reveal that the city's tax burden was divided into fixed quotas for each parish. Residents paid in the parish in which they lived with their wives and children, although the city complained about those who moved to more lightly taxed parishes whenever a subsidy was imposed. Merchants, bakers, hostelers and weavers executed the job of collection during Henry V's reign, with such vigor that in 1420 they even collected from a suburb usually considered within the North Riding.[43] How hard these collectors pressed their own friends and neighbors for payment is less easy to determine.

Records of the lay subsidy provide another test for the veracity of poverty pleas. Plaintive complaints of being unable to collect the tax pepper York's city council records during the 1490s. York's cries of poverty had increased in eloquence and urgency over time, so that by 1492 even the king agreed that the parish quotas had to be adjusted to ease the burden. Although this was done, six years later the collectors still complained they could raise no money and that the poor were bearing too much of the burden and wealthy civic officials not enough.[44] Parish assessments of 1334 had obviously not kept pace with the redistribution of wealth of the post-plague economy, and to their critics civic officials appeared undertaxed.

The collectors had few powers and fewer thanks for their services. No one in Nottingham complained when Edward IV notified town officials that he had canceled collection of a subsidy after he dissolved his military expedition of 1475 and came to terms with the French king.[45] Unsuccessful collectors faced the wrath of their neighbors, Exchequer clerks, Chamber receivers, and the king himself. Unpaid by the central government, they received wine and minor payments from city councils: a reward of one mark from Exeter's council, and two marks from Norwich, doubtless in addition to bribes advanced by inhabitants.[46] The collectors were empowered to distrain property if citizens did not contribute, and municipal sheriffs could imprison the recalcitrant.[47] Payment of the subsidies could extend over several Exchequer terms, but in general 80% of the money was collected a year after most fifteenths and tenths were granted.[48]

The greatest drawback to the lay subsidy was its fixed quotas, inhibiting the wealthier from taking on a greater share of the burden than the poor. However, the alternative forms of direct taxation devised to effect proportioned contributions proved difficult and unprofitable to collect. The most notorious, the poll taxes of the 1370s and 1380–1, were marked by evasion as well as by violent resistance. In 1377, York paid £120, which at 4d. *per capita* indicated at least 7200 taxable residents. The total national yield of only c. £22,000 encouraged the disappointed government to impose graduated assessments, then to combine them with the original flat rate, a move that sparked the Great Revolt of 1381. It is well known that the returns recorded a marked diminution of population too great to be explained by death or migration. Some historians have interpreted the discrepancies as evasions (44% in York, somewhat less in the other three boroughs), although a more sanguine school argues for deliberate exclusion in order to spare the very poor.[49] Whatever the truth of the matter, the government's overwhelming lack of success with poll taxes inhibited innovation for the rest of Richard II's reign. In 1404, Henry IV revitalized feudal aids for the marriage of his daughter, to which York (the only city mentioned on the writ) seems to have contributed 10s.[50] Taxes on knights' fees and the value of landholdings and incomes affected boroughs throughout the reigns of Henry IV and Henry VI. The 1428 levy on householders within parishes raised over £23 from York, less than half that from Norwich, and just over £5 from Nottingham, for a national total of less than a quarter of the anticipated £12,291.[51] Levies on incomes from land, offices, and annuities netted about £9000 in 1436, and two-thirds that sum in 1450-51.[52] Such taxes identified and mulcted the wealthiest urban subjects, whose goodwill and voluntary contributions were too valuable to make this form of assessment more than a temporary expedient. Parliament was so chary of these unusual taxes that its members usually refused to record them in detail and barred them from creating a precedent. It remained the opinion of the commons that the fixed and largely underestimated sums of the fifteenth and tenth comprised "the moost easy, redy and prone payment of any charge to be born within this Realme."[53]

Towns also took responsibility for the collection of taxes on alien merchants. Throughout the fifteenth century, the Crown kept close watch on non-English merchants and craftsmen. Aliens had to petition for letters of denization and privileges of landholding and property inheritance, while in 1436 they were required to take oaths of fealty before bailiffs and other urban officers.[54] In 1440, the Crown collected its first alien subsidy, the proceeds earmarked for naval defense. Alien householders paid 16d., and residents 6d.; if all had paid dutifully, the Crown would have been richer by c.£700. Only half that sum was realized, and the subsidy never affected the wealthier merchants who had been given exemptions in exchange for their commerce and their loans. Valid for two years, the grant was renewed in 1442 and upon several other occasions into Henry VII's reign.[55] In general, however, the returns tell us more about the distribution and origin of aliens in England than about financial contributions. Natives of Iceland and Scotland predominated in York; Norwich hosted craftsmen from the Low Countries; and French and Irish resided in Devonshire. The sums collected in boroughs were usually under £1.[56] Mayors, sheriffs and aldermen received orders from Chancery to record the names of aliens and collect the money, so small a contribution to Crown resources that surveillance of foreigners may have been the more practical result of the levy.[57]

Whatever their ease of collection and general public acceptance, these examples of direct taxation created an extra burden for town budgets. Table 8 indicates how heavy that burden could be even if measuring only the lay subsidies and extending their demands evenly over an entire reign. Although the actual borough contributions formed a very small part of the national total (less than 1% in each of the four cases), the sums had to be found without excessive delay or excuse. York's assessment of £162 per subsidy meant that for every grant parliament approved it had to raise an amount slightly in excess of its annual fee farm. Exeter's and Nottingham's assessments (slightly more than £36 and £37 respectively) were very modest, and even Norwich's subsidy of over £94 was less than either its fee farm or its average local receipts.

Tax burdens varied from monarch to monarch, as the progress of war with France influenced parliamentary grants. As expected during a reign requiring heavy support of military activity, towns paid most, in the shortest period of time, under Henry V, who was granted more than one levy for each year on the throne. This meant that in theory Exeter, for example, had to find an extra £38 *per annum* to pay the subsidy, equivalent to more than 80% of the fee farm sum the Crown also expected to be paid annually. Specifically, the years 1416–20 were hardest on towns, for over six grants were made during those years. Although Adam of Usk reported contemporary complaints about the tax levies, expressed with "murmurs and with smothered curses...from the hatred of the burden,"[58] the four boroughs did not complain for over a decade. Simple pride in the king's achievements may have carried even stretched urban budgets into Henry VI's reign, when both military and economic stalemate proved discouraging. In 1433, pleas of poverty throughout the realm convinced the government to return to stricken areas £4000 from each levy. Complaints continued, and in 1445 the reduction had to be raised to £6000 per grant.[59] York had the most reason to appreciate the rebates: its obligation was reduced at first by almost £17 and later by more than £25, and still the collectors could come up empty-handed. Even Exeter, whose economy benefited from a healthy cloth trade and population growth even in the 1440s, received small waivers of £5 to £8.[60] Nevertheless, York excepted, the boroughs raised the money with little more than stereotypical grumbling. The number of lay subsidies granted was never excessive, and actually decreased during the

Table 8: Lay subsidies required of the four boroughs, 1377–1509 (drain on town economy in pounds *per annum*)

	Total number of subsidies	Exeter: average share, per annum	Norwich: average share, per annum	Nottingham: average share, per annum	York: average share, per annum
Richard II 1377–1399	12.5	£21	£54	£21	£ 92
Henry IV 1399–1413	8	£21	£54	£21	£ 92.5
Henry V 1413–1422	10.33	£38	£98	£38	£167
Henry VI 1422–1432	3.83	£13	£33	£13	£ 56
1433–1444	5.5[1]	£14	£39	£17	£ 66
1445–1461	4.5[2]	£ 8	£22	£10	£ 38
Edward IV 1461–1483[3]	5[2]	£ 6.5	£18	£ 8	£ 31
Henry VII 1485–1509[3]	7[2]	£ 8	£23	£11	£ 40

[1] £4000 returned from each grant to neediest areas.
[2] £6000 returned from each grant to neediest areas.
[3] For calculations including alternative subsidies and income taxes granted during the reign, see below.

Note: before reductions, one fifteenth and one tenth yielded approximately c.£37,429 18s. J. F. Ramsay (*Lancaster and York*, 1:152) estimates that each subsidy netted the Crown £36,000, allowing for losses due to collectors' remuneration, permitted exemptions and deductions, and bad debts. R. S. Schofield ("Parliamentary Lay Taxation 1485–1547," p. 416) estimates that the net yield on the reduced subsidies of Henry VII's reign was c. £29,000.

Continued next page

Table 8—*Continued*

Borough shares before reductions: Exeter, £36 12s. 4d. per subsidy (0.098% of national total); Norwich, £94 12s. 0d. per subsidy (0.25%); Nottingham, £37 1s. 0d. (0.099%); York, £162 (0.43%). By way of contrast, London was assessed at £733 6s. 8d. (2%).

course of the fifteenth century as monarchs found other sources of revenue. That the towns' own representatives had agreed to the grants, and used their full power (*plena potestas*) to bind their communities to their decisions, may also have reconciled the boroughs to their financial fate.

Loans

Cash loans to the Crown constituted one of the most unpredictable drains upon urban resources. Although London rather than the four provincial boroughs received the most demands, any town found it as difficult to refuse a loan to a monarch as it was to deny him troops or hospitality. Whether the occasion was the French threat to Gascony, a royal marriage, or a spurious attack on Calais, "it is spoken of as an urgent necessity, a threat to the safety of the realm, or an opportunity for removing such a threat," and was expressed in stereotypical phrases that changed little between 1377 and 1509. Requests for loans also allowed monarchs to redress the imbalance between urban assessments for the lay subsidy and actual town wealth.[61]

Lending was not a problem that affected only the governors of a town. In 1409, Norwich lent 500 marks to the king, 60% of which was raised out of common funds. The remainder had to be assessed by a general levy that affected all but the poorest citizens.[62] However, loans were negotiable to a greater extent than the lay subsidies. Monarchs commissioned men of standing and wealth in each county to persuade others, including towns, to provide support. Boroughs conferred among themselves as well, as in 1475 when Norwich sent a representative to Bury St. Edmunds to determine how much money other burgesses were prepared to lend the king.[63] When the amount was decided, the money could flow from chamberlains' surplus, general levies, or the personal generosity of aldermen and other civic officials interested in advertising their wealth and increasing their local stature.[64]

Methods of repayment depended upon the nature of the need and the reign in which the loan was made. A study of London corporate loans from 1400 to 1450 reveals that the city lent money out of a sense of duty and in response to the king's necessity, eschewing interest payments in the hope that the loans would be viewed "as oil to lubricate the machinery of royal favor and privilege."[65] Before 1450, monarchs took seriously their promises to repay, often providing lenders with tallies of assignment on the wool subsidy, the customs from a nearby port, or the lay subsidy next levied on the community that offered the money. Throughout his reign, Henry IV rewarded corporate and individual lenders with the right to export wool without paying duty, a method of repayment convenient only to those who participated in the trade.[66] Repayment plans exemplified the truism that it takes money to make money. During reigns with frequent tax levies, subjects lent frequently, for repayment could be made from the next fifteenth and tenth. At the end of Henry VI's reign, for example, when parliament granted few taxes, individuals and boroughs showed more reluctance to lend because reimbursement could not be so easily guaranteed, especially in a contracting economy.[67]

The system did not always work smoothly. In 1436, Norwich lent the Crown £100, which failed to be covered as promised by the fifteenth from the county of Essex. Four years later, the citizens sued in Exchequer for its recovery, for they hoped to give the sum to the duke of Gloucester who was planning a visit.[68] The use of jewels as sureties caused problems as well. Henry V pledged swords, crowns and ornaments to raise money from boroughs, whose officers were burdened with the safekeeping of these objects and the dilemma whether to sell them if the king defaulted. In 1415, Henry pledged a tabernacle of jeweled silver gilt, raising a total of 860 marks, one hundred of which came from Exeter. Civic officials shared the care of the item with Devon abbeys and gentry, and had to answer in Exchequer for it, at a cost of 3s. 4d each trip. Although licensed to dispose of the tabernacle if the king did not repay the loans, the caretakers did not do so, and in 1422 carriage of the object back to London cost Exeter officials an extra 20d.—petty sums entailing maximum annoyance.[69] Norwich officials shared this reluctance to sell one of Henry V's gold coronets. In 1417–18, they sent a representative to Exchequer to sue for the money due them. When this move failed, the jewel itself made the trip south in 1420, but again the city (along with Lynn, which shared responsibility) failed to obtain payment. In 1424, Norwich officials began a suit in Exchequer and approached urban patrons Sir Thomas Erpingham and the bishop of Norwich for advice, but five years later they succeeded only in redeeming the circlet for 60% less than their advance. The unhappy experience did, however, prevent Henry V from demanding further loans from them for the remainder of his reign.[70]

Despite these bad experiences, almost totally confined to the reign of Henry V, Ricardian and Lancastrian borrowing fulfilled an immediate need and adequately secured repayment. Loan demands were never cheerfully welcomed by boroughs, but town officials calculated such outlay as shrewd investments. When at all possible, town governments tried to respond positively if incompletely to the king's call for funds. In many cases, the loans acted as another form of urban patronage, more effective than gifts of wine or small pensions in convincing the monarch to extend his favor and grant a desired charter or privilege. Lending money may also have helped many subjects feel a part of the government and its actions, a welcome impression as Crown machinery adopted the attributes of bureaucracy and fell out of touch with local conditions and needs. Still, not every borough lent money. Given Exeter's burgeoning economy, we might expect it to have provided more cash than the records describe. The city did not escape Henry V's demands, but otherwise its resources remained underutilized. However, an unspecified loan extended in 1448 for victualing and furnishing three ships to transport soldiers to Brittany reminds us of the port city's responsibilities towards England's naval forces in the Hundred Years' War.[71] Exeter and its wealthier mercantile citizens provided men, ships, and supplies, which may have excused the borough from more frequent offerings of cash gifts.

But boroughs could have very specific and selfish reasons for lending. Anxious for increases in chartered privileges, Norwich lent an average of £39 *per annum* during Richard II's reign (almost half of it during his final decade); £90 p.a. under Henry IV; and £100 p.a. to Henry V (see Table 9). Cries of poverty lay in the future: in 1397, when a few citizens rashly promised the king a corporate loan of 500 marks, the city hoped he could accept less, yet found the money when asked. A town aspiring to county status could do no less, one reason why Norwich advanced 1000 marks to Henry IV soon after his accession.[72] Direct benefits such as the acquisition of municipal offices and trading privileges also persuaded York to lend money during this period. Richard

II received two loans of £200 each in addition to gifts and hospitality during his visits, and over £1300 was granted to Henry IV corporately during the first five years of his reign. These loans also provide insight into the borough's attitude towards the Lancastrian usurpation. In 1398, York's mayor and sheriffs joined the king's serjeant-at-arms to obtain payment from various citizens pledged by letters obligatory to pay the king £2000. Their unwillingness to pay may have encouraged the city to support Henry of Bolingbroke with 500 marks upon his landing at Ravenspur, followed by another 1000 marks after his accession for household expenses.[73]

Borrowing patterns changed under the Yorkist monarchs, affecting boroughs' responses to demands. By modifying both the reasons given for advances and the ways in which the money was collected, the Yorkists discovered that funds did not always have to be repaid. The urban protestations of poverty that convinced a weaker predecessor had less effect upon the propagator of benevolences. Edward IV was quick to remind his subjects that "by the lawe we may call and lawfully compelle [you] to go with us . . . into any place of this land for the defens of the same against outward enemyes." He defined the loans he called benevolences as little more than the equivalent of such personal service, and no more likely to be repaid. Whether through commissioners or more effectively during personal visits, the king reminded urban subjects in particular how he was sparing them the inconvenience of personal military service, only asking for what they "list give of their free will."[74] Fortunately for town governments, the Yorkists and the first Tudor found it more profitable to approach wealthy individuals rather than reluctant city councils. As a result, York (a heavy contributor to the Scottish campaigns) was corporately responsible for no loan during Edward's reign and Norwich for less than £250.[75] This strategy provides yet more evidence of the straitened circumstances of borough corporations and the underassessment of the king's wealthiest urban subjects.

Although repayment was unpredictable and interest nonexistent (unless built into the original sum borrowed), boroughs tried hard to respond positively to Crown demands for support. Whatever the reality of their cries of poverty, the towns rarely demurred even if they could provide only part of the sum requested with major contributions coming from individuals rather than the corporation. For towns still intent upon augmenting chartered liberties, the loans acted as another form of urban patronage, although the records are mostly silent when it came to noting

Table 9: Urban loans, 1378–1482

	Exeter	Norwich	Nottingham	York
Richard II:				
1378		400 marks		
1379			100 marks[1]	
1380			100 marks	
1385		250 marks		£163
1386		£100	£50	£200
1397		500 marks	100 marks	£200
Henry IV:				
1400				1500 m.[2]
1402		1000 marks		
1403				500 marks
1404			100 marks[1]	£200[1]
1407			100 marks	
1409		500 marks		
1412		400 marks		
Henry V:				
1415	100 marks	500 marks		
1417		1000 marks		£454[3]
Henry VI[4]:				
1430		£94 12s.		£162[1]
1434		£200		
1436	300 marks	800 marks	£106	1000 m.[5]
1437		£100		
1442				100 marks
1446				100 marks
1448	?[6]			
1452		100 marks		
1454		£100		£100
Edward IV:				
1465				£46 13s.[1]
1481		£200		
1482		50 marks		

[1] Raised by individuals, not corporately
[2] One-third given before Henry IV's accession

Continued next page

Table 9—*Continued*

[3] Total for Henry V's entire reign; may include individual loans as well: Anthony Steel, *Receipt of the Exchequer, 1377–1485* (Cambridge: Cambridge University Press, 1954), p. 196. My own examination of receipt rolls and other sources has not confirmed this high a figure.

[4] Steel, *Receipt of the Exchequer*, pp. 196, 265, 349, notes that for the period 1422–32, Norwich lent £266 and York £162. Between 1432 and 1442, Norwich lent £300, and £38 for the period 1442–52. From 1452 to 1462, Norwich lent 100 marks and Nottingham £153 3s. 2d. The figures do not agree with my own examination of local and Crown records, listed above.

[5] The Crown requested these sums from the boroughs as loans for the army in France under the duke of York's command, February 1436: Nicholas H. Nicolas, ed., *Proceedings and Ordinances of the Privy Council of England*, 7 vols. (London: Record Commission, 1834–37), 4:316–21. They may not have proffered as requested; Norwich's records and the Receipt Rolls reveal that the city lent £100, which the royal government did not repay: P.R.O., E.401/748; N.R.O., 16-d, Assembly Book I, ff. 14r-v.

[6] Unspecified loan from Exeter for victualing ships to Brittany: D.R.O., Bk. 51, f.308v.

urban reasons for and reactions to the loans that were extended.[76] Lending money may have helped many subjects feel a part of the government and its actions. In 1421, for example, a complex and costly system of commissions raised £9000 by contributions from over five hundred sources (towns, wapentakes, vills and individuals) whose collective nature swelled the number of people actually involved.[77] As shown above, the large number of tax levies during the reign freed lenders from worry about repayment, but something less mercenary may have been at stake. By way of loans, a large proportion of the country became directly involved in the regime and its military ventures, and could identify future actions as ones partly of their own making.

"Total" Demands

The precise nature of Crown claims on urban finances will never be known, but further analysis can be made from the preceding material and a study of Crown documents. Despite some outdated material copied onto the rolls for years without question or correction, as well as the later reliance upon Chamber financing, the Exchequer's pipe and memoranda rolls usefully record towns' basic debts to the central government. The rolls reveal what proportion of the money was actually paid in or previously alienated, and how much (if any) the local officials still owed. Pipe roll sums included the borough fee farm, in addition to a small amount of miscellaneous rents and farms of Jews' houses, mills, and plots of land taken into Crown hands. In York, the basic debt varied from £17 to £83 above the fee farm; in Norwich, payment for land surrounding the castle and taken over by the city increased the figure on average £30 above the fee farm debt of £113.[78]

Crown demands can be compared to local revenues in a number of different ways (Tables 10A, B & C). Although fee farms, taxes and loans were raised separately from the revenues earmarked for internal expenses, towns had a limited number of sources from which to derive payments. In lieu of city sheriffs' accounts, which no longer survive in quantity for the four boroughs, local receipts and expenses provide our only sources for comparison. The results bring us closer to an assessment of urban financial health and pleas of poverty during the period.

The calculations on Table 10A indicate that to satisfy pipe roll clerks alone, the four boroughs had to find sums equal to or exceeding three-quarters of the amount of local receipts listed on chamberlains' accounts (Tables 4–7). Exeter's figures are undoubtedly too low, based as they are only on the borough farm in the absence of detailed entries on the pipe rolls. Nottingham's loss of local records, on the other hand, leaves us only with its modest Crown demands. Norwich experienced the most frustrating times during Henry VI's reign when its liberties were seized, for the inability to pay the fee farm or large fines meant that charges accumulated until all debts were waived. The figures reflect that final disposition, as do those of York under Henry VII, when confusion over the fee farm debt and royal waivers incurred arrears from which the city never entirely recovered.

These figures alone might persuade us to conclude that each borough shouldered at least a modest burden in order to satisfy the royal Exchequer. We know that borough officials complained about raising money for local expenses; Crown clerks demanded that no washing jug or cooking pot be overlooked in the search for sums comparable to what satisfied internal creditors. But Table 10B reveals that with few exceptions city sheriffs met their Exchequer debts in full and on time. Pipe roll entries show that payments and tallies cleared the officers of their charges and sometimes left a minuscule surplus. Delinquency in payment resulted less from outright poverty than from claims of waivers which required due process, although York's fee farm troubles combined

Table 10A: Royal financial needs—Pipe Roll demands by reign averaged *per annum*, and the demands expressed as percentage of local receipts (where available)

	Exeter[1]	Norwich	Nottingham	York
Richard II **1377–1399**	35%	£160, 80%	£114[2]	£177[2]
Henry IV **1399–1413**	32%	£155, 83%	£68[2]	£186[2]
Henry V **1413–1422**	31%	£132, 75%	£76[2]	£225[2]
Henry VI **1422–1432**	33%	£132, 68%	£68[2]	£179[2]
1433–1444	38%	£157, 76%[3]	£65[2]	£179, 77%
1445–1460	33%	£135, 59%[3]	£67[2]	£183, 86%
Edward IV **1461–1483** **and Richard III** **1483–1485**	32%	£139, 95%	£72, 53%	£185, 76%
Henry VII **1485–1509**	24%	£137, 83%	£76[2]	£243, 107%[4]

Sources: P.R.O., E.372 series, Pipe Rolls; Tables 4–7, *supra.*

[1] Exeter does not have a listing separate from Devonshire on the Pipe Rolls. The figures presented here based only on annual Crown demand of £45 12s. 6d. for the fee farm.

[2] Insufficient local financial data.

[3] Excludes the extraordinary debts listed between 21–30 Henry VI (1442–51), when the Pipe Rolls recorded that the fee farm debt was not paid while the city's liberties were seized by the king, and demanded an ever-increasing amount from urban sheriffs. During those years, Pipe Roll demands averaged £517 19s. *per annum*, or 243% of local receipts.

Continued next page

Table10A—*Continued*

[4] Based on corrected figures noted on Pipe Roll entries. The original notations for the first two years of Henry VII's reign included demands for the fee farm (waived by Richard III) and other archaic financial payments. During those two years, the Pipe Rolls demanded £376 12s. (1–2 Henry VII) and £498 4s. (2–3 Henry VII), averaging 199% of local receipts. Although Pipe Roll clerks eventually recognized their error, they nevertheless appear to have hounded York's sheriffs and recorder for the money.

Table 10B: Percentage of debts on Pipe Rolls unpaid to Crown at time of remittance[1]

	Norwich	Nottingham	York
Richard II 1377–1399	3.0%	44.0%	0.3%
Henry IV 1399–1413	6.5%	0%	9.0%
Henry V 1413–1422	0%	0%	10.0%[2]
Henry VI 1422–1460	0%[3]	0%	10.0%
Edward IV 1461–1483 and Richard III 1483–1485	0%	0.9%	1.0%
Henry VII 1485–1509	1.6%	11%	16.0%[4]

Sources: P.R.O., E.372 series

[1] Exeter omitted because its payment history is not discussed at any length under the entries for Devonshire.
[2] Results skewed by unpaid account of 99% of debt, 1419–20; other years of Henry V's reign witnessed 0–2% unpaid balances.
[3] Based on normal demands and payments, not those for the waived fee farm and penalty payments 1442–50, when 52% of the Pipe Roll demands went unpaid each year.
[4] Excludes unpaid balance of over £327 in 1485–86, waived the following year.

Table 10C: Total Crown demands *per annum* (Pipe Roll information plus lay subsidy and loan data)

	Average payments due Crown per annum	Crown demands as percentage of local receipts	Crown demands as percentage of net local expenses
EXETER:[1]			
Richard II	£67	51%	68%
Henry IV	£67	46%	52%
Henry V	£90	62%	72%
Henry VI			
1422–1432	£59	42%	53%
1433–1444	£76	63%	81%
1445–1460	£54	40%	59%
Edward IV	£52	37%	44%
Henry VII	£54	28%	32%
NORWICH:			
Richard II	£253	127%	170%
Henry IV	£299	160%	197%
Henry V	£330	188%	237%
Henry VI			
1422–1432	£174	89%	99%
1433–1444	£229	112%	—[2]
1445–1460	£170	74%	113%
Edward IV	£168	115%	125%
Henry VII	£160	97%	138%

Continued next page

Table 10C—*Continued*

NOTTINGHAM:			
Richard II			
Henry IV	£140	—[2]	—[2]
Henry V	£93	—[2]	—[2]
Henry VI	£114	—[2]	—[2]
1422–1432			
1433–1444	£81	—[2]	—[2]
1445–1460	£91	—[2]	—[2]
Edward IV	£77	—[2]	—[2]
Henry VII	£80	59%	62%
	£87	—[2]	—[2]
YORK:			
Richard II	£295	—[2]	72%[3]
Henry IV	£388	—[2]	—[2]
Henry V	£437	—[2]	—[2]
Henry VI			
1422–1432	£235	—[2]	—[2]
1433–1444	£306	131%	171%
1445–1460	£231	109%	102%
Edward IV	£216	89%	99%
Henry VII	£283	124%	126%

Sources: P.R.O., E.372 series; Tables 8–9 *supra*

[1] Pipe Roll portion of Exeter's payments based only on fee farm sum: see Table 10A, above

[2] Insufficient local data

[3] Based on gross total expenses provided for one accounting year only

the two. We have already seen that lay subsidies and loans found their way to royal coffers without excessive delay. With the addition of the pipe roll evidence, we can conclude that the basic royal financial demands constituted a burden bearable as long as a borough possessed all of its privileges and could document all of its releases.

One last calculation remains to be made. Table 10C adds to the pipe roll figures the average annual drain made by the lay subsidy, and by the average annual burden of loans to the Crown. The results indicate that in order fully to satisfy the Crown's needs for money each year, a borough had to raise all over again the amount it gathered just for local debts. Total royal needs exceeded net local expenses most consistently in Norwich and York. Exeter's modest demands remain affected by our lack of data beyond the fee farm, although we have already seen that the subsidy and loan burdens there were small and befitting a borough that had not yet achieved incorporation. During reigns with frequent tax levies or fee farm problems, however, Crown requests could deal a crippling, though not fatal blow.

Pleas of Poverty

The apparent precision of statistics can distract historians from a complete appreciation of how medieval citizens assessed their fiscal health. The figures alone cannot persuade us to conclude that urban poverty was a fantasy imagined by greedy boroughs and ignored by central machinery whose demands were fully met. Cries of poverty expressed more than simple economic stress. Social historians have begun to trace pervasive changes in medieval concepts of poverty and the poor, noticing that during the fourteenth and fifteenth centuries, attitudes towards the destitute hardened, which led to the fear and loathing lying behind sixteenth-century legislation against vagabonds and beggars.[79] Further study is needed to determine what factors contributed to these changes in attitudes: real fiscal hardship especially from the mid-fifteenth century; the deleterious financial effects arising from internal violence and the national unrest of the Wars of the Roses; civic officials' fear of failing to safeguard their towns from plunging into poverty if expenses got out of hand; uncertainty concerning the balance between corporate responsibility for the poor and private benevolence expressed in wills and bequests. Until these factors can be weighed, we can only conclude that officials' stereotypical claims of poverty expressed fears about the financial, social, and psychological state of town life, fears no less real for being impossible to quantify.

Fifteenth-century claims of poverty have become one of the most studied topics in English medieval urban history.[80] Since historians are unable to agree on the financial nature of even one city such as York, there seems little hope for a consensus of opinion about English boroughs in general.[81] Undeniably, some boroughs prospered during the fifteenth century, especially if they hosted clothworkers, served as regional distribution centers for county products, or engaged in foreign trade. While York's losses of the wool and cloth trades give credence to its claims of poverty and decay, the other three boroughs in this study possessed stronger fiscal histories and healthier commercial profiles. The evidence of urban building projects throughout the century also indicates less decline and decay than has been thought. Despite problems with loss of trade contacts, Southampton and Lynn continued to build both public and private edifices; Norwich's destructive fires of 1505 and 1508 interrupted a minor building boom (although thereafter the wealthy may have moved to the suburbs); and York's churches and guildhalls benefited from rebuilding in the 1440s and 1450s thanks to individual wealthy merchants.[82]

But contemporary interpretation of the economy and the proper response to poverty should not be ignored. Investigating comments about the perceived severity and extent of poverty reveals cultural attitudes about social class and responsibility impossible to discern from chamberlains' accounts. For example, despite the provable strength of Exeter's economy at the end of the fifteenth century, in 1496 the trustees of Mayor Thomas Calwodeley's estate were convinced the opposite was true. They gave the city a manor and lands specifically for the relief of poor inhabitants burdened by fee farms, tallages, and other royal demands.[83] At least five other Exeter almshouses saw foundation during the fifteenth century, accommodating over fifty individuals unable to weather bad trade cycles and market trends.[84] Early in Henry IV's reign, Norwich citizens of wealth and prominence left bequests to the city to help with public works and the payment of a city tax, necessary actions that too heavily taxed the poorer elements of the town, even with an increase in receipts. By mid-century, such bequests were even more gratefully received and their benefactors remembered with annual ceremonies, "the poverty and need of the city having been considered."[85]

Conspicuous personal wealth and political prominence made civic officials of all boroughs the appropriate figures expected to take action against poverty. Such expectations were made clearest by York's burdened populace. In 1498, when collectors of a subsidy came up empty-handed, officeholders did not deny that the poor were bearing too much of the tax burden and the lord mayor and his brethren not enough.[86] Payments were made by parish, and civic officials generally resided in quarters that contributed the most money, although underassessment was a reality of medieval tax collection. But it can have been no secret that

York's mayors and aldermen owned extensive properties, not just in their parish of residence but in the surrounding county as well, in addition to their commercial interests, and that these sources of wealth contributed nothing to alleviate the city's tax burden. Westminster writs and statutes had already raised awareness of the existence of vagabonds and the unemployed, and the threats they constituted to peacekeeping.[87] In such an environment, it is not surprising to read in civic officials' wills extensive arrangements to feed and house the destitute on the proceeds of the very property and wealth that contributed insufficiently to urban payments to the Crown.[88] Whatever the inadequacy of their responses while alive, civic leaders' responsibilities towards the less fortunate of their borough continued beyond the grave and secured the salvation of testators and the grateful poor given reason to bless their memory.

Clearly, medieval complaints about financial inequity sheltered complex assumptions about identifying poverty and employing methods to ameliorate it. As medieval Coventry's historian has noted, pleas of poverty "enshrined truths which seemed self-evident to contemporaries, however inaccurate may have been their rounded sense of either retrospective chronology or the exact orders of magnitude involved when describing physical decay."[89] The Crown responded as seriously as possible to such pleas, regardless of the elements of fiction they may have contained. Civic officials who claimed difficulties in collecting a subsidy or extending a loan communicated more than unwelcome fiscal information to the royal government. Financial vitality underpinned Crown actions in military affairs and diplomacy, in relations with the nobles of the realm, and in the creation and maintenance of the royal image. The city that defined itself as destitute and decayed blemished the realm, however small its share of contributions. Such extreme pleas sought immediate attention from the king, to restore health to a relationship scarred by inequities.

Urban financial planning during the later Middle Ages required the maximum amount of foresight and ingenuity from the amateur officers in charge of budgets. Extensive military campaigns, bankrupt monarchs, and fluctuations in trade and manufacture all conspired to exhaust the traditional sources of urban wealth. But despite such challenges, accounting to the royal government on one's own had always embodied the cornerstone of urban chartered liberties that the four boroughs continued to pursue throughout the period. Abundant resources provided the means to extend patronage to the influential and hospitality to the monarch, to participate in the realm's military ventures, and to build the physical borough that best expressed its sense of identity. Diminution of the resources threatened a borough's position within a complex network of relationships ranging from local noble to foreign leader.

Whether examining local receipts and expenses, or the sums due the royal government, the comparative method of this study maximizes the sheer number and variety of records while also avoiding shallow conclusions. The contrasting pace and direction of economic growth in the four towns warns against formulating broad generalizations about urban development in post-plague England. Urban officials may have shared a language of complaint, but they did not share all experiences and challenges. Towns like York which had once been provincial capitals with lively economies experienced change for the worse as commercial and industrial patterns shifted. Smaller towns like Nottingham experienced neither spectacular growth nor debilitating decline, thanks to their continued role in cloth manufacturing and transport. New centers such as Norwich already knew financial fortune, while Exeter's economic boom remained in its early stages.

Whatever their direction of growth and volume of complaint, the boroughs displayed a surprising ability to pay all but the most overwhelming and unfair charges. Their ability to acquit themselves hints at greater flexibility of local resources than recorded in the rolls and turned into statistics. Two factors helped the situation: the timely generosity of wealthy individuals able to extend loans and assist the poor, and the Crown's tolerance of tardy payments, even two or three years after they were first due. Slightly surprising is the fact that none of the four boroughs during this period took the opportunity of discovering what the Crown would do if civic officials paid only a small portion of their debts, or refused payment altogether. In 1292, Edward I had seized York's liberties because the city had had trouble paying its debts to the Crown for over twenty years.[90] Memory of that seizure may have remained strong enough to convince all towns to pay as promptly and as fully as possible, without jeopardizing hard-won liberties. For Crown demands simply were not ignored, even if the farms and taxes that composed such requests were established decades earlier when boroughs enjoyed greater levels of wealth.

Despite fragmentary archives created for purposes other than our own, modern historians can derive at least a dim picture of urban economy. Its very obscurity acts as salutary warning of the limitations of statistics and the pitfalls of generalization. The rolls leave us with more than debits and credits. Equally important as factors are the innovative actions of the authors of those records. Leaving no washing jug unturned, they hunted down the pennies that paid local bills and tied provincial towns to kings, their annuitants, and their foreign conquests. We may be doomed never to know urban officials' thoughts on the ease or difficulty with which they raised money, much less the exact reason why Exeter's mayor felt the need for a half-gallon of wine while making his accounts. Equally elusive are the long-term effects of Henry V's demands for military funding, followed closely by decades of costly urban legal battles and contributions to the Wars of the Roses, all within a context of national economic contraction. We are only beginning to recognize the complex relationships between pleas of poverty and balanced budgets, between retainers' fees and Exchequer accounts, between royal visits and a bureaucrat's understanding of the nature of urban resources. When the picture sharpens, we may find that the mayor of Exeter and leaders of other towns could make their accounts and pass the wine with pleasure, rather than as painkiller.

NOTES

[1]   D.R.O., Receivers' Roll, 7–8 Henry V. He ordered a pottle, equal to a half-gallon, but because the number of officials present at the accounting was not noted, how much wine each man drank remains unknown. For the social and cultural role of wine in urban government, a commodity that "made civic participation less painful," see David Gary Shaw, *The Creation of a Community: The City of Wells in the Middle Ages* (Oxford: Clarendon Press, 1993), pp. 199–200.

[2]   For general discussion, see N. J. G. Pounds, *An Economic History of Medieval Europe* (New York: Longman, 1974), esp. ch. 6 and 10; and John Hatcher, "The Great Slump of the Mid-Fifteenth Century," *Progress and Problems in Medieval England: Essays in Honour of Edward Miller*, ed. Richard Britnell and John Hatcher (Cambridge: Cambridge University Press, 1996), pp. 237–72, esp. pp. 266–70. A. J. Pollard, *North-eastern England during the Wars of the Roses: Lay Society, War, and Politics 1450–1500* (Oxford: Clarendon Press, 1990), pp. 43–52, 71–73, examines the crisis in the context of regional economies, with extensive references. As will be shown below, Exeter and large parts of southern England had less to worry about

than the north: Marjorie K. McIntosh, "Local Change and Community Control in England, 1465–1500," *Huntington Library Quarterly* 49 (1986): 219–23.

3 For the 133-year period spanning 1377–1509 (the reigns of Richard II through Henry VII), Exeter has 121 Receivers' Rolls surviving; Norwich has 105 accounts (a mixture of treasurers' rolls, chamberlains' rolls, chamberlains' account books, and apprenticeship indentures, only 67 of which contain totals for both receipts and expenses); Nottingham has 10 surviving accounts (3 with both expenses and receipts) beginning only with Edward IV's reign; and York has 17 chamberlains' rolls. The Nottingham material is scattered through volumes 2 and 3 of *Records of the Borough of Nottingham*, ed. W. H. Stevenson, 5 vols. (London: Bernard Quaritch, 1882–1900); for references, see Table 6. The York material through 1500 has been published more coherently: R. B. Dobson, ed., *York City Chamberlains' Account Rolls 1396–1500*, Surtees Society, vol. 192 (Gateshead, 1980).

4 York's accounts are unusually helpful in separating "real" expenditures from the *superplusagium* entries which represented deficits carried over from the previous year: Dobson, *Chamberlains' Accounts*, p. xxv.

5 For discussion of the ways in which Exeter's prosperity and growth can be measured, see Maryanne Kowaleski, *Local Markets and Regional Trade in Medieval Exeter* (Cambridge: Cambridge University Press, 1995), pp. 89–95, 325–333.

6 *Norwich Records*, 2:xxxv–xxxix.

7 N.R.O., 16-d, Assembly Book I, f.73; A. P. M. Wright, "The Relations between the King's Government and the English Cities and Boroughs in the Fifteenth Century," (D.Phil. thesis, University of Oxford, 1965), pp. 184–85.

8 *Norwich Records*, 2: cxxxvi–cxxxvii, 74–75. In obtaining the grants, Norwich was bucking a national trend that saw a decline in fairs after 1350: S. R. Epstein, "Regional Fairs, Institutional Innovation, and Economic Growth in Late Medieval Europe," *Economic History Review*, 2d series, 47 (1994): 459–82.

9 N.R.O., 17-d, Apprenticeship Indentures, ff. 19v–22r. The unusual expenses consequent upon Queen Margaret's visit in 1453 provide the exception that proves the rule: see above, p. 76.

10 Dobson, *Chamberlains' Accounts*, pp. xxvi–xxxi.

11 *York House Books*, p. 300; Dobson, *Chamberlains' Accounts*, pp. xxxvii–xxxix (and see p. xxv for comments on the fictitious nature of such accounts).

12 Dobson, *Chamberlains' Accounts*, pp. xxxi–xxxii; *York House Books*, p. 674. Fees for the mayor and recorder were reduced, retainers for legal advisors scrutinized, and fines imposed on tardy officials, "forsomuch as the cite is in greit det...". For economic analysis of the period 1510–60, see David Palliser, *Tudor York* (Oxford: Oxford University Press, 1979), pp. 211–25.

13 Susan Reynolds, *An Introduction to the History of English Medieval Towns* (Oxford: Oxford University Press, 1977), p. 198; Thomas Madox, *Firma Burgi* (London: W. Bowyer, 1726), p. 18. From 1462, fee farms and other revenues were collected by special receivers for payment to the Chamber, but this did not affect the ways in which the farms were collected on the borough level: *CPR, 1461–67*, p. 519; B. P. Wolffe, *The Royal Demesne in English History* (London: George Allen and Unwin Ltd., 1971), p. 149.

14 *Nott. Records*, 1:197, 311–13; Nt.R.O., CA7476, Account of Hugh Wyllughby, Sheriff of Nottinghamshire, to the Exchequer (the borough had not yet received

county status, and still accounted to the Crown through the royal sheriff). The farm
was set at £54 12s. until reduced £20 in 1462 for twenty years, in reward for services
extended to Edward IV: *Nott. Records*, 2:248–49, 254–55.

[15]   Madox, *Firma Burgi*, p. 263; *Norwich Records*, 1:42; 2:74–75.

[16]   For queens, see *CCR, 1381–85*, p. 264; *1422–29*, pp. 19–22; *Rot. Parl.*, 5:261–62;
CPR, 1461–67, p. 430; *1485–94*, pp. 75–77. Dowager queen Elizabeth Woodville
even received over £20 per annum from Norwich's farm at the start of Henry VII's
reign as residue of her dowry: William Campbell, ed., *Materials for a History of the
Reign of Henry VII*, 2 vols., Rolls Series, vol. 60 (London, 1873, 1877), 1:347. For
the unemployed, see *CCR, 1441–47*, p. 182; *1454–61*, p. 467; *1461–67*, pp. 43, 47,
89; *CPR, 1446–52*, pp. 35, 233; Rosemary Horrox and P. W. Hammond, eds.,
British Library Harleian MS. 433, 4 vols. (London and Upminster: Alan Sutton
Publishing for the Richard III Society, 1979–83), 1:130; A. R. Myers, *The
Household of Edward IV* (Manchester: Manchester University Press, 1959), p. 131.

[17]   Holy Trinity priory received from Exeter over £25 *per annum*, except during the
costly jurisdictional litigation when payment was ignored in order to cover court
fees: H. Lloyd Parry, "The Fee Farm of Exeter," *Transactions of the Devonshire
Association* 81 (1949): 197–99. The remaining £20 benefited Poitiers veteran John
de Suly during the 1360s and 1370s; Richard II's doctor; the king's half-brother
John Holand; and in 1415, the Beaufort duke of Exeter: *CPR, 1377–81*, p. 193; *ibid.*,
1396–99, p. 537; *CCR, 1396–99*, p. 34; D.R.O., Book 51, f.299v. For Nottingham's
payments to religious from its farm of £54 12s., see *CPR, 1391–96*, p. 503 and Ann
K. Warren, *Anchorites and Their Patrons in Medieval England* (Berkeley and Los
Angeles: University of California Press, 1985), pp. 170–71, 175 (anchorite); *CPR,
1399–1401*, p. 322 (prioress and convent of St. Mary de Pratis, Derby); *ibid., 1467–
77*, p. 586, and *Harl. 433*, 3:196 (Westminster recluse, granted £4 p.a. by Edward IV
from the borough's issues).

[18]   For the jewels, see *CPR, 1461–67*, p. 96; P.R.O., E.368/235, Precepta, Michaelmas
2 Edward IV, rot. 1v.

[19]   *York House Books*, pp. 270–71; A. R. Bridbury, "English Provincial Towns in the
Later Middle Ages," *Economic History Review*, 2d series, 34 (1981): 11.

[20]   *Norwich Records*, 1:342–43. Fee farm and other payments to the Crown were not
interrupted when the king first seized the city's liberties 1437–38; however, the city
did not make its customary payments during the 1443–47 seizure and accumulated a
debt of over £440, as well as a fine of one thousand marks. The fee farm debt was
eventually canceled in 1452 after Norwich brought its case to the court of the
Exchequer. For the documents of these financial problems at the Crown level, see
PRO, E.28/71, E.28/72; E.159/220, Brevia directa, Trinity 22 Henry VI, rot.12v;
E.159/221, Brevia directa, Trinity 23 Henry VI, rot.1v; E.368/216, Precepta,
Michaelmas 22 Henry VI; E.368/224, Communa, Michaelmas, rot.23; E.372/288;
KB.27/746, rex 29, ff.175–76. Local documentation of the seizure of the liberties
and its financial cost to the city includes N.R.O., 9-d, 1–11, 14–17; 17-b, Book of
Pleas, ff.16v–20v, 81v–85v. Henry VI's examination of the records of Norwich's
behavior during the first seizure is noted in Nicholas H. Nicolas, ed., *Proceedings
and Ordinances of the Privy Council of England*, 7 vols. (London: Record
Commission, 1834–37), 5:242–43.

[21]   The following episode is related in detail in my article, "The King's Interest—

York's Fee Farm and the Central Government, 1480–1492," *Northern History* 17 (1981): 24–43. Corrections made in the text below do not alter the general conclusions drawn in that work. The nature and efficiency of the late medieval Exchequer is the subject of controversy, interpreted by some historians as antiquated and sterile (e.g., Frederick C. Dietz, *English Government Finance 1485–1558*, University of Illinois Studies in the Social Sciences, vol. 9 [Urbana: University of Illinois Press, 1920], pp. 60–67, and W. C. Richardson, *Tudor Chamber Administration, 1485–1547* [Baton Rouge: Louisiana State University Press, 1952], pp. 41–59), and by others as flexible and self-improving (J. D. Alsop, "The Exchequer in Late Medieval Government, c.1485–1530," *Aspects of Late Medieval Government and Society: Essays Presented to J. R. Lander*, ed. J. G. Rowe [Toronto: University of Toronto Press, 1986], pp. 179–212). See David Grummitt, "Henry VII, Chamber Finance and the New Monarchy," *Historical Research* 72 (1999): 229–43 for new evidence of the first Tudor's complex Chamber management.

22 John F. Benton, ed., *Town Origins: The Evidence from Medieval England* (Boston: D. C. Heath and Co., 1968), pp. 98–101; Madox, *Firma Burgi*, pp. 3–4, 18–19.

23 *CPR, 1317–21*, p. 29. William also received £100 p.a. from the farm of Lincoln: J. F. W. Hill, *Medieval Lincoln* (Cambridge: Cambridge University Press, 1948), p. 243. York's share rose to £120 p.a. in the fifteenth century.

24 *CCR, 1385–89*, p. 9; *1422–29*, pp. 417–18; *1429–35*, p. 71; *CPR, 1441–46*, p. 445. For Clarence, see *CPR, 1461–67*, p. 115; *1476–85*, p. 521; *Complete Peerage*, 11:105–107.

25 *Rot. Parl.*, 6:193–95; *CCR, 1476–85*, p. 144.

26 *CFR, 1471–85*, no.155 contains a brief history of the payment.

27 *CPR, 1476–85*, p. 123; *CFR, 1471–85*, p. 239.

28 *York House Books*, p. 271.

29 *Ibid.*, pp. 295, 729.

30 "[I]t is soo that now of late at oure being in oure said Citee for gret causes us specialy moving, We have disposed the said Fee ferme aswelle to the Releef and socouring of the said Citee as otherwise, so that the saide annuite ne may be paiable there...": Horrox and Hammond, *Harleian MS. 433*, 2:18. Richard arranged for the Michaelmas installment of Savage's pension to be paid from the revenues of the county palatine of Chester. More permanent arrangements followed in September for the money to be paid from the king's lands in the Welsh marches: *Harl. 433*, 1:90–91; P.R.O., C.81/1392/5. The signet letter was delivered to the lord chancellor and enrolled on 4 February 1484: *CPR, 1476–85*, p. 413.

31 See above, pp. 96-97 note 68, for discussion of more skeptical views about Richard's intentions. For Savage's holdings, see *CPR, 1467–77*, pp. 490, 497, 524, 526, 572; *1476–85*, pp. 94, 319; James Gairdner, *Henry the Seventh* (London: Macmillan and Co., 1899), p. 27. For the 1484 release, see *CPR, 1476–85*, p. 409. The mayor's pension of £18 5s. was also confirmed.

32 P.R.O., E.372/329; E.372/330.

33 *York House Books*, pp. 328, 333, 348 (quotation). Metcalf received a reward of forty shillings for his pains in Westminster. The new grant came early in 1485, when the king ordered the treasurer and chamberlains of the Exchequer to quit the city sheriffs of over £60, but it had no lasting effect: P.R.O., E.404/78/3/42 (31 January 1485).

[34]   P.R.O., E.372/331.

[35]   P.R.O., E.372/332 (total debt of £498 4s. 1 1/4 d.). The chancery warrant confirming Richard's grants survives (C.82/11/20) but Henry's letter patent was not enrolled.

[36]   *Rot. Parl.*, 6:300; *York House Books*, pp. 507–10 (where the sum is given incorrectly as £120; see P.R.O. E.159/262, Recorda, Trinity 1 Henry VII, rot. 19v, 22 for the correct sum of £112 13s. 4d), 603–4. Given the poor communications exhibited by all parties, Henry could have been working more in ignorance than in malice.

[37]   *York House Books*, pp. 517–18, 522, 524 (quotation), 528–29. Upon Henry's accession, the Chamber and receiver system of accounting was in shambles with no recovery noted before the late 1480s. The barons of the Exchequer, with whom the York authorities had always been dealing, resumed their powers of audit denied them in many cases by the Yorkist monarchs: Wolffe, *Royal Demesne*, pp. 199–200.

[38]   E.g., P.R.O., E.372/333–335, 341–43, 351–53. The release is not mentioned on the roll for 1508–1509: E.372/354.

[39]   Lord Roos was unable to manage his own affairs, so his guardian Sir Thomas Lovell took charge and enjoyed revenues from fee farms of York and Lincoln. Roos claims were taken up by the family's heir George Manners (who wielded influence being married to a cousin of Henry VII's queen), and continued into Henry VIII's reign by Manners's heirs the earls of Rutland: *York Civic Records*, 3:42–43, 81–82, 94, 110, 113, 116–17, 139, 146, 150, 152, 165, 167, 169, 174; *Complete Peerage*, 11:106–108; Nicholas Harris Nicolas, ed., *Testamenta Vetusta.*, 2 vols. (London: Nichols and Son, 1826), 2:528–29; Palliser, *Tudor York*, pp. 215–17; Steven Gunn, "Sir Thomas Lovell (c.1449–1524): A New Man in a New Monarchy?" in *The End of the Middle Ages? England in the Fifteenth and Sixteenth Centuries*, ed. John L. Watts (Stroud: Sutton Publishing, 1998), p. 143.

[40]   A. G. Dickens, "Tudor York," in P. M. Tillot, ed., *The Victoria History of the Counties of England: A History of Yorkshire, The City of York* (London: Oxford University Press, 1961), pp. 123–24; Palliser, *Tudor York*, pp. 216–17. The problem was eventually resolved by an act of parliament in 1536 which compounded the Rutland payment and reduced support of ecclesiastical foundations. Earlier (1523–24), York's fee farm was among those revenues earmarked for payment to the general surveyors of the crown lands, not the barons of the Exchequer: Richardson, *Tudor Chamber Administration*, pp. 478–83.

[41]   P.R.O., PSO.2/1/17; PSO.2/3; *CPR, 1461–67*, p. 186; I. S. Leadam, ed., *Select Cases before the King's Council in the Star Chamber, Volume I: 1477–1509*, Selden Society, vol. 16 (London, 1903), pp. cxliii–cxlvii.

[42]   Dietz, *English Government Finance 1485–1558*, p. 13; Robin E. Glasscock, ed., *The Lay Subsidy of 1334*, British Academy Records of Social and Economic History, n.s. 2 (London: Oxford University Press, 1975), pp. xvi, 49, 192, 227, 357; J. F. Hadwin, "The Medieval Lay Subsidies and Economic History," *Economic History Review*, 2d series, 36 (1983): 214; R. S. Schofield, "Parliamentary Lay Taxation 1485–1547" (Ph.D. diss., University of Cambridge, 1963), pp. 7–8, 413–24. A lucid summary of direct and indirect taxation is found in Goronwy Edwards, *The Second Century of the English Parliament* (Oxford: Clarendon Press, 1979), pp. 17–43. By the end of the fifteenth century, gross yield was c.£31,000 and net yield £29,000. I am grateful to Professor W. Mark Ormrod of the University of York for advice on the calculations found in this section.

43   Schofield, *ibid.*, pp. 102–103, 469; W. A. Morris and J. R. Strayer, eds., *Fiscal Administration*, vol. 2 of *The English Government at Work, 1327–1336* (Cambridge, Mass.: The Mediaeval Academy of America, 1950), p. 36; *York Mem. Bk.*, 1:178–79, 2:73, 76, 91–92.

44   *York Civic Records*, 2:81–84, 89, 129–30, 134–38. See below, p. 179 note 86.

45   Nt.R.O., CA 4506, privy seal letter dated 6 October 1475; see *Nott. Records*, 2:418 for its context. Waiving taxes could buy support of greater value than the assessment: in 1389, Richard II "of his own mere motion, without advice from anyone," remitted the second installment of a subsidy soon after declaring himself of age, and the new king Henry IV remitted the third moiety of a subsidy granted during Richard's 1397–98 parliament: Nigel Saul, *Richard II* (New Haven and London: Yale University Press, 1997), pp. 235, 260–61.

46   For example, D.R.O., Receivers' Rolls, 5–6 Henry IV, 1–2 Henry VI; N.R.O., 7-c, Treasurers' Rolls, 3–4, 6–9 Henry V, 1–2 and 8–9 Henry VI; 18-a, Chamberlains' Account Book, 1384–1448, 5–6 Henry V, ff.122–23.

47   Schofield, "Parliamentary Lay Taxation 1485–1547," pp. 102–103; *CCR, 1422–29*, pp. 51–52.

48   P.R.O., E.179/217/61 (33 Henry VI). A study of Exchequer receipt rolls, records of daily payments to the Crown, reveals that tiny amounts of the levies continued to trickle into the central government fifteen months to two years after they were first granted: e.g., E.401/760 *sub* 4 February 1439 (17 Henry VI).

49   *Rot. Parl.*, 3:90; R. B. Dobson, ed., *The Peasants' Revolt of 1381* (London: Macmillan, 1970), pp. 55–57; Miller, *VCH*, p. 66; P.R.O., E.179/149/62, E.179/159/34, E.179/217/13, 15 and 16; Edwards, *Second Century of English Parliament*, pp. 28–29; N. Bartlett, ed., "Lay Poll Tax Returns for the City of York in 1381," *Transactions of the East Riding Antiquarian Society* 30 (1953), n.p.; J. I. Leggett, "The 1377 Poll Tax Return for the City of York," *Yorkshire Archaeological Journal* 43 (1971): 128–46. For calculations of evasion, see John A. F. Thomson, *The Transformation of Medieval England, 1370–1529* (London and New York: Longman, 1983), Table A.4, pp. 384–85. The more positive view, included in an analysis of the demographic evidence of the poll tax returns, can be found in P. J. P. Goldberg, "Urban Identity and the Poll Taxes of 1377, 1379, and 1381," *Economic History Review*, 2d series, 43 (1990): 194–216, esp. 205–8.

50   *CFR, 1399–1405*, pp. 147–49; P.R.O., E.372/248 (3–4 Henry IV).

51   *Rot. Parl.*, 4:318. Exeter's payment was silently subsumed under Devon's heading. The returns for 1428 are printed in *Feudal Aids*, 6 vols. (London, 1899–1920), 1:xxvii–xxviii, 473; 3:603–606 (Norwich); 4:142 (Nottingham); 6:352–54 (York). For additional material on York's collection, see *CFR, 1422–30*, p. 216; and *York Mem. Bk.*, 2:130–31. The 1428 levy aided Jacqueline of Hainault, or more likely her husband the duke of Gloucester's defense of her holdings: J. S. Roskell *et al.*, eds., *The History of Parliament: The House of Commons, 1386–1421*, 4 vols. (Stroud: Alan Sutton Publishing for the History of Parliament Trust, 1992), 1:118 n.120. For debate on the yield, see Ralph A. Griffiths, *The Reign of King Henry VI* (Berkeley and Los Angeles: University of California Press, 1981), p. 125 note 63.

52   For the first levy, see *Rot. Parl.* 4:486–87; T. B. Pugh and C. D. Ross, "The English Baronage and the Income Tax of 1436," *Bulletin of the Institute of Historical Research* 26 (1953): 1–28; Griffiths, *Henry VI*, pp. 118, 125 n.72. York's record of

the subsidy's collection, P.R.O. E179/217/38, not only lists the city's payment of
£32 7s., but includes assessments of citizens and their holdings, including those of
nine women and the vicars choral. For the latter levy, see Roger Virgoe, "The
Parliamentary Subsidy of 1450," *Bulletin of the Institute of Historical Research* 55
(1982): 124–38. The survival of Norwich's return provides valuable information
about urban social structure and the Crown's reliance upon towns' financial help:
see Virgoe, "A Norwich Taxation List of 1451," *Norfolk Archaeology* 40 (1989):
145–54. Norwich was originally assessed at £63 11s. but paid £55 15s., the largest
sum for any provincial city with county status. York paid the next largest sum of £47
13s. 6d. (its assessment included fewer wealthy landholders of gentry status).
Nottingham paid the modest sum of £8 14s. 6d. See P.R.O., E.179/238/78
(Norwich), E.179/217/56 (York), and E.179/159/83 (Nottingham).

53   Roskell, *House of Commons 1386–1421*, 1:118; *Rot. Parl.*, 6:151 (quotation).

54   E.g., P.R.O., C.1/24/25; *CPR, 1429–36*, pp. 112, 116; *1436–41*, p. 549; *Rot. Parl.*,
      4:387.

55   *Rot. Parl.*, 5:6; Sylvia Thrupp, "A Survey of the Alien Population of England in
      1440," *Speculum* 32 (1957): 263–67; M. S. Giuseppi, "Alien Merchants in England
      in the Fifteenth Century," *Transactions of the Royal Historical Society*, 2d series, 9
      (1895): 91–93.

56   P.R.O., E.179/217/46; E.179/149/124–126 and 130; E.179/95/100; E.179/95/102. In
      1452, York officers admitted to four alien householders and five residents, paying a
      total of 7s. 10d. One year later, the city had gained one householder and two
      residents, for a total payment of 10s. 2d. Norwich in 1455 claimed nine
      householders and five residents, and collected £2 3s. 6d.: P.R.O., E.179/217/60 and
      E.401/825 *sub* 12 May 1452; E.179/217/64 and E.401/831 *sub* 30 July 1453;
      E.179/149/163 and E.401/847 *sub* 19 November 1455.

57   E.g., *CFR, 1437–45*, pp. 238–39 (directions to Norwich and York, 12 November
      1442).

58   Cited in Pamela Nightingale, *A Medieval Mercantile Community: The Grocers'
      Company and the Politics and Trade of London 1000–1485* (New Haven and
      London: Yale University Press, 1995), p. 383.

59   *Rot. Parl.*, 6:535–40; *CFR, 1430–37*, pp. 185–88; *1445–52*, pp. 30–33; W. G.
      Hoskins, "The Wealth of Medieval Devon," in *Devonshire Studies*, ed. W. G.
      Hoskins and H. P. R. Finberg (London: Cape, 1952), pp. 228–29, 247. In 1433,
      York was returned £16 19s. 7 3/4d., Norwich £9 18s. 3/4d., and Exeter £6 13s. 4d.
      In 1445, York received £25 9s. 5 1/2d. and Norwich £14 17s. 1d. See the following
      note for discussion of Exeter's rebate.

60   Hoskins, "The Wealth of Medieval Devon," p. 247, discusses the 1489–90 county
      reassessment and argues that Exeter had been excused £10 in 1445 and only £8
      under Henry VII, a sign of its economic growth. This contradicts notations on
      subsidy rolls, which indicate that Exeter was excused £8 in 1440 (P.R.O.,
      E.179/95/84), and only 100s. on a subsidy and a half grant in 1446 (E.179/95/99; see
      also E.179/95/109 [1449]). E.179/95/28 confirms Hoskins' observation that Exeter
      was excused £8 in 1489. Devonshire's rebate totaled £99 19s. 5.5d. from 1433, and
      £149 19s. 2.25d. from 1445: *CFR, 1430–37*, pp. 185–88; *1445–52*, pp. 120–22.

61   G. L. Harriss, "Aids, Loans and Benevolences," *Historical Journal* 6 (1963): 4, 8,
      16; W. M. Ormrod, "The Crown and the English Economy 1290–1348," in *Before*

the Black Death: Studies in the "Crisis" of the Early Fourteenth Century, ed. Bruce M. S. Campbell (Manchester and New York: Manchester University Press, 1991), pp. 157–58.

[62] Francis Blomefield, *A Topographical History of the County of Norfolk*, 2d ed., 11 vols (London: William Miller, 1805–10), 3:125.

[63] N.R.O., 18-a, Chamberlains' Account Book, 1470–90, f.75v; in 1481, representatives went to Lynn: *ibid.*, 1479–88, f.20v.

[64] D.R.O., Receivers' Roll, 1–2 Henry V; N.R.O., 16-d, Assembly Book I, f.19; *Norwich Records*, 2:48–49. Individuals in York expected to lend money in 1436 and promised repayment from the lay subsidy included the dean of York, the mayor, the recorder, and a legal advisor: *CPR, 1429–36*, pp. 528–30.

[65] Caroline Barron, "The Government of London and Its Relations with the Crown, 1400–1450" (Ph.D. diss., University of London, 1970), pp. 423, 440, 451–52.

[66] *Ibid.*, p. 21; *CPR, 1399–1401*, pp. 251, 353–55; *1401–1405*, pp. 403, 416–17; P.R.O., E.404/2/261.

[67] Griffiths, *Henry VI*, p. 109. In 1430, a loan of £162 raised by individuals in York was repaid out of the city's lay subsidy payment due at the end of the year: *CPR, 1429–36*, p. 60. Likewise, York's loan of 100 marks made on 26 October 1442 was covered by the second half of the lay tax from the East Riding, paid into the receipt of the Exchequer the following day: P.R.O., E.401/780.

[68] P.R.O., E.401/748, *sub* 3 May 1436; N.R.O., 16-d, Assembly Book I, f.14 (October 1440). Gloucester did not appear, but the duke of Norfolk took his place and when he asked for a loan on behalf of the Crown, Norwich told him it was too poor to lend: *Norwich Records*, 1:283.

[69] D.R.O., Receivers' Rolls, 5–6, 7–8 Henry V, 1–2 Henry VI; Rymer, *Foedera*, 9:285; *CPR, 1413–16*, p. 354; Richard A. Newhall, *The English Conquest of Normandy, 1416–1424* (New Haven: Yale University Press, 1924), p. 147 n.13.

[70] N.R.O., 18-a, Chamberlains' Account Book, 1384–1448, ff.122–23; 7-c, Treasurers' Accounts, 7–8, 8–9 Henry V; *Norwich Records*, 2:62, 64. A crafty individual could turn possession of royal jewels to his own advantage: see K. B. McFarlane, "At the Deathbed of Cardinal Beaufort," in *Studies in Medieval History presented to F. M. Powicke*, edited by R. W. Hunt, W. A. Pantin, R. W. Southern (Oxford: Clarendon Press, 1948), pp. 412, 416, 418.

[71] D.R.O., Bk. 51, f.308v.

[72] *Norwich Records*, 1:lx, 2:45; Rymer, *Foedera*, 8:9–12; *CPR, 1396–99*, pp. 180–81; Blomefield, *History of Norfolk*, 3:119.

[73] Rymer, *Foedera*, 8:152; *CPR, 1396–99*, pp. 363–64, 368; *1399–1401*, p. 353. Henry IV gained another 500 marks for a Welsh campaign in 1403, and £200 pledged by six individuals in 1404: Nicolas, *Proceedings Privy Council*, 1:200–203; Miller, *VCH*, p. 67.

[74] Nicolas, *Proceedings Privy Council*, 5:418–21; Harriss, "Aids, Loans and Benevolences," 10. The reluctant were forced to give an increased amount.

[75] N.R.O., 16-d, Assembly Book I, ff.111, 112v, 114.

[76] Caroline Barron, "London and the Crown 1451–61," in *The Crown and Local Communities in England and France in the Fifteenth Century*, ed. J. R. L. Highfield and Robin Jeffs (Gloucester: Alan Sutton Publishing, 1981), pp. 92–94.

[77] Anthony Steel, *Receipt of the Exchequer, 1377–1485* (Cambridge: Cambridge

University Press, 1954), p. 163. The large number of sources and individual negotiations raised the collection and administration costs of such a loan, whose outreach to so many subjects must have been a major consideration.

[78] Norwich acquired land surrounding the castle in 1345 in order to extend its jurisdiction into an area haunted by fugitives from borough justice: *Norwich Records*, 1:xlii, 23–27; *Rot. Parl.*, 3:322; P.R.O., E.372/248 (3–4 Henry IV).

[79] Michel Mollat, *The Poor in the Middle Ages*, trans. Arthur Goldhammer (New Haven and London: Yale University Press, 1986), especially pp. 191–293. Miri Rubin, *Charity and Community in Medieval Cambridge* (Cambridge: Cambridge University Press, 1987), studies changing forms of charitable giving and the role of hospitals in the later Middle Ages. My article, "Preparation for Death in Sixteenth-Century Northern England," *Sixteenth–Century Journal* 13 (1982): 37–66, focuses on sixteenth-century charitable behavior, showing through the use of wills that bequests to the poor occupied the minds of individual testators and that private charity was an important aspect of medieval and early modern culture.

[80] Susan Reynolds, "Decline and Decay in Late Medieval Towns," *Urban History Yearbook 1980*, 76–78, provides a guide to the literature of urban poverty as well as valuable bibliographic information (through 1979) in its notes. Since then, important contributions to the topic include Stephen H. Rigby, "English Provincial Towns in the Later Middle Ages," *Economic History Review*, 2d series, 34 (1981): 1–24; Rigby, "Urban Decline in the Later Middle Ages: The Reliability of the Non-statistical Evidence," *Urban History Yearbook 1984*, 45–54; Rigby, "Late Medieval Urban Prosperity: The Evidence of the Lay Subsidies," *Economic History Review*, 2d series, 39 (1986): 411–16; A. R. Bridbury, "Dr. Rigby's Comment: A Reply," *ibid.*, 417–22; J. F. Hadwin, "From Dissonance to Harmony in the Late Medieval Town," *ibid.*, 423–26; Alan Dyer, *Decline and Growth in English Towns 1400–1640* (Cambridge: Cambridge University Press, 1995); and most recently *Towns in Decline AD100–1600*, edited by T. R. Slater (Aldershot: Ashgate, 2000).

[81] For York, see J. N. Bartlett, "The Expansion and Decline of York in the Later Middle Ages," *Economic History Review*, 2d series, 12 (1959): 17–33; R. B. Dobson, "Urban Decline in Late Medieval England," *Transactions of the Royal Historical Society*, 5th series, 27 (1977 for 1976): 1–22; D. M. Palliser, "A Crisis in English Towns? The Case of York, 1460–1640," *Northern History* 14 (1978): 108–25; Jennifer I. Kermode, "Urban Decline? The Flight from Office in Late Medieval York," *Economic History Review*, 2d series, 35 (1982): 179–98; Palliser, "Urban Decay Revisited," in *Towns and Townspeople in the Fifteenth Century*, ed. John A. F. Thomson (Gloucester: Alan Sutton, 1988), pp. 1–21. Other important statements on poverty within specific boroughs include Charles Phythian-Adams, *Desolation of a City: Coventry and the Urban Crisis of the Late Middle Ages* (Cambridge: Cambridge University Press, 1979); Gervase Rosser, *Medieval Westminster 1200–1540* (Oxford: Clarendon Press, 1989), pp. 169, 171, 176–77, 325; A. F. Butcher, "Rent, Population, and Economic Change in Late-Medieval Newcastle," *Northern History* 14 (1978): 73–75; Shaw, *Creation of Community*, pp. 101–103.

[82] Reynolds, "Decline and Decay," 77; Hatcher, "The Great Slump of the Mid-Fifteenth Century," pp. 250–51; *Norwich Records*, 2:lxxi; N.R.O., 16-c, Assembly Minute Book I, ff.121v, 124; J. L. Bolton, *The Medieval English Economy 1150–1500* (London: J. M. Dent and Sons, 1980), p. 252; Bridbury, "English Provincial

Towns in the Later Middle Ages," 14; Miller, *VCH*, p. 107; Jennifer I. Kermode, *Medieval Merchants: York, Beverley and Hull in the Later Middle Ages* (Cambridge: Cambridge University Press, 1998), pp. 151–52; *Norwich Records*, 2:cxxiv–cxxv, 131–32.

[83] D.R.O., Documents D267, 282, 283; Hoskins, "Wealth of Medieval Devon," pp. 234–41. For early sixteenth-century Exeter, Hoskins estimates that about 7% of the taxable population owned nearly two-thirds of the taxable wealth: "English Provincial Towns in the Early Sixteenth-Century," *Transactions of the Royal Historical Society*, 5th series, 6 (1956): 18.

[84] Wallace T. MacCaffrey, *Exeter 1540–1640: The Growth of an English County Town*, 2d ed. (London and Cambridge, Mass.: Harvard University Press, 1975), pp. 102–5.

[85] *Norwich Records*, 2:cvi–cvii, 92–93.

[86] *York Civic Records*, 2:134–38. Two years later, mayor William Nelson and former mayor (1490) John Gilliot were cited for declining knighthood despite holding lands or rents worth at least £40 *per annum*: Walter J. Kaye, "Yorkshiremen Who Declined to Take Up Their Knighthood," *Yorkshire Archaeological Journal* 31 (1932–34): 362.

[87] In 1461, Chancery ordered Exeter and other boroughs to arrest "seditious vagabonds" and dissidents: *CPR, 1461–67*, pp. 35, 101, 232. From 1482, York's officials pronounced against vagrants and poor people entering the city, and Henry VII spent the first Christmas Eve of his reign ordering the city to imprison and punish "vacabundes, idel people, mighty and valiant beggers and othre suspect personnes," in the first of many Tudor decrees on the subject: *York House Books*, pp. 258, 394. Norwich set its beggars in stocks, as directed by statute: *Norwich Records*, 2:153 (1496), 11 Henry VII, c.2. "True" beggars, distinguished from "sturdy" (i.e., undeserving) beggars, received badges from parish constables under Henry VIII and could remain in York: *York Civic Records*, 3:46, 66, 111, 118.

[88] An examination of the wills of men who held the mayoralty under Henry VII helps to explain why the officials of 1498 did not deny the accusation. If we assume they resided in and were taxed in the parishes in which they requested burial, then it is clear they lived in areas paying the highest assessments, some even higher than the 1428 assessment (*York Mem. Bk.*, 2:131–35). St. Michael Ousegate, St. Michael le Belfry, and All Saints' Pavement were popular for mayoral burials, and paid the highest amounts in 1492 (£12, £9 18s., and £7 respectively; however, of the three, only St. Michael Ousegate was valued higher [£2 more] than in 1428). But mayoral wills also show possession of extensive urban, suburban, and county properties, as well as charitable arrangements to assuage local conditions. Some of the best examples in print include the wills of Sir William Todd (mayor 1487), John Stockdale (1501), and John Petty (1508): James Raine, ed., *Testamenta Eboracensia, Volume 4*, Surtees Society, vol. 53 (1869), pp. 212–13, 256–57, 333–35. John Carre (mayor 1448 and 1453, died 1487) and Sir Richard York (mayor 1469 and 1482; died 1498) also provided for extensive charitable works (*maisons dieu*, almshouses, dowries, bedding) financed by their properties: *ibid.*, pp. 26–30, 134–37. The topic deserves a more thorough analysis than can be provided here. For further comment, see Kermode, *Medieval Merchants*, pp. 20, 133–34, 141–45, 278–91.

[89]   Charles Phythian-Adams, "Urban Decay in Late Medieval England," in *Towns in Societies*, ed. Philip Abrams and E. A. Wrigley (Cambridge: Cambridge University Press, 1978), pp. 161–62.
[90]   Miller, *VCH*, p. 35.

CHAPTER 6
DEFENSE OF THE REALM

The golden age of urban militias belonged to a time and place other than that of late medieval England. The Reconquest forces described in the twelfth-century Iberian *fueros*, and the frontier troops mentioned in the Angevin *établissements* defended and extended territory with an effectiveness that rivaled their kings' own forces.[1] For better or worse, borough militias never aided or threatened English monarchs in a comparable manner. To judge from town records, English urban troops consisted of small bands of badly trained amateurs, reluctant to join battles, not much use when they got there, and lacking in the money and expertise needed to defend even their own homes from attack. The numbers such troops contributed to forces in France, Scotland, and in the domestic battles of the Wars of the Roses were extremely small. Nevertheless, medieval English kings expected their urban subjects to assist in the defense of the realm, with their bodies as well as with the supplies and fortifications imperative to campaigns. The frustration or fulfillment of these expectations reveals a great deal about society and identity in late medieval towns.

From a modern perspective, urban troops lost little by avoiding combat, particularly those campaigns supporting England's fruitless claims for overseas territory. That medieval monarchs, however, limited their participation in the age's foremost occasions for heroic and financial aggrandizement speaks directly to town militias' inadequacies in combat. Although English towns had been called upon for supplies and naval assistance for centuries, and were expected to defend themselves in case of attack, citizens' skills in physical combat had not been particularly honed. They did not share their French counterparts' interest in chivalric exercises in either peace or wartime.[2] Unlike towns on the Iberian and French frontiers, not to mention the border with Wales, most English boroughs had known neither constant threat to survival nor great inducement to territorial expansion, and their inhabitants had not augmented their commercial duties with the military chores of the feudal elite. Without such catalysts, the English Crown would have been foolish to build up urban militias as capable of turning on their king as on his enemies.

The varied sizes and fortunes of the boroughs studied here reveal flexible strategies on the part of both Crown and town. Requirements of men and supplies were tailored to each site, but enthusiasm or reluctance to serve had as much to do with patronage patterns and expectation of royal reward as with geography or economics. Moreover, the financial difficulties of the fifteenth century meant that towns faced an interesting dilemma when asked to provide the Crown with military aid. Giving the king the troops and equipment he demanded reminded the government of borough loyalty and could lead to an extension of town privileges, but providing men and supplies placed a strain on urban revenues. The royal government sometimes helped a town repair the walls and buy the guns needed for national defense, but Crown-assisted local measures constitute less than half the story. From the king's point of view, the best thing about urban contributions was that towns had to raise, train, and equip the troops they provided for the defense of the realm, and feed and pay them at least while they remained within county boundaries or to a specified muster point.[3] The system may not have produced bands of urban heroes systematically trained and utilized, but it did present a bargaining ground on which both king and borough negotiated for suitable expressions of urban loyalty and cooperation. However negligible the contributions, town participation in military projects provided the monarchy with a way to connect local concerns to national issues, a broadening of outlook from which both could benefit.

Preparations for Combat

The rapid and efficient distribution of news and propaganda was essential to any king's military plans. The royal government not only saw boroughs as sources of troops and supplies, but recognized towns as efficient centers for the distribution of such information. As entrepôts and leading market centers with concentrated and at least marginally literate populations, towns received early notice of foreign and domestic policy that sometimes led to armed conflict. The Crown used civic officials as the most convenient mouthpieces by which news and instructions could be communicated to all subjects. In the late fifteenth century, messages could contain such vital information as the identity of the current king and the status of leading nobles. Early in March 1461, for example, the sheriffs of London and provincial towns received orders to proclaim the accession of Edward IV and ban the military support of Henry VI, news repeated in 1471 upon Edward's return to power.[4] The current status of men likely to lead troops also needed to be communicated promptly, such as when York and Norwich received word in 1471 declaring the duke of Clarence and the earl of Warwick traitors and offering reward for their capture.[5]

Towns also received prompt word of international news and diplomatic advancements promising peace. In 1415, the mayor and bailiffs of Exeter were ordered to join officers of other towns in Devon in announcing a ten-year general truce between England and France. Exeter's port also received a Crown-appointed conservator of the truce, empowered to preserve the pact, to issue safeconducts, and specifically to punish those who ignored the truce and persisted in attacking the king's new-made allies.[6] The York records contain full texts of Henry VII's letters concerning international affairs of the 1490s, including offers of peace and treaties with the Hansa and Austrian merchants which were of great importance to northern traders.[7] York naturally received the bulk of messages about Anglo-Scottish affairs, but not all of them required urban subjects to arm themselves. In 1501, Henry warned York officials that ambassadors from Scotland would soon visit the city to begin negotiations that resulted in Margaret Tudor's marriage to James IV. Messengers received small rewards for their pains, although the amounts could depend on the nature of the news broadcast.[8]

Upon declaration of war, towns could be charged with the financing of troops, or more commonly with the provision of supplies and transport. During the fourteenth and early fifteenth centuries, towns received orders from the Crown to build and rig barges and balingers, sometimes levying taxes specifically upon the wealthy to cover costs.[9] Barge provision could be made a condition of royal charter confirmation, at such heavy expense that some towns shared the burden of construction. In later years, monarchs requisitioned the vessels they needed from merchants, although Edward IV purchased his own ships and expected cities such as Norwich to do the same on his behalf.[10]

The fourteenth and fifteenth centuries found even provincial English towns experimenting with ordnance. Norwich was especially well prepared with artillery. Town accounts of 1384–85 show that the threat of French invasion had encouraged citizens to begin buying saltpeter and sulfur from London, and to assess the wards to purchase guns.[11] As keeper of the city of York after Henry IV seized its liberties in 1405, William Frost received orders to send the king saltpeter from urban supplies.[12] Urban command over artillery almost exceeded that of the monarchy, for the royal government did not appoint a Master of the King's Ordnance until 1456. Part of his job was to insure that artillery scattered across the realm in castles and walled towns was ready for use, but his death in 1460 cut short the attempt at organization.[13]

The threats of Lambert Simnel and Perkin Warbeck during Henry VII's reign show the rate of progress towns had made in ordnance and its distribution over the years. Exeter's financial records speak of gunpowder and gunners after 1483, measures used to good effect against Warbeck's rebels.[14] By way of contrast, York's precocious development of urban artillery had declined and defensive measures lay unfulfilled in the ruins of the castle. Sometime after 1450–51, York gained its first recorded keeper of the city's ordnance, but John Craven was dismissed from office in 1484 for neglecting his stock. For defense against Simnel in 1487, the city prepared to transfer gunpowder and twelve serpentines from Scarborough, for not even in the remains of their castle could civic officials find sufficient equipment.[15] Threat of insurrection after the earl of Northumberland's murder two years later forced the city to collect a benevolence to pay for iron gates and posterns, more traditional means of defense.[16]

Walls, gates and towers were not only more old fashioned, passive means of defense than guns and cannon, but repair and extension of wall fabric made constant demands on urban finances. It did not help when monarchs, intent on refurbishing and fortifying castles like Warwick and Nottingham, invited criticism when they did not carry out their plans: Richard III pulled down York's castle with every intention of rebuilding it, but work halted at the end of his reign and the site was left in ruins.[17] As well as expressing civic pride and enhancing communal images, towns showed their loyalty to the Crown by maintaining their defenses to defend themselves and keep the king's peace, precisely the argument used by Norwich in 1253 when its citizens petitioned the king for the right to build walls.[18] Town governments always welcomed outside help to finance wall construction, and often the best protection could only be assured by royal assistance. Towns helped themselves by scheduling annual inspections by urban officials, an activity recorded on financial records as much for the wine consumed in the process as for the notation of sums needed for repair.[19] The impetus for inspection could also come from the Crown itself, as in 1458 when the Norwich mayor and his sheriffs were ordered to repair broken walls. In 1491, Henry VII pointedly reminded York officials they almost lost their city to Simnel's forces because of walls in poor repair.[20]

Wall repair consumed a moderate but important portion of local budgets. Exeter spent between £30 and £60 annually on mending during the 1380s (23% to 46% of average annual receipts), and over £50 after Perkin Warbeck's attack a century later (26% of annual receipts). York's costs were somewhat lower, ranging from 13s. 11d. to over £12 *p.a.* after Simnel's attack.[21] During the 1450s when Norwich found its walls in ruins and its regular contributions from each ward inadequate, city officials planned on levying a general subsidy on citizens until they were saved by a timely legacy from a former mayor.[22] To provide funds, the royal government granted towns licenses of mortmain to raise money, as well as direct grants from customs and cloth aulnage receipts.[23] A typical grant was murage, the Crown's gift of the right to levy local taxes, such as a toll on merchandise entering town gates. Although eagerly adapted by civic officials to their internal budgets, grants of murage were clearly controlled by the king. Most clearly specified the commodities that could be taxed, the duration of the grant, and the groups or individuals exempt from it. A few towns such as York succeeded in gaining the proceeds in perpetuity, but in general the royal government retained control over a source of revenue that guaranteed both local and national security and prosperity.[24]

Such grants could prove to be a mixed blessing. The possibility that the toll charges that composed murage were a burden and a hindrance to trade had to be balanced against the benefits they brought to defense. During the royal progress of 1483, Richard III recognized the inconvenience murage could cause. He sought York's favor by agreeing to the request civic officials had made a few months earlier to abolish tolls on merchandise entering the city, not realizing that in doing so he deprived York of a significant source of their income and murage.[25] Financial accounts show that on average murage accounted for about £22 or 10% of total annual receipts, and that expenses for repair were usually (and perhaps negligently) quite small. Richard later recompensed the city with a £20 annuity specifically for wall repair, but his initial concession so confused both local and Crown authorities that more harm than good was done to city finances and tempers.[26] The correct assessment of local needs, and particularly the value of investment in defensive measures, often required more acuity than either civic officials or kings possessed. Nevertheless, it was clear to all parties that urban commercial prosperity could be harnessed to improve the safety and amenities of a town, upon which depended the wealth and security of the entire realm.

Troops

The organization of human beings provoked greater challenges than the provision of supplies and defensive measures. When the king declared war, towns not only had to raise and pay troops, but deal with the men authorized to lead the forces. The responsibility for organizing urban troops could rest with the king himself or, more usually, the nobles to whom he delegated such duties. In periods of civil disturbance, conflicts over leadership had national repercussions.

Towns that found themselves led into battle by local nobles known to and patronized by civic officials usually had little complaint, but this was not always the case. Magnates who mustered on their own, perhaps for their own aggrandizement, were not unknown. In 1419, Sir Henry de Athedill asked York for troops to reinforce the Scottish east march, guarded by the earl of Northumberland. Civic officers doubted whether the earl or the king had authorized the increment and sent messengers northwards to inquire, discovering that the earl had no knowledge of the request. York decided to keep ten men-at-arms and twenty archers in readiness in case a royal command was given, an act of preparedness Norwich was not ready to copy.[27] Its civic officials refused to help the earl of Warwick in 1457 when as captain of Calais he appealed without royal authorization for troops against an alleged French attack.[28] Thirty years later, the mayor and sheriffs made their reluctance explicit when in response to Lord FitzWalter's request for troops against the earl of Lincoln, they pointed out that mustering would commence only upon the receipt of a royal commission.[29] Edward IV's problems with Warwick and Clarence resulted in several unauthorized musters, forcing the king to advise his towns in 1469 not to raise soldiers unless in receipt of orders with the king's privy seal, signet, or sign manual.[30] On the whole, civic officials showed an understandable reluctance to raise and pay troops without royal approval. But there was little a town could do to prevent a determined noble from gathering forces and giving them his livery, as Thomas Percy Baron Egremont showed in 1453 when he convinced unemployed York craftsmen to attack his family's enemies the Nevilles.[31]

Who were the men willing to forsake home and friends for a campaign season or longer? When Coventry raised troops for the 1481 campaign against Scotland, officers relied upon "strangers" from towns as distant as thirty miles, and faced the task of feeding and housing them while awaiting royal orders.[32] Norwich musters of the mid-fourteenth century listed servants, hostelers, and tailors, mostly inadequately equipped.[33] The York jobless who flocked to Egremont's cause were probably typical, hoping to improve their financial lot by some combination of wages and plunder. The soldiers who rebelled against York's policy of payment during the Scottish campaigns were named and arrested by civic officials, including a gentleman whose higher status persuaded the others to take the lead first in criticizing urban policy and then apologizing.[34] Mustering went to the very heart of a town's notion of self-identity: the dispute over suburban legal jurisdiction found the city of Norwich and the cathedral prior also at odds over the correct distribution of able-bodied soldiers from the wards in question.[35]

The financing of urban troops provided late medieval civic officials with their greatest challenges. Pre-paid troops were so much the norm that when the Lancastrian Bastard of Fauconberg invaded the realm in 1471, he expected the Kentish troops who joined him to provide their own wages.[36] The chronicler John Warkworth even blamed too-frequent mustering for Edward IV's loss of the crown in 1470, because over the previous decade the common people had "at yet at every battle to come ferre oute [of] there countreis at ther awn coste."[37] Royal demands for military contributions forced some officials into creative financing: in 1451, the mayor of Nottingham let to lease a meadow in the town's common field for the £20 needed to pay the wages of troops sent the year before against Jack Cade's rebels.[38] Early in the spring of 1460 when Norwich assessed citizens by ward to pay for soldiers to resist the Yorkists, town officials deliberately excused the poor from contributing, a charitable consideration repeated in other boroughs such as York. But before the end of the year, Norwich officials decided that the poor existed in such numbers that they had to ask the Crown for full release from a commission requesting more troops.[39]

The officials' difficulties in raising funds were not always appreciated by the troops. During the 1460s and 1470s, many towns found it necessary to increase wages to overcome reluctance to serve. After 1462, Norwich could no longer find willing troops at the customary rate of 6d. *per diem*, while Nottingham's troops commanded 8d. *per diem*. Likewise, Coventry's soldiers demanded a raise from eight to twelve pence *per diem* between 1468 and 1470. Twelve pence was also the daily rate York's officials had to pay the eighty men sent to Richard III's last campaign at Bosworth. Not only did some troops expect jackets and other equipment to be provided, but monetary rewards for good service upon their return were especially appreciated.[40]

Despite the strain on local budgets, officials careful of their town's image in royal eyes offered support in addition to the expected salaries. Although few boroughs attempted to victual the troops apart from wine or ale consumed before they left town, arrangements for food and drink were vital. The men were expected to use the wages they received in advance to buy food along the way: not only did kings warn troops against plundering their own countryside, but both the Crown and civic officials ordered local victualers to provide adequate supplies at reasonable prices when troops passed through their markets.[41]

Captains to lead the soldiers and equipment to aid their tasks usually were provided by the towns. Mayors and sheriffs sometimes performed the leadership task, but lesser men with reputations for competence and trustworthiness were more frequently chosen: York entrusted its macebearer John Brakenbury with the task during Edward IV's reign; Nottingham, its sheriff.[42] York officials also covered the costs of the standard, pavilion, harness and jackets for troops bound for Scotland in 1481, not requiring the citizens to contribute further.[43] Training, however, receives little mention: the ruins of York's second castle, the Old Baile, witnessed the assembly and disciplining of troops late in the sixteenth century; a century earlier, men from the Ainsty mustered in the pasture of Knavesmire outside the city; and York's contingent was ordered to assemble before the mayor and officers outside Bootham Bar. But exactly how urban inhabitants were trained to be useful soldiers, if they were instructed at all, remains unclear.[44]

Even when a town raised all or part of the money needed for expenses, disputes continued to arise. Troops were customarily paid only partly in advance: before the 1420s, captains paid soldiers in the French campaigns half a year in advance, and forced them to subsist on the sum for nine months, after which the men were paid at the end of each succeeding quarter.[45] Towns had similar systems of disbursement, and heard similar complaints. In June 1461, Norwich troops remarked to the duke of Norfolk that the city was cheating them by refusing to pay for service given earlier that year. Edward IV himself intervened on the troops' behalf, and when city soldiers joined him for a campaign two years later he demanded they be paid for a full nine weeks of service, three weeks longer than customary.[46] Norwich was still slow to pay troops after the battle of Tewkesbury in 1471: eleven months later some soldiers still had not been paid for their service on the field, and in 1474 payment was finally given to one citizen for riding to London at the time of the battle.[47]

York took special care with troops' wages, but was unable to avoid problems. Payment for the Scottish campaign of 1481 was to have been gathered by the constables of each parish and delivered to the wardens, who were to distribute the money to the troops' captain. A month after this system was devised the mayor decided to intercede between the wardens and the captain, avoiding discontent by paying each soldier 10s. on his first day, "and that so fully spendit to delyver more." Civic generosity was pressed to the limit six weeks later when two soldiers arrayed from other areas arrived in York destitute, requiring a loan from the officers to convey them to Newcastle.[48] No less expensive was the conflict that arose in 1482 when three soldiers bound for Scotland demanded not an advance for fourteen days but their full wages for twice that long, refusing to move until they had been paid. Civic officials feared an insurrection if all the troops joined the protest so they imprisoned the three instigators for over a week. Upon investigation, they learned that a conspiracy was not afoot, but to save the campaign the mayor and his brethren paid the troops for the full term of twenty-eight days. Care with finances continued upon urban militias' return from battle, when officers carefully examined accounts and directed any money left over to be repaid to the parishes that had originally raised it.[49]

Correctly mustered and paid in advance, soldiers could still cause trouble by refusing to join their companies. Deserters and soldiers who were A.W.O.L. created problems for every campaign, but the most reluctance was shown towards overseas assignments. Late in 1380, the mayor and bailiffs of Exeter and nine other southern towns received orders to retain "under honorable and not rigorous arrest" all soldiers found within their jurisdictions who had withdrawn from royal service in France and Brittany.[50] During the first half of the fifteenth century, officers in Norwich and Exeter were advised to watch both for citizens who avoided service and for other soldiers who illegally tarried in the two cities: Calais and Picardy seem to have been particularly unwelcome assignments.[51] Scotland was little more attractive to some soldiers. Several York residents refused to leave the city and take up victualing chores at Berwick, while a Hingham (Norf.) merchant spent the spring of 1476 in Norwich instead of joining the earl of Northumberland on the Scottish border.[52] From 1439, chief officers in ports were obliged under statute to arrest tarrying troops and detain them for inquiry by justices of the peace, but their efforts seemed to have little effect.[53] Not every subject was convinced by his government's demands for his attendance in battle far from home and livelihood, and a few gambled that anonymity could be found in urban settings.

Medieval Campaigns

The Continent

Although borough troops formed no great part of the musters for the Hundred Years' War, monarchs expected town forces to be in readiness for French campaigns both announced and only rumored. For example, Nottingham contributed five slingers to the 1359 French campaign. During the same decade, inspections of arms and arrays in one Norwich ward revealed over two hundred men in various stages of preparedness, ranging from civic officials in plate armor to servants with staffs and coutels. The city could turn out close to one thousand men for combat, but in terms of able and equipped forces Norwich frequently provided the Crown with 120 soldiers.[54] In 1385, forty men-at-arms, forty archers, and an equal number of mariners prepared to resist an imminent French invasion, the troops' wages covered by a double subsidy (about £189) Norwich levied on and by itself. Norwich was also responsible that year for contributions to the royal navy, although local records dedicated much more space to the guns, a standard, and red and white hoods and tunics the men wore.[55] The French threat of 1386 led to preparation not only in Norwich but also in Exeter, Nottingham, and five other urban centers. Richard II asked for men-at-arms with wages for a month, or a loan which he promised to repay from the next lay subsidy. The threatening force soon disbanded but the close call angered many about the ineptitude of English foreign policy and formed part of the charges that led to Chancellor Pole's impeachment.[56] Despite truces that marked the later years of Richard II's reign, urban mustering for France continued. Days after Henry of Bolingbroke returned from exile, Guardian of England Edmund duke of York ordered York sheriffs to stop arraying men for French campaigns and to keep the troops in the north, ready to discourage the Scots from invading at a time of national weakness.[57]

Local records took little interest in even the major engagements of the fifteenth-century French campaigns. The battle of Agincourt goes unnoticed in such sources, although records of Salisbury mention its veterans passing through the city and picking a fight with the residents.[58] However, Exeter's proximity to the continent guaranteed its participation in a variety of preparations for combat. During the 1340s, Welsh troops had passed through the city on their way to France, causing the officers additional cost "for watching and other expenses...." Exeter's receivers' roll of 1417–18 preserves the expenses incurred during the victualing of troops for Henry V's Lower Normandy campaign. The soldiers may have been raised by the city, or the civic officials may have been ordered to provision royal troops who passed through town on the way to the coast. The men and supplies of Exeter also nourished a force of about 13,000 to annex large portions of Normandy and capture Rouen in 1419.[59]

If later monarchs showed any interest in utilizing urban troops in innovative ways for French campaigns, local records preserve no trace. During 1425–26, when English conquest had reached its fullest extent, Exeter's mayor and bailiffs inspected city troops and their equipment, an occasion noteworthy only for the officers' consumption of four gallons of wine in the process.[60] Threats to Calais required troops from Norwich, Nottingham, York and Hull between 1436 and 1453.[61] Enemy vessels sighted off the Norfolk coast frightened Paston correspondents throughout the 1450s and 1460s, but Norwich was not called upon to respond. The city saved its resources for a petition from the burghers of Great Yarmouth, who asked the city for aid in 1457 against the French threat. Norwich sent two hundred men and assessed "a reasonable aid" on every citizen to pay the troops for eight days.[62] Later campaigns, such as Edward IV's abbreviated invasion and Henry VII's expeditions, were undertaken with town money instead of manpower. Exeter citizen William Floier indented to serve the duke of Clarence and to supply archers in 1475, but the city itself left no record of corporate action. Edward expected York, Norwich and Nottingham to contribute to a subsidy for archers, but the money proved so hard to collect that one-and-three-quarters lay subsidies were levied instead.[63] Throughout the period, English urban troops maintained a narrow field of activity, making no significant contributions to their realm's activities on the Continent. They missed the glories and the indignities of foreign combat, reserving their strengths for battlefields closer to home and livelihood.

The Scots

Although truces with Scotland were not unknown, English monarchs throughout the period relied upon military means to claim overlordship, control lands and fishing rights along the marches, and wrest the fortress of Berwick permanently from the Scots. Fierce raiding through the thirteenth and fourteenth centuries had depopulated the northern counties and resulted in reduced tax assessments. By the late fourteenth century, the Crown established that wars conducted against the Scots and Welsh constituted domestic defensive action and hence troops' services, at least to the point of muster, should be paid by their communities.[64] Henry IV and later kings clarified their subjects' duties by requiring military aid of all men, lords and yeomen alike, who had received any lands or annuities from the Crown, or risk forfeiture of the grants.[65] But the weight of this burden was not imposed equitably. Their geographic proximity to the enemy meant that York and to a lesser extent Nottingham bore much of the responsibility for defense against the Scots throughout the fourteenth and early fifteenth centuries: during the early years of Edward III, for example, York routinely raised one hundred men for Scottish campaigns.[66] Not only did mustered troops and supplies have a shorter distance to travel to the front to be organized by the wardens of the marches, but monarchs counted on these towns' defensive motivations, retaliatory impulses against neighboring raiders, and the lure of nearby plunder. Southern and eastern towns such as Norwich did not routinely contribute paid troops and equipment to Scottish campaigns until obliged to by the Yorkist kings.[67]

Financial and judicial measures, however, involved a greater variety of boroughs in royal policy against Scotland. In 1400, Henry IV asked the leading officials of five major towns to lend money for his Scottish war, appointing as receivers of the funds York notables Archbishop Scrope, the abbot of St. Mary's, Mayor William Frost, and former mayor and parliamentary representative Thomas Graa.[68] Henry's antagonism towards Scotland increased when the earl of Northumberland and Lord Bardolf escaped over the border after their rebellion in 1405. The following year, the civic officers of Nottingham were named to a commission of inquiry concerning the "people of the north" who pretended to take up arms on behalf of the king and the Prince of Wales, but who actually worked against the king's peace.[69] The unofficial and partial mustering that occurred in 1419 after Henry de Athedill's plea for help was not the only step York took against the northern enemy. A month after the muster, the city passed stringent rules against resident Scotsmen, and throughout the period York residents always responded quickly to deny that most insulting and dangerous slander, being called a Scotsman.[70]

English kings throughout the fifteenth century all struggled with the Scottish enemy and the domestic preparations needed to combat him. Henry VI's campaigns were tightly linked to the political factionalism engendered by his greater nobles. Edward IV's early campaigns demanded modest resources from his realm, but boroughs were not excused from contributing. The city of Norwich specifically provided troops to sieges of Lancastrian-held Northumbrian castles and to general campaigns against the Scots as well, spending almost £300 during the first three years of Edward's reign.[71] York continued to carry the greatest burden, however, working in concert with commanders such as the earl of Warwick, and later Richard of Gloucester and the earl of Northumberland.[72]

The truces that marked the 1470s could not solve the deep disputes between Scotland and northern English society, and a renewal of war was inevitable. Although Edward IV and James III discussed peace terms sincerely and planned the marriages of their offspring and siblings, continuing border raids and the pressure of family members (the dukes of Albany and Gloucester in particular) prompted a return to hostilities.[73] The city of York found itself in a particularly difficult position, as its officers were reluctant to oppose a favorite project of their good lord Gloucester, but suffered too many economic problems to be open-handed in their support. Entries describing preparations for war survive in the midst of complaints of debt, restrictions on foreign merchants and vagrants, and the problems of collecting tolls.[74] The detailed accounts of the raising of men and money for a nearby theater of war under the command of the nobleman long seen as a patron are fascinating in themselves. Their value is increased because they take place within a complex socio-economic context, revealing how problems of mustering complicated the borough's assumptions about the nature of patronage, financial constraints, and duties to the Crown.

After August 1479, the withdrawal of marriage arrangements, renewed border raids, and rumors of a Franco-Scottish rapprochement prompted Edward to return to war. His appointment of his brother Richard as Lieutenant General with the power to summon troops in the area led directly to York's mustering of forces throughout the summer of 1480. On 8 September, probably in response to a raid on Bamburgh by the earl of Angus, Richard of Gloucester demanded York troops assemble at Durham within a week of receipt of his orders.[75] The retaliatory raid that ensued did little harm to Scotland, but it persuaded James to petition Louis XI for artillery and gunners with which to fight the English.[76] York's loyal mustering for the campaign earned the king's praise as well as a request the following February to array 120 men from the city and the Ainsty, for a two-month Scottish campaign led by Edward himself. The promise of royal leadership and pressure from the Prince of Wales's council convinced Coventry as well to contribute a grant of 200 marks and the wages of sixty men-at-arms, but the strain on city finances resulted in threatening assemblies and vocal discontent. York avoided similar displeasure by dividing financial responsibilities. City constables collected money for wages from the parishes, and prepared victuals, transport, and scouts for leaders Gloucester and Northumberland. Council members relieved part of the burden by determining that although salaries were covered by the citizenry, the chamber alone would pay for jackets and equipment.[77] Although a moderate degree of efficiency marked both urban and royal preparations, the campaign degenerated into uncoordinated raids. Both Edward and James blamed papal intervention for the cessation of full-scale war, but in reality neither side could afford more than sporadic attacks.[78]

The 1482 campaign was plagued with difficulties for both the king and his urban troops. After the previous two campaign seasons, York believed it could no longer maintain the same level of loyal support.

Unrest broke the city's peace and on one occasion the officers allowed Gloucester to punish the perpetrators himself; this usurpation of municipal privilege may have been intended to honor York's good patron or simply to involve the figure prompting the insurrection. City officers asserted that York's finances could not support another campaign at previous levels, and decreased the number of archers they usually provided. Gloucester sent word of this change to the king, who at the start of the campaign in April acknowledged "ye be not of such richesse as ye have been in tyme past." Nevertheless, Edward looked forward to the usual 120 archers and carts to carry food to the front, requiring that the officers lay all costs and charges only upon the wealthier citizens and not the poor commoners.[79] This admonition required the officers to pledge personal support for a total of thirty-nine troops, to gather money for the wages of the remainder, and to excuse the poorest parishes from contributing at all.[80]

Such efficient preparations, however, did not result in total success on the battlefield. Although the campaign was invigorated when the duke of Albany joined the English, the expedition soon became troubled. Edward IV decided against taking personal leadership of the army, renewing Gloucester's command instead; Albany's defection prompted peace negotiations which forced Gloucester to retreat from Edinburgh before he had accomplished all he desired; and even the successful capture of Berwick was considered by some a waste of resources.[81] Raids upon Dumfries and Edinburgh may have allowed York troops to profit from pillaging, but the city's force as a whole ran out of money in August, requiring local parishes to raise more funds. Troops ready for departure that month acted on the financial problems when they threatened insurrection demanding full wages in advance. Upon their return, the soldiers' performance was openly criticized. One man slandered the troops by asserting "tha dyd nothyng for [their wages] bot made whypys of thar bow strynges to dryve cariage with...."[82] Richard himself came in for rebuke by local men in June 1482 and February 1483, an indication that his role as military hero and borough patron had its critics.[83] To the Crown, however, Richard had become indispensable, praised by parliament and rewarded richly by the king with a permanent wardenship and lands along the frontier. York could bask in his reflected glory grateful it had managed to provide some of the resources of his victories. Future gifts and concessions to the northern capital, particularly those granted by Richard himself, were consciously based upon the loyal contributions made to Scotland's bloody fields.[84]

Edward IV's successors took a more cautious approach to Scotland. Once king, Richard could not afford continued warfare in the north: recognizing the link between York's poverty and its military support, his major grant to York during his royal progress specifically mentioned those contributions at Dumfries and Edinburgh. His 1484 alliance with James III allayed his fears of French intervention while casting a dignified light of conciliation upon a usurper's regime.[85] Even the small number of Scots troops given Henry Tudor by the French king for Bosworth persuaded the new monarch of the value of Anglo-Scottish accord. But conciliation was not bound to please inhabitants of the north, direct victims of border raids and beneficiaries of plundering parties who recalled with increasing nostalgia Richard's leadership against the Scots. Within a month of his accession, Henry VII wrote to York, pardoning all but a handful of northerners, and expressing respect for the sacrifices they had made for his "uncle" Henry VI and for the indispensable military service they always contributed against Scotland. He particularly feared that the Scots would attack Berwick with the help of Yorkist loyalists, and in an effort to reconstitute northern resistance he restored the earls of Northumberland and Westmorland to their positions in the east march and the county palatine of Durham.[86] In April 1488, the restored Northumberland called upon the city of York for troops for a surprising turnaround in diplomacy: the defense of James III's realm against violent factionalism erupting on the border. If the city complied, they left no trace of it in their records, and were helpless to avert the king's murder in June at Sauchieburn.[87]

The new king, James IV, brought a greater challenge to the realm of the first Tudor by his support of the pretender Perkin Warbeck. During James's early years on the throne, Henry annoyed the young ruler by reinforcing his rebels with boatloads of munitions and refusing to punish merchants guilty of piracy against the Scots. Although the monarchs continued to exchange gifts and maintain a pretense of peace, James began to take seriously messages from Margaret, Dowager Duchess of Burgundy, that she was ready to conspire against Henry and wanted his help.[88] James's interest resulted in Warbeck's arrival in Scotland in 1495, after the pretender had failed to raise Ireland and France on his behalf but had gained the mischievous backing of Yorkist Duchess Margaret and Maximilian I. James lavished money and supplies upon Warbeck, but his tentative raid across the border in September 1496 failed to convince even northerners heartily dissatisfied with Henry to join the enemy Scots.[89] As acting warden of the east marches, the earl of Surrey ordered York to raise and finance sixty archers for the ten-day campaign. This request was repeated (and the number of men doubled) the following spring with orders to collect taxation voted by parliament in January; York apparently had no difficulty in complying, but Norwich so resented the imposition it raised only twenty men.[90] Nevertheless, Henry's serious response to the threat and the urban militias' participation prompted James to withdraw support from Warbeck and abandon him to his ultimate fate in the west country. After a flurry of border raids designed to save face with his subjects, James began serious peace negotiations with Henry. They resulted in 1497 in the landmark Truce of Ayton, making possible the Scottish king's 1503 marriage to Princess Margaret. Once more, urban militias had contributed their small part to border warfare and international diplomacy, creating the precedents that maintained York as an important center for Scottish campaigns through the mid-sixteenth century.[91]

Dynastic Disputes

Internal rebellion inflicted strains upon urban resources which exceeded the merely financial. The violent encounters of kings, their rival claimants to the throne, and the noble factions supporting them forced civic officials to make shrewd decisions about the nature of military support able to be mustered and the side to which it should be given. A king had every right to demand soldiers when his throne was threatened, but how were the towns to fulfill their obligations when the very identity of the king was in question? A borough's survival in legal as well as physical terms depended upon the discerning judgment its officials showed when called upon for support.

Although civil discord in the period found its most concentrated expression during the second half of the fifteenth century, examples of internal rebellion occurred earlier. Towns could not ignore the change in dynasty when Henry IV took the throne from Richard II: in January 1400, the new king demanded military aid from Nottingham and several other midland towns, to counter an attack threatened by Richard's followers. The boroughs' ready compliance with the new regime helped

Henry keep his throne, although the show of force for the former king assured Richard's demise within a few weeks.[92] But as the fifteenth century progressed, the choices became more difficult and the stakes higher, although generosity in civic patronage sometimes assured friends in all possible camps. Actual combat conditions between 1455 and 1497 may have occupied no more than four hundred days and England was spared the devastation Europe knew throughout the century, but few people went totally untouched by the disorder and uneasiness engendered by civil conflict.[93] Civil combat not only brought the usual problems of finance and training, but the enemy was no longer of a different nationality, easy to ridicule and safe to hate. When, for example, Lancastrian lords passed through Nottingham in 1459, dissension arose even though the town was not immediately called upon to muster for a campaign, for townsmen took sides in a fierce political quarrel that drove them to borough court.[94]

During the early years of the Wars of the Roses, the issues appeared clear-cut and the king's pleas for help received timely and generous responses from towns. From December 1459 to February 1460, Henry VI's government established commissions of array commanding men and archers at community expense for the defense of England against the Yorkists. Exeter equipped more than thirty men; Nottingham raised over £23 for expenses; and the wealthier and more populous Norwich aimed for the sum of two hundred marks while exempting the poor from contributing.[95] Even after the duke of York and his party arrived in England in June 1460 and the subsequent battle of Northampton resulted in a Yorkist victory and the capture of the king, towns loyally continued to raise troops for Henry VI. Urban patronage to Yorkist relatives helped balance town policy to some extent, but in matters of actual defense civic officials recognized no alternative to the king.[96] During Henry Tudor's reign, the city of York claimed it had been consistently devoted to the Lancastrian cause, sending 400 men to fight at Wakefield in December 1460, another 400 for Queen Margaret's march south, and 1000 men for the battle of Towton in March 1461. The numbers are in the realm of fiction, but the city's financial records do show accumulated debts that stem partly from frequent mustering.[97]

The months of transition between the Lancastrian and Yorkist regimes demanded tact and forethought from towns. Their comments in local records are confined to issues of local resources, although occasionally choices in regnal dating reveal a borough's gambling streak.

Early in January 1461, a commission of array came to Norwich in Henry VI's name and after "mature consideration" the city agreed to raise 120 men for a term of six weeks at the cost of 6d. *per diem*. The following month, the earl of Warwick wrote in Henry's name, praising the contribution and asking that the term of service be extended a month.[98] Local records do not indicate whether the troops were present at either the February Yorkist victory at Mortimers Cross or the Lancastrian triumph two weeks later at the second battle of St. Albans, but those are likely venues. The next entry in the Assembly Book simply announced Edward IV's accession early in March and was followed later that month by a call for all men between the ages of sixteen and sixty to array themselves for the new king's cause. Norwich agreed to send Edward a "competens numerus" of troops and levied half of a tenth (about £47) to pay for victuals, its quiet acquiescence perhaps due in part to the Yorkist duke of Norfolk's relationship with the city.[99] None of the towns exhibited Lancastrian sympathies in the early years of Edward's reign, complying instead with his frequent requests for aid against the Lancastrian-held north.[100] In 1462, Norwich received royal praise and some psychological pressure in recognition of the burdens it had borne over the preceding two years. The king commented that the officers had done such a good job, he knew he could rely upon them to help array his new fleet.[101]

By 1469, the strain of such frequent mustering began to show. During that year, numerous local risings occurred and Edward IV was taken prisoner by Warwick. Norwich's recorder rode to the duke of Norfolk, empowered to array all subjects in the county, to discuss the realm's violence and ask to be excused from providing troops. The recorder believed that if the duke reminded Edward of Norwich's hospitality shown the royal family that year, the city would gain a pardon. The ploy had limited effect, for Norwich eventually sent forty men clothed in jackets to quell Lord Welles and the Lincolnshire rebellion of March 1470. The men received 12d. *per diem* for five weeks, but Edward kept them another fourteen days and asked the city to send him the extra wages so he could pay the men. Soldiers' wages rose again in the autumn of 1470, when Edward asked not for an "adequate number" but for as many as Norwich could spare: the frequent demand for their services gave soldiers the ability to demand 16d. *per diem* for the campaign against Clarence and Warwick.[102]

Towns kept a low profile during the months of Edward's exile (September 1470 to March 1471) and obediently dated entries in their records with Henry VI's regnal year. Evidence of Yorkist sympathies is not only slight, but apparent only some weeks after the Yorkist king returned and could be considered something more than a friendless exile. Norwich sent out messengers in April 1471 to determine Edward's return and progress south. The officers, like those of London, waited for news of Yorkist victory at Barnet before offering troops, although they begged permission to keep them at home in case the Bastard of Fauconberg attacked the Norfolk coast.[103] Nottingham showed the most interest in the Yorkist restoration, mustering soldiers only two weeks after Edward landed at Ravenspur, raising over £26 in one day, and optimistically dating the entry in their records with Edward's regnal year.[104]

After 1471, towns expressed their fatigue and poverty more forthrightly in attempts to win release. Even York's civic officials, desirous as they were of a close relationship with the Yorkists, could not make contributions without considering local strains and dissension. Nevertheless, they intended to start out on the right foot when they responded to one of Richard's first appeals for troops June 1483 when he claimed protectorship of the realm. The mayor gathered two hundred men of the city and one hundred from the Ainsty and paid them 12d. *per diem*, though they arrived too late to help Richard in the way he intended.[105] Tardiness marked York's last contribution to Richard as well, when in August 1485 its officers sent only eighty men to the king at Bosworth, too late for them to help in battle.[106] Lacking such a personal relationship, Norwich retreated to the Edwardian system of benevolences, offering Richard £40 to be excused from raising troops against enemies such as Buckingham during the early months of his reign.[107] Yet *not* being asked to muster troops could be an equally upsetting experience. When Richard sent commissions of array to various Norfolk gentlemen in March 1484, Norwich was left out and wondered how to act. Its counselors advised the city to ignore the county commissions, and merely to warn citizens that an assessment might be made in the future and to have their money ready.[108]

Henry VII's problems with pretenders challenged towns on several different levels. Civic officials were never tempted to believe the claims of Simnel or Warbeck, or at least did not reveal as much in local records. Rather, the conditions of Henry's accession made it imperative for them to act with positive dispatch to confirm their loyalty to the Tudor regime.

In 1487, although Norwich could plead poverty and send £40 to the king instead of soldiers,[109] York had to exhibit greater willingness to serve the new king. Diehard Yorkists Lord Lovell and the earl of Lincoln petitioned the city for permission to enter as Simnel's vanguard and counted on York's support, but its officers merely passed the letter to the earl of Northumberland who was raising royal troops. Percy mustered sufficient forces on his own, leaving local soldiers in the city to defend it against attacks by the Lords Scrope of Bolton and Masham. York celebrated the royal victory at Stoke that June with services in the Minster, quelling royal doubts of lingering civic sympathy for the Yorkist cause. The extensive account recorded after the fact in the city's council minutes further placed the officers' loyal response in the best light possible.[110]

Henry took Warbeck's claims to the throne seriously, not least because of the threat they constituted to diplomatic relations with France and Spain. By the 1490s, foreign rulers such as Ferdinand and Isabella respected Henry enough to negotiate a marriage with his heir, but they withheld final approval (and the bride) until Henry terminated all threats to his realm. The variety of battlefields Warbeck chose prompted the king to compel several urban militias to participate. York's soldiers could be counted on for service when the pretender invaded from the north with Scottish support, but Norwich troops resented being sent so far away.[111] Local threats moved them to raise troops to assist Great Yarmouth when Warbeck planned to land in East Anglia during the summer of 1495, but they responded with less enthusiasm when asked two years later for men to resist his landing in Cornwall.[112] By way of contrast, Exeter, the city at the center of Perkin's 1497 invasion, not only was the object of Henry's concern but adequately defended itself on the king's behalf without being compelled or threatened. With the support of the earl of Devon, the citizens held Exeter against the rebels and used town ordnance to turn them away.[113] Henry and his realm remained free of Yorkist threats until the winter of 1501–2, when Edmund de la Pole earl of Suffolk took umbrage at his treatment by the new regime and fled to Maximilian's court to raise support for an invasion. Norwich raised forty troops and £40 to counter this threat but they were unlikely to be employed as Suffolk did not return to England until 1506, when he was delivered directly into Henry's captivity.[114] The first Tudor's survival was assured only in small part by the willingness of urban troops to support their king, but their role in demonstrating loyalty and acquiescing to shrewd leadership was an essential one.

The defense of the realm involved towns in a complex network of contributions and obligations. Kings expected civic officers to act upon royal calls for aid with measures ranging from soldiers and ships to gunpowder and pigs. Urban subjects fought overseas and in neighboring counties, and when the men did not go themselves, they contributed instead supplies, transport, or money. The benefits kings gained are clear, despite the anecdotal evidence of recalcitrant and untrained forces who cannot have been easy to lead into battle. But towns themselves also gained from the experience of war, however consistently they complained of the cost and trouble. Royal musters of men and supplies forced towns into a state of preparedness, and compelled them to survey their means for defense. Reviews of the men and equipment they possessed for their share of the defense of the realm created the opportunities for urban subjects to request royal assistance. Mustering against a common enemy provided cohesion within urban society, and forced citizens to think beyond local preoccupations to the realm's higher policies.

The comparative method employed in this study allows us to survey the responses of several towns in various stages of economic and legal development. York's significant contribution to the Anglo-Scottish campaigns came at a time in its history when it had developed the written records able to preserve the full variety of urban responses to royal demands. The difficulties it faced in balancing real financial hardship with its personal relationship to the campaign's leader are largely unmatched by the other boroughs and their records. Norwich's assembly books also provided an opportunity to record complaint and comment, revealing that its growing economic status did not inhibit townspeople from grumbling about being removed from their homes and livelihoods to distant battlefields for questionable causes. As military duties increasingly fell to professionals in this period, and requirements for expensive artillery grew, urban complaints should be seen less as selfish whining than as shrewd commentary on appropriate military preparedness. But despite all the criticism, one cannot help but be impressed by the cooperation shown by large and small boroughs when a military summons arrived, as the loyal mustering of an Exeter or Nottingham reveals. Unable to provide professionals in the field or the latest in combat technology, towns nevertheless hurried to fulfill the Crown's orders. But one cannot ignore the implications of John Warkworth's comment on the link between increased mustering under the Yorkists and national discontent so severe that Edward IV temporarily lost his throne. The financial pressure that the towns of this study experienced as a consequence of military preparedness was merely the local reaction within a full context of civil disturbance.

Towns' willingness to supply the commander in chief with his requirements thus had serious consequences for urban development. When the king petitioned for assistance, he invariably argued for the necessity of defensive measures, an imperative that touched the welfare of the entire realm. Subjects could not refuse: poverty might force them to excuse themselves, but as long as the king clearly stated both the danger to every subject as well as the cooperation of his council, outright refusal was not a possible response.[115] But towns were not without choices and alternatives, as the integration of royal and urban records reveals. Towns unable to fulfill royal expectations had to devise crafty excuses to avoid the monarch's displeasure, but underneath the formulaic explanations of nonconformance lie vivid statements about urban well-being in these years. To die for one's king on campaign was a heavy charge, but equally weighty (especially for civic officials) was the financing and organization required for the initial investment. The messengers who brought news to late medieval boroughs carried more than declarations of war and developments in diplomacy. They simultaneously delivered challenges to urban loyalties, budgets, and principles.

NOTES

[1] James F. Powers, *A Society Organized for War: The Iberian Municipal Militias in the Central Middle Ages, 1000–1284* (Berkeley and Los Angeles: University of California Press, 1988); Pierre Clément Timbal, *La Guerre de cent ans vue à travers les registres du parlement (1337–1369)* (Paris: Centre National de la Recherche Scientifique, 1961), pp. 172–74.

[2] French comparisons are examined in Richard W. Kaeuper in *War, Justice and Public Order: England and France in the Later Middle Ages* (Oxford: Clarendon Press, 1988), pp. 190–91. For a discussion of the earlier period, see Charles R. Young, *The English Borough and Royal Administration, 1130–1307* (Durham, N.C.: Duke University Press, 1961), ch. 5. Henry II's Assize of Arms 1181 demanded that burgesses be equipped with quilted doublets, iron headpieces, and a lance, and

provide service if possessed of chattels or rents to a certain value: David C. Douglas and George W. Greenaway, eds., *English Historical Documents II, 1042–1189* (New York: Oxford University Press, 1968), pp. 416–17.

[3] Only when the soldiers were needed for foreign campaigns did the Crown have to pay the men's wages, usually from the time the troops left their counties until they returned: James F. Willard and William A. Morris, eds., *Central and Prerogative Administration*, vol. 1, *The English Government at Work 1327–1336* (Cambridge, Mass.: Mediaeval Academy of America, 1940), p. 361; Michael Prestwich, *Armies and Warfare in the Middle Ages: The English Experience* (New Haven and London: Yale University Press, 1996), p. 126; Anthony Goodman, *The Wars of the Roses* (London: Routledge and Kegan Paul, 1981), pp. 138–39.

[4] *CCR, 1461–68*, pp. 54–55; Rymer, *Foedera*, 11:703. The 1471 news came between the battles of Barnet and Tewkesbury. See C. A. J. Armstrong, "Some Examples of the Distribution and Speed of News in England at the Time of the Wars of the Roses," in *Studies in Medieval History Presented to Frederick Maurice Powicke*, ed. R. W. Hunt *et al.* (Oxford: Clarendon Press, 1948), pp. 429–54, for general discussion of communications.

[5] *Rot. Parl.*, 6:233–34. Land valued at £100, or £1000 in ready cash, was offered as a reward.

[6] *CCR, 1413–19*, pp. 280–81; Dorothy M. Gardiner, ed., *A Calendar of Early Chancery Proceedings relating to West Country Shipping 1388–1493*, Devon and Cornwall Record Society, n.s., vol. 21 (Torquay, 1976), pp. xiv–xvi.

[7] *CPR, 1485–94*, pp. 351–52, 475; *York Civic Records*, 2:94–96, 123–25.

[8] Robert Davies, "Margaret Tudor at York," *Yorkshire Archaeological Journal* 7 (1882): 306–7; *York Civic Records*, 2:167–69, 172. Word of peace between England and Castile in 1410 brought a serjeant-at-arms 3s. 4d. in reward from Norwich, while the news of the 1415 truce with France earned a messenger £2: N.R.O., 7-c, Treasurers' Rolls, 11–12 Henry IV, 3–4 Henry V.

[9] D.R.O., Receivers' Roll, 1–2 Richard II; *CCR, 1377–81*, pp. 32–33, 43, 51, 57, 181. Norwich citizens of slender means complained to the king in 1378 that they had been charged more heavily than the wealthy, prompting Richard to dictate taxation only of those worth £10 or more in goods and lands: *CCR, 1377–81*, p. 51. The terms barge and balinger were often used interchangeably, but usually a balinger was the smaller vessel, about forty tons and bearing both masts and forty to eighty oars. Both types of vessel were common in western ports and could be used in coastal waters to carry bulky cargoes or as sea-going craft: Dorothy Burwash, *English Merchant Shipping 1460–1540* (Toronto: University of Toronto Press, 1947), pp. 103–13; James W. Sherborne, "English Barges and Balingers of the Late Fourteenth Century," *Mariner's Mirror* 63 (1977): 109. Cf. Prestwich, *Armies and Warfare in the Middle Ages*, p. 265.

[10] For sharing of barge construction, see *CCR, 1399–1402*, pp. 238–39; Rymer, *Foedera*, 8:172–74. For examples of mercantile requisitions, see *CPR, 1391–96*, pp. 518, 521; *CCR, 1399–1402*, p. 169; Gardiner, *Early Chancery Proceedings*, p. xiii; Colin Richmond, "English Naval Power in the Fifteenth Century," *History* 52 (1967): 6–9, 13; Prestwich, *Armies and Warfare in the Middle Ages*, pp. 268–69. Merchant ships avoided active combat, ferrying noble commanders to and from French battlefields instead, the vessels' owners bearing most of the cost: *CPR,*

1436–41, pp. 149, 273, 313, 372; *1441–46*, pp. 79, 105; Alexander Jenkins, *The History and Description of the City of Exeter and Its Environs* (Exeter: P. Hedgeland, 1806), p. 76. For Norwich's search for an appropriate vessel to buy and victual for the king, see N.R.O., 16-d, Assembly Book I, ff.53v–54; *Norwich Records*, 2:95–96.

[11]   N.R.O., 7a-b, Treasurers' Roll, 8–9 Richard II; 18-a, Chamberlains' Account Book, 1384–1448, f.4; Richard Howlett, "Norwich Artillery in the Fourteenth Century," *Norfolk Archaeology* 16 (1905): 48–49, 56, 63–75.

[12]   P.R.O., E.28/22/7; *CCR, 1381–85*, p. 285; *1419–22*, p. 166; *1468–76*, p. 376; *CPR, 1467–77*, p. 462 (with Nottingham, for Edward IV's French expedition); Michael Powicke, *Military Obligation in Medieval England* (Oxford: Clarendon Press, 1962), p. 219. Throughout the period, York stores also contributed feathers for royal arrows, and Norwich supplied arrows and bowstrings: *CPR, 1429–36*, pp. 531, 600; N.R.O., 18-a, f.17v.

[13]   Goodman, *Wars of the Roses*, pp. 160, 191.

[14]   D.R.O., Receivers' Rolls, 1–2 Richard III, 12–13 Henry VII; Goodman, *Wars of the Roses*, p. 190; Lorraine Attreed, "A New Source for Perkin Warbeck's Invasion of 1497," *Mediaeval Studies* 48 (1986): 518.

[15]   *York House Books*, pp. 307, 556, 562; Dobson, *Chamberlains' Accounts*, pp. 153–54; *York Mem. Bk.*, 2:299.

[16]   *York House Books*, pp. 655, 662.

[17]   *Harl. 433*, 2:152 (commission to hire workers on York Castle, 23 July 1484).

[18]   D. M. Palliser, "Town Defences in Medieval England and Wales," in *The Medieval Military Revolution: State, Society, and Military Change in Medieval and Early Modern Europe*, ed. Andrew Ayton and J. L. Price (London and New York: Tauris Academic Studies, 1995), pp. 115–16; Christopher Allmand, "Taxation in Medieval England: The Example of Murage," in *Villes, bonnes villes, cités et capitales*, ed. Monique Bourin (Caen: Paradigme, 1993), p. 225.

[19]   E.g., N.R.O., 16-d, Assembly Book I, f.8; D.R.O., Receivers' Rolls, 4–5, 6–7 Henry VI; *Norwich Records*, 2:49.

[20]   *York Civic Records*, 2:66–67; *CPR, 1452–61*, p. 441. York officials had tried to alert the royal government of its problems early in Henry VI's reign, when they asked for help with repairs as the walls in their current state could allow the enemy in to destroy the city: P.R.O., SC.8/153/7623.

[21]   D.R.O., Miscellaneous Roll 6; Receivers' Rolls 11–12, 13–14, 16–17, 19–20 Henry VII; Dobson, *Chamberlains' Accounts*, pp. 29, 78–79, 89, 96–98, 112–13, 130–31, 153–54, 189.

[22]   N.R.O., 16-d, Assembly Book I, ff.27, 31–32, 35v, 37v. The legacy, of two hundred marks, proved inadequate, and Norwich had to assess a full tenth (over £94) to pay for a section of wall repair.

[23]   *CPR, 1391–96*, p. 121; *1408–13*, pp. 194–95.

[24]   Hilary L. Turner, *Town Defences in England and Wales* (London: John Baker Ltd., 1971), pp. 110–15, 129–38, 191–96; Allmand, "Taxation in Medieval England," pp. 227–29. Exeter's murage accounts were kept separately from the receivers' rolls, and the account for 1341–42 (during which over £28 of the nearly £32 collected was spent on repairs) has been printed: Margery M. Rowe and John M. Draisey, eds., *The Receivers' Accounts of the City of Exeter 1304–1353*, Devon and Cornwall

Record Society, n.s., vol. 32 (Exeter, 1989), Appendix II. See also D.R.O., Miscellaneous Roll 72 (*tempore* Edward III), for the collection of nearly £23 in murage, and Ian Burrow, "The Town Defences of Exeter," *Transactions of the Devonshire Association* 109 (1977): 34–36.

[25] Such a decrease in trade affected town and king alike: the burgesses of thirteenth-century Shrewsbury deducted construction costs from their fee farm payment when murage tolls cut trade: Young, *The English Borough and Royal Administration*, pp. 103–104. For Richard's concern, see *York House Books*, pp. 282 (petition of 24 April 1483), 729 (Richard's grant of 17 September 1483); Lorraine Attreed, "Poverty, Payments, and Fiscal Policies in English Provincial Towns," in *Portraits of Medieval Living: Essays in Memory of David Herlihy* (Ann Arbor: University of Michigan Press, 1996), p. 346; and above, p. 147.

[26] Dobson, *Chamberlains' Accounts*, Appendix II; *CPR, 1476–85*, p. 409. In 1453–54, murage rose to £29, or one-seventh of the total receipts.

[27] *York Mem. Bk.*, 2:84.

[28] N.R.O., 16-d, Assembly Book I, ff.32v.

[29] *Ibid.*, f.129v. In July of the same year, Henry VII asked for 100 men for war in northern parts: f.130.

[30] Mary D. Harris, ed., *The Coventry Leet Book*, 2 vols., Early English Text Society, o.s., vols. 134–35, 138 & 146 (London, 1907, 1913), 1:342–3.

[31] P.R.O., KB.9/148/1, mm. 7, 8, 13, 16; KB.9/148/2, mem. 32; KB.9/149/1, mm. 34, 37, 39, 89; A. J. Pollard, *North-eastern England During the Wars of the Roses: Lay Society, War, and Politics 1450–1500* (Oxford: Clarendon Press, 1990), pp. 256–62.

[32] In a group of sixty identified in Coventry's records, over 40% were drawn from the city's cloth and leather trades with the remainder representing lesser crafts: Harris, *Coventry Leet Book*, 1:478–80, 483–89. Edward IV was dissatisfied with such small numbers, which the town raised to one hundred archers, but delays in the expedition kept them all at home: Christine Carpenter, *Locality and Polity: A Study of Warwickshire Landed Society, 1401–1499* (Cambridge: Cambridge University Press, 1992), p. 541.

[33] *Norwich Records*, 1:cxliv, 390–404.

[34] *York House Books*, pp. 263, 265. See below, p. 189.

[35] N.R.O., 13-a-2 (1511 muster).

[36] Colin Richmond, "Fauconberg's Kentish Rising of May 1471," *English Historical Review* 85 (1970): 684–89.

[37] John Warkworth, ed., *A Chronicle of the First Thirteen Years of the Reign of King Edward the Fourth*, ed. James O. Halliwell, Camden Society, o.s., vol. 10 (London, 1839), p. 12.

[38] *Nott. Records*, 3:409–11.

[39] N.R.O., 16-d, Assembly Book I, f.42v. Similarly, York's poorer citizens were exempted by Edward IV from contributing to the campaign of 1482: *York House Books*, pp. 696–97.

[40] *Norwich Records*, 1:406; *Nott. Records*, 3:414–15; Harris, *Coventry Leet Book*, 1:343, 355; *York House Books*, pp. 221, 368. By way of comparison, archers during the 1340s received 6d. *per diem*: H. J. Hewitt, *The Organization of War Under Edward III* (Manchester and New York: Manchester University Press, 1966), p. 34.

41   Goodman, *Wars of the Roses*, pp. 154–55; Paul L. Hughes and James F. Larken, eds., *Tudor Royal Proclamations: 1. The Early Tudors, 1485–1553* (New Haven and London: Yale University Press), p. 13. York received detailed instructions early in 1481 concerning the provision of flour and other foodstuffs along the route to Scotland, and victualers robbed or attacked by the king's enemies were promised recompense by the Crown. In 1487, civic officials communicated Henry VII's proclamation to victualers, and set a price limit on wine of 10d. per gallon: *York House Books*, p. 585–86, 694–96.

42   *York House Books*, pp. 225, 236, 244, 260, 262; *Nott. Records*, 2:377. Brakenbury, described as both esquire of the mace and gentleman servant, frequently rode to London and the residences of Richard duke of Gloucester with correspondence between the city and the king. For his family's relations with Gloucester in County Durham and after Richard's accession, see Pollard, *North-eastern England*, p. 332, and Rosemary Horrox, *Richard III: A Study of Service* (Cambridge: Cambridge University Press, 1989), pp. 53, 190–91, 237, 260.

43   *York House Books*, p. 242.

44   Angelo Raine, *Mediaeval York* (London: John Murray, 1955), pp. 25, 260, 304; *York House Books*, p. 262. In 1482, York's assembly point was outside the chapel of St. Mary Magdalene's hospital at 9 a.m., on the road to Newcastle and the north. In 1503, civic officials accompanied Henry VII's daughter Margaret to the same boundary when she left the city to ride to Scotland and her bridegroom: *York Civic Records*, 2:189.

45   Protest brought about monthly payment after the first quarter, which was paid in advance: Richard A. Newhall, *The English Conquest of Normandy, 1416–1424* (New Haven: Yale University Press, 1924), pp. 242, 244. The change may have occurred as early as 1418.

46   Distrust of civic paymasters as well as a notion of their own value may have prompted the troops to demand as well a raise from the traditional rate of 6d. *per diem*: N.R.O., 16-d, Assembly Book I, ff.47, 49, 54v, 55, 57v.

47   *Ibid.*, ff.90v, 97v.

48   *York House Books*, p. 242.

49   *Ibid.*, pp. 262–65, 267, 269, 272.

50   Those with special leave certified in Chancery were excused, but others had taken their wages and fled home, an act "which might tend not only to contempt of the king but to the peril of him and of his captains and to dispersal of his army": *CCR, 1377–81*, p. 485.

51   *CPR, 1405–1408*, p. 139; *1422–29*, p. 532; *1436 41*, pp. 275, 341; *1441–46*, pp. 179, 312; *1446–52*, pp. 202, 275, 305, 462–63, 558; *1452–61*, pp. 197, 205, 229, 275, 326, 427; *1461–67*, pp. 272, 321, 406, 470, 485, 526; *1476–85*, p. 335.

52   *CPR, 1446–52*, p. 150; *1452–61*, p. 334; *1467–77*, p. 591.

53   *Statutes of the Realm*, 2:314–15.

54   Prestwich, *Armies and Warfare in the Middle Ages*, p. 133 (citing P.R.O., E.101/393/11, f.116); *Norwich Records*, 1:cxliv, 390–94. The latter contains muster rolls of various Norwich wards dating from c.1355 to c.1365. Fuller editions can be found in William Hudson, "Norwich Militia in the Fourteenth Century," *Norfolk and Norwich Archaeological Society* 14 (1900): 263–320.

208 The King's Towns

55 CPR, 1381–85, p. 598; N.R.O., 7a-b, Treasurers' Roll, 8–9 Richard II; Norwich Records, 1:272; Hudson, "Norwich Militia in the Fourteenth Century," 284.

56 CCR, 1385–89, p. 60; CPR, 1385–89, p. 216; Maurice Keen, England in the Later Middle Ages (London: Methuen and Co., Ltd., 1973), pp. 276, 279.

57 CCR, 1396–99, p. 518; May McKisack, The Fourteenth Century, 1307–1399 (Oxford: Oxford University Press, 1959), pp. 475, 477, 492; J. J. N. Palmer, "English Foreign Policy, 1388–99," in The Reign of Richard II: Essays in Honour of May McKisack, ed. F. R. H. Du Boulay and Caroline Barron (London: Athlone Press, 1971), pp. 77–79, 82–83.

58 A. R. Malden, "An Official Account of the Battle of Agincourt," Ancestor 11 (1904): 26–31. Northern subjects believed they were more needed at home in defense against the Scots: Neil Jamieson, "The Recruitment of Northerners for Service in English Armies in France, 1415–50," Trade, Devotion and Governance: Papers in Later Medieval History, ed. Dorothy J. Clayton, Richard G. Davies, and Peter McNiven (Stroud: Alan Sutton Publishing Ltd., 1994), p. 112.

59 Rowe and Draisey, eds., Receivers' Accounts, pp. xxii, 22 (Welsh troops); D.R.O., Receivers' Roll, 5–6 Henry V. For the earlier campaign, four men-at-arms received 3s. 4d. each, and eighty-seven archers each were paid 20d., to cover expenses until they left England. Exeter spent over £50 to carry dozens of loaves of bread, tuns of wine, and six pigs downstream to Topsham for the voyage across the Channel to Cherbourg. In 1419, costs totaled £52 9s. 8d., about 37% of total expenses for the year. For assessments of the importance of the campaign, see Christopher Allmand, Henry V (Berkeley and Los Angeles: University of California Press, 1992), pp. 113–27; Newhall, English Conquest, pp. 54–59, 92, 194, 202; and E. F. Jacob, The Fifteenth Century (Oxford: Oxford University Press, 1961), pp. 171–75.

60 D.R.O., Receivers' Roll, 4–5 Henry VI.

61 CPR, 1429–36, p. 523; 1452–61, p. 410; Rot. Parl., 5:231–32. The 1453 commission was not implemented for over four years. It requested 152 archers from York, 121 (sic) from Norwich, 30 from Nottingham, and 1137 from London. Henry had initially been granted 20,000 men, to serve six months, but he dispensed with 7000.

62 Norman Davis, ed., Paston Letters and Papers of the Fifteenth Century, 2 vols. (Oxford: Clarendon Press, 1971, 1976), 1:32, 237–38, 265–66, 289; N.R.O., 16-d, Assembly Book I, ff.44r–v; Norwich Records, 1:404–405. Norwich met a similar request three years later with only sixty soldiers, costing £6 13s. 4d.

63 Rot. Parl., 6:111–19; D.R.O., Receivers' Roll, 14–15 Edward IV. York's contribution to the total sum of over £50,000 was established at £254 12s. 6 3/4d.; Norwich's, £172 4s. 1d.; Nottingham's, £65 9s. 1 3/4d.

64 J. F. Willard, "The Scotch Raids and the Fourteenth-century Taxation of Northern England," University of Colorado Studies 5 (1906–08): 237–42; G. L. Harriss, "Aids, Loans and Benevolences," Historical Journal 6 (1963): 10.

65 Men who had received lands from Edward III, Richard II, John of Gaunt, or Henry himself had to provide service, as announced by the sheriffs of Norwich and other counties in 1407: CPR, 1405–1408, p. 362. See Goodman, Wars of the Roses, pp. 132–33 for a discussion of Henry VII's expectations.

66 A. E. Prince, "The Strength of English Armies in the Reign of Edward III," English Historical Review 46 (1931): 355, 357.

67 N.R.O., 16-d, Assembly Book I, f.54v.

68 At Henry's specific request, Coventry lent £300, a debt still unpaid in his grandson's reign, while York offered 1000 marks to be repaid out of the wool customs and subsidy of the port of Kingston-upon-Hull: P.R.O., E.101/42/36; *CPR, 1399–1401*, p. 356; Rymer, *Foedera*, 8:152–53; Harris, *Coventry Leet Book*, 1:60–64.

69 *CPR, 1405–1408*, p. 229; James Hamilton Wylie, *History of England Under Henry the Fourth*, 4 vols. (London: Longmans, 1884-98; rpt., New York: AMS Press, 1969), 2:382–92. The earl was defeated at Bramham Moor after invading England in January-February 1408.

70 Scotsmen could not hold office, act as jurors, assemble together, or even enter the common hall where city business could be overheard: *York Mem. Bk.*, 1:84, 86; *York House Books*, pp. 109–10, 131, 238, 356, 511, 515, 520–21, 524, 728–29; James Raine, ed., *A Volume of English Miscellanies Illustrating the History and Language of the Northern Counties of England*, Surtees Society, vol. 85 (Durham, 1890), pp. 35–52. Nor was Norwich free of hatred of the Scots: see P.R.O., C.1/24/25 for the case in 1455 of Mayor Richard Broun's violent attacks against a Scotsman.

71 N.R.O., 16-d, Assembly Book I, ff.56v, 57v; 21-f, 9-58, Kirkpatrick Notes, *sub* 1462.

72 Dobson, *Chamberlains' Accounts*, pp. 110, 114–15. Throughout 1462, for example, the city equipped soldiers for Warwick's campaigns, expeditions that not only achieved a brief truce with Scotland but extricated English castles from Lancastrian control. City troops received red and white jackets, and Ainsty men red and white scarves, at the cost of just over £4. Edward visited York in November on his way to the battlefront, but missed his chance at leading his men when he fell ill with measles: Cora L. Scofield, *The Life and Reign of Edward the Fourth*, 2 vols. (London: Longmans, Green and Company, 1923), 1:263–64. The war in the north is analyzed in detail in Philip A. Haigh, *The Military Campaigns of the Wars of the Roses* (Stroud: Alan Sutton Publishing Limited, 1995), pp. 69–77.

73 James III's son was to marry Edward's daughter Cecily, and installments were paid on her dowry 1475–79; James's sister Margaret was to marry Edward's brother-in-law Anthony Earl Rivers, and the city of York was told to expect the princess on her journey to meet her bridegroom. Neither marriage took place, and it is likely that Edward was deeply insulted by Margaret's seduction by a Scottish nobleman: *York House Books*, p. 196; David Dunlop, "King Edward's War: The Anglo-Scottish Conflict of 1480–84," pp. 1–2, 4. Dr. Dunlop kindly shared with me a photocopy of this unpublished essay.

74 *York House Books*, pp. 222, 230, 257, 271.

75 *CPR, 1476–85*, p. 205; *York House Books*, pp. 220–21, 699. York may have received at nearly the same time a letter from the earl of Northumberland dated 7 September (no year), requiring the city to prepare its forces and march them thirty-two miles to Northallerton within three to four days, a task stretching the capacities of an urban amateur army. If the earl's letter also dates to 1480, and the city hesitated in sending troops, this may explain why the Scots were free to raid the borders for three days: Dunlop, "King Edward's War," pp. 6–7. See my comments on the dating of the two September letters, *York House Books*, pp. 698–99.

76 *Calendar of State Papers, Milan: Volume I, 1385–1618*, ed. Allen B. Hinds (London: His Majesty's Stationery Office, 1912), pp. 244–45.

77   Harris, *Coventry Leet Book*, 1:474–86; *York House Books*, pp. 231, 233, 240, 242,
     244, 694–96, 700. Tenants of Ainsty hundred bore responsibility not only to York
     but to various lords, who prevented their tenants from executing the city's demands.
     Ainsty representatives later compromised and paid the costs of forty men: *ibid.*, pp.
     236–37, 239, 241.

78   On 20 May 1481, Edward wrote the pope he regretted not being able to join in a
     European campaign against the Turks because the Scots kept invading his territory,
     a complaint the pope was to use to pressure James to cease fighting: *Calendar of
     State Papers, Venetian, 1202–1509*, ed. Rawdon Brown (London: Her Majesty's
     Stationery Office, 1864; Nendeln: Kraus Reprint, 1970), pp. 142–43.

79   *York House Books*, pp. 251, 254, 696–97.

80   *Ibid.*, pp. 256–57, 260, 702.

81   For criticism, see Nicholas Pronay and John Cox, eds., *The Crowland Chronicle
     Continuations: 1459–1486* (London: Alan Sutton for Richard III and Yorkist
     History Trust, 1986), p. 149.

82   *York House Books*, pp. 262–63, 265, 273; James Gairdner, *The History of the Life
     and Reign of Richard III* (Cambridge: Cambridge University Press, 1898), pp. 39–
     42; Scofield, *Edward the Fourth*, 2:344–49; Charles Ross, *Edward IV* (London:
     Eyre Methuen, 1974), pp. 288–90.

83   *York House Books*, pp. 696, 707.

84   *Rot. Parl.*, 6:204–5; Pollard, *North-eastern England*, pp. 239, 242–43. Pollard
     asserts (p. 242) "above all else this was Gloucester's war."

85   *York House Books*, pp. 712, 729; Charles D. Ross, *Richard III* (London: Eyre
     Methuen, 1981), p. 193.

86   *York House Books*, pp. 371–72; Pollard, *North-eastern England*, pp. 369–71; A. F.
     Pollard, *The Reign of Henry VII from Contemporary Sources*, 3 vols. (London:
     Longmans, Green, 1913), 1:19–22. The king did, however, make clear by the
     restrictions placed upon them and by the resumption of Berwick into royal control
     that overmighty nobles would not be tolerated either in the north or in the new
     regime.

87   R. L. Mackie, *King James IV of Scotland* (Edinburgh and London: Oliver and Boyd,
     1958), pp. 39–44.

88   Agnes Conway, *Henry VII's Relations with Scotland and Ireland 1485–1498* (New
     York: Octagon Books, 1972), pp. 21–32. See David Dunlop, "The 'Masked
     Comedian': Perkin Warbeck's Adventures in Scotland and England from 1495 to
     1497," *The Scottish Historical Review* 70 (1991): 97–128, for details of James's
     support of the pretender.

89   The Nottingham civic records contain mention of a vengeful servant who accused
     her master of vowing to support the king's enemies, but the remarks were dismissed
     as gossip: *Nott. Records*, 3:401. For Warbeck's Scottish support, see Ian Arthurson,
     The Perkin Warbeck Conspiracy 1491–1499 (Stroud: Alan Sutton Publishing Ltd.,
     1994), pp. 121–25, 144–49.

90   *York Civic Records*, 2:128–33; S. B. Chrimes, *Henry VII* (Berkeley and Los
     Angeles: University of California Press, 1972), pp. 88–91. York officers agreed in
     May that eighty soldiers could be supported. Norwich's twenty soldiers were so
     recalcitrant that the earl of Oxford scolded civic officials for permitting such
     procrastination and urged them to imprison the most stubborn until they changed

their minds and volunteered for service. The officials themselves paid for eleven of the twenty men: N.R.O., 16-c, Assembly Minute Book I, ff.66v–70v; 16-d, Assembly Book II, ff.23, 24v, 25, 27.

[91] For details, see David Palliser, *Tudor York* (Oxford: Oxford University Press, 1979), pp. 51–52, 260, 270.

[92] *CCR, 1399–1402*, p. 34; Keen, *England Later Middle Ages*, p. 304.

[93] Goodman, *Wars of the Roses*, pp. 221–22, 227–28; John Gillingham, *The Wars of the Roses* (Baton Rouge: Louisiana State University Press, 1981), pp. 5, 13, 15, 28, 255.

[94] *Nott. Records*, 2:368–69; Goodman, *Wars of the Roses*, pp. 203–4.

[95] D.R.O., Book 51, f.313; Nt.R.O., CA7452, f.1; N.R.O., 16-d, Assembly Book I, ff.42r–v; *Norwich Records*, 1:405; *CPR, 1452–61*, p. 561; Scofield, *Edward the Fourth*, 1:68.

[96] For patronage patterns, see above, pp. 108–109, 117, 121.

[97] In 1462–63, the chamberlains inherited a debt of over £250 from their immediate predecessors in office, and a campaign that year led by Hastings and Warwick in the north further added to the deficit: *York House Books*, pp. 390–91; Dobson, *Chamberlains' Accounts*, pp. 107, 110–15.

[98] Forty were paid by the aldermen and former sheriffs, and the remainder by the commonalty, at the rate of 6d. *per diem*: N.R.O., 16-d, Assembly Book I, f.47v; *Norwich Records*, 1:405–6; Goodman, *Wars of the Roses*, p. 146.

[99] N.R.O., 16-d, f.48. See above, p. 117.

[100] Nottingham's troops earned 8d. *per diem* and new red and white jackets when they followed Lord Hastings to Northumberland: *Nott. Records*, 2:377; 3:415.

[101] N.R.O., 16-d, f.50; 21-f, 9-58, Kirkpatrick Notes, *sub* 1461 and 1462.

[102] N.R.O., 16-d, ff.83–84; 18-a, Chamberlains' Account Book, 1470–90, ff.5v, 7v–8v. See above, p. 77.

[103] N.R.O., 18-a, ff.27r–v; 16-d, f.87v *bis*, 90v, 97v.

[104] Nt.R.O., CA7452, ff.2v, 3v, 4v.

[105] *York House Books*, pp. 284–86, 713–14. The troops arrived too late to be useful against "the quene, hir blode adherenttes and affinitie," whom Richard named as his enemies, although they may have reinforced his bid for the throne. York forces were also offered later in the year against Buckingham's threat: *ibid.*, pp. 413–14.

[106] *Ibid.*, pp. 367–69, 734–35.

[107] N.R.O., 16-d, f.122; 18-a, Chamberlains' Account Book, 1479–88, f.51v.

[108] N.R.O., 16-d, f.122v, *pace* A. P. M. Wright, "The Relations between the King's Government and the English Cities and Boroughs in the Fifteenth Century" (D.Phil. thesis, University of Oxford, 1965), p. 329, who argues that the Yorkist monarchs had a tighter, more menacing control over towns than the Lancastrians.

[109] N.R.O., 16-d, f.130. The city calculated that full military participation would have cost more than £140.

[110] *York House Books*, pp. 570–73, 577.

[111] N.R.O., 16-c, Assembly Minute Book I, 1492–1520, ff.33v, 34, 40, 43, 64.

[112] Davis, *Paston Letters and Papers*, 2:472–74. For the East Anglia background, see Arthurson, *Perkin Warbeck*, pp. 111–12. Norwich raised twelve men for the Cornish campaign: six of the twelve were paid for by the aldermen, four by the wards, and two by the commonalty: N.R.O., 16-c, Assembly Minute Book I, ff.70v–71v.

113   Attreed, " Perkin Warbeck's Invasion," 514–21, esp. 518, n.10; Arthurson, *Perkin Warbeck*, pp. 183–88. See below, pp. 303–304.

114   N.R.O., 16-c, Assembly Minute Book I, ff.89r–91r; Chrimes, *Henry VII*, pp. 92–94. The capture was arranged by Archduke Philip in repayment of hospitality Henry showed him and his wife Juana of Castile when adverse winds drove their ship ashore early in 1506. Henry executed Edmund in 1513 when Louis XII recognized him as Richard IV.

115   Harriss, "Aids, Loans and Benevolences," 5–7.

CHAPTER 7
COMMERCIAL RESOURCES

Trade and commerce provided the undeniable basis for the urban prosperity upon which royal government relied. The measurement of that trade, however, and the proper study of its human and social dimensions raise significant problems. When one town's mercantile profile during a mere twenty-year period can be the subject of a significant and detailed study, the appropriate selection of commercial activities becomes critical to illuminate a broader examination of urban and Crown relations. However valuable it may be to track one town's total trading patterns, or produce even partial statistics from national customs accounts, the focus of this study must remain on the ways in which urban subjects and royal government interacted to preserve and extend profits.

Town residents rarely hesitated to point out the ways in which the royal government could assure mutual benefits. They sought chartered liberties and grants to increase their markets and tame the physical elements that impeded trade, and they utilized the Crown's legal venues to assure those conditions that contributed to profit. Although the merchants of London dominated trading patterns with their lower transaction costs and easier access to markets and financial networks, provincial merchants persisted in their endeavors. They, too, pursued foreign markets often at the risk of their own investments and safety, and even at home they endured competition from foreign traders. The king's urban subjects and their trading patterns made small but significant contributions to local, national, and international patterns of commerce. From those patterns, the Crown received much more than could be reflected on customs accounts or any other single record of revenue collection. Fully to understand the commercial aspects of this relationship, the study must range more broadly to examine dimensions beyond the purely financial.

Facilitating Trade

Trade contributed substantially to the wealth that made urban subjects valuable to the Crown, so that the king was naturally concerned for the facilities—both natural and man-made—that encouraged commerce. Citizens often complained that they alone could not insure the conditions that maximized profit for both town and Crown. Physical elements conspired against them: rivers could become clogged with weirs, bridges and streets fall into disrepair, and mills break down. For those privileges for which towns claimed an urgent need, such as fairs and recognizance of debt, only royal charters and ordinances would suffice. In such instances, limited urban resources needed royal assistance in order for trade to resume and profit subject and Crown alike. Town officials found this a successful argument in dealing with the royal government, and invented creative variations on the plea to attract attention and assistance. Their failure to achieve all of their ends tells us much about royal policy regarding not only towns but also national issues of balanced trade and healthy commerce.

Keeping rivers clear and navigable, for example, was a major task for town officials. Norwich chamberlains' accounts record large expenditures for cleaning the River Wensum and cutting weeds from its banks. The costly but necessary task also attracted private, charitable funding: in 1456, a wealthy citizen left £10 in his will for such work to be undertaken.[1] Occasionally, the task was so great, or a town's neighbors so offensive, that civic officials had to ask for Crown assistance. But royal intervention had its limitations, as in the case of Exeter's battle with the earls of Devon. The Courtenay family erected the first obstruction to river traffic during the 1240s, and for the following three centuries a barrier of some fashion rested in the waters of the Exe, blocking trade and passage. Local antiquary John Hoker asserted that the citizens tried to overturn Courtenay power with the help of royal writs and inquisitions, but they had little effect until the family fell from power in the 1530s.[2]

Nottingham obtained several royal commissions to clear the Trent, one of the realm's major waterways. Richard II explained his interest in Nottingham's problems because his consort Anne enjoyed its revenues. In 1383, he ordered men of the town and county to investigate the offending blockages erected by Richard Byron of Colwick, a village less than four miles east of Nottingham.[3] The commission met with little success, so that eight years later, the mayor and bailiffs acted on their own accord and dismantled the Byron weir. Richard and his wife Joan complained to parliament that such an action deprived them of their inheritance, and investigation recommenced.[4] In June 1392, an inquest was held in the town, to hear the testimony of various individuals who asserted that Byron diverted the waters of the Trent at Colwick by planting willows and fixing piles in the river. The new trench assisted Byron's mill, but prevented ships from reaching the town and, most important, from bringing merchandise to town and castle, to the contempt of the king, the damage of the queen, and the cost of the burgesses. Although Byron argued that an ancestor of his wife won from the town the right to have such a mill and weir, Nottingham's argument was the more powerful. Byron lost the case and the weir was ordered removed by the county sheriff.[5]

No more was heard of the Byrons, but the Trent continued to be the subject of dispute. In 1432, merchants of Nottingham, York, Hull and Lincoln demanded that a royal commission investigate river blockages ranging from weeds to cattle driven through the river in summer.[6] A later case involving Sir Henry Pierrepont was more difficult because of the knight's local connections. Sir Henry had fought for Edward IV at Towton and Tewkesbury and served the county as sheriff and justice of the peace from the 1460s through the 1490s. In 1467, his weir in the Trent caused enough obstruction to encourage Nottingham's mayor to take steps. The two men agreed to abide by the arbitration of a serjeant-at-law and royal attorneys, under penalty of £200. The arbitrators ruled in favor of the town and ordered Sir Henry to remove his piles and foundations, although his right to passage in the Trent and the Leen was not disputed.[7]

Of the four towns, York experienced the worst problems with river obstructions. Its distress combines themes of trade, royal profits, and the city's search for active patrons. Although statutes suppressing weirs existed from the thirteenth century, local landholders and religious houses in particular persisted in erecting traps and wicker "rooms" in which to catch large quantities of fish, thus impeding navigation and reducing the amount individuals could catch with hook and line. When royal courts were transferred to York in 1392, the city took the opportunity to file complaints against various offenders. City jurors argued that the River Ouse was a highway used by merchants who came up the Humber and assured the "great increase of the kingdom and especially of York, Yorkshire, and other counties and towns in the north parts."[8] The most serious offenders against such profit were the powerful York abbey of St. Mary's and the tenants of the duchy of Lancaster.

York's complaints to the Crown often resulted in the issue of letters patent, ordering the mayor and aldermen to head commissions of inquiry, but permanent results were not forthcoming. The North's experience of the agrarian crisis of the 1440s and the contraction of trade and industry provide a context for York's obsession with clearing fishgarths and safeguarding its remaining commerce. The city chamberlains' rolls include two accounts for the years 1444–46, which trace York's litigation against St. Mary's Abbey and the expense it involved.[9] Although the exact nature of the proceedings is unknown, the "divers discords and debates" mentioned most likely refer to the weirs that the abbey had erected on the shores of the Ouse, along which St. Mary's had extensive property holdings. In 1444–45, the royal council heard the problems and ordered the city and the abbot to keep the peace, but the attempted compromise was not successful.[10] Not until 1462 did the mayor and corporation gain statutory power to remove offending weirs from the Ouse and its tributaries.[11]

For successful opposition to the powerful interests erecting weirs, York needed the assistance of an equally powerful friend. In 1475, when the city gained an act of parliament establishing yet another commission of inquiry, civic officials took the precaution of first showing it to Richard of Gloucester. The decision immediately bore fruit: Gloucester ordered his bailiffs and tenants to remove all weirs they had erected, and he allowed the city to refer to his interest and support when York wrote the bishop of Durham complaining about the latter's weirs.[12] From that time Gloucester's interest in fishgarth obstruction formed an important part of his relations with the city and the northeast. In 1476, the city council sent a letter to the king noting the great loss the Crown suffered when local economies were cheated of their deserved wealth, prompting Edward IV to put his younger brother more officially in charge of investigating the problem. Richard was commanded to "take a view and oversight of the fishgarths and weirs" when next he came home to Yorkshire, and to direct the destruction of likely impediments to urban trade.[13] These commands inspired the events of the spring of 1479, when civic officials spent over £21 inspecting the rivers, identifying offending traps, and sending messengers to Richard and to local nobleman Henry Percy earl of Northumberland for their assistance.[14] Despite such diligence, the problem was not easily or quickly solved. In 1482, violence broke out in Snaith, south of York, over the destruction of a fishgarth, and two summers later a party of civic officials who examined northern rivers discovered numerous traps still operated by the major bishops, abbots, and nobles of the region. Even worse, the Crown owned a few fishgarths itself in the rivers of the Duchy of Lancaster, and duchy tenants of Gowdall on the Aire stubbornly resisted attacks on their traps.[15]

This persistent problem continued after good patron Richard became king. In 1484, a city sheriff and two of the chamberlains rowed the Ouse looking for traps and reporting their owners to the mayor. The men found forty-six fishgarths of varying size, operated by fifty-six tenants of powerful lords including the archbishop of York, the bishop and prior of Durham, the abbots of Selby and St. Mary's, and the duke of Suffolk.[16] Whatever Richard's personal or royal interest in the case, he was unable to overcome the persistence of such powerful vested interests. Late in Henry VII's reign, the mayor resorted to a yearly inspection of the Ouse and surrounding rivers in accordance with a royal commission that allowed civic authorities to bring owners of offending weirs before King's Bench.[17] By no means a petty annoyance of small importance, the problem of the fishgarths was symptomatic of the northeast's distressed economic condition, and of the lengths to which an ambitious local lord would go to help the area and himself in the process.

Bridges were no less important than the unimpeded waterways they spanned. Recent studies have emphasized the high quality and efficient placement of medieval bridges and causeways necessary for active internal trade.[18] Exeter's thirteenth-century Exe bridge collapsed in the 1370s after heavy rains, and civic officials spent the following century rebuilding and repairing the edifice. In 1447, it occurred to Mayor John Shillingford that because bridge maintenance had become too heavy a burden upon city revenues, an alternate source of funding could be found in Cardinal Beaufort's will. Shillingford petitioned the cardinal's executors, reminding them that since the bridge's collapse a ferry had to be used "as in olde tymes, to the great peril and charge of the people," and to the desolation of Exeter's trade and royal profits. Shillingford was certain that such a contribution could be interpreted as a gift of alms for the benefit of the cardinal's soul, but unfortunately the mayor died before the plan came to fruition.[19] Wills of less exalted persons also contained help for public works. In 1472, civic officials of Norwich took steps to carry out the will of former mayor John Gilbert, whose executors were instructed to spend £30 for bridge repairs.[20]

Nottingham's problems with Leen Bridge had less to do with finances than with matters of principle and commitment. The town insisted that the county was responsible for maintenance of seven-eighths of the bridge's structure, and that Nottingham itself had charge of only forty-six and one-half feet on the northern side. In 1458, after almost a century of complaints, Henry VI appointed local knights and counselors to join civic officials in determining the condition of the flood-torn structure.[21] Inquiries under oath revealed that six townships should have pooled resources and arranged for maintenance, but they had refused to do this for almost fifty years. Even giving testimony before King's Bench and suffering distraint of goods did not move the Nottinghamshire men to repair the bridge. An inquisition held at Nottingham in 1501 revealed that the case had continued so long, two of the defendants had died, and the heir of one was too young to take on his father's responsibilities.[22]

Nottingham's problems may have been solved more quickly had town officials stressed economic losses to the realm over principles and promises. The financial argument had achieved success in 1422, when merchants in York, Nottingham, and other north midland towns united to complain about Yorkshire's "Turnbridge." The men pointed out that the timber bridge on a tributary to the Ouse some eighteen miles south of York was too narrow and low for safety: "ther may no shippes passe under the seid Brigge . . . to the grete hurt and damage as wel to the Kyng in his customs and subsidys."[23] The reference to the loss of royal profit and the merchants' offer to pay for a new bridge themselves convinced Henry VI to give his permission for the old wooden structure to be replaced.[24]

Riverside mills had value for the revenue they added to town coffers, but they needed special care and raised issues of unfair competition. When Nottingham residents complained about the Byron weir, the townspeople were equally upset about the mill benefiting from the diverted waters. Nottingham citizens' own mills also disturbed Henry IV, who in 1402 and 1407 issued writs to determine whether John Wryght's private horse-driven mill competed unfairly with royal mills at the castle, thus depriving the Crown of revenue. Issues from these royal structures were given as gifts and annuities to favorites such as Henry IV's chamberlain and to Edward IV's brother George, and the Crown was loath to lose the profits.[25]

Norwich's problems with its New Mills, located on the Wensum in Ultra Aquam ward, formed part of the city's jurisdiction battles with local religious houses. In 1441, after prolonged election interference and withdrawal of the city's liberties for eight months, the earl of Suffolk once more intervened in Norwich affairs. As in 1437, the earl defended former mayor Thomas Wetherby and furthered the latter's policies by promoting dissension between the city and those local houses already at odds with Norwich over rights of jurisdiction. Following the proceedings of a commission of oyer and terminer established to investigate those local quarrels, Suffolk acted as arbitrator and ordered the city to destroy its New Mills and to stand to bond with the abbot of St. Benet's under penalty of £100. The abbot complained that the mills had been newly erected ten years earlier and were damaging his livelihood and his right of passage on the river. Although the city argued that similar structures had always existed on the spot, neither Suffolk nor the abbot was convinced. Civic officials refused to seal the bond, and the situation degenerated into riotous gatherings and theft of the city's seal to prevent its use. While the mayor traveled to London to explain matters to the king, suffering imprisonment there for six weeks, Wetherby and Suffolk took advantage of his absence to seal the bond and destroy the mills.[26] Their action precipitated decades of litigation as the city continued to claim both land and resources as essential to urban prosperity and integrity.

After Wetherby's death in 1445 and Suffolk's murder five years later, Norwich politics knew comparative quiet until Edward IV's reign, during which time the New Mills were rebuilt. Litigation began again in 1478–79 with a plea filed by the abbot of St. Benet's, and within three years urban defense expenses (including timely gifts to well-placed patrons) had risen to over £67.[27] The abbot revived the earlier charges against the mills, asserting that they had caused damage to his neighboring property in Heigham, northwest of the city, and to the rights of passage he and his predecessors enjoyed on the Wensum. Moreover, although the four New Mills were located within city limits, they were especially damaging to abbey profits because they kept Heigham waters above the level needed to grind grain, and had also flooded the meadows. The abbey had relied upon Suffolk's award of 1441 and the destruction of the mills that had occurred two years later, but the citizens had since repaired the mills to cause more damage than ever. In conclusion, the abbot told the king that the abbey had suffered £2000 in damages.[28]

Civic officials, of course, had their own version of events. In an answer to the abbot's bill of complaint to the king, the citizens asserted that mills had occupied that spot on the river since the Conquest and had only recently been rebuilt. Norwich had deliberately refused to obey Suffolk's award because compliance would have deprived the city of those profits from corn-grinding that composed a quarter of the city's fee farm, to the detriment of both town and Crown. The reference to the king's revenue loss was a clever one, but the abbot for one did not believe it. As he argued in his reply, Norwich had paid the fee farm before the mills were erected in the 1420s, and could have made use of six good mills within half a mile of town to augment revenue. Although the illegal sealing of the 1441 award was noted, litigation and its attendant costs continued for several decades.[29] The king's brother-in-law Anthony Woodville Earl Rivers acted for a time as arbitrator with Chief Justice of King's Bench William Huse in proceedings that included a visit to the site of the mills, and even Edward IV seemed to side with the city, particularly after receiving a painted map showing the boundaries determined by one of the viewings of the mills.[30]

Well into Henry VII's reign, Norwich worried about its relations with the abbey and the need to repair damaged mills.[31] Clearly, a change in dynasty did not bring about a change in tactics. The length and bitterness of the suit, one small part of the jurisdictional problems, shows that the divisions and violence had yet to be overcome. Connecting local disputes to national issues of revenue and commerce had secured some measure of Crown intervention, but it rarely delivered the sweeping changes Norwich or any of the four boroughs craved. As these cases and following examples will show, the royal government had broader ends and wider responsibilities in mind than those which served only its urban subjects.

Legal Recourse

Formal regulation of commerce required assistance from charters and statutes granted by the king and his government, while the problems that arose with trade demanded recourse in a variety of legal venues. By the later Middle Ages, boroughs had honed to perfection their appeals for help, citing the reduction in revenue not only the town but the king himself would suffer if a grant were denied or a plaintiff defeated. But perfect arguments did not guarantee full satisfaction. Any grant or decree made to an individual merchant or borough affected a larger network of commercial contacts, some with international ramifications. Urban merchants could afford to focus only upon local trade balances; the royal government risked diplomatic disaster if its gaze were too parochial.

The granting of fairs constituted one of the least abrasive relationships between town and Crown. Post-plague Europe saw an increase in regional fairs, as commercial demands grew and states provided legal recognition and legitimization of the events created to serve them.[32] Although England in general experienced decline in the number of fairs after 1350, provincial towns fearful of poverty and decay seized upon such grants as panaceas for their budgets. They could be purchased by civic officials for modest sums paid to Chancery, or given as components of royal charters, although areas of intense commercial activity supported fairs without Crown sanction. In 1482, for example, Edward IV gave Norwich a parting gift of two fairs at the end of his visit. Unfortunately, the grant did not increase town revenue as expected, and by 1486 the fairs showed no profit and hardly any participants at all.[33] On the other hand, Exeter initiated five new fairs between the 1370s and 1463, bothering to receive chartered confirmation only of the last one. All five, and two older ones, survived at least into the sixteenth century, rivaling the earl's and priory's venues. They enjoyed sufficient business particularly from a growing fishing industry to contribute to the healthy economic state of the western port.[34]

York's economic challenges cast fairs in a different light. The city enjoyed two fairs from at least the thirteenth century, its Pentecost gathering extended and postponed a week by a grant of 1449. In 1501, civic officials successfully petitioned the king to grant two more fairs "to be gettyn toward the upholdyng of this citie whiche is in gret ruyn and decaye." The gatherings, focusing on sales of cattle and cloth in particular, were proclaimed widely to attract merchants throughout the northeast.[35] One of these fairs disappeared from the record soon after the grant but the other survived into the modern period, one of several venues for the sale of horses both inside and outside the city walls.[36]

The money exchanged in urban commercial ventures was another source of concern for the Crown. The four towns had housed royal and ecclesiastical mints since the twelfth century or earlier, and statutes throughout the later Middle Ages confirmed the centers as places of coinage and exchange.[37] Recoinage and debasement of currency occurred rarely, so that the Crown more typically directed civic officials to help guard the quantity and purity of English currency. Loss of native bullion through foreign trade and credit worried all medieval monarchs. In 1379, Richard II directed Exeter and eleven other ports to forbid the export of gold and silver and to deliver to the Tower all precious metals that arose from wool sales.[38] During Henry VI's reign, mayors and bailiffs of York, Norwich, and five other boroughs had the legal power to restrict sales of precious metals and enforce standards set by their London counterparts. Mayors and sheriffs were similarly advised to take special care with foreign coins, Irish and Scottish money particularly considered suspect.[39]

Even worse than foreign coin was counterfeit specie. Henry V had shown great concern over coinage and the flow of bullion in 1414, and two years later statutory measures were taken to protect currency. The Statute of Treasons was updated to condemn manipulation of valid coin as well as outright counterfeiting, and gave to all justices of the peace in counties and mayors and bailiffs in towns the power to investigate both foreign and false coins, sending suspicious examples to the justices of assize.[40] Nearly forty years later, York officials discovered that their problems with a local counterfeiter raised significant questions about borough legal privileges. Recently chastised for ignoring the powers of Richard III's special local creation, the Council of the North, the officers quickly advised the king's lieutenant on that body of their discovery of false coins and a father and son team of counterfeiters. The case was a difficult one, for no one was certain whether the creation of French and Dutch coin was as treasonous as the counterfeiting of English specie. Letters to the king's lieutenant reveal York's anxiety that incorrect procedure would endanger their liberties and franchises, which nonetheless demanded that the city punish the offender if the Council found him guilty.[41]

Far more common violations concerned the use of false measures which cheated customers of the goods they selected. Any borough's records could produce examples of civic officials' efforts to enforce the use of proper weights and measures, but the Crown had more than an indirect interest in such compunction.[42] Even privately owned measures had to meet national standards, and by statute of 1429, every city and town had to employ balances and weights in accord with the common standard set by the Exchequer. Kept by the mayor or constables, these measures could be used freely by citizens or for a small sum paid by foreign merchants.[43] Despite the officers' influence, the system was not without fault, and frequent complaints convinced Henry VII at the start of his reign to declare all old measures defective and to distribute new ones. All four towns were chosen to receive the new standard weights (which were replaced again in 1496) and town officers had their powers of inspection renewed.[44]

Local scales and monopoly on their use provoked serious complaints and royal intervention late in the fifteenth century between York officials and merchants and miners of Richmondshire lead. City custom decreed that the lead could not be shipped out of the north without first stopping in York to be weighed on the common crane. Moreover, a foreign merchant (one not possessing the freedom of the city) could not buy the lead and sell it to another foreigner without a citizen acting as middleman, nor could a citizen avoid the city crane and its costs by making his transactions at the lead's point of origin. Adding to the distress was the rising cost of weighing the goods: in 1490, use of the crane cost 6d. for each fother of lead (usually 2100 lbs.), a price that rose sharply within a decade to reach 14d. per fother in 1499. Given these demands, miners and merchants found much to complain about, and some did not hesitate to take their grievances to the equity court of the Council in Star Chamber. In 1499, the lead miners charged York officers with using faulty measures and not the standard weights ordered by statute. For every five-hundred-weight of lead placed on the scale, the miners complained the measurement was in excess of thirty to forty pounds, thus raising the total price.[45]

The Star Chamber suit proved costly and time-consuming for York. Not only did the king take an unwelcome interest in the city's local commercial policy, but he required aldermen and the recorder to ride to London to meet with the chancellor. His appointment of the abbot of St. Mary's as arbitrator could not have pleased civic officials given the long history of disputes between city and abbey. Local authorities turned for help to the king's attorney James Hobart, rewarding him with gifts and dinners, but still the case dragged on without resolution. The final decision was not recorded, although it was later determined that London and Newcastle merchants could override local custom and avoid York's crane.[46]

These were not isolated examples of Crown interest in local trade. The problem of urban craft guilds and their status within a town provides further examples. No town was free of troubles from the local organizations dedicated to economic profit and social pleasure. During the 1450s in Exeter and the 1490s in York, cordwainers and weavers waged battle over which group took precedence in local processions, while during the entire fifteenth century York and Nottingham weavers suffered such financial losses from lack of work that they had difficulty making payments required by the boroughs.[47] By a statute of 1436, town officers had control over the recording of guild charters, but some crafts avoided consulting mayors and councilors in the search for increased autonomy.[48] The tailors of Exeter, for example, won special privileges from Edward IV early in his reign, culminating in 1466 with letters patent. The grant provided a charter of incorporation for the tailors' guild of St. John the Baptist, complete with livery, a seal, government by a master, and self-inspection of the craft's work by wardens throughout the city and its suburbs.[49]

The city objected not to the incorporation, but to two of its effects: not only did guildsmen violently attack city tailors to force them to join the guild and pay its fees (so charged the city), but the group admitted men from other crafts who were not freemen of Exeter. What remained unstated but no less true was the city rulers' resentment over such a challenge to their own power. They viewed the situation as a threat to the peace of the city and the harmony of its economic practices, until then preserved by the mayor and his council empowered by a variety of royal charters. In 1477, the city complained to Edward IV's council but achieved only a compromise by which the tailors were forced to restrict the scope and aggression of their inspections.[50]

Friction continued between the groups until 1482, when the civic officials petitioned parliament to curtail guild privileges. The complaint stated that only the mayor had the right to oversee and govern the city's merchants, tailors, and all other craftsmen, without competition from any of the guilds; the offensive charter had exacerbated the tailors' "bad disposition" so that they could not be ruled by the mayor.[51] Until the king's letters of 1466, the mayor had done his job quietly and without contradiction, but since the charter was granted the mayor found it increasingly difficult to rule the city and prevent the tailors' violence and illegal gatherings that daily threatened the king's peace. This argument, however exaggerated, proved far more effective than an appeal to monetary losses that affected either town or Crown. The city's expenditure of almost £40 in London succeeded in annulling the charter, payment that no doubt helped Edward recognize how recklessly the craft had interpreted his grant, and how an autonomous guild threatened the integrity of royally-granted privileges, urban peacekeeping, and the realm's security.[52]

Urban subjects did not always find the king's justice so hard to come by. Citizens pursued a variety of mercantile problems in both the court of Common Pleas and the equity courts of Westminster, and were also provided with the means for arbitration. Long-distance trade in particular, which could involve foreign languages and need for technical knowledge, made reliance upon local courts difficult. Some cases began in local borough courts but obviously did not end to one of the parties' satisfaction, and some wealthy urban subjects thought the extra expense and long-distance negotiations worth the effort. Fears of local prejudice drove some merchants to Chancery, as in the case of a Bristol resident who was sued by an Exeter citizen and believed he could not get justice in the latter city.[53] Foreign merchants were especially wary of local courts of common law, while other cases involved shoddy goods, stolen merchandise, and broken agreements.[54] But royal intervention did not bring advantages alone for a borough that courted it: justice sought outside a town took a broader view of economic health than many urban subjects found advantageous.

Revenues and Their Uses

The actual cash payments generated by mercantile activity, and the records that kept track of them, offer a tempting bank of data from which secure conclusions and reliable statistics seem easily derived. The merest acquaintance with medieval recordkeeping should disabuse historians of such sanguine confidence. Nevertheless, revenues from tolls and from customs and subsidy payments made important contributions to urban and royal budgets, although we may never know with certainty the magnitude of their share. The problems towns encountered in levying and collecting these revenues, and enjoying the share that was theirs, provided additional reasons to seek legal assistance and guiding advice from the royal government.

Local tolls levied on goods entering towns caused conflict and litigation during the later Middle Ages. Most royal charters granted urban merchants freedom from toll throughout the kingdom, but a monarch's personal gift to a borough sometimes was not respected by other towns. To avoid such problems, Exeter along with other towns kept and updated lists of boroughs whose freemen enjoyed exemptions. In cases of severe dispute, borough courts handled some of these cases, but litigants distrustful of the justice they could receive there sought resolution in the royal equity courts.[55]

Exeter's toll problems, involving a larger and more important opponent, drove its merchants and civic officials to Star Chamber.[56] In 1499, three local merchants took linen to London and were told the cloth was liable to scavage duty, levied on merchandise foreign to the city. At Ludgate, servants of the London sheriffs accosted the merchants and took from them fifteen shillings in gold and five pieces of linen in lieu of payment. The merchants returned home outraged, prompting Exeter's mayor to address the king and council. He claimed exemption from scavage on the grounds that Exeter was ancient demesne. In Hilary term 1500, London's mayor and commonalty answered, claiming the right to take scavage on merchandise from beyond the sea. They argued that the Exeter merchants had brought in packs of foreign linen to be sold in London, and were duly charged thirteen (*sic*) shillings on it. When they refused to pay, their money and cloth were seized. Rights and privileges granted by the Crown to two different boroughs were clearly in conflict, and London claimed precedence.

To defend themselves, Exeter officials sent to London various local merchants old enough to recall appropriate precedents. John Bonyfant, for example, was not only a venerable sixty year old, but he had served as bailiff and receiver of Exeter throughout the 1480s and 1490s: his testimony, that his own foreign linen and Gascon wine had always been free of scavage, thus carried considerable weight.[57] Bonyfant was joined by seven other senior merchants and civic officials, all of whom testified they had traded in London since Edward IV's day and never been troubled with scavage tolls. When an illiterate London toll collector then testified that he had collected scavage from Exeter merchants for eleven years, the court concluded that until Henry VII's day the toll had not been levied regularly. The collector could not recall how much Exeter merchants paid, "butt thay paid it without grugge or contradiccion or clayme to be quyte of payment therof...." London merchants then testified, all of them claiming knowledge of Exeter traders' uncontested payments during the 1490s. In 1502, the chancellor ordered London officials to return money and goods confiscated in lieu of scavage.[58] Two years later, an act of parliament declared that scavage could no longer be levied under penalty of £20. The money Exeter officials had spent on litigation since 1499 (c.£30) seemed to have achieved this welcome decision, but when recorded in the statutes a proviso was added exempting London from the prohibition. The Crown could not risk alienating the capital and its merchants, or threatening its fiscal resources. Nor should we underestimate the strength of London's trading networks and markets which had eclipsed northern merchants in the lead, cloth and wine trade by the mid-fifteenth century.[59]

Nottingham's central location and access to the Trent awarded the town a large share of toll problems prompting recourse to the central courts. Its most prolonged problems lay with the town of Retford. Since the early fourteenth century, the burgesses of Retford were obliged to pay Nottingham twenty-five marks a year for the toll of Merrils Bridge across the Trent. In 1477, Nottingham went to the court of Common Pleas to force Retford to pay the rent and its arrears, plus damages, for a total of over £90. The court declared for Nottingham, but two years later the town still had not received payment. Attempts to gain recompense by force had failed, and burgesses complained to the chancellor that Retford kept its goods "in such secrete places that non execucion can be hadde [by distraint] of any part therof without the assent of the same bayllyves...."[60] Westminster policy urged that local problems be settled on the local level if at all possible, so that town officials agreed to abide by the counsel of arbitrators, who in 1482 decided for Nottingham.[61] But Retford paid no more attention to this decision than to any other, forcing Nottingham to choose new arbitrators within two years who once more decided in Nottingham's favor. Retford again ignored the decision, claiming exemption by ancient demesne. Nottingham's attorney searched Domesday Book but could not find evidence for such a claim, and the problems continued into Henry VII's reign.[62] Although its annoyance level was high, the case was not serious enough (or the evidence strong enough) for either side to win final resolution. Central courts gave Nottingham the verdict it required, yet seemed unable or unwilling to force the defendant to respect it, and local measures such as arbitration proved little more effective. Legal recourse to the royal government constituted only one step in a series of moves calculated to air issues and advertise complaints, but generally avoid decisions that could harm larger patterns of commerce.

The royal customs accounts have long been minutely examined to shed light on international trade patterns and the wealth they brought

England. They are far from being a perfect, full, or reliable source of information. Even provincial town records contain complaints from kings and citizens alike about concealment and farming of customs, smuggling and fraud, and incorrect copies sent to Westminster.[63] By the fifteenth century, some merchandise valuations became conventional, hiding the true size and changing nature of trade. More frustrating for historians of towns and their unique contributions to national wealth, the inclusion of several ports under one heading obscures the share of trade pertaining to any single urban center. [64]

To judge by the royal customs accounts alone, the port of Exeter (which included Dartmouth, Barnstaple, and at times Plymouth) made minuscule contributions to international trade patterns, handling some of the smallest amounts of wool England exported.[65] However, its cloth exports rose from 0.6% of the national total at the start of the fifteenth century, to 3% by mid-century, and ranged from 4% to 12% during Henry VII's reign.[66] In terms of monetary contributions, Exeter's share was similarly small, ranging from one-quarter of 1% of Crown revenue in 1432–33, to 4% late in Henry VII's reign.[67]

Not only do these figures fail to tell us about Exeter's particular contribution to national wealth, but extensive work on late medieval Exeter reveals the shortcomings of relying primarily upon the national records.[68] Some 70% of Exeter's import trade came via coastal not foreign trade routes. National port customs accounts did not record such commerce, just as they omitted the light, cheap cloths the southwest manufactured in large number. A fuller picture of Exeter's total commercial activity is possible because the city is blessed with the most comprehensive set of local customs accounts of any English town. They tell us that while cloth exports fell in the late fourteenth century and stagnated through the 1420s, recovery began by the following decade and continued into the sixteenth century despite some setbacks in the 1450s. They indicate the full scope of trans-shipments of foreign goods from other redistribution centers, and remind us that coastal trade, being safer and cheaper than overseas commerce, allowed more men to participate in trade and enjoy its profits.[69] This potential for a broader spread of wealth joins other factors to explain a lack of political tensions in Exeter city government as well as its ability to balance the internal budget nearly every year. Furthermore, it provided the foundation for the city's growth in the sixteenth century, a development rather more puzzling when illustrated only by Exeter's modest trade profile as recorded in national accounts.

Without comparable local data, citing customs revenues for Norwich (out of the port of Great Yarmouth) or York (out of Hull) would be nearly pointless. National accounts certainly have their utility in providing an index of direct overseas trade, but even that plays a small role in a study of Crown-town relations. Nor are we much better off by examining aulnage records to determine how many cloths were approved and sealed for sale. To an even greater extent than customs returns, aulnage accounts have been condemned as fraudulent.[70] At best, the accounts show the distribution of clothmaking rather than the true size of the home market, revealing that by the early fifteenth century, the textile industry had departed the boroughs and their restrictions for the rural areas of the west country, East Anglia, and Yorkshire.

We are on firmer ground with customs and aulnage returns when we analyze the use kings made of the money. Collectors were officers who not only produced money regularly at the Exchequer, but who paid it out locally as well upon receipt of Exchequer-issued tallies from individuals deserving of annuities or debt repayment. The primary utilization of customs revenues in this manner was for defense. Throughout the fourteenth and fifteenth centuries, cloth and wool subsidies paid for military campaigns in general as well as for specific measures like noble and mercantile plans to safeguard the seas.[71] Exeter customs in particular paid the salary of Edward IV's Keeper of Ships, rewarded a yeoman of the Crown for capturing an enemy (Scottish) vessel, and reimbursed a local customer loyal to Richard III for resisting the duke of Buckingham's followers.[72] In the 1460s, Exeter and Dartmouth customs contributed £30 *per annum* to the latter's defenses, a sum that rose to £40 under Henry VII.[73] Customs and aulnage payments also helped to pay the Crown's debts. Henry VI owed Sir John Radclyf, seneschal of Aquitaine and constable of Fronsac castle, over £7000 in back payments. Part of the debt was treated as a fictitious loan to the Crown while the rest was repaid through Exeter and Dartmouth customs.[74]

Customs and subsidies also provided annuities and salaries. Wages for royal serjeants-at-arms came from west country ports, as did payments to the tutor of Edward IV's sons, the king's tailor, his French secretary, a Windsor gardener, and the Clarenceux herald. In 1497, the earl of Surrey acted as keeper of the east march towards Scotland, receiving a salary of £1000 composed of contributions from most of

England's ports, including £300 from Exeter and Dartmouth.[75] Enrolled accounts and other Exchequer documents may disappoint those in search of accurate, consistent information about a city's role in national trade, but one fact emerges clearly. By tracing the number of alienations made on the ports' contributions, it is apparent that customs and to a lesser extent aulnage payments provided a valuable and reliable source of income that the Crown could tap to pay its debts and reward its followers.[76]

Foreign Trade and Traders

The evidence of trade and its revenues presented so far indicates that the royal government rarely allowed local issues and needs to dominate national and especially international patterns of commerce. The delicacy and importance of these patterns is best seen in English towns' problems with foreign merchants and pirates. The Devonshire coast was particularly prone to illegal attacks, being riddled with coves and harbors in which lawbreakers could hide. Exeter merchants knew more than their share of pirate attacks, by both foreign traders and denizens, in addition to smuggling activities designed to by-pass customs collection.[77] Mayors of towns were obliged to assist customs officials' inquiries into illegal activities and to arrest the goods of suspects, but between 1377 and 1509 there was no noticeable improvement in law enforcement. Early in Richard II's reign, Exeter's mayor had joined with the Admiral to bring two local pirates to justice, but the city was still plagued by attacks when Henry VII commanded its governors to join him in planning measures to take against "diverse evill-disposed persones...nowe lieing upon the See as commyn pyrates...."[78] During the intervening decades, kings established commissions to investigate reports of attacks and ordered the nation's customs officials to arrest ships and help individuals such as Devonshire natives Sir Philip Courtenay and William Bonville resist pirates.[79] There is no evidence such measures had the slightest effect. The most famous example occurred in 1414, when Henry V's commission of oyer and terminer was thwarted in its investigation of attacks on Breton shipping. Local juries refused to indict their own mariners even when breach of an Anglo-Breton truce was at stake.[80]

The problem of pirates and attacks upon the high seas grew more complicated whenever foreign seamen were involved. English merchants attacked foreign shipping not just for personal gain, but to achieve compensation for losses of their own goods. The Crown was torn between defending native merchants and preventing foreign governments from becoming so offended that they removed their profitable presence from English ports. It did not help that medieval towns treated alien traders from other countries with deep suspicion: throughout the period, London in particular witnessed bitter attacks upon aliens, whose movements and mercantile activities were severely restricted. In 1378, Norwich citizens obtained from the Crown prohibitions against alien retailing in return for building the king a barge, while York's charter of 1442 contained similar restrictions. Customary law in thirteenth-century Exeter decreed it lawful to distrain the goods of an alien's countrymen if he himself fell into debt.[81] Ports like Exeter hosted special keepers enjoined to detect enemy ships, arrest vessels, and prevent the arrival and departure of all but known and licensed merchants. During the 1420s and 1430s, the keepers also prevented the export of food, helped watch for bullion leaving the country, and demanded that alien importers spend the money they received from their own sales only on English goods.[82]

Of all alien merchants, Hanseatic League traders contributed the most wealth to the nation's economy. In addition to London, they were most active in the ports of Hull and Lynn, in which York and Norwich merchants respectively contributed significant business. Compared to other foreign traders, Hansa merchants participated in unrestricted retail sales and trade amongst themselves while residing in England. This freedom made all the more galling those injustices inflicted upon English merchants in Prussia, Norway and the Baltic, areas in which the Hansa traded and resented English intrusion.[83] London merchants in particular wanted the Hansa's privileges curtailed, on the grounds that despite a treaty of 1377, English traders "when they came into [German] parts with merchandise [had not been] as amicably and fairly treated there...as by the liberties contained in the charter the Almains exercise their trade here."[84]

The early years of Richard II's reign witnessed inconsistent government policy resulting in retaliatory raids by both Hansa and English merchants. In response, the king ordered confiscated all Prussian goods in England, writing to the officials of Norwich and York to forward his council's complaints about Prussian attacks.[85] Between 1386 and 1388, the Crown planned to send an embassy to the Grand Master of Teutonic Knights, its costs to be levied from the goods arrested. York merchant and wool exporter Thomas Graa was ordered "to leave all else and ceasing every excuse" come before the king and council for business concerning the estate of the realm. Graa was appointed co-leader of the embassy with Walter Sybil of London, and given ships in which to return the confiscated merchandise. York merchants claimed the Prussians owed them almost £100, a figure later adjusted to £1636; Norwich traders claimed just over £60; while Nottingham men set their loss at £2 16s. 8d. Prussian goods confiscated in England were returned to show goodwill, and some return of English merchandise was effected, although the Crown tapped all gains to pay for the embassy.[86]

Richard achieved for his merchants conditions of near-parity in their relations with the League, but trouble with Hansa merchants and illegal seizures continued during the fifteenth century. In 1451, after four years of particularly fierce disturbances, Henry VI decided to send ambassadors to a diet at Utrecht. Mayors of London, York, Norwich, and port towns received orders to cease attacking the Prussians for the time being and to send their complaints about the Hansa to the planned diet.[87] The meeting accomplished little, and a Norwich merchant lost cloth and tin in further seizures on Danzig-bound ships two years later. English losses overseas were reduced only after Edward IV took the throne and initiated "an uneasy Anglo-Hanseatic dialogue" resulting in the Treaty of Utrecht (1474).[88] The higher customs they paid on exported goods and the markets they provided in Europe for English cloth made the Hansa merchants difficult to dispense with, much less to punish. Only periods of insecurity during the late 1460s forced Edward to abandon his own inclination to balance Hansa and English demands and honor the wishes of the more xenophobic London merchants upon whose fortunes and goodwill he relied. York merchants complained about unfair competition, but even Edward IV's successors such as Henry VII continued his policy of favoring the Hansa by confirming their privileges, further evidence of the vital role these merchants played in a national context that would always take precedence over the local and urban.[89]

Scandinavian countries provided markets and friction in almost equal proportions. In the 1390s, a York merchant complained to the Crown of a Danish attack on his ship when it was blown off course during a storm. He requested that the mayor and bailiffs of Hull arrest the Danish merchant responsible, who was presently residing in the northern port, as punishment for theft of his cargo and the ransom demanded for his crew.[90] Henry VI continued to have problems with the Danes, who took approximately £5000 worth of goods from York and Hull merchants in a single year, and £20,000 worth from the rest of England's merchants (the figures are likely to have been inflated for effect).[91] Although relations degenerated into open attacks on English shipping in 1468, the profits of such trade were sufficient to persuade Norwich merchant John Belles to shape a new Anglo-Danish mercantile treaty of 1490 which provided English shipping with freedom of navigation.[92] Relations were no easier with Iceland, to which English traders had been welcomed since early in the fifteenth century. Violence and piracy combined to convince the Crown in 1444 to prohibit all commerce with the island, although the ban was sometimes ignored.[93] Edward IV gave licenses to sail to Iceland as rewards after Towton, but Richard III considered the danger so great that he ordered all Iceland-bound ships to travel in convoy.[94]

Relations with close neighbors proved no easier. England's disputes with Scotland on land were matched by those on the sea and between merchants. In 1392, a tentative and temporary peace had no sooner been agreed between the two realms than the earl of Northumberland as guardian of the truce was required to investigate several petitions. The citizens of York and the burgesses of Nottingham demanded the earl and his fellow wardens of the marches investigate the loss of over £100 worth of herring and eels. The cargo was waylaid along the coast of Scotland by subjects of that country who had no respect for the truce, so the accusation was made. The Crown sought a solution to the problem in Yarmouth, where bailiffs were ordered to unload the goods from several Scottish merchants' ships and entrust the merchandise to local men, certifying its value in Chancery. No record remains of the ultimate decision, but five weeks after receiving their orders Yarmouth men were told to sell any perishable goods found on board.[95]

No country had unblemished trade relations with England. The close rolls contain numerous complaints about foreign piracy, as well as notice of local English commissions established to investigate claims and return stolen goods. Truces may not necessarily have brought out the worst in a medieval merchant, but neither did they effectively control piracy. The embassies established to seek justice did little to punish individual offenders, but they did preserve international relations and prevent isolated incidents from threatening trade networks.

Residents in each of the four towns studied here relied upon trade and commerce to make significant contributions to personal and corporate prosperity. They were well-aware that commercial revenues kept their town budgets balanced and helped to satisfy royal demands for payments. They fully exploited the link between local profit and royal prosperity, reminding the king at frequent intervals that timely assistance benefited both parties. While successful petitions could result in helpful charters and grants, full participation in commerce brought with it added responsibilities for urban subjects, particularly those wealthy merchants most likely to hold local office. Such men played essential parts in national and international trade, tracking counterfeit coins, sealing cloths, collecting customs, and negotiating with foreign traders.

In numerous commercial venues, urban subjects relied upon the royal government to defend their interests and safeguard their investments. They pursued justice in royal courts and in royally-constituted embassies with an enduring optimism that the personal and local could receive the same attention as the national and international. Their disappointments were numerous, but their confidence serves as testimony to the success of the monarchy in uniting its component parts and clarifying the contribution even the humblest urban merchant made to the realm's wealth and diplomacy.

NOTES

[1] *Norwich Records*, 2:cxxix–cxxx, 92, 102, 318–19; N.R.O., 7-c, Chamberlains' Account Roll, 6–7 Henry VII.

[2] See above, p. 105; Hoker, *Description of the Citie*, 3:657; A. M. Jackson, "Medieval Exeter, the Exe, and the Earldom of Devon," *Transactions of the Devonshire Association* 104 (1972): 57–72; Philip C. De la Garde, "On the Antiquity and Invention of the Lock Canal of Exeter," *Archaeologia* 28 (1839): 8, 14, 16; D.R.O., Miscellaneous Roll 3, no. 7.

[3] *Nott. Records*, 1:199–201, 227–29. For the queen's interest in revenues derived from a borough's fee farm, see above, p. 145.

[4] *Rot. Parl.*, 3:298; *CCR, 1389–92*, p. 528; *CPR, 1391–96*, p. 79.

[5] Nt.R.O., CA7384; *Nott. Records*, 1:412–21; C. T. Flower, ed., *Public Works in Mediaeval Law, Volume II*, Selden Society, vol. 40 (London, 1925), pp. 113–14.

[6] *CPR, 1429–36*, p. 202. See also the commission of 1466: *CPR, 1461–67*, p. 552.

[7] Nt.R.O., CA4488, 4489, 4490; 7452, f.2v; *Nott. Records*, 2:380–83; William E. Hampton, *Memorials of the Wars of the Roses* (Upminster: Richard III Society, 1979), p. 145; Joel Rosenthal, "Feuds and Private Peace-making," *Nottingham Medieval Studies* 14 (1970): 84–90.

[8] P.R.O., KB.9/144; Flower, *Public Works*, pp. 253, 258; *CPR, 1377–81*, p. 524; *1396–99*, p. 52. A statute of 1352 (25 Edward III, st.3, c.4) prohibited all weirs

erected since the time of Edward I, but it had little permanent effect.

9 *CPR, 1441–46*, p. 200; Dobson, *Chamberlains' Accounts*, pp. 37–58; see above, p. 120. A. J. Pollard, *North-eastern England During the Wars of the Roses: Lay Society, War, and Politics 1450–1500* (Oxford: Clarendon Press, 1990), pp. 71–73, 333, explores the economic context of weir clearance.

10 Nicholas H. Nicolas, ed., *Proceedings and Ordinances of the Privy Council of England*, 7 vols. (London: Record Commission, 1834–37), 5:225, 232. The city spent over £130, raised by assessments quite separate from local receipts and royal tallages and subsidies.

11 Dobson, *Chamberlains' Accounts*, pp. 61–62; David Palliser, "York under the Tudors," in *Perspectives in English Urban History*, ed. Alan Everitt (London: Macmillan, 1973), p. 43; Y.C.A., Charter A.25.

12 *CPR, 1461–67*, p. 572; *York House Books*, pp. 9–10.

13 *York House Books*, pp. 128–30.

14 Dobson, *Chamberlains' Accounts*, pp. 163–64. The sum constituted 9% of total receipts.

15 *York House Books*, pp. 269, 307, 318–20; Rosemary Horrox and P. W. Hammond, ed., *British Library Harleian MS. 433*, 4 vols. (London and Upminster: Alan Sutton Publishing for the Richard III Society, 1979–83), 1:192; P.R.O. E.368/255, mem.49.

16 *York House Books*, pp. 318–20. Two to four "rooms" were usual, but one weir contained twenty-nine compartments.

17 *York Civic Records*, 2:191; *Statutes of the Realm*, 2:572.

18 D. F. Harrison, "Bridges and Economic Development, 1300–1800," *Economic History Review*, 2d ser. 45 (1992): 240–61; James Masschaele, "Transport Costs in Medieval England," *idem* 46 (1993): 266–79.

19 D.R.O., Miscellaneous Rolls 3 & 6; Book 51, ff.289v, 308; Stuart A. Moore, ed., *Letters and Papers of John Shillingford, Mayor of Exeter, 1447–50*, Camden Society, n.s., vol. 2 (London, 1871), pp. xxiv, 141–42; W. G. Hoskins, *Two Thousand Years in Exeter* (Exeter: James Townsend and Sons Ltd., 1960), p. 28.

20 N.R.O., 17-a, *Liber Albus*, f.14. For York examples of donations in wills, see Jennifer I. Kermode, *Medieval Merchants: York, Beverley and Hull in the Later Middle Ages* (Cambridge: Cambridge University Press, 1998), pp. 150–51. Churches asked for prayers for those who made and repaired bridges and streets: T. P. Cooper, "The Medieval Highways, Streets, Open Ditches and Sanitary Conditions of the City of York," *Yorkshire Archaeological Journal* 22 (1912–13): 280–81.

21 Nt.R.O., CA4771, 4477, 4518; *Nott. Records*, 2:222–41; *CPR, 1381–85*, p. 257; *1401–1405*, p. 197; *1422–29*, p. 193; James Granger, *Old Nottingham: Its Streets, People, etc.* (Nottingham: Nottingham Daily Express Office, 1902), p. 79. As justices, the men had the power to hold inquiries under oath to determine exactly who should repair the bridge.

22 P.R.O., KB.9/351, mm. 30–31; KB.29/109, f.13v; KB.9/363, mm. 5–6; KB.29/112, f.29v; KB.29/124, f.13v; KB.29/132, f.8.

23 P.R.O., SC.8/27/1330; SC.8/198/9891.

24 *Rot. Parl.*, 5:43–44. Henry, however, took twenty years to respond since the initial plea.

25 *CCR, 1399–1402*, p. 557; *1405–1409*, p. 258; *CPR, 1408–13*, p. 370; *1461–67*, pp. 226, 460. See also *CPR, 1467–77*, p. 470, and P.R.O., C.1/27/365, for an example

from Exeter; and SC.6/1088/18, for one from York.

[26] *Norwich Records*, 1:348–54. See below, p. 263.

[27] N.R.O., 18-a, Chamberlains' Account Book, 1470–90, ff.117v; Account Book 1479–88, ff.30–34.

[28] N.R.O., 9-e, and 17-a, *Liber Albus*, ff.82v–83v.

[29] N.R.O., 9-e; 17-a, ff.83v–88; *Norwich Records,* 1:353.

[30] N.R.O., 9-e; 18-a, Account Book 1479–88, ff.30–34. For the painted map, see N.R.O., 21-F, 9–58, *sub* 1482: "and so it was that the said Abbot never prevailed in his suit." Lord Howard, the bishop of Norwich, and Justice William Jenney were also approached for their favor, while local men between the ages of 78 and 95 gave testimony, some for the city and others for the abbot.

[31] N.R.O., 16-d, Assembly Minute Book II, ff.3, 4, 6.

[32] S. R. Epstein, "Regional Fairs, Institutional Innovation, and Economic Growth in Late Medieval Europe," *Economic History Review*, 2d series, 47 (1994): 460, 469; R. H. Britnell, *The Commercialisation of English Society 1000–1500* (Cambridge: Cambridge University Press, 1993), pp. 10–22, 81–85, 88–90. See also Anne Lombard-Jourdan, "Fairs," *Dictionary of the Middle Ages*, ed. Joseph R. Strayer, 12 vols. (New York: Charles Scribner's Sons, 1982–89), 4:582–90. For a full review of the English literature on fairs, see Maryanne Kowaleski, *Local Markets and Regional Trade in Medieval Exeter* (Cambridge and New York: Cambridge University Press, 1995), p. 42, note 2.

[33] *Norwich Records*, 1:42–43; 2:cxxxvi–cxxxvii, 74–75; *CPR, 1476–85*, p. 326. See above, p. 143, for the effect of the fairs' decline on urban finances.

[34] One of the five was a refounding of an older fair dating from before 1240: Kowaleski, *Local Markets and Regional Trade*, pp. 65–68, Appendix 2 Table A2.1.

[35] *York Civic Records*, 2:166, 170, 172, 174–76; *CPR, 1494–1509*, p. 257; H. G. Richardson, *The Medieval Fairs and Markets of York*, St. Anthony's Hall Publication 20 (York, 1961), pp. 21–22.

[36] K. J. Allison, "Markets and Fairs," in P. M. Tillot, ed., *The Victoria History of the Counties of England: A History of Yorkshire, The City of York* (London: Oxford University Press, 1961), pp. 489–91.

[37] E.g., *Statutes of the Realm*, 2:213 (1422), and P.R.O., C.1/69/28. See also Alice Beardwood, "The Royal Mints and Exchanges," in *Local Administration*, vol. 3, *The English Government at Work, 1327–1336*, edited by James F. Willard, William A. Morris and W. H. Dunham, Jr. (Cambridge, Mass.: The Mediaeval Academy of America, 1950), pp. 35–66.

[38] *Statutes of the Realm*, 2:17–18; *CCR, 1377–81*, p. 193; J. L. Bolton, *The Medieval English Economy 1150–1500* (London: J. M. Dent and Sons, 1980), pp. 298–300.

[39] *Rot. Parl.*, 4:256–57; *Statutes of the Realm*, 2:87, 223–24, 457; *CCR, 1385–89*, p. 441; *CPR, 1494–1509*, pp. 178–79.

[40] Exchequer memoranda rolls record how seriously the magistrates took their duty: in 1445, Mayor John Shillingford reported in detail that Exeter was free of false coin and had not exported bullion: P.R.O., E.368/218, Communa, Michaelmas, mem. 4v. See also *Statutes of the Realm*, 2:191, and Edward Powell, *Kingship, Law and Society: Criminal Justice in the Reign of Henry V* (Oxford: Clarendon Press, 1989), p. 259, for discussion of the social and judicial context of this extension of the 1352 statute.

41   *York House Books*, pp. 345–47.

42   For examples, see *Nott. Records*, 3:37–39, and Kowaleski, *Local Markets and Regional Trade*, pp. 189–90.

43   *Statutes of the Realm*, 2:242, 283. Four years later, mayors and constables gained the power to enforce all statutes concerning measures. I. S. Leadam, ed., *Select Cases before the King's Council in the Star Chamber, Volume I: 1477–1509*, Selden Society, vol. 16 (London, 1903), pp. cxlvii–cli includes a concise history of this legislation.

44   *Ibid.*, 2:570–71, 637–38; Francis Blomefield, *A Topographical History of the County of Norfolk*, 2d ed., 11 vols. (London: William Miller, 1805–10), 3:141.

45   Palliser, *Tudor York*, pp. 186–87; *York Civic Records*, 3:23; Leadam, *Select Cases Star Chamber*, pp. 69–71.

46   *York Civic Records*, 2:142–45; Dobson, *Chamberlains' Accounts*, p. 204. The city council agreed that the mayor should take Hobart some fish, but concluded that if the attorney cited his impartiality he should be provided with dinner by the council at his own lodging. For Hobart's actions as an urban patron, see above pp. 118–19.

47   D.R.O., Mayor's Court Roll, 1458–59, f.29; *York Civic Records*, 2:70–71, 90, 93, 97–100; *Nott. Records*, 3:56–59; *CPR, 1485–94*, p. 109. The York weavers' guild's fee farm of £5 *per annum* was eventually waived in 1486.

48   *Statutes of the Realm*, 2:298–99.

49   *CPR, 1461–67*, p. 543; Toulmin Smith, ed., *English Gilds*, Early English Text Society, o.s., vol. 40 (London, 1870), pp. 299–301; Joyce A. Youings, *Tuckers Hall Exeter* (Exeter: University of Exeter Press, 1968), p. 11. The letters patent cost the tailors forty shillings.

50   Smith, ed., *English Gilds*, pp. 302–9; Leadam, *Select Cases Star Chamber*, pp. cli–clii, 1–6. A statute of 1437 (15 Henry VI, c.6) had deterred guilds and fraternities from making ordinances that infringed upon royal and municipal corporate privileges, but it had lapsed with the deposition of Henry VI and was not renewed until 1504 (19 Henry VII, c.7).

51   P.R.O., SC.8/30/1462; Smith, ed., *English Gilds*, pp. 309–12.

52   *Rot. Parl.*, 5:390–91; 6:219–20; D.R.O., Book 51, ff.62–63; Receivers' Roll 22 Edward IV–1 Richard III; Alice S. Green, *Town Life in the Fifteenth Century*, 2 vols. (London and New York: Macmillan and Co., 1894), 2:167–89; May McKisack, *The Parliamentary Representation of the English Boroughs during the Middle Ages* (Oxford: Clarendon Press, 1932), p. 134; Kowaleski, *Local Markets and Regional Trade*, pp. 100–101, 156. History repeated itself in 1550 when the promise of improved peacekeeping persuaded the royal government to grant Exeter a more comprehensive charter following violent attacks on civic officials by members of the tailors' guild: Robert Tittler, *The Reformation and the Towns in England: Politics and Political Culture, c.1540–1640* (Oxford: Clarendon Press, 1998), pp. 177–79. For an example of London tailors ignoring the statute of 1436 and obtaining a royal charter of incorporation, see R. Harold Garrett-Goodyear, "Revival of Quo Warranto and Early Tudor Policy towards Local Governors, 1485–1540" (Ph.D. diss., Harvard University, 1973), pp. 137–44.

53   P.R.O., C.1/46/60. See also C.1/46/448, C.1/46/262. For mercantile affairs settled by arbitration, see Carole Rawcliffe, "'That Kindliness Should be Cherished More, and Discord Driven Out:' The Settlement of Commercial Disputes by Arbitration in

Later Medieval England," *Enterprise and Individuals in Fifteenth-Century England*, ed. J. I. Kermode (Stroud: Alan Sutton Publishing, 1991), pp. 99–117.

[54] P.R.O., C.1/32/74, C.1/31/33, C.1/2/17. For the arbitration achieved in 1446 by Chancellor John Stafford to settle a dispute between merchant of York William Bowes and Bawdewyn Sahenny of Epinal in France, see *CCR, 1441–47*, pp. 444–45.

[55] Kowaleski, *Local Markets and Regional Trade*, p. 197. See N.R.O., 16-d, Assembly Book I, f.92, for details of the case of two Norwich aldermen claiming exemption from toll before the royal council.

[56] Details of the following case can be found in Leadam, *Select Cases Star Chamber*, pp. 71–95.

[57] P.R.O., STAC.1/2/78/8.

[58] D.R.O., Miscellaneous Roll 82; Book 55, ff.68–70; Book 51, f.36.

[59] D.R.O., Receivers' Rolls, 15–16, 16–17, 18–19 Henry VII; Leadam, *Select Cases Star Chamber*, pp. cxlii–cxliii; Kermode, *Medieval Merchants*, pp. 252–53.

[60] *Nott. Records*, 2:310–17; 3:426–27; Nt.R.O., CA4217, 4218, 4219, 5536, 4562A.

[61] *Nott. Records*, 3:427; Nt.R.O., CA4517C.

[62] *Nott. Records*, 2:396, 398, 421; 3:266; Nt.R.O., CA4441.

[63] For examples in Exeter records, see D.R.O., Book 51, ff.320v, 330. The returns survive in two different forms: the particular accounts made in each port by royal officials recording every detail of ships arriving or departing; and enrolled accounts made in the Exchequer and noting only total quantities or values of goods, Michaelmas to Michaelmas of each succeeding year. The particular accounts are the more valuable because they describe the goods passing through each port, but survivals are scarce: E. M. Carus-Wilson, and Olive Coleman, *England's Export Trade 1275–1547* (Oxford: Clarendon Press, 1963), pp. 7–8; Anthony Saul, "English Towns in the Late Middle Ages: The Case of Great Yarmouth," *Journal of Medieval History* 8 (1982): 77–78.

[64] T. H. Lloyd, *Alien Merchants in England in the High Middle Ages* (New York: St. Martin's Press, 1982), p. 7; A. R. Bridbury, *England and the Salt Trade in the Later Middle Ages* (Oxford: Oxford University Press, 1955), pp. 104–105; Carus-Wilson and Coleman, *England's Export Trade*, pp. 194–95.

[65] Eileen Power and M. M. Postan, eds., *Studies in English Trade in the Fifteenth Century* (London: G. Routledge and Sons, Ltd., 1933), pp. 337–39.

[66] Carus-Wilson and Coleman, *England's Export Trade*, pp. 80–113, 122–23, 128–29, 132–33, 138–39, 144–45, 146–47, 154–55.

[67] Anthony Steel, *Receipt of the Exchequer, 1377–1485* (Cambridge: Cambridge University Press, 1954), pp. 203, 292; Carus-Wilson and Coleman, *England's Export Trade*, pp. 94, 102. Under the first Tudor the customs revenue constituted 1.7% of total royal income, falling to 1.4% in the sixteenth century not necessarily because of a decline of trade but because Henry found alternate sources of revenue: Dietz, *English Government Finance*, p. 80; Michael Van Cleave Alexander, *The First of the Tudors: A Study of Henry VII and His Reign* (Totowa, New Jersey: Rowman and Littlefield, 1980), p. 69.

[68] For what follows, see Kowaleski, *Local Markets and Regional Trade*, especially pp. 28, 224–25. This entire work shows how such records can inform a broad analysis of urban and regional trading patterns. Some of the accounts themselves are printed in

Maryanne Kowaleski, *The Local Port Customs Accounts of the City of Exeter 1266–1321*, Devon and Cornwall Record Society, n.s., vol. 36 (Exeter, 1993). See also Henry S. Cobb, "Local Port Customs Accounts prior to 1550," *Journal of the Society of Archivists* 1 (1958): 214 n.4; W. B. Stephens, "The Origins and Nature of the Exeter Town Customs Duties," *Devon and Cornwall Notes and Queries* 28 (1961): 247–49.

[69]   Kowaleski, *Local Markets and Regional Trade*, pp. 237, 329.

[70]   E. M. Carus-Wilson, "The Aulnage Accounts: A Criticism," *Economic History Review* 2 (1929): 114, 122; Carus-Wilson and Coleman, *England's Export Trade*, p. 20. A. R. Bridbury, *Medieval English Clothmaking: An Economic Survey* (London: Heinemann Educational Books, Ltd., 1982), pp. 47–53, 59, believes the records may at least suggest some broad patterns of trade. For aulnage in general: Herbert Heaton, *The Yorkshire Woollen and Worsted Industries*, 2d ed. (Oxford: Clarendon Press, 1965), pp. 69, 85, 127.

[71]   E.g., *Rot. Parl.*, 3:35, 88, 124; 4:200, 302; 5:504; *CCR, 1405–1409*, pp. 45–46; *1447–54*, p. 461–62, 474; Steel, *Receipt of the Exchequer*, p. 218.

[72]   P.R.O., E.404/78/3/29, E.404/77/3/41, E.404/78/3/25; Horrox and Hammond, *Harleian MS. 433*, 1:248; M. Oppenheim, ed., *Naval Accounts and Inventories of the Reign of Henry VII, 1485–88, and 1495–97*, Navy Records Society, vol. 8 (London, 1896), pp. 3–5.

[73]   *CPR, 1461–67*, p. 75; *1476–85*, p. 251; *1485–94*, p. 111; Horrox and Hammond, *Harleian MS. 433*, 1:167, 194; P.R.O., E.368/258, E.368/261.

[74]   *CPR, 1436–41*, pp. 247, 542; *1441–46*, p. 440; Steel, *Receipt of the Exchequer*, p. 212. Sir John died before he was fully reimbursed, but his executors continued to collect, forcing other "lenders" to the Crown such as the earl of Salisbury to wait their turn. For further examples, see P.R.O., E.401/744, *sub* 11 November; E.401/748, *sub* 17 June; E.401/756, *sub* 24 May.

[75]   P.R.O., E.368/260, Status et visus, Michaelmas, rot. 7; E.404/82 (10 April 1497); *CPR, 1467–77*, p. 184; *1476–85*, pp. 46, 311, 389; *CCR, 1476–85*, nn. 1, 1100; Horrox and Hammond, *Harleian MS. 433*, 3:193–94; William Campbell, ed., *Materials for a History of the Reign of Henry VII*, 2 vols., Rolls Series, vol. 60 (London, 1873, 1877), 1:302, 525–26.

[76]   Nor should it be forgotten that kings alienated traded goods as well as cash payments. The royal ancient prise of wine required two tuns (over 500 gallons) be set aside for the king from each cargo of twenty tuns or more. Edward IV alienated part of his prise, two tuns a year from the ports of Exeter and Dartmouth, to Joan, widow of Yorkist knight Sir John Dynham, a grant that continued under Henry VII until Joan's death in 1497: *Complete Peerage*, 4:377–78; Colin Platt, *Medieval Southampton* (London: Routledge and Kegan Paul, 1973), p. 74; *CPR, 1467–77*, p. 154; *CCR, 1485–1500*, no. 238; P.R.O., E.101/83/1. For Dynham's loyalty, see above, pp. 109, 110, 111.

[77]   Neville Williams, *Contraband Cargoes: Seven Centuries of Smuggling* (London: Longmans, 1959), p. 13; Peter Ramsey, "Overseas Trade in the Reign of Henry VII," *Economic History Review*, 2d ser., 6 (1953): 173–75; Charles L. Kingsford, *Prejudice and Promise in XVth Century England* (Oxford: Oxford University Press, 1925), p. 82; Edward Gillett and Kenneth A. MacMahon, *A History of Hull*, 2d ed. (Hull: Hull University Press, 1989), pp. 48–51.

78   *CPR, 1377–81*, p. 356; D.R.O., Letter 1. For background on piracy, the inefficacy of the Admiral, and participation of Exeter's elite in illegal activities, see S. Bhanji, "The Involvement of Exeter and the Exe Estuary in Piracy," *Transactions of the Devonshire Association* 130 (1998): 23–30.

79   *CPR, 1436–41*, p. 411; *1452–61*, p. 258; *1467–77*, pp. 168–69.

80   Powell, *Kingship, Law and Society*, pp. 201–8.

81   *Rot. Parl.*, 3:41; *CChR*, 6:30–31; *York Mem. Bk.*, 3:130–31. See above, p. 37. Pamela Nightingale, *A Medieval Mercantile Community: The Grocers' Company and the Politics and Trade of London 1000–1485* (New Haven and London: Yale University Press, 1995), contains extensive analysis of alien conflict throughout the Middle Ages, particularly in chapters 11, 13–14, 19. See also M. S. Giuseppi, "Alien Merchants in England in the Fifteenth Century," *Transactions of the Royal Historical Society*, 2d series, 9 (1895): 78, 80, 84–85; Mary Bateson, ed., *Borough Customs*, 2 vols., Selden Society, vols. 18, 21 (London, 1904, 1906), 1:117–18; Leadam, *Select Cases Star Chamber*, pp. 114–18.

82   Frances A. Mace, "Devonshire Ports in the Fourteenth and Fifteenth Centuries," *Transactions of the Royal Historical Society*, 4th series, 8 (1925): 112; *CCR, 1399–1402*, pp. 38, 76, 554; *1402–1405*, pp. 93, 263, 421–22; *1422–29*, pp. 85–86; *1429–35*, p. 199; *1447–54*, pp. 9–10; *Statutes of the Realm*, 2:257; *Rot. Parl.*, 3:396.

83   Hyman Palais, "England's First Attempt to Break the Commercial Monopoly of the Hanseatic League, 1377–1380," *American Historical Review* 64 (1959): 852–57; John D. Fudge, *Cargoes, Embargoes, and Emissaries: The Commercial and Political Interaction of England and the German Hanse 1450–1510* (Toronto and London: University of Toronto Press, 1995), pp. 7–10, 163; Power and Postan, *Studies in English Trade*, p. 106.

84   *CPR, 1377–81*, p. 57; *Rot. Parl.*, 2:367; Ralph Flenley, "London and Foreign Merchants in the Reign of Henry VI," *English Historical Review* 25 (1910): 646, 654–55.

85   *York Mem. Bk.*, 2:1–4; *CCR, 1385–89*, pp. 67–68.

86   *CCR, 1385–89*, pp. 163, 194–95, 388, 416, 481, 529, 565–66. For biographical information on Graa, see Kermode, *Medieval Merchants*, pp. 50–51.

87   *CCR, 1447–54*, p. 267; Rymer, *Foedera*, 11:282–83; Fudge, *Cargoes, Embargoes, and Emissaries*, p. 19.

88   Fudge, *Cargoes, Embargoes, and Emissaries*, p. 22, 184; Power and Postan, *Studies in English Trade*, pp. 136–38.

89   Edward did, however, salvage future negotiations by continuing to favor the Cologne merchants when others of the Steelyard suffered arrest and confiscation. He returned to his more balanced policy early in the 1470s: Fudge, *Cargoes, Embargoes, and Emissaries*, pp. 54–57, 74–76, 90, 98; *York Civic Records*, 2:123–25; James Gairdner, *History of the Life and Reign of Richard III* (Cambridge: Cambridge University Press, 1898), pp. 277–79; P.R.O., E.101/414/6, f.23v. For the argument that the Lowland markets were far more important to York and Hull merchants than Hansa towns, and that many of the complaints of losses in the Baltic were more rhetorical than actual, see Fudge, *Cargoes, Embargoes, and Emissaries*, pp. 98–100, 122, 128.

90   *CCR, 1392–96*, pp. 200, 207.

91   *Statutes of the Realm*, 2:273; *Rot. Parl.*, 4:402–403.

[92]   Fudge, *Cargoes, Embargoes, and Emissaries*, pp. 25–27, 99, 195.

[93]   E. M. Carus-Wilson, "The Iceland Trade," in Power and Postan, *Studies in English Trade*, pp. 157–65; E. M. Carus-Wilson, "The Overseas Trade of Late Medieval Coventry," *Économies et Sociétés au Moyen Ages: Mélanges offerts à Edouard Perroy* (Paris: Publications de la Sorbonne, 1973), pp. 377–78; G. J. Marcus, "The First English Voyages to Iceland," *Mariner's Mirror* 42 (1956): 316–17; P. Heath, "North Sea Fishing in the Fifteenth Century," *Northern History* 3 (1968): 62–63; W. R. Childs, "England's Icelandic Trade in the Fifteenth Century: The Role of the Port of Hull," *Northern Seas Yearbook* 5 (1995): 11–31; P.R.O., E.30/1096/2, E.30/1096/4. For the 1465–66 attacks on Iceland and retaliation against English traders, see Fudge, *Cargoes, Embargoes, and Emissaries*, pp. 25–27.

[94]   Heath, "North Sea Fishing," 62; Horrox and Hammond, *Harleian MS. 433*, 1:132, 241, 262, 266; 2:99–100, 106–7, 146. Hull traders invested more heavily in the Icelandic trade than York merchants: Kermode, *Medieval Merchants*, p. 273.

[95]   *CCR, 1389–92*, pp. 426, 433–34, 455–56, 473; P.R.O., SC.1/43/45.

PART IV, CHAPTER 8
THE PURSUIT OF JUSTICE

U rban subjects never had to travel far or wait long to pursue justice in a royal court. Towns regularly played host to royal justices on circuit hearing possessory assizes and delivering the jails, occasions that provided opportunities for patronage and consultation. More important, since the twelfth century their charters had provided towns with their own courts and excused residents from having to plead local cases outside city walls.[1] Late medieval borough court records preserve the variety of cases heard in such venues: property disputes, brawls, pleas of debt, petty theft, and bonds for good behavior all received attention within town courts. Charters provided officials with the powers of justices of the peace, authorized to pursue those violations injurious to subjects' and king's profit and peace. Delegated powers by an over-burdened monarchy, mayors and other officers arrested vagabonds, transported offenders to Westminster, and sat with assize justices to hear cases. Civic officials jealously guarded such privileges, viewing their task of helping to maintain the king's peace as a key component in their relations with the Crown.[2] Under the strictest interpretation, the cases undertaken in a mayor's or sheriff's court exemplify the intersection of urban needs and Crown-granted powers. But they do not illuminate the full story of town relations with royal justice.

In truth, not all townspeople were content to make their complaints and seek compensation on the local level alone. Crown records reveal the frequent appearance of urban litigants who preferred to pursue justice in the central courts. Such individuals were undeterred even by local legislation that prohibited certain cases from leaving the town.[3] Motives for transferring a case, even when recorded, varied widely and avoided the complete truth: some litigants feared an unfair or manipulated verdict at home, others preferred equity jurisdiction for issues ignored by the common law, while some sought to pressure their opponent with a costly and time-consuming process at Westminster. Common to all royal subjects were high expectations of a judicial system that had grown in scope and purview over three centuries, but promised more order and fairness than it could deliver. The very popularity of royal courts clogged them with petitions that impaired their ability to provide quick and efficient verdicts. Judicial personnel drawn from the same elite groups that contributed much disorder to medieval society threatened more violence than many subjects thought tolerable. Late medieval literature of satire and complaint contained extensive criticism of royal justice and its failings, reflecting the disappointment many subjects felt about the judicial process and its servants.[4] Yet residents of town and country alike continued to flock to the royal courts in the sincere but misguided belief that justice to their own liking could be found there. Closer examination of the kinds of cases removed to Crown courts and the precise nature of the litigants' expectations of royal justice thus provides further insights into the complex nature of towns' relations with the central government.

Complementary to royal justice available in the central courts was dispute settlement achieved through extra-judicial recourse to negotiation, mediation, and arbitration.[5] Recent studies of arbitration in particular have revealed it as no less sophisticated or respected than any process administered by the central judiciary. At the very least, it could often be used in conjunction with litigation, and the latter could be pursued or threatened as a preliminary or accompaniment to arbitration. Frequently organized by key figures in the royal courts, it exhibited no great sense of distance from the philosophies and assumptions current at Westminster, though it was freer in its ability to apply them to local situations.[6] Whether arbitration was conducted informally by one's neighbors, with greater impact by local magnates, or at the instigation of the lord chancellor himself (and sometimes with his participation), it required that the arbitrators be individuals of moral authority with an instinct for natural justice and sufficient influence to persuade the disputants to accept the settlement.[7] The voluntary nature of the procedure urged opposing parties to acknowledge that love—the principle of self-regulation representing common sense, compromise, and bonds of affection—was complementary to law with its strict application of the rules, and equally essential to placid public relations especially valued in urban settings.[8]

The four towns of this study all turned to combinations of royal juridical process and arbitration to solve problems over land claims. During the fifteenth century, they all experienced threats to the legal rights they asserted over lands within and without city walls, territory desperately needed to augment annual revenue or to provide pasture. Their charters did not always specify which suburbs belonged to a particular borough, and neighboring religious houses which claimed them were especially jealous of both their own holdings and the liberties they enjoyed in the towns themselves. Confused by conflicting claims of jurisdiction and anxious to extend their legal rights, the boroughs petitioned the Crown for help and argued their cases in central courts or before arbitrators appointed by the king. As often as possible, the towns were careful to point out to the monarch that the broader their claims of jurisdiction, the greater the monetary profit for the Crown and the greater the area brought under the king's peace.

The four towns' experience of arbitration unites themes of identity and patronage previously developed in this work. Boroughs of the later Middle Ages not only continued to seek expansion of their chartered privileges, but they also worked for the enlargement and strengthening of their physical size. They did not yet know the limits of their own growth or full nature of their identity, and their claims and explorations formed part of their maturing process. Towns sought protection and help from the patronage patterns carefully established with magnates and civil servants. Just as bastard feudalism has only recently been appreciated as a positive force in late medieval society, arbitration has increasingly been viewed as an opportunity whereby magnates could enhance their prestige by acting justly and bringing peace, and litigants could obtain solutions unavailable by other avenues.[9]

These familiar themes combine in a new context that explores townspeople's trust in royal justice. As the specific cases reveal, initial desires for a decisive ruling were gradually replaced by an appreciation of what local mediation could provide. Like the medieval litigants themselves, modern historians slowly have come to praise the nature of settlements which stressed compromise over the clear victories and losses more apparent at the common law. Diplomatic handling by the arbitrators could assuage anger, soothe wounded pride, and disguise an unpalatable decision as the shrewd counsel of a freely-chosen superior. Arbitrators also had more freedom to consider evidence and arguments that strayed from the point at hand yet invaluably illuminated the context of a dispute. They did not have to conform to the methods or previous decisions of other courts, and thus could bring a fresher and broader perspective to a conflict.[10] Although the urban cases studied here will present some caveats to such sanguine conclusions, civic officials recognized that they had much to gain by this particular recourse to the law. As a result, these legal cases played important roles in the maturing of the boroughs' relations with society outside their walls.

External Recourse

Urban litigants who took their cases to royal courts had a number of choices to make before initiating proceedings. Those who chose the crowded common law courts experienced so much delay that one must assume that harassment and frustration of the defendant were the plaintiff's main intention. The writs to start proceedings, find the defendant, distrain goods, or outlaw an offender all cost money, further advantaging wealthy litigants over the poor. The large number of incomplete cases on the records can best be explained by parties pressured by these tactics into settling by other means.[11] Nor was it always clear what kind of legal problem would be pursued in which court. Claiming that an act had been committed with violence and in breach of the king's peace (*cum vi et armis et contra pacem*) could bring even minor incidents to royal attention, whether the description fit reality or drifted into fiction.[12]

Perhaps a systematic and statistical study of all urban cases brought to the court of Common Pleas will reveal important patterns in the search for justice, but the material is not promising.[13] Like other suitors throughout the entire time span of the study, townspeople brought cases of debt, detinue, disputed property, and unfulfilled contracts. Representation by an attorney mitigated the long-distance commuting involved to pursue a case through several terms. York citizens Robert and Emma Savage were typical of urban subjects who employed an attorney (their kinsman William) to settle a debt of £2, owed by Robert de Santon of Hull to the estate of Hugh de Hanley, for which Emma acted as executrix.[14] During the same term, Michaelmas 1385, widow Alice Latryngton fought John Beverlay for three York messuages she claimed John had given her.[15] Almost a century later, former mayor Richard York and three city chamberlains were called to the bench to answer a chaplain retained by the York officers to celebrate services for a year. The chaplain was unable to finish his term of service but demanded his whole annuity, because "the contract was entire."[16] Crown records did not preserve the verdicts in these cases, if indeed they had them. Disputes involving friends, neighbors, family, and employees could find far more satisfactory settlement out of court, especially if prodded by the inconvenience and threat of centralized judicial process.

Such examples as cited above are rich in anecdote, but ultimately they frustrate attempts to derive patterns of urban litigation. A more rewarding field of inquiry tracks the townspeople who exploited the opportunities for redress offered by equitable jurisdiction, since the late fourteenth century a supplement to the common law, a fulfillment of its true aims, and a corrective for its worst abuses. Equity, or what was termed conscience, circumvented the long and cumbersome procedure so effectively that Chancellor John Morton was able to promise during Henry VII's reign that "no one who came to Chancery should leave the court without a remedy."[17] The growth of business in the equity courts has been used by some historians as evidence of the strengthening of monarchical power, starting with Edward IV and Henry VII and culminating under Henry VIII and Wolsey. Although there is much to commend the theory, this study has shown that townspeople had a long history of reliance upon king and Crown for justice and privileges. And as equity cases themselves will show, not all final resolutions emerged from the courts or the king, but resulted when the local community itself was urged to settle its own affairs.

As Morton's statement suggests, Chancery was the main equity court, although other venues such as the Council in Star Chamber were available. Perhaps 20% of all pleas were handled in equity courts. Equity was considered to be the most rational and flexible expression of natural law, able to settle disputes which had not found answers at common law, with competence over all lands under the English Crown. Plaintiffs who believed they could not find remedy by the course of common law, or who were convinced that other courts could not deal with innovations such as uses, filed a bill of complaint addressed to the chancellor or to the king in council.[18] The speed with which a problem could be dispatched, the power with which the courts could compel defendants to appear, and the predominance of the rule of proof were obvious advantages, although the process was not inexpensive.[19]

The chancellor presided over the most accessible court of equity, its jurisdiction derived from the council and its judicial functions considered an extension of the king's own role. As Wolsey later argued, he had the obligation to set aside or mitigate the common law of the land because the rule of conscience must prevail. The chancellor not only provided equitable solutions, but during the later Middle Ages continued to help litigants find solutions at common law, often counseling and arranging for arbitration on the local level. Equity's superior and more flexible machinery led to more rapid resolutions and ones possibly less susceptible to local influence. Decisions were rarely noted on the records, and as in common law courts final verdicts may not have been the object of all suits. But the popularity of the court indicates that the chancellor was filling a need with dispatch and efficiency, especially for those with the resources to travel to Westminster and maintain a visible presence there. [20]

Towns used the court of Chancery frequently, for mercantile and commercial disputes as well as for those problems of uses and enfeoffment which sent the majority of individual plaintiffs to equity. Urban disputes over property mainly concerned contested title to messuages and illegal detention of deeds and other records, pleas that brought ordinary property cases to the equity court. [21] Equally troublesome to urban plaintiffs were cases of debt and bond, problems which could have been tried at Common Pleas but came to equity for more rapid resolution. Executors of estates, like Exeter mayor John Shillingford's son William, complained of friends of the deceased who claimed money not due them; others told stories of assault and imprisonment resulting from non-payment. [22] Peter Mannyng, a worsted weaver of Norwich, told Chancery a familiar story, claiming that he had faithfully paid his debt of £8 but that his creditor failed to destroy the bond and was suing for a second payment in the local sheriffs' court. [23]

Charges of civic officials' prejudice or incompetence, as well as mercantile disputes and problems with trade, had their part to play. [24] The mixed demographic composition of towns created particular problems appropriate for Chancery view. Individuals non-resident in the boroughs in which a debt occurred found themselves particularly vulnerable in local courts. Early in Edward IV's reign, Norwich baker Edmund Turnour fell into debt to John Dasshe, and when Dasshe started proceedings against him in the Guildhall in Norwich, Turnour retaliated with several suits of trespass. Dasshe was forced to drop the suit on the local level, for as a non-resident dwelling outside the city he could not ask that a citizen's goods be distrained, and he feared further retaliation if he pressed his suit. His fears were echoed by other "foreigners" who appealed to the chancellor for various remedies unavailable locally. Alien merchants took their cases there as well, acting on their right to sue and be sued according to the law of nature.[25]

Courts of equity addressed not just civil complaints but criminal actions brought to their attention by the bills of private petitioners. From the late fifteenth century, the Council in Star Chamber possessed criminal jurisdiction and took special note of those problems to which the labels "riot" and "with force and arms" were attached, with or without due cause. However, most of its business consisted of more commonplace civil suits or disputes over municipal franchises.[26] In addition to complaints of riot, petitions to the king in council used the same (probably rhetorical) phrases heard in the court of Chancery: other remedies have failed or are not available; the applicant is poor and cannot obtain justice elsewhere; local influence of his opponent makes it impossible to get a fair trial at home, etc. As in Chancery, pledges were used to assure the sincerity of the appeal. But decisive resolutions did not always result from the process.

Town cases in general formed only a small part of Star Chamber proceedings.[27] This study will examine how all four of the boroughs used the court for eight different disputes between 1471 and 1500. Half of the cases claimed riot or assault, the grievances traditionally associated with Star Chamber.[28] Most helpfully, the records of five of the cases provide either the decree handed down or an indication of where plaintiffs proceeded after leaving the court, thus revealing not only why urban subjects used the Crown court, but also how the royal government reacted and attempted to define its judicial relations with town dwellers. In four of the cases discussed below, the court urged a compromise so unsatisfactory to the urban petitioners that other means of settlement were sought.

Three of the cases have already been studied in the context of trade and commerce: York's conflict with miners over the weighing of lead, Exeter's dispute with its tailors' guild, and Exeter merchants' claims of exemption from scavage tolls on linen.[29] In 1499, Yorkshire lead miners became angered by not only being forced to weigh the metal in York, but by the city's use of what they claimed were false weights and measures. The miners sued in Star Chamber and achieved a modest, preliminary victory when civic representatives were forced to journey to the council for examination. But the first steps toward resolution had to be made locally. Shortly thereafter, the chancellor ordered the abbot of St. Mary's, well-known although hardly well-liked by the city, to select an "indifferent person" to weigh the lead and keep the money received for the service until it was determined to whom the money belonged. Dissatisfied with this decision, civic officials placed more of their hopes in patronage, sending gifts to London with their representatives and offering fish and dinner to the visiting royal attorney so that he would show them favor. At the end of the year, the records reported that no Westminster court could put an end to the dispute and that all arguments had been postponed until the following term.[30]

Exeter officials brought two important cases to Star Chamber but neither found satisfactory resolution there. In 1477, their first complaint to the council stated that the local tailors' guild's acquisition of royal letters patent was a direct threat to their chartered powers. This resulted in a compromise that urged the tailors not to infringe civic liberties nor to induct its members so violently that they broke the king's peace. Civic officials were so little satisfied by the decision that they petitioned parliament to curtail guild privileges. Their argument that the guild prevented the mayor from ruling the city and from keeping the king's peace so convinced Edward IV that he annulled the tailors' letters.[31] In 1500, Exeter officials again petitioned the council, outraged by London's demands for scavage duty on packs of linen they brought into the capital. After hearing testimony from Exeter's oldest merchants, who claimed to know no precedents for the imposition, the chancellor ordered London officials to return the goods they had confiscated in lieu of the duty and quit them of scavage. However, no attempt was made to set policy or to forbid London from imposing the duty again. The situation remained in this unsettled state until 1504, when an act of parliament declared the imposition of scavage on denizens illegal—except within the city of London, whose merchants were too wealthy and powerful for the king to offend.[32]

A fourth example of an unsatisfactory compromise emerging from this equity court involved Norwich's complex jurisdiction dispute. By 1491, Crown justices informed the royal council that various suburbs of Norwich, long claimed by both the city and the cathedral priory, lay within the liberties of the borough and belonged to no one else. The council accepted this verdict, but urged that the prior be allowed to purchase jurisdiction within the contested areas. When Norwich refused to consider this suggestion, the case went to Star Chamber. Recognizing that there was no way to make the city give up land which was already confirmed as its own, the court gave no decree. The case then went to the arbitration of the king's attorney, but still failed to reach an accepted settlement. After several riots between citizens and priory monks, Cardinal Wolsey stepped in with a composition the citizens ultimately accepted.[33]

All of these cases involved complex disputes between differently, but no less validly, constituted powers. The compromises attempted to respect the nature of their rights and privileges, particularly those granted to boroughs by the Crown, while defusing the conflict. They are marked by moderation and in none of these urban cases do they reveal a monarch eager to impose upon a local authority. In each case, one of the parties perceived the decrees to be unsatisfactory, although complete resolution was rare even with recourse to further arbitration or the legislative ability of parliament.

There were even some cases Star Chamber refused to consider at all, following other courts in its ability to return some cases to home ground. One such case late in Edward IV's reign involved Exeter citizens John Tayllour and John Atwyll. The men had been at odds before, in 1478 when Tayllour sued Atwyll for repayment of a debt while the latter was serving in parliament.[34] Three years later, when Atwyll served on a commission to investigate concealments of customs and subsidies, he used the opportunity to retaliate. Atwyll and his brother Philip forged a bill against Tayllour, customer of the ports of Exeter and Dartmouth, alleging that Tayllour concealed valuable quantities of canvas and sailcloth. As half of the value should have gone to the Crown, Tayllour could have been in serious trouble. Luckily, he learned of the deception before Atwyll could pursue the case in the court of Exchequer. When jurors swore the bill was untrue Tayllour sent their statements to the king, demanding justice from king and council. Edward IV replied by returning the letter and the case to the mayor and bailiffs, telling them to imprison the Atwyll brothers if the charges were true. The civic officials indeed took that decision, their confidence in local process buoyed by the king's trust in their ability.[35] Royal trust in local justice was even more explicitly expressed in 1504 when Henry VII reserved punishment of those York citizens involved in election riots expressly for the lord mayor and his brethren, permitting recourse to members of his own council only if the civic authorities could not prevail.[36]

Returning cases to their points of origins was also a prerogative of the Council of Requests. This body originated in the Yorkist period to handle the cases of the poor and complaints against royal officials, but in reality it was open to any complaint a subject might direct to the king. [37] In 1498, civic authorities complained to the council that the incumbent mayor of Exeter's staple had unlawfully appointed his successor without recognizing either statute or the results of an election. Although municipal staples had lost much of their power after the establishment of Calais, they were able to retain the right to take recognizance of debt and try commercial cases by the law merchant. Statutes passed during Edward III's reign provided for the election of staple officers who were to have previously served as municipal mayor. Exeter's mayor denied that these conditions had been met, pointing out that the true winner of the election was being ignored.

The council refused to make a decision, and in the following year remitted the case to Exeter's mayor and common councilors. They proceeded to make short work of the case, dismissing the man they had considered a usurper all along. The Crown even called in a local noble patron, namely the earl of Devon, to help settle the case. The case is not clearly described, but it appears to be another example of Crown recognition that the local community best knew how it was supposed to work, and especially how it should relate to royal officers. To Crown courts, the situation may have seemed as volatile as Atwyll and Tayllour's problems—and therefore best decided by the people who knew the most about the participants and local customs.

These cases contain elements of malicious private suits made worse by a clash of personalities. Although participants and even civic officials may have appreciated the attention of an impartial judge in far-off Westminster, and the monarch may have benefited from recognition of his superior council-centered justice, no king imposed that justice in a blindly authoritarian manner. He knew the disputants had to go on living and working together in the same town after a decision was made. In returning the case to the local venue, three benefits resulted: the royal council had its judicial machinery respected but spared a hotly disputed investigation; local officials had their own power and jurisdiction confirmed by the Crown; and the combatants could possibly receive the kind of informed judgment by their neighbors and peers that would lead to more peaceful relations.

The royal creation of the Council of the North attempted to bring all of these benefits to an area plagued by violence. The roots of its power were several. Richard III organized it officially in July 1484 as an arm of the king's council, "for his surety and the wealth of the inhabitants" of the north parts. He specifically told the city of York to treat it as a court of first instance, designed to ease Westminster's burden and to keep the peace and punish riots. The court was attended by the earl of Northumberland and various retainers and counselors formerly in attendance upon the duke of Gloucester. Centered at Sandal but holding quarterly sessions in the city of York, the Council of the North had both civil and criminal jurisdiction, and served the king's political purposes directly to control the northeast. Henry VII retained the Council on the same grounds, but after its re-establishment by Wolsey in 1525 it ranged more widely into problems of administration and local politics.[38]

In October 1484, the Council became involved in a problem initiated by a royal decree. York residents had rioted over enclosure of common areas, a deprivation carried out at Richard III's express command. The king chided the townspeople for resorting to violent means rather than turning to members of the Council of the North: the earl of Lincoln (the king's lieutenant in the north following the death of the Prince of Wales) and the earl of Northumberland had not been consulted, and the latter was particularly angered. Percy wrote to civic officials, coldly wondering how they had attained their power when they were obviously ignorant of how to uphold the law and whom to consult in emergencies. In response, the officials seem to have submitted the problem of enclosures to the Council within a month, with the attitude of chastened children unable to manage their own affairs.[39]

York's officers accepted the assistance of the Council with better will when it served to clarify difficult points of law or determine rival jurisdictions. The city happily sent the Council a local counterfeiter accused of making foreign coin, an act no one in York could decide was as treasonous as forging native coin. A second case was similarly difficult for civic officials to determine. In May 1485, a resident of the forest of Galtres attacked a citizen in the Bootham suburb. The criminal was later rescued and removed by several of his friends from the forest. The civic officials did not feel that their power was as valid in that area as within city walls, and asked the Council to command the individual return to York.[40] The Council's rare reticence to intervene in borough matters was also appreciated. During most of Henry VII's reign, as the city struggled with the Minster over common lands in the suburbs, the Council provided York with arbitrators to help the citizens decide the matter and end the violence that had ensued. It also refused to change York's chartered right to the election of city sheriffs, preferring to uphold the strictures of Richard II's grant.[41]

The Council of the North had been created by a king who prided himself on the close and sympathetic relationship he developed with the major borough of the area. Rivaling its liberties (the most recent of which he had granted), much less depriving it of them, was not his intention. But by the late fifteenth century, no town was so secure in its privileges that the existence, much less the close proximity, of an alternate form of justice did not cause some apprehension. Local records of all the boroughs throughout the fifteenth century contain references to civic officials who nervously and extra-legally kept cases and defendants in town courts rather than allow Chancery to deprive them of chartered legal privileges.[42] Nevertheless, the central courts appeared willing to respect borough process, even during the reign of kings like Henry VII noted for his suspicion of rival jurisdictions. Crown courts of common law and equity provided urban litigants with increased opportunities to find justice in an unfair and violent world, but they also served to remind townspeople of the utility of their own courts and internal judicial process. The use they made of both venues allowed citizens and their institutions further occasions for growth and maturity.

Arbitration: Four Case Studies

Each of the four towns disputed with local religious bodies over lands both inside and outside of city walls, and each combined arbitration with recourse to common law and equity courts. For some towns, the disputes centered on simple claims for pasture and common land, reminding us of the importance of livestock holding and access to grazing even among urban residents. Other towns viewed legal jurisdiction in suburbs and particularly in urban neighborhoods as an essential component of their own government and of the peacekeeping tasks delegated to them by the Crown. Control over those districts created town identity distinct from other incorporated bodies. But the claimants to rival jurisdictions did not evaporate from view even when the law decided in a town's favor. Competitors continued to live in close proximity, and the renewal of peaceful relations made the generous and even-handed nature of arbitration particularly valuable.

Nottingham

Nottingham's jurisdiction problems were the most straightforward of the four, resulting in a satisfactory resolution for civic officials. The land in dispute was a close called Corner Wong, in the field of Basford three miles northwest of the center of town. In 1271, Archbishop of York Walter Giffard gave the burgesses right of pasturage in the field, although the town had to pay thirty marks for damages and expenses to the rival claimant, the prior of Shelford.[43] This award was confirmed in 1483, when the local Mickletorn jury responsible for claims of encroachments on public lands heard the complaints of John Mapperley. The report of Mapperley's claims is confused, but it appears that not only did he claim Corner Wong, but for three years he had refused to return to Shelford Priory the evidence he had borrowed to prove his case. The prior spoke with Mapperley in April of that year, threatening to ask for Richard of Gloucester's help in the matter when the latter arrived in Nottingham that day.[44] As the prior later explained to town officials, Mapperley had asked in 1480 to see priory documents pertaining to Corner Wong, on surety of £20. The prior lent the evidence, assuring him that the town had full right to common pasture. Despite the bond, Mapperley never returned the papers.[45]

Dissatisfied with local response, and in full possession of all documentation, John Mapperley petitioned the king for help. He argued that the Mapperley family had been seised of Corner Wong close for over a century, and only recently had the mayor pretended interest in the land. That interest had not been expressed in a friendly manner: Mapperley accused the mayor of bringing two hundred people and entering the close by force to dispossess him. Moreover, he claimed the mayor tried to delay his suit of *novel disseisin* and daily menaced him. The king was specifically asked to send for the mayor and town officers, to force them to answer to the Crown.[46]

Nottingham's officers preferred to settle the matter by arbitration rather than the common law, particularly if they could interest a friend and patron in acting as arbiter. They settled upon Gervase Clifton, a retainer of William Lord Hastings and well known in the county as justice of the peace, commissioner of array, and sheriff.[47] In July 1484, Mapperley agreed (under penalty of £100) to obey any award given by Clifton and Sir Charles Pilkington, a former county sheriff then acting as constable of the castle.[48] As a result of arbitration in February 1485, Clifton and Pilkington awarded Corner Wong to the mayor and brethren, forcing Mapperley to relinquish to the town all the deeds and writings pertaining to the close. Gifts of wine made to the gentlemen three days earlier may have increased their appreciation of the justice of the town's case. The town had won its jurisdictional battle, but in one sense John Mapperley was the ultimate victor: to this day the area in question is called Mapperley Closes.[49]

York

The need for common pasture similarly caused jurisdiction problems for the city of York, whose battles for territorial control intertwined with the evolution of self-government. York was honeycombed with private fees: the liberty of St. Peter, controlled by the Minster, came into existence by 1086, and was soon joined by liberties of St. Mary's Abbey and St. Leonard's Hospital, all consisting of lands both within and without city walls. The tenants of these exempt fees were excluded from city jurisdiction, free of the obligation to appear in city courts or help raise troops, contribute to murage or repair walls in their wards. Civic officials' distress over these exemptions, particularly during fifteenth-century economic contraction, was compounded by York's need for open fields for livestock. The same pastureland that the city required frequently belonged to a private liberty, which could either restrict the city's access to the ground or force York officials to pay for the privilege.[50] The city's legal ground was shaky: since the 1270s the Minster had been secure in the king's unambiguous recognition of the liberty's legal and geographical rights.[51] This did not stop citizens from making claims, occupying desired territory, and citing custom as their justification. Matters worsened when social rifts emerged. One way the city council found to raise money was to extinguish the pasture rights it did possess in exchange for payment from clerical landholders.[52] This provoked some of the poorer freemen, whose livelihood depended upon the livestock they barely kept under control in the best of times. Social rebellion was the natural result of such friction between the city council and those beleaguered citizens convinced that their leaders did not have their best interests at heart.[53]

York's disputes with neighboring religious bodies were complicated by a number of factors. St. Mary's Abbey, just outside city walls, possessed considerable prestige, but its rivalry with the borough over jurisdiction in the suburbs and fishgarths in the river often resulted in violence and ill-will. Its abbot served on important judicial commissions, including the Council of the North, making civic officials fearful of retaliation he could show the city. York Minster itself also served as an important venue for civic ceremonies.[54] The civic officers and many of the citizens had cordial social relations with the residentiary canons, the dean, and other Minster dignitaries, relations threatened by these disputes.[55] Those men in addition to the archbishop of York acted as arbitrators and advisors to the city on many occasions. The archbishops themselves played important roles in the royal government, often acting as chancellor of England, and thus were well-placed to convey York's needs to the source of urban liberties and privileges.[56] But it is equally true that cathedral servants and especially the vicars choral were guilty of attacking, slandering, and even murdering citizens: a colorful case occurred in 1490 when a canon's servant verbally abused the city sheriffs from the safety of the Minster's liberty, and the frustrated sheriffs could only poke their axes through the fence managing seriously to wound the man.[57] But even in the most violent cases, church dignitaries worked hard to restore peaceful relations with York and instill respect for the law.[58]

Several different quarrels over jurisdiction erupted by the 1470s. In 1479, Lord Francis Lovell opposed the city over part of abbey-controlled Knavesmire, claiming pasture for his own tenants and winning his case in 1483 when he was honored, and perhaps favored, as the king's chamberlain.[59] Between 1480 and 1484, a bitter dispute raged between the city and St. Mary's Abbey over rights in the common at Fulford. Arbitration by the recorder and other counselors settled the conflict, although the award was not preserved in the city archives.[60] Moreover, Richard III himself precipitated one of the most serious jurisdictional disputes in 1484 when he asked the city council to relinquish common rights in a close belonging to St. Nicholas Hospital. The council concurred, "if the commons will agre to the same." Far from agreeing, the commonalty violently opposed the loss of the land, expressing their displeasure by rioting early in October 1484. The controller of the royal household read to the assembly a letter from Richard expressing his disappointment in the civic officials.[61] The commons themselves were scolded by the king for taking matters into their own hands instead of bringing their case either to the mayor and his brethren, to local lords and members of the Council of the North such as the earls of Lincoln or Northumberland, or even to the king himself. In the end, Richard could not risk losing the support of an important borough, and canceled the grant of the common pasture to the hospital.[62]

The most violent conflicts concerned the citizens' claims to "winter common rights" within fields lying northeast of the city and belonging to the Minster's vicars choral. These men, often local in origin, performed services on behalf of absent canons, and lived (often with concubines and children) in economically-impoverished circumstances within the Minster liberty. In brief, the citizens were determined to exercise their ancient right to place livestock on the Vicars' Lees field from October through March, and the vicars were equally determined to preserve the integrity of their land and the tenants on it.[63] The city turned to mediation to settle the dispute, but disliked the fact that the king appointed as arbitrator the abbot of St. Mary's: not only had the city and abbot experienced centuries of disputes over suburban jurisdiction, but only the previous year civic officials had disputed the abbot's right to determine by arbitration a dispute between local guildsmen.[64]

Matters came to a head in November 1494 when the citizens forced entry, breaking hedges that the vicars immediately rebuilt. Worse yet, eyewitnesses saw two vicars and their servants striking York sheep, two of which later turned up dead. The city's discovery that the abbot and the Minster's dean told the vicars to beat the animals soured relations with the cathedral. Civic officers boycotted Minster services and dinners with canons. Called into Henry VII's presence, they endured a scolding that detailed how their behavior had threatened the peace and prosperity of the king's city. Henry recognized their unwillingness to stomach rulers other than those freely elected in York, but he argued, "I may not see the citie go in utter ruyne and dekaye in defaute of you that shuld rewle, for rather of necessite I most and woll put in other rewlers that woll rewle and govern the citie accordyng to my lawez."[65] Renewed arbitration by the abbot and the Council of the North's earl of Surrey suggested that the city accept a yearly payment to relinquish common rights. Evidence suggests that the city accepted the fee, although recalcitrant citizens continued to claim common rights every October, and one mayoral candidate was said to have lost support when it was recalled that when he last held the office, "he lost the Vicars Lees."[66]

Distrust of the abbot of St. Mary's also exacerbated quarrels with the abbey over the suburb of Bootham, directly outside the western gate of the city. Established as a free borough in 1275, Bootham returned to limited city control in 1350 when York successfully argued that its loss reduced revenues necessary for the king's fee farm.[67] Violent disputes erupted in 1500 and lasted over three years. In June 1500, the city sent both a bill of petition to Henry VII and letters of complaint to the duke of York and royal councilor Sir Reginald Bray among others, asking them to be "tender lords" to York in the disagreement between the city and the abbey. William Sever, abbot of St. Mary's and bishop of Carlisle, had erected enclosures and a round tower in the suburb, offending civic officials and city tenants. The opposing parties agreed to stand to the arbitration of two serjeants-at-law, who would be replaced by a chief justice if they could not agree. By the end of the year, no decision had been reached, although peace was temporarily assured by prohibiting the bishop from making any more enclosures. The parties turned to arbitration again early in 1501, prompted by the commons' threat that they would not hold the mayoral election unless justice was done.[68] Although the election was held as usual, civic officers soon after rode to London to put the case directly to the king. The royal council permitted the abbot to continue occupying the land, a decision not pleasing to civic officials. They refused the abbot's offer of further arbitration, and turned to the council of the king's son, the eleven-year-old Henry duke of York. The case remained unsettled, despite intervention of the council in Star Chamber, a state of affairs perhaps more pleasing to the officers than a decision made in favor of the abbot.[69]

A dispute between the city and the dean and chapter involved issues of even broader import. Citizens claimed the winter common in fields held by a prebendary of the Minster.[70] In 1486, the prebendary decided to hold the land, called Tanghall, in severalty, recognizing no one else's joint interest or rights. The canon in question was a man of prestige and influence, potentially of assistance to the city. Henry Carnebull served as assistant to Archbishop of York Rotherham and frequented London and the king's court. Civic officials and especially York's legal advisor urged the citizens not to press their rights until the case was examined and

Carnebull soothed. They restrained themselves until December, when they took possession violently and prompted an extended attempt at arbitration, once more with the unwanted participation of the abbot of St. Mary's.[71] The city refused to extinguish its rights of pasture, but because the prebend changed hands frequently the issue did not go away. In 1489, civic officials finally agreed to accept a fee in exchange for common rights, because the prebendary then was Henry VII's secretary who had promised to be a good friend to the city. However, this agreement was not to set a precedent, and citizens' livestock returned to Tanghall in subsequent years.[72] Even when the nephew of Henry VII's favored councilor Reginald Bray held the prebend, and the grant was interpreted as a gift to the elder Bray, the waiver of common rights was limited.[73] When the prebend fell to Cardinal Wolsey's chaplain, however, the pressure on the civic officials intensified. Citizens continued to clamor for pasture rights, but financial problems and trade losses tempted the authorities to please Wolsey, then archbishop of York.[74]

Norwich

Norwich's problems with property claims have recently been studied within the context of medieval violence.[75] Modern historians now doubt that violence was as bloody or as prevalent as medieval records described in order to receive attention at the law or to legitimate one social group over another. Blood and wound measurement aside, it is clear from local records as well as Crown reports that medieval subjects, particularly those of towns, were extremely troubled by even the potential of riot and unrest. They were sensitive to the threat they constituted to their economic livelihood and to their chartered liberties, which had been and were again taken into the king's hands when he could no longer trust civic officials to keep his peace. Influenced by challenges to the local election process and exacerbated by urban factionalism, Norwich's property disputes challenged civic officials to try a variety of legal means not just to establish ownership but to calm relations with citizens and neighbors.

As in York, Norwich's problems began in the thirteenth century. In 1205, the citizens disputed the prior of Norwich's right to pastures in Lakenham and Eaton, suburbs south of the city. The dispute was settled when the citizens agreed that the fee belonged to the prior, who would let them use the land for a small fine and for permission to allow the prior to put forty acres under cultivation.[76] Almost half a century later, city and priory fought again, both claiming access to Holmstreet, Ratonrowe, and Tombland, areas surrounding the cathedral fee within the city.[77] The argument became violent, forcing Henry III to visit and eventually to seize city liberties in punishment. At the start of the fourteenth century, Edward I decreed that the cathedral fee properties were separate from the city, suffering only the attendance of royal (not urban) officers.[78]

Matters were made worse by the charter of incorporation granted in 1404. When the city of Norwich was separated from the county of Norfolk, the citizens assumed that the grant carried with it an extended area of suburban jurisdiction. The ambiguous language of the charter encouraged their belief. Without specifying the areas concerned or calling them by name, Henry IV's charter granted the city all its land within its liberty, with its suburbs and hamlets, and assured Norwich that the change of city title would not prejudice the citizens or residents or compromise the liberties granted to them by his progenitors.[79] For the next century and more, these words persuaded Norwich citizens to claim as many suburbs as they wished, certain that they had been granted them if not by Henry then by his predecessors. The suburbs and villages of Bracondale, Trowse, Lakenham, and Eaton became the sources of the most bitter dispute. Only in 1524 was a composition made between the chief combatants, the citizens and the prior, by which the city released all claim to certain suburbs and received in return eighty acres of land.[80]

Norwich's fifteenth-century disputes began indirectly, when the prioress of Carrow charged the prior of Norwich with taking cattle from her lands along the River Wensum outside the southeast corner of the city. Her plea was heard at Westminster in 1416, and her argument that Carrow belonged to the city of Norwich upheld in two consecutive terms.[81] Carrow and Bracondale's direct connection to the city emerged the next year, when the prior obtained from the king an inquisition at Cringleford to inquire into the citizens' alleged encroachments in those areas and in Trowse as well. Civic coroners had laid claim to those areas by hearing cases in them, forcing residents' debt cases into city courts, and also by claiming fishing rights in Trowse by actually going on a fishing expedition there and distributing their catch to the citizens. The Cringleford jury upheld the prior's claims to the suburbs and discouraged any possibility of dispute settlement.[82]

For almost two decades, citizens worked quietly but ineffectually to restore the suburbs to city control. Royal officials at both the shire and Westminster levels received payments for "showing favor" and for quashing writs brought by the prior.[83] City counselors combed royal records for pertinent precedents, while Norwich officials went to the prior to discuss the inquest findings.[84] Any attempts at arbitration have left no trace in the records. Late in 1429, the mayor and the prior sealed an indenture acknowledging the city's encroachments and confirming many of the prior's territorial rights. The document not only disappointed many townspeople, but it stood at the heart of a constitutional debate over election practices and officeholding fraught with social conflict and factionalism among the urban elites. An older group of powerful citizens was ready to admit many of the prior's claims; a younger group, at the peak of their political careers, fought such claims as a threat to the integrity of city jurisdiction and identity.[85]

The pace quickened after 1437, when a new prior was elected and the younger group of citizens gained temporary power within the city. The prior brought actions in King's Bench against citizens and officers who had encroached upon lands in Trowse and elsewhere, prompting the city council to authorize a levy of 6d. on each commoner to help bear the cost of defending the allegation.[86] Following an *inspeximus* of his charters and rights, the prior obtained a special commission of oyer and terminer to investigate "errors, defects and misprisions in the city of Norwich for lack of good governaunce." The justices who sat at Thetford in July 1441 included William Paston, well-known to the city but accepting a retainer's fee from the prior as well as from other magnates in the area. They heard tales of Norwich officials' illegal activities in priory suburbs, stereotypically described as invading suburbs arrayed for war and insisting upon holding inquests on the dead. Municipal sheriffs also were criticized for arresting suburban residents for matters (usually of debt) that did not concern them: those civic officers and even mayors also were described as acting *cum vi et armis*.[87]

The existence of the 1429 indenture confirming priory claims gave the officers little leverage before the commission. They asked the bishop of Norwich to meet with them and all disputing parties, which by this time included not only the prior but also two abbots of Norfolk houses. Out of that request developed an arbitration by the earl of Suffolk, awarded in June 1442, for "the more norisshyng and kepyng of good loue and peas" between all parties. Affection was not the citizens' first reaction when they learned that the earl ordered demolition of the New Mills that offended one of the abbots, bound the city in costly obligations to the religious, confirmed some of the prior's claims, and advised the city to go to King's Bench to settle disputed points and discover the truth "by fourme and esie processe in the lawe." They postponed signing the award by appealing to their "good lord" Suffolk for further clarification.[88]

Stalling tactics lasted until January 1443, when a bitter council meeting resulted in those citizens opposed to the award stealing the common seal so that the indenture could not be ratified. The unrest and riots that ensued, and particularly the destruction of the prior's stocks, prompted the Crown to seize Norwich liberties for four years and impose heavy corporate and individual fines.[89] An inquisition held later in 1443 confirmed the 1429 findings that the suburbs and areas in question had never belonged to the city. Nevertheless, friction between Norwich and the priory lasted for several decades, with frequent attempts at arbitration defusing the tension but lacking definitive solutions. City coroners continued to examine dead bodies in distant suburbs, while the prior complained about daily attacks on his person and threatened the mayor with a privy seal writ.[90]

During 1491–92, Norwich citizens appeared before the king and his council in Star Chamber. The king expressed regret that the city and the prior had not been able to make peace, "but the same grigge and variaunces ben dayly renewed and therby great enconveniencez ben lykly to ensue...." The hearing at last resulted in a victory for the city, but the achievement was hollow. The justices informed the royal council that the territories so long disputed truly lay within the liberties of the city and county of Norwich. However, the council urged Norwich to exclude the priory from civic jurisdiction by accepting the prior's offer to offer monetary compensation. The love and good-will that had been unable to be achieved by arbitration were now being offered the city by the Crown itself. But Norwich refused to consider the suggestion, and matters were not settled even in Star Chamber.[91]

Henry then directed city officers to submit to the mediation of one of his councilors, Sir John Heydon, and of his attorney general James Hobart. Norwich legal counsel met with the two men, and the city later made Hobart its recorder, but on matters of jurisdiction the mediators had no influence. No settlement was achieved during the rest of Henry's reign, and problems even worsened in 1506 when an assault on a city sheriff by priory monks resulted in bitter riots between citizens and cathedral staff.[92] Not until Cardinal Wolsey's personal intervention in 1524 did Norwich know for certain the physical extent of its legal jurisdiction. So strong were some citizens' concepts of what the city should look like, and how wide its officers' powers should be, that they refused all attempts to diminish that identity, even when those attempts included an honorable means to assure civic harmony.

Exeter

Exeter's jurisdiction battles contained the clearest examples of the benefits of arbitration as well as some of the strongest incidents of urban resistance to settlement.[93] Like York, Exeter contained rival jurisdictions that thwarted the officers' execution of their legal and financial duties. The most notable liberties were those of the cathedral: an extra-mural liberty of the dean and chapter, and the bishop's fee of St. Stephen. The latter had little physical integrity, being composed of the cathedral church, its churchyard, and individual tenements held by the bishop but widely scattered within city walls. In such a liberty, no matter how compact or dispersed, civic officials had no rights. Miscreants from the city's liberty could escape apprehension by absconding into the episcopal liberty, sometimes as easy as crossing a street. Urban officials were helpless to enforce their laws and (as they complained to the Crown) had difficulty in maintaining the king's peace. A totally separate judicial system prevailed there, not necessarily cooperative with that of the city. Moreover, merchants and craftsmen of the episcopal liberty did not have to take up expensive city franchises in order to practice their trades, and their wares were not subject to urban quality controls. A city's financial loss, so mayors and aldermen argued, was a loss for the Crown as well.

Both liberties created problems for the developing city from the thirteenth century, but only the more compact fee of the dean and chapter found satisfactory definition by act of Parliament in 1436.[94] St. Stephen's fee remained a problem, erupting in 1445 after a scuffle involving a cathedral servant and the mayor's serjeant. The ensuing disagreement over who hit whom and in whose jurisdiction the blows had been exchanged persuaded Bishop Edmund Lacy to seek royal help. He acquired a royal charter granting him wide powers of jurisdiction in Saint Stephen's fee, and a letter patent excluding civic officials from the cathedral church and yard of the fee and exempting the bishop's tenants from contributing to royal taxation.[95] To the city, this was an insulting action which threatened the power of their own chartered privileges. They began to collect evidence that would bolster their case and levied a special tax to pay for potential litigation. The bishop, in fact, initiated that litigation in the spring of 1447, when he obtained a privy seal writ ordering Mayor John Shillingford and the commonalty to appear before the chancellor and the chief justices of Common Pleas and King's Bench on 20 June, under penalty of £1000.[96]

Unlike many urban subjects who valued equity jurisdiction and direct royal intervention in their problems, Exeter's officers sought to escape the bishop's choice of venue by pleading for a hearing at common law. Lacy's representatives had used the intervening months to gather evidence and advice from Westminster courts, and the mayor himself had admitted that the cathedral party's case was a strong one. As a consequence, the city may have wished for the slower process and narrower purview available at common law. They may also have wished to avoid appearing before Chancellor John Stafford, archbishop of Canterbury and former prebendary of Exeter cathedral, a man both parties could expect would be partial to Lacy's side.[97]

Shillingford's oft-quoted letters from London to his officers in Exeter provide an understanding of how this situation turned in the city's favor and how arbitration became an alternative. The mayor appeared before the chancellor and justices on the dictated June date, and within a few weeks had agreed with the cathedral party to abide by the arbitration of Stafford and Justices Fortescue and Newton.[98] The chancellor frequently advised arbitration for petitioners, and the cathedral party may have hoped for this alternative when the bishop first obtained his writ.[99] But Michaelmas term saw the problem postponed on several occasions, providing Shillingford with the opportunity to win friends in unexpectedly high places. He frequented the Westminster law courts, Lambeth Palace, and the Temple, taking every opportunity to greet the chancellor and justices, express the city's hope for a rapid settlement, and send gifts of fish and fruit to individuals likely to advance his case.[100] As reported at length in the letters, the mayor and the chancellor had good rapport, and the latter observed shrewdly that the main points of disagreement were local and fairly petty, and that stubbornness on either side would result only in increased distress at home. When the cathedral representatives responded to the city's articles of complaint with what amounted to a slanderous attack on Shillingford himself ("they have spatte out the uttmyst and worste venym that they coude seye or thynke by me"), the mayor was delighted to record that the chancellor struck out the offending passages himself, and continued to share with the mayor his wine cup and reminisce with him about his own experiences in Exeter.[101]

By the end of the year, however, the chancellor's words struck a new tone, making Shillingford feel uncertain about his chances. Stafford expressed regret that arrests of any nature had to take place in the cathedral, God's house, as would happen frequently if the area were included in the city's jurisdiction. In reporting the chancellor's comment, the mayor lost some of his confidence and confessed to the officers at home "y fere therof bot the courte be so hard against us...," for reasons which may have more to do with respect for ecclesiastical institutions than with points of law. The chancellor had, in fact, begun to raise the difficult issue of the sacred nature of the land in dispute. Delays in delivery of the fish Shillingford found so useful to season his relations with the chancellor did not improve the mayor's state of mind. Before the end of the year, both parties were told to return to Exeter and settle their dispute there; if they failed to do so by Candlemas 1448, the chancellor and justices would impose a settlement.[102]

Meanwhile, the cathedral party had made good use of its time at Westminster, examining Domesday Book and a *quo warranto* roll of 1281 for evidence that the city possessed none of the courts and powers of jurisdiction it claimed.[103] Armed with this proof and suspicious of the close relations established between the mayor and the chancellor, Lacy brought an action at common law over arrests Exeter bailiffs had accomplished within his fee.[104] The new proceedings upset both Shillingford and the chancellor, who advised Lacy fruitlessly not to take such a path. Stafford in particular feared that a common law decision would prove excessively harsh and expensive, would sour relationships within the city, and satisfy one party at the expense of the other. In a telling moment that illuminates the medieval understanding of justice, he exclaimed to Shillingford that if the common law path were chosen, "God hit forbede, then sholde ye never love, and that were pyty."[105] However, both attempts at arbitration and the bishop's common law case suffered postponements until Michaelmas 1448, when the latter was granted a writ of *nisi prius* for a trial at Barnstaple in December.[106] Given the relationship between common law litigation and arbitration, this may be an example of the use (or threat) of the former to achieve settlement at the latter. Certainly the varied nature of the evidence put forward by both sides dictated the most flexible adjudication possible.

Throughout these months, both parties had sought the advice and good-will of the county's leading magnates and legal counsel. Although money was not spared to reward nobles, clerks, and jurors, neither party spent themselves into bankruptcy to secure favor.[107] Despite strained relations dating back several centuries, the city sought the friendship of Thomas Courtenay earl of Devon with gifts of money and food. Nor was Devon's rival in the shire, Sir William Bonville, forgotten when it came to gifts and courtesy.[108] These men also had relations with the cathedral, Bonville being a patron of various parish churches and the Courtenays holding manors from the bishop and intervening with the king on behalf of the poor priests of the cathedral.[109] Their position within local and court society made them the natural choice to arbitrate this bitter case. Thus, by early December 1448, the disputants agreed to accept Courtenay and Bonville's arbitration.

The composition was signed 12 December 1448. Although the settlement strongly favored the bishop and acquiesced to almost all of his demands, the rights of civic officials were not totally ignored. The arbitrators agreed that the bishop's common law case should proceed as planned four days hence at Barnstaple. They anticipated that the bishop would receive monetary damages, but in a spirit of compromise they ordered the sum to be remitted to the city.[110] The bishop and his successors were confirmed in Saint Stephen's fee, defined as including the cathedral church and yard. They did not, however, take this opportunity to define and measure the full geographical extent of the fee. Civic officials were required to confine their arrests to public areas outside the churchyard, but the cathedral party also had to agree not to arrest citizens within that space. Most of the powers of jurisdiction Lacy wanted (i.e., court leet, court baron, view of frankpledge) were granted to him, except for the very broad claim to "all pleas real, personal, and mixed" listed in the 1445 charter. Cathedral tenants were required to keep watch in the city with other residents, provided the mayor gave them reasonable warning, and to pay the king's tenth and other taxes, although the bishop's bailiff was allowed to make the actual collection. The charters Lacy obtained in 1445 and 1446 were declared null and void, and both sides were prohibited from changing the nature of their jurisdiction by purchasing new grants. Finally, civic officers and their successors were permitted to bear their maces within the bishop's fee without interference. This is a concession highly communicative of the power of symbolism and public ceremony in urban life, and it also suggests that the city's theoretical rights within the fee were ultimately undeniable.[111]

To the fullest extent possible, the arbitrators tried to acknowledge the cathedral party's claims without ignoring the civic officials' duties towards the citizens and their king. The decision reflects the arbitrators' comprehension of the long and complex history of the dispute, and of the need to offer advice in the spirit of equity and balance. It was a sensitive decision unlikely to be achieved at other legal venues. But it was not perfect, for its lack of precision permitted further disagreement. The bishop himself violated the composition by obtaining a new charter, almost identical to the document annulled by the arbitrators and bearing the same 1445 date.[112] Civic officials continued to try to extend their judicial and financial rights into the liberty, petitioning Parliament fruitlessly into the 1520s to expand their privileges. A partial victory was obtained in 1535 when the mayor, recorder, and aldermen became justices of the peace for the city with superior judicial rights over any immunities held by the cathedral.[113]

Two years later, in the wake of rebellions in the provinces, Exeter became a county in its own right and extended the king's law further into local society.[114] It thus became vital to determine the exact boundaries of the new legal entity. Dissatisfied with the imprecision of arbitration and compromise, the citizens petitioned Henry VIII for an act of Parliament to determine the boundaries once and for all. As pleased as they were to receive an act that granted the city both Saint Sidwell's and Saint Stephen's fees, the decree (granted in the next reign) once more compromised and guaranteed that the cathedral party would not be deprived of any privileges by its provisions.[115] Familiar charges of civic intrusion and episcopal disobedience continued for over a century, as the city's new county status had not obliterated certain episcopal privileges. Although the courts and views the bishop claimed became increasingly anachronistic, the loss of power and income Exeter cathedral suffered during the Reformation and the inflationary sixteenth century made ecclesiastics maintain even meaningless rights with increased ferocity well into the nineteenth century.[116]

However full and detailed the urban charters granted by kings, no town could pursue justice within its own precincts and courts alone. The boroughs and their liberties had developed in a society that increasingly credited the monarch with the task of keeping the peace, applying the law, and providing the means by which all subjects could find justice. The very crowding of the common law and equity courts is testimony to the prevalence of this belief, just as criticism of the system's failures became a natural corollary.

Urban subjects voluntarily approached royal courts for a number of reasons. Some sincerely wanted decisive verdicts, desiring clear-cut definitions and a termination to their problem, all guaranteed by the power of the monarch. Others sought common-law justice in particular for the length of its process, hoping either to harass defendants or to pressure them into settling elsewhere. Fearful of local prejudices and favoritism, still others looked to distant courts to obtain a fair hearing amongst strangers. Equity courts were especially popular, not only hearing cases not covered by common law but utilizing a more expeditious process. But no matter how eagerly urban plaintiffs worked for definitive decisions, Crown courts themselves respected borough courts and the environment from which the dispute arose. Although the Council of North defended its right to hear cases, there is no evidence that any of these courts negated borough privileges or denied a town the opportunity to settle matters on the local level.

This is best seen in the royal government's attitude towards arbitration. Such dispute settlement should not be seen as the last resort of a burdened judicial system anxious to cut its case load. Rather, arbitration was considered to be the natural starting point for the resolution of disputes, whether it was conducted by a local guild, neighboring magnates, or supervised by the lord chancellor. Beginning the healing process between two quarreling individuals or institutions was arbitration's most important contribution, and one that could not be obtained if the strict interpretations and definitions of common law were applied. It is a measure of medieval society's wisdom and sophistication that arbitration was valued for just these reasons.

Likewise, it is a measure of towns' increasing maturity that they cooperated so often in this process. Their disputes over territory and rights required civic officials to think and act more than locally. They gained experience mustering evidence, weighing the advantages of equity over common law, guiding suits through Westminster courts, identifying and rewarding helpful patrons, and maximizing city gains from arbitration. They had always had to balance local needs and concerns with their responsibilities to the king and the royal government, but these cases brought new challenges to that relationship. But even the closest relationship with the king did not assure a town the unfettered exercise of its will, for the other residents such as the clergy cherished their autonomy as well, and all hoped to live in peace. The checks these presented to towns caused civic officials to examine their claims, their actions, their rights and traditions more closely. This process of self-analysis was vital to the institution's maturity, as towns continued to grow into their liberties and privileges, and define for themselves what it meant to be urban.

NOTES

[1]   For example, see *CChR*, 3:431, for Exeter's 1320 charter protecting citizens from having to plead outside the city. Norwich received the privilege in 1194, York in 1256, and Nottingham in 1314: Adolphus Ballard, ed., *British Borough Charters 1042–1216* (Cambridge: Cambridge University Press, 1913), pp. liv–lv, 115–21.

[2]   *Statutes of the Realm*, 2:185–86, 426–29, 510–12; *CPR, 1461–67*, pp. 35, 101, 232; *1413–16*, p. 222; *1422–29*, pp. 361, 363; *CCR, 1461–68*, pp. 327, 371, 379, 431, 437. Henry VII's great statute (3 Henry VII, c.12) listed in detail the crimes and abuses JPs were responsible for suppressing, evincing no great confidence that his peace was being kept: *Statutes of the Realm*, 2:536–37.

[3]   In 1502, York's city council agreed that cases of debt and trespass between any of the aldermen or councilors or any franchised citizens could not be taken to the king or to a central court before being shown to the mayor. Transfer to another court could take place only if local courts could not reach an agreement after forty days: *York Civic Records*, 2:173. See above, pp. 43–44. The Crown, however, could preserve business for its central courts: a statute of 1504 (renewing one of 1437) prohibited fraternities and guilds within boroughs from preventing their members from suing to the king or his courts: *Statutes of the Realm*, 2:652–53 (19 Henry VII, c.7). See above, p. 254, for further examples.

[4]   These topics are discussed in full in Richard W. Kaeuper, *War, Justice and Public Order: England and France in the Later Middle Ages* (Oxford: Clarendon Press, 1988).

[5]   By self-help and negotiation, the parties involved settled the dispute without outside help; by mediation, a neutral party helped the disputants bring about a settlement, which was not legally binding; by arbitration or adjudication, the disputants submitted to an umpire and surrendered their power to negotiate a settlement directly: Edward Powell, *Kingship, Law and Society: Criminal Justice in the Reign of Henry V* (Oxford: Clarendon Press, 1989), p. 93. For more general discussion, see

Simon Roberts, "The Study of Dispute: Anthropological Perspectives," *Disputes and Settlements: Law and Human Relations in the West*, ed. John Bossy (Cambridge: Cambridge University Press, 1983), pp. 11–12.

6   For a negative view of arbitration, see R. L. Storey, *The End of the House of Lancaster* (London: Barrie and Rockliff, 1966; rpt., Gloucester: Alan Sutton Publishing, 1986), p. 155. For threats of litigation in order to make an opponent come to terms, see Edward Powell, "Arbitration and the Law in England in the Late Middle Ages," *Transactions of the Royal Historical Society*, 5th ser., 33 (1983): 62; and *idem, Kingship, Law and Society*, pp. 100–101. Cf. J. H. Baker, ed., *The Reports of Sir John Spelman*, 2 vols., Selden Society, vol. 94 (London, 1977), 2:91. J. B. Post describes the various courts and procedures used in a property dispute in "Courts, Councils, and Arbitrators in the Ladbroke Manor Dispute, 1382–1400," in *Medieval Legal Records*, R. F. Hunnisett and J. B. Post, gen. eds. (London: Her Majesty's Stationery Office, 1978), p. 290, and explores the resemblance between equity and arbitration, pp. 296–98.

7   J. B. Post, "Equitable Resorts before 1450," in *Law, Litigants and the Legal Profession*, ed. E. W. Ives and A. H. Manchester (London: The Royal Historical Society, 1983), pp. 74–77; Carole Rawcliffe, "The Great Lord as Peacekeeper: Arbitration by English Noblemen and Their Councils in the Later Middle Ages," in *Law and Social Change in British History*, ed. J. A. Guy and H. G. Beale (London: The Royal Historical Society, 1984), pp. 40. The disputants could also agree to a loveday, a day on which the dispute could be settled without recourse to courts or formal arbitration: Josephine W. Bennett, "The Mediaeval Loveday," *Speculum* 33 (1958): 354. The increasingly formal processes of self-help, mediation, and formal arbitration and adjudication are studied in S. Roberts, *Order and Dispute* (Harmondsworth: Penguin, 1979), pp. 69–71. Urban governments and guilds offered arbitration as the first step in problem-solving: for examples, see Edward Powell, "Arbitration and the Law," 53–54; Toulmin Smith, ed., *English Gilds*, Early English Text Society, o.s., vol. 40 (1870; reprint, London: Oxford University Press, 1963), pp. 21, 76, 96, 115, 158–59, 279, 322–23, 426; A. H. Thomas, ed. *Calendar of Select Pleas and Memoranda of the City of London, 1381–1412* (Cambridge: Cambridge University Press, 1932), pp. xxix–xxx.

8   Michael Clanchy, "Law and Love in the Middle Ages," in *Disputes and Settlements*, ed. Bossy, pp. 47–48, 50, 52, 61–62 explores the meaning of these terms in medieval society, focusing on the contrast between self-regulation and decisions imposed by the central administration.

9   Nobles anxious to raise their public standing and build a loyal following were especially careful to render fair decisions: Joel Rosenthal, "Feuds and Private Peace-Making: A Fifteenth-Century Example," *Nottingham Mediaeval Studies* 14 (1970): 86–87. See also Ian Rowney, "Arbitration in Gentry Disputes of the Later Middle Ages," *History* 67 (1982): 371–76; Michael Hicks, "Restraint, Mediation and Private Justice: George, Duke of Clarence as 'Good Lord'," *Journal of Legal History* 4 (1983): 56–57, 61–63; Powell, "Arbitration and the Law," 55; Simon J. Payling, "Law and Arbitration in Nottinghamshire 1399–1461," in *People, Politics and Community in the Later Middle Ages*, ed. Joel Rosenthal and Colin Richmond (Gloucester, England and New York: Alan Sutton Publishing and St. Martin's Press, 1987), pp. 140–160; David Tilsley, "Arbitration in Gentry Disputes: The Case of

Bucklow Hundred in Cheshire, 1400–1465," in *Courts, Counties and the Capital in the Later Middle Ages*, ed. Diana E. S. Dunn (New York: St. Martin's Press, 1996), pp. 53–70.

[10] Fredric L. Cheyette, "*Suum Cuique Tribuere*," *French Historical Studies* 6 (1970): 293–95; Stephen D. White, "'*Pactum...Legum Vincit et Amor Judicium*': The Settlement of Disputes by Compromise in Eleventh-Century Western France," *American Journal of Legal History* 22 (1978): 300–302; Edward Powell, "Settlement of Disputes by Arbitration in Fifteenth-Century England," *Law and History Review* 2 (1984): 36, 39.

[11] By Henry VII's reign, Common Pleas heard about 10,000 actions each year, King's Bench over 2500 (and business in both courts was not what it had been earlier in the fifteenth century): Alan Harding, *The Law Courts of Medieval England* (London: Allen and Unwin, 1973), pp. 76–77, 84; DeLloyd J. Guth, "Notes on the Early Tudor Exchequer of Pleas," *Tudor Men and Institutions*, ed. A. J. Slavin (Baton Rouge, 1972), p. 106. For specific problems with these courts, see Marjorie Blatcher, *The Court of King's Bench 1450–1550: A Study in Self-Help* (London: Athlone Press, 1978), pp. 66, 72–73; and Margaret Hastings, *The Court of Common Pleas in Fifteenth-Century England* (Ithaca, N.Y.: Cornell University Press, 1947), pp. 158, 212.

[12] Powell, *Kingship, Law and Society*, pp. 47–49.

[13] In addition to the records' great bulk, the fictional quality of some narratives, their omission of resolution, and the minimal information provided about the parties and disputes, several rolls for the fifteenth century are in poor condition and readers are denied access to them. For further comments on the difficulty of using these and other legal records over wide spans of years, see Christine Carpenter, *Locality and Polity: A Study of Warwickshire Landed Society, 1401–1499* (Cambridge: Cambridge University Press, 1992), pp. 705–9; Timothy S. Haskett, "The Medieval English Court of Chancery," *Law and History Review* 14 (1996): 280–85; Alan MacFarlane, *A Guide to English Historical Records* (Cambridge: Cambridge University Press, 1983), pp. 45–46, 50; Blatcher, *Court of King's Bench*, p. 34; N. Neilson, *Year Books of Edward IV: 10 Edward IV and 49 Henry VI, 1470*, Selden Society, vol. 47 (London, 1930), pp. xvii–xviii. For the following paragraph, a sample of the available CP.40 Common Pleas rolls was used for the period under study. Records of all terms for every third year were checked, as were years immediately preceding and following an accession, to examine whether a change in monarch had any effect on petitions and process.

[14] P.R.O., CP.40/499, mem.102 (Michaelmas 1385).

[15] *Ibid.*, mem. 388.

[16] P.R.O., CP.40/838 (Hilary 1471), cited in Neilson, *Year Books of Edward IV*, pp. 163–65, 191. No verdict is given on the rolls, but Neilson believes the decision went against the civic officials.

[17] W. T. Barbour, *The History of Contract in Early English Equity* (London, 1914), p. 152, citing Year Book 4 Henry VII, 4.8; MacFarlane, *Guide to Records*, pp. 51–53. The origins of Chancery's equitable jurisdiction can be found in Nicholas Pronay, "The Chancellor, the Chancery, and the Council at the End of the Fifteenth Century," in *British Government and Administration: Studies Presented to S. B. Chrimes*, ed. H. Hearder and H. R. Loyn (Cardiff: University of Wales Press, 1974),

pp. 87–103; and in Haskett, "Court of Chancery," 245–313. Although equity as a fully-developed legal concept dates only to the sixteenth century, the term will be used for the earlier period as well.

[18] Franz Metzger, "The Last Phase of the Medieval Chancery," *Law-Making and Law-Makers in British History*, ed. Alan Harding (London: Royal Historical Society, 1980), p. 82; Christine Carpenter, "Law, Justice and Landowners in Late Medieval England," *Law and History Review* 1 (1983), 212, associates equity with natural law. Powell, "Settlement of Disputes by Arbitration," 40, gives the range of equitable resorts. The bill was in English, not formulaic Latin. After the bill of complaint was filed, a subpoena was issued to compel the defendant to appear and answer the charge. Reply was made under oath; no juries were necessary; and even complex evidence could be presented without the constraints known at common law. After an exchange of answers and replications and perhaps an examination of witnesses either in London or elsewhere by the use of commissions, the court handed down its decision. Unfortunately, not all of those decisions survive (decree rolls began 1543–44), as precedent did not influence the rulings.

[19] Harding, *Law Courts*, p. 105; Margaret Avery, "The History of the Equitable Jurisdiction of Chancery before 1460," *Bulletin of the Institute of Historical Research* 42 (1969): 132, 134; William P. Baildon, ed., *Select Cases in Chancery 1364–1471*, Selden Society, vol. 10 (1896), pp. xiii, xiv, xxii. The court's power to punish the guilty also was not great: it could not inflict capital punishment, so that crimes worthy of such a sentence were directed back to common law, usually a commission of oyer and terminer composed of council members.

[20] Metzger, "Last Phase of Medieval Chancery," p. 89. The chancellor as a figure of transition and accommodation is studied in Pronay, "The Chancellor, the Chancery, and the Council." The following paragraph is derived from Avery, "History of Equitable Jurisdiction," *ibid.*, and Dorothy M. Gardiner, ed., *A Calendar of Early Chancery Proceedings relating to West Country Shipping 1388–1493*, Devon and Cornwall Record Society, n.s., vol. 21 (1976), pp. x–xi, xviii.

[21] The difficulty of counting all Chancery cases, many of which survive in bill of complaint only, creates divergent conclusions about the court's business. By the mid-fifteenth century, some historians assert 90% of cases concerned uses (Harding, *Law Courts*, p. 101), while others put the figure much lower (Pronay, "The Chancellor, the Chancery, and the Council," p. 92). Urban and commercial are synonymous to some historians, who have noticed that urban mercantile cases peaked under the Yorkists and dropped throughout the mid-sixteenth century: J. A. Guy, "The Development of Equitable Jurisdictions, 1450–1550," *Law, Litigants and the Legal Profession*, ed. E. W. Ives and A. H. Manchester (London: Royal Historical Society, 1983), p. 83; Pronay, *ibid.*, pp. 92, 94. This method of computing does not recognize that towns could bring property disputes to the court just as easily. Detinue of deeds became a formula to bring into Chancery land cases not ordinarily heard there: for examples, see Jennifer I. Kermode, *Medieval Merchants: York, Beverley and Hull in the Later Middle Ages* (Cambridge: Cambridge University Press, 1998), p. 109.

[22] P.R.O., C.1/31/9, C.1/6/55.

[23] P.R.O., C.1/32/407. For pleas of debt in print, see Patricia M. Barnes, "The Chancery corpus cum causa file, 10–11 Edward IV," in *Medieval Legal Records*, ed.

R. F. Hunnisett and J. B. Post (London: HMSO, 1978), numbers 28, 91, 115, 208, 209.

24 For complaints against civic officials, see above, pp. 48–49; for mercantile disputes in towns, see above, p. 225.

25 P.R.O., C.1/32/362; see also C.1/32/374 (concerning the arrest of a foreigner for debt), C.1/16/578 and C.1/46/448. The rights of alien merchants and of the chancellor to ignore common law in dealing with them are discussed in Pronay, "The Chancellor, the Chancery, and the Council," pp. 96–97; and Mark Beilby, "The Profits of Expertise: The Rise of the Civil Lawyers and Chancery Equity," in *Profit, Piety and the Professions in Later Medieval England*, ed. Michael Hicks (Gloucester: Alan Sutton, 1990), p. 81.

26 Bryce Lyon, *A Constitutional and Legal History of Medieval England*, 2d ed. (New York: Norton and Co., 1980), p. 616; Harding, *Law Courts*, pp. 106–107; S. B. Chrimes, *Henry VII* (Berkeley and Los Angeles: University of California Press, 1972), pp. 147–49. Its structure is described in Stanford E. Lehmberg, "Star Chamber: 1485–1509," *Huntington Library Quarterly* 24 (May 1961): 196, and J. A. Guy, *The Court of Star Chamber and its records to the reign of Elizabeth I*, Public Record Office Handbooks No. 21 (London: HMSO, 1985), pp. 37–48. The court of Star Chamber, most active and notorious in Henry VIII's day and later, is not discussed here.

27 Exactly how many cases were heard during Henry VII's reign is a matter of some dispute. Earlier this century, proceedings for 194 cases were found: C. G. Bayne and W. H. Dunham, eds., *Select Cases in the Council of Henry VII*, Selden Society, vol. 75 (1956), pp. lxxiii. Lehmberg, however, discerned that there were only 128 complete sets of Star Chamber proceedings for the period: "Star Chamber," 191. The most recent archival study has increased the number of cases to about 300: Guy, *Court of Star Chamber*, p. 5.

28 The earliest case claiming violence dates from 1471, when Nottingham's mayor and officers complained about riots and violence engendered by Lord Grey's retainers. Edward IV demanded the men appear before the king rather than be committed to the town jail: *Nott. Records*, 2:384–87. Also dating from Edward IV's reign is Exeter's case against the tailors' guild, described below. The third case addressed Exeter's mayor in 1495, charging him with the cruel and unjust imprisonment of a Devonshire woman. The plaintiff argued that she had been violently seized and subjected to harsh physical conditions while in city prison. By the time the suit got to court, the mayor had died and was represented by his widow, who laid claim to the woman's land. The widow argued that she could not be held responsible for her husband's actions, and there is no record of the court's decree: Bayne and Dunham, *Council of Henry VII*, p. clix; I. S. Leadam, ed., *Select Cases before the King's Council in the Star Chamber, Volume I: 1477–1509*, Selden Society, vol. 16 (London, 1903), pp. cxxxvi–cxxxvii, 51–54; and see above, pp. 48–49. A fourth case, dating from Henry VII's reign, resulted after a riotous attack on a royal sheriff sent to investigate violence in York: P.R.O., STAC. 1/2/55. A possible fifth case involved the city of York in 1504 after election riots disrupted the peace (the case did not follow normal procedure): see above at p. 259.

29 See above, pp. 223, 224–25, 226–27.

30 Leadam, *Select Cases Star Chamber,* pp. 69–71. William Sever (or Senhouse), abbot of St. Mary's and successively bishop of Carlisle (1495-1502) and Durham (1502-5), also acted as Henry VII's receiver and surveyor of the king's prerogative rights in the northern parts from October 1499, and was active in chamber administration before his death in 1505: Chrimes, *Henry VII*, p. 130; W. C. Richardson, *Tudor Chamber Administration, 1485–1547* (Baton Rouge: Louisiana State University Press, 1952), pp. 135–40; R. B. Dobson, "Cathedral Chapters and Cathedral Cities: York, Durham, and Carlisle in the Fifteenth Century," *Northern History* 19 (1983):43.

31 Leadam, *Select Cases Star Chamber*, pp. lxxii, 1–6; P.R.O., SC.8/30/1462; *Rot. Parl.*, 5:390–91; 6:219–20; D.R.O., Book 51, ff.62–63; Receivers' Roll 22 Edward IV–1 Richard III; Maryanne Kowaleski, *Local Markets and Regional Trade in Medieval Exeter* (Cambridge and New York: Cambridge University Press, 1995), pp. 100–101, 156.

32 Leadam, *Select Cases Star Chamber*, pp. 71–95; Bayne and Dunham, *Council of Henry VII*, p. clxiv; P.R.O., STAC.1/2/78/8.

33 Wolsey began to take an interest in 1517: N.R.O., 16-d, Assembly Minute Book II, f.94. In 1524, the city released its claim to certain suburbs in exchange for eighty acres of common land: N.R.O., 16-c, Assembly Minute Book I, ff. 38, 39, 45v; 17-a, *Liber Albus*, ff. 104–24; 9-e; 21-f, 9-58, Kirkpatrick Notes, sub 1493; Bayne and Dunham, *Council of Henry VII*, p. clxi. See below, at p. 263.

34 Above, p. 60. For what follows, see Leadam, *Select Cases Star Chamber*, pp. lxxiii–lxxvii, 6–15.

35 The Atwyll brothers suffered imprisonment, although Philip escaped and John suffered only a short arrest in the castle. Their local reputations remained unscathed: John Atwyll became mayor of Exeter for the third of five times in 1485, and Tayllour kept his post as customer until Bosworth, after which he worked overseas to restore Yorkists to the throne: see below, p. 312 note 92. A similar case occurred in Coventry when Henry VII returned to local courts a citizen who had slandered the mayor and tried to incite the people to riot: Bayne and Dunham, *Council of Henry VII*, pp. cl–cli.

36 *York Civic Records*, 3:3 (10 April 1504).

37 Lehmberg, "Star Chamber," 211–12. For what follows, see I. S. Leadam, ed., *Select Cases in the Court of Requests 1497–1569*, Selden Society, vol. 12 (1898), pp. lxxiv–lxxvi, 3–6.

38 Rachel R. Reid, *King's Council in the North* (London: Longmans, 1921), pp. 44–47, 59, 64, 66, 92–190 *passim*, 490, 492; F. W. Brooks, *York and the Council of the North*, St. Anthony's Hall Publications, vol. 5 (York, 1954), pp. 3–12; Charles D. Ross, *Richard the Third* (London: Eyre Methuen, 1981), 182–83; A. J. Pollard, *North-eastern England During the Wars of the Roses* (Oxford: Clarendon Press, 1990), pp. 356–57. The proposed nature of the Council is most fully described in Rosemary Horrox and P. W. Hammond, eds., *British Library Harleian MS. 433*, 4 vols. (London and Upminster: Alan Sutton Publishing, for the Richard III Society, 1979–83), 3:114–15.

39 *York House Books*, pp. 335–37, 340–41.

40 *Ibid.*, pp. pp. 345–47 (counterfeiter), 361–62 (attack).

41   *York Civic Records*, 2:101, 105–7, 112, 113, 117, 130 (arbitration); 3:8–9 (election).
     For the role of Thomas Howard earl of Surrey as head of the Council 1490–99 and
     his patronage relationship with York, see above p. 123.

42   In 1448–49, Norwich paid a Chancery clerk 3s. 4d. for a writ of *procedendo* to
     enable civic officials to continue trying locally a man who farmed the common quay
     and who was presently in prison for arrears: N.R.O., 17-d, Apprentice Indentures,
     ff.7v–12. Almost thirty years later, Norwich paid their legal advisor and four
     serjeants-at-law to keep a rebellious citizen in the local courts where his prosecution
     for tax evasion would serve as an example to others: N.R.O., 16-d, Assembly Book
     I, f.103v; 18-a, Chamberlains' Account Book, 1470–90, f.95. Similarly, the mayor
     of York tried to preserve local privilege in 1470 when he ignored a *habeas corpus
     cum causa* writ to release to the chancellor a merchant who had slandered him:
     Barnes, "Chancery corpus cum causa file," p. 433 and number 197.

43   Nt.R.O., CA4529, 4530; *Nott. Records*, 1:48–53; William Page, ed., *The Victoria
     History of the County of Nottingham*, 2 vols. (London: Archibald Constable and Co.,
     Ltd., 1906; London: Dawsons of Pall Mall, 1970), 2:117–20. The priory of Austin
     Canons, founded *tempore* Henry II, was located six miles east of Nottingham.

44   *Nott. Records*, 2:392–94. Gloucester was on his way to intercept Edward V at
     Northampton and Stony Stratford: Rhoda Edwards, *The Itinerary of King Richard
     III 1483–1485* (London: Alan Sutton Publishing for the Richard III Society, 1983),
     p. 1. The prior threatened to talk to the mayor, but the latter was occupied waiting
     for the duke's arrival. See above, p. 121.

45   *Nott. Records*, 2:332–37.

46   *Ibid.*, 345–46; Nt.R.O., CA4532.

47   William E. Hampton, *Memorials of the Wars of the Roses* (Upminster: Richard III
     Society, 1979), pp. 144–45; Horrox and Hammond, *Harl. 433*, 1:183, 226, 228.
     Chamberlains' accounts for 1484–85 show how frequently the town contacted
     Clifton: *Nott. Records*, 3:233–34, 239–41. See above, p. 122.

48   Nt.R.O., CA4527; Hampton, *Memorials*, p. 148; Horrox and Hammond, *Harl. 433*,
     1:144, 183, 226, 228, 230, 287. To cover all bases, town representatives spent much
     time and money at Westminster, countering Mapperley's restoration to the close and
     the need to sue at common law: *Nott. Records*, 3:232–34, 397–98.

49   *Nott. Records*, 1:48–49, 49 n.3; 2:398–400, 437; 3:239–41.

50   Miller, *VCH*, pp. 38, 76–77, 498–99; David Palliser, *Tudor York* (Oxford and New
     York: Oxford University Press, 1979), p. 29. Southwest of the city, Knavesmire
     provided some pasture, but St. Mary's Abbey laid claim to much of the area; the
     abbey also regulated civic access to the township of Clifton, northwest of York, and
     to Fulford to the southeast. In Heworth township to the northeast, York eventually
     gained the right to six months of pasturage from the archbishop.

51   Francis Drake, *Eboracum* (London: W. Bowyer, 1736), pp. 553, 556; R. B. Dobson,
     "The Later Middle Ages 1215–1500," in *A History of York Minster*, ed. G. E.
     Aylmer and Reginald Cant (Oxford: Clarendon Press, 1977), pp. 102–3.

52   K. J. Allison, "Common Lands and Strays," in P. M. Tillott, ed., *Victoria History of
     the Counties of England: A History of Yorkshire, The City of York* (London: Oxford
     University Press, 1961), p. 500; *York Civic Records*, 3:151 (18 Feb. 1533 complaint
     by the citizens that common lands were being leased far below their true value, to
     the damage of city finances as well as the loss of their common privileges). See

Mary D. Harris, "Laurence Saunders, Citizen of Coventry," *English Historical Review* 9 (1894): 633–51, for a parallel case in that town. Heather Swanson, *Medieval Artisans: An Urban Class in Late Medieval England* (Oxford and New York: Basil Blackwell, 1989), pp. 123, 137 analyzes citizens' needs for grazing areas.

53 Unlike other boroughs, York found that the Reformation provided few opportunities for the city to extend its jurisdiction. Henry VIII priced Church lands beyond the means of an impoverished city council, sold land and buildings to rich country gentry, and suppressed only six prebends; the city gained little more mid-century when chantries and guilds were dissolved: Dickens, "Tudor York," pp. 117–18; Palliser, *Tudor York*, pp. 237–39; George Benson, *Later Medieval York: The City and County of the City of York from 1100 to 1603* (York: Coultas and Volans, 1919), pp. 116–17, 123.

54 Dobson, "The Later Middle Ages," in *A History of York Minster*, pp. 45, 108; *idem,* "Cathedral Chapters and Cathedral Cities," 39. For religious and political ceremonies held in the Minster, see *York House Books*, 5 (religious service and formal procession of officers), 282 (services on death of Edward IV), 382 (taking oath to Henry VII), 475 (hearing letters from the king), 577 (thanksgiving services for military victory), 588 (officials escort Henry VII to archbishop's palace).

55 R. B. Dobson, "The Residentiary Canons of York in the Fifteenth Century," *Journal of Ecclesiastical History* 30 (1979): 164–65.

56 During the fifteenth and early sixteenth centuries, four men served as chancellor while archbishop of York: John Kemp (1426–32, 1450–54), George Neville (1460–67, 1470–71), Thomas Rotherham (1474–75, 1475–83, 1485), and Thomas Wolsey (1515–29). Thomas Langley was chancellor while dean of York 1405–7 and bishop of Durham from 1406.

57 *York Civic Records*, 2:59–62. Frederick Harrison, *Life in a Medieval College: The Story of the Vicars-Choral of York Minster* (London: John Murray, 1952), pp. 32, 60, 68–72, and Dobson, "Cathedral Chapters and Cathedral Cities," p. 36, contain details of the vicars' worldly behavior.

58 In 1483, a brewer in the dean's household received punishment from the city council for striking a franchised citizen: *York House Books*, pp. 279–80, 307. The Minster masons who killed a York tiler were incarcerated in the sheriffs' jail in 1490: *York Civic Records*, 2:77. In 1511, the city and Minster cooperated over a claim to sanctuary, and in 1517 the Dean and Archdeacon allowed one of their tenants to be punished for slander by the city council: *York Civic Records*, 3:35, 62–63.

59 *York House Books*, pp. 193–94, 294.

60 *Ibid.*, pp. 213–14, 243–44, 280–81, 294, 320–21.

61 The mayor pointed out that he had imprisoned the ringleaders, but the mass of the rioters refused to be silenced. They submitted to the controller a bill of complaint against the mayor, "but in every poynt [he] layde his lawfull excuse and disproved the said bill in every article and poynt therof": *ibid.*, pp. 303, 335–37, 340–41.

62 *Ibid.*, pp. 440–41.

63 A letter from the vicars to Henry VIII early in his reign stated that the dispute started in 1485 and continued every October thereafter, but council records indicate problems as early as 1482: *York House Books*, p. 264; Harrison, *Life in a Medieval College*, p. 320.

64   *York Civic Records*, 2:97–98 (May 1493), 105–8 (February to October 1494). York's problems with the monks and abbot centered on control over the land directly outside their western gate. They were not settled by the Reformation and Dissolution because the abbey was partially sold privately and also used as the residence of the Lord President of the Council in the North. The area around the abbey became part of the North Riding until the 1884 York (City) Extension Act: *York Civic Records*, 3:139; Dickens, "Tudor York," pp. 117–18; George Benson, *York from the Reformation to the Year 1925* (York: Cooper and Swann, 1925), pp. 113–14.

65   *York Civic Records*, 2:111–17 (quotation p. 115).

66   Y.C.A., B7, ff.133r–134r, 138; *York Civic Records*, 3:36 (5 November 1511; George Kirk had been mayor in 1495); Harrison, *Life in a Medieval College*, p. 321.

67   The city's control of Bootham was limited in that the abbot and monks could not be arrested there except on charges of felony and trespass, and the tenants were to pay their share of royal taxation not to the city but to county collectors of the North Riding of Yorkshire: Miller, *VCH*, pp. 39, 68; *York Mem. Bk.*, 3:185; Dobson, *Chamberlains' Accounts*, p. 51.

68   *York Civic Records*, 2:155–58, 163, 165.

69   *Ibid.*, pp. 166, 169–70, 173, 180–81, 191–93; *York Civic Records*, 3:1–7; Bayne and Dunham, *Council of Henry VII*, p. clxii; Palliser, *Tudor York*, p. 45. See above, p. 52.

70   The prebend of Fridaythorpe was worth over £38 per annum in 1535, ranking it fifteenth of the Minster's thirty-six prebends. It survived the Reformation with twenty-nine others, to be held by Cardinal Wolsey's son, and later by Queen Elizabeth's physician as a pension: Dobson, "The Later Middle Ages," *A History of York Minster*, pp. 55–56; Claire Cross, "From the Reformation to the Restoration," *ibid.*, pp. 196, 202, 205, 222, 225.

71   *York House Books*, pp. 513, 515–19, 522, 524–26.

72   *Ibid.*, pp. 623, 655. In 1499, the prebend was held by Richard Nykez, who was allowed to hold Tanghall in severalty for an annual fee because the city needed his friendship on Henry VII's council. However, the citizens were allowed to put their animals in to graze for one day, to register the city's claim to the common: *York Civic Records*, 2:143–44.

73   *York Civic Records*, p. 170. The favor to Bray was renewed (with one day open grazing to preserve citizens' rights) in 1502: *ibid.*, p. 178. For Bray's influence in royal government, see above, p. 136 note 108.

74   *York Civic Records*, 3:96–102 (October-November 1524). The city retained some right to Tanghall through the sixteenth century. In 1837, a private citizen purchased it, and in 1919 the city acquired it for a housing development: Angelo Raine, ed., *York Civic Records, Volume 6*, Yorkshire Archaeological Society Record Series, vol. 112 (Wakefield, 1946), pp. 3–6, 100; Allison, "Common Lands and Strays," p. 501.

75   For example, Philippa C. Maddern, *Violence and Social Order: East Anglia 1422–1442* (Oxford: Clarendon Press, 1992). For criticism of Maddern's approach, see Ben R. McRee, "Peacemaking and its Limits in Late Medieval Norwich," *English Historical Review* 109 (1994): 831–66, esp. 854 note 1.

[76] N.R.O., 17-a, *Liber Albus*, f.12v; Norman Tanner, "The Cathedral and the City," in Ian Atherton, *et al.*, eds., *Norwich Cathedral: Church, City and Diocese, 1096–1996* (London and Rio Grande: The Hambledon Press, 1996), pp. 258–59. Tanner provides a helpful map of the suburbs and liberties on page 257.

[77] *Norwich Records*, 1:lxxx. Tombland and Ratonrowe were in front of the cathedral prectinct, Holmstrete on its northern edge, and the priory also claimed the liberty of Normanslond in the Ultra Aquam ward: see Maddern, *Violence and Social Order*, p. 178, Map 6.1.

[78] N.R.O., 17-a, ff.62v, 63v; Tanner, "Cathedral and the City," p. 262.

[79] "We have granted...that the said city and all the land within the said City and the Liberty thereof with its suburbs and hamlets and their precinct and the land in the circuit of our said City of Norwich (the castle and the shirehouse excepted) shall be separated from the said County of Norfolk": *Norwich Records*, 1:lxxxi, 31–36. In fairness to Henry, he was more concerned to separate the city from royal and shrieval jurisdiction than that of the priory. See above, p. 40.

[80] *Norwich Records*, 1:43; 2:cxxxviii.

[81] *Ibid.*, 1:319–20; N.R.O., 9-b, nn. 1 & 2; 17-b, ff.39v–41r.

[82] *Norwich Records*, 1:320–24; N.R.O., 9-b; 17-b, ff.34v–39v. Maddern, *Violence and Social Order*, p. 181, calls the inquisition "a weapon used by the priory to fend off the claims of the city."

[83] N.R.O., Treasurers' Rolls: 7-c (6–7, 7–8, 8–9 Henry V); 7-d (1–2, 2–3, 3–4, 4–5 Henry VI); 18-a, Chamberlains' Account Book I, f. 145v (1423–24). For William Paston's role in these actions, and a justification of the choice of the word "quashing," see above, p. 131 note 60. Part of the delay was due to the royal escheator's death, as the king himself had to petition the deceased's executors to relinquish the Cringleford writs and records: N.R.O., 17-b, Book of Pleas, f.30v (February 1428); *Norwich Records*, 1:324.

[84] They spent almost £70 in the process during the late 1420s to no great effect: N.R.O., 7-d, view of account 1429–30; Treasurers' Roll, 8–9 Henry VI.

[85] *Norwich Records*, 1:lxxxii; Maddern, *Violence and Social Order*, pp. 183, 200–201.

[86] P.R.O., KB.27/708, mem. 17r; N.R.O., 16-d, Assembly Book I, f.9v; 17-a, *Liber Albus*, ff.31v–33v; 17-b, Book of Pleas, ff.48–49v; *Norwich Records*, 1:lxxxvii.

[87] P.R.O., KB.9/240, mm. 35–37. A statute of 28 Edward III allowed neighboring counties to investigate unrest in boroughs. The Thetford bench also included Chief Baron of the Exchequer John Fray and Justice of King's Bench William Goderede, as well as former city keeper Sir John Clifton, and the earl of Suffolk's steward Sir Thomas Tuddenham: *Norwich Records*, 1:326–28; N.R.O., 9-c, transcript of pleas.

[88] N.R.O., 9-c. The King's Bench action, brought Michaelmas 1442, can be found on P.R.O. KB.27/726, mem. 39r. For the New Mills, see above, p. 219.

[89] *Norwich Records*, 1:350–56.

[90] *Ibid.*, 1:lxxxii, 328; N.R.O., 9-d (indentures 1450); 9-e; 17-a, ff.124–25; 21-f, 9-58, Kirkpatrick Notes, *sub* 1490 (coroners' inquiry in Lakenham).

[91] N.R.O., 16-c, Assembly Minute Book I, ff.38, 39, 45v; 17-a, ff.104–24; Bayne and Dunham, *Council of Henry VII*, p. clxi. See above at p. 251.

[92] N.R.O., 9-e; 21-f, 9-58, Kirkpatrick Notes, *sub* 1493; 13a no. 2 (in 1511 the city claimed the ability to muster troops from the disputed wards and suburbs). See also Bayne and Dunham, *Council of Henry VII*, p. clxi; R. Harold Garrett-Goodyear,

"Revival of Quo Warranto and Early Tudor Policy towards Local Governors, 1485–1540" (Ph.D. diss., Harvard University, 1973), pp. 133–34.

93 A fuller study of Exeter's case can be found in Lorraine C. Attreed, "Arbitration and the Growth of Urban Liberties in Late Medieval England," *Journal of British Studies* 31 (1992): 205–35. For background details, see also Muriel E. Curtis, *Some Disputes between the City and the Cathedral Authorities of Exeter*, History of Exeter Research Group, monograph 4 (Manchester: Manchester University Press, 1932), pp. 17–23.

94 Parliament defined the boundaries of Saint Sidwell's fee, gave the dean and chapter a court baron and view of frankpledge for the area, but allowed civic officials to claim toll on the tenants' mercantile and commercial activity: D.C.A, Nos. 503, 2890, 2892, 4720; D.R.O, Book 55, Freeman's Book, ff. 71v–74v; P.R.O., C1/12/243; *CPR, 1429–36*, pp. 358–59.

95 *CChR*, 6:60; *CPR, 1441–46*, pp. 451–52. The letter patent is dated 14 July 1446; the charter was granted 14 November 1445 and allowed the bishop and his successors to hold "before their steward and bailiffs all assizes of novel disseisin, fresh force and mort d'ancestor and all pleas real personal and mixed from their fees, possessions, lands and tenements and those of the Dean and Chapter of Saint Peter's, Exeter, and of the canons and vicars thereof, lying within the city of Exeter and its suburbs...." It is evident that neither the king nor his government checked to see that these privileges did not conflict with those granted to the city over previous centuries. Henry himself confirmed the city's charters 1 June 1447, and missed a second opportunity to check for conflicts: D.C.A., No. 2335.

96 D.R.O, Receivers' Roll 24–25 Henry VI; D.C.A, No. 3679 (evidence of the special rate, beginning Easter 1446 and meant to last three years, to maintain the suit between the city and the cathedral); Stuart A. Moore, ed., *Letters and Papers of John Shillingford, Mayor of Exeter 1447–50*, Camden Society, n.s., vol. 2 (London, 1871), pp. 2, 133–35 (privy seal writ).

97 Moore, *Letters and Papers*, p. 58. The city cited Magna Carta and a statute of Edward III that confirmed a number of Magna Carta's clauses, and reaffirmed a subject's right to justice at the common law before being required to answer before the king or his council: *Rot. Parl.*, 2:295. See Carpenter, "Law, Justice and Landowners," pp. 229, 235, for the use of Magna Carta by those adverse to equitable resorts.

98 D.C.A, No. 2334; Moore, *Letters and Papers*, p. 135. The parties also bound themselves on pain of £500.

99 Powell, "Arbitration and the Law," pp. 54–55, 65. Arbitration was formally encouraged in canon law, and Bishop Lacy's registers reveal him to have advocated that alternative on several occasions: G. R. Dunstan, ed., *The Register of Edmund Lacy, Bishop of Exeter, 1420–1455, Registrum Commune*, 5 vols. (Torquay, 1963–72), 1:144–47, 167–75, 195–96; 2:134–39; 3:245–55, 271–72, 290–96, 311–15.

100 Moore, *Letters and Papers*, pp. 6–7, 9. For details of the gifts and the highly-placed men who received them, see above, p. 125. No record survives indicating that the noblemen took any interest in the case, but Shillingford was pleased to have called their attention to its existence.

[101] *Ibid.*, pp. 12–14, 16–19. These actions may have been mere gestures, since Stafford was known by his contemporaries for his "almost boundless hospitality": *D.N.B.*, 18:863.

[102] Moore, *Letters and Papers*, pp. 20–23.

[103] D.C.A., no. 2977, pieces 17 (Domesday Book), 19; no. 2337 (*quo warranto* roll).

[104] Curtis, *Some Disputes*, p. 29. The arrests involved the cathedral chancellor's servant and two clerks, all taken by city bailiffs *cum vi et armis* while in the churchyard. Included also was a charge that in 1430, civic officials illegally seized a pair of knives belonging to a tenant of the bishop's fee. Harassment of town authorities may have been Lacy's primary intention.

[105] Moore, *Letters and Papers*, pp. 40–42, 68, and above at p. 244.

[106] Printed in Hoker, *Description of the Citie*, 2:190–205. See Moore, *Letters and Papers*, pp. 45–46, for delays and postponements in March 1448, pp. 59–63 for April delays, and p. 65 for the bishop's complaint to King Henry that he was ready to settle and had met with Shillingford personally but arbitration was broken off. Shillingford often played for time and refused to consider suggestions for settlement he found awkward, because (as he wrote) of his "sympelnesse and poverte."

[107] The city's finances are discussed above, pp. 138, 142. The cathedral's financial records include an account for December 1448, showing expenses exceeding £187 and carefully distributed to Justice Nicholas Ashton, his servants and clerks, the bishop's counselors and solicitors, and jurors: D.C.A., no 2977, piece 21.

[108] For the history of the city's relations with the Courtenays and Bonvilles, see above, pp. 101, 105-110.

[109] For Bonville, see Dunstan, *Register of Edmund Lacy*, 2:71, 166, 248, 313. This activity continued during the 1450s, when Bonville could also be found acting with Bishop Lacy to swear in the sheriff of Devonshire, and acting with his ally Sir Philip Courtenay of Powderham to keep the peace in the area: Dunstan, *Register,* 3:54–55, 137, 160–61. For Courtenay, see D.C.A., No. 3498; Dunstan, *Register*, 1:281–82, 292; 2:24, 107–8, 169–70, 193–94, 291–92, 354–55. David N. Lepine, "The Courtenays and Exeter Cathedral in the Later Middle Ages," *Transactions of the Devonshire Association* 24 (1992): 41–58, explores the link the family maintained with the cathedral, including providing four canons and a bishop of Exeter (1478–87). Bishop Lacy also wrote to the duke of Exeter asking the "right worshipful and excellent prince…to be brothyr to the Churche of Exeter." The letter of 8 October bears no year; John Holand, who bore that title and others, died 5 August 1447, leaving as heir his seventeen-year-old son Henry who was the duke of York's son-in-law and ward. Lacy could have been addressing John, or trying to establish relations with the new well-connected duke, who does not seem to have replied: *CPR, 1446–52*, p. 86; *Complete Peerage*, 6:653–54; *D.N.B.*, 9:1042–44.

[110] The Barnstaple jurors did indeed find for the cathedral party and awarded one thousand marks for the trespass and court costs, from payment of which the city was immediately excused: Hoker, *Description of the Citie*, 2:205.

[111] Moore, *Letters and Papers*, pp. 136–41. In accepting the final concord, both parties bound themselves under penalty of £2000. Copies of the composition continued to be made throughout the spring of 1449, as well as rewards for the clerks who made the records: D.C.A., No. 2977, piece 16, part 4.

112 D.C.A., No. 2977, piece 2a, indicates that the new patents were sealed on 10 February 1449 at the cost of 40s., and the old document cancelled 20 February for 6s. 8d. The new charter is examined in Muriel E. Curtis, "A Note on the Dating of an Exeter Charter," *English Historical Review* 45 (1930): 290–91. The bishop's motives here are suspect: did he believe the new charter would be adopted without question if it bore the 1445 date?

113 D.R.O., City charters, No. 32. The cathedral party's rights were not expressly protected. See Joyce Youings, *Early Tudor Exeter: The Founders of the County of the City* (Exeter: University of Exeter, 1974), pp. 12–18, for analysis of the disturbances surrounding Protestant sermons which sparked Henry VIII's government to grant the city expanded judicial powers to keep the peace.

114 D.R.O., City charters, No. 33.

115 D.C.A., No. 2899 (1538 petition to Henry VIII); Record Office, House of Lords, London, 2 and 3 Edward VI, No. 49, "An act for the enlarging of the liberties of the city of Exeter." The act, passed in 1548, defined the city and suburbs of Exeter as part of the county of the city of Exeter, with its own officers who were permitted to serve writs and initiate judicial processes, *excepting* those which were prejudicial to the rights of the bishop and his successors. Exeter's loss of diocesan income, from £1500 *per annum* to £500, is examined in Wallace T. MacCaffrey, *Exeter 1540–1640* (Cambridge, Mass.: Harvard University Press, 1958), pp. 185–87, 200–201.

116 See Curtis, *Some Disputes*, pp. 43–54, for a review of the dispute between 1535 and 1826. Stanford E. Lehmberg, *The Reformation of Cathedrals: Cathedrals in English Society, 1485–1603* (Princeton: Princeton University Press, 1988), discusses the strained cathedral finances of the sixteenth century, especially in chapter 7.

CHAPTER 9
CUM VI ET ARMIS

D
espite recent studies that diminish the role of violence in late
medieval society, there can be no doubt that urban discord
brought town and Crown into closer relations, whether the
disorder arose from local circumstances or had external causes. Although
it may be true that phrases like *cum vi et armis* were legal strategies more
than descriptions of reality, many members of society expressed distress
over threats to the king's peace and the means required to restore it.
Expectations of peacekeeping may have been unreasonably high, but this
recognition should not blind us to the deep and sincere concern
expressed in royal proclamations and town records alike. What urban
subjects described as a riot may indeed have been little more than a
shoving match adorned with meaningful vocabulary to achieve Crown
intervention.[1] It is likely that the royal government was as aware of the
exaggeration as are modern students of the period, but on no occasion
could it afford to ignore even a potential threat.

In the period under study, the four towns provided the king with
numerous occasions of discord and several of outright violence. The five
case studies that follow examine key periods in English medieval history
and the disorder they produced in towns. Whatever their magnitude, such
disturbances threatened the basis of the relationship between monarch
and urban subjects, mocking the king's role as guarantor of peace and
harmony while disturbing the fiscal prosperity essential to town dwellers
and monarchs. The unrest resulted from complex combinations of many
of the themes addressed so far: internal administrative privileges
extended to only part of the urban populace, the pressures of the post-
plague economy, noble patrons' abuse of their urban relationships, and
the national events of royal dynastic change after 1460.

If the royal responses to these threats lacked consistency, the nature
of each regime and the character of the monarch himself must be

considered. The reactions of the first Lancastrian or Tudor battling opposition early in a reign differ greatly from the ineffective will of Henry VI and the hesitant enforcement of his council. Nevertheless, the fact that such incidents of violence arose from more than purely local and internal causes made royal attention imperative. However anxious urban subjects may have been for a clean end to these disturbances, royal intervention also proved to be an unwelcome reminder that they had somehow failed in the responsibilities delegated to them. Whether solved by royal decree or settled by internal efforts, incidents of violence and urban disorder marked important milestones in the growth of English towns and in their process of maturity.

The Great Revolt 1381

In the period under study, urban violence first caught inspiration from national events at the time of the Great Revolt of 1381. Of the four towns, Norwich copied most directly the lessons of lawlessness taught by Wat Tyler and the rebels in the south, suffering assaults that underline the interpenetration of town and countryside, and of national and local interests. On 14 June, the very day on which Richard II was conferring at Mile End and royal servants including Archbishop Sudbury were losing their lives, several bands of insurgents rose in Norfolk, setting off incidents of mob violence. In eastern Norfolk, there arose as "king of the commons" a Felmingham dyer, Geoffrey (or John) Litster, who entered Norwich on 17 June and won mass support among the poorer residents. As the days passed and the novelty of revolt wore thin, the rebels decided to use money extorted from the city to buy a charter of manumission and pardon from Richard II. By 24 June, the bishop of Norwich had gathered enough forces to recapture the town and rout the rebels. The bishop absolved Litster himself and accompanied him to his traitor's execution, after which part of the rebel's body adorned Norwich's walls. By this grisly act, the city showed it was no longer the passive victim of insurgence, but an entity ready to assume the more fitting role as the leading county town, loyal to the king and active in the suppression of disorder.[2]

York's experience during Richard II's reign was more complex, with origins pre-dating the Great Revolt. Violence resulted when long-standing factional disputes and splits within the ruling oligarchy encountered an atmosphere of social unrest common to both urban and rural locales. As described in parliament, the "horrible deed" done at York in November 1380 arose out of personal ambitions and local animosities whose ferocity and similarity to other threats to the Crown led inevitably to royal involvement.[3] Problems centered on Mayor John de Gisburne, a wealthy merchant with court connections who had served as mayor three times during the 1370s, and whose terms witnessed incidents of peculation, arbitrary imprisonment, and general malpractice.[4] Insurgents, mostly city craftsmen, forced him from office and supported his rival Simon Quixley, whom they proclaimed mayor after breaking into the Guildhall. Quixley had the grace to protest against this unorthodox appointment but the commons paid no heed. Their actions directly rebelled against the local administration from which most of them were barred.

This attack on elected representatives and borough custom led to Crown intervention. Before the end of 1380, twenty-two of the rioters were ordered to the Tower of London, and early in the new year, Quixley was called to appear before the king's council to answer for his part in the uprisings.[5] In the meantime, Richard had officially restored Gisburne to the mayoralty he later relinquished to the duly-elected Quixley on 3 February 1381. How deeply the citizens resented Crown intervention remained to be seen. Whatever their previous records, leading citizens Gisburne and Quixley were the king's most natural choices to investigate local disorder. In May 1381, both the former mayor and the incumbent were named members of a commission required to investigate disputes of the previous year in the neighboring town of Beverley. Soon after, Gisburne's judgment was again required, this time in his own defense, during the testimony of forty York citizens who each had entered into bonds of £40 to keep the peace they shattered six months earlier.[6]

Into this maelstrom came news in June of insurrection in Kent and Essex. There followed an assault on religious houses within York, which neither Gisburne nor Quixley could have countenanced. Rebellious commons, perhaps inspired by the successes of their southern brethren, also destroyed the earthen ramparts of the walls and carried off two of the gates of York's Dominican friars, mirroring attacks elsewhere on religious institutions' property. Chancery ordered Mayor Quixley to repair the damage, while he and his fellow officers struggled to keep control of the city's legal rights by fining anyone who attempted to transfer to an external royal court any plea belonging to the city's own jurisdiction.[7] Nevertheless, Quixley's reputation as a peacekeeper received a harsh blow in July when Gisburne and his followers attacked Bootham Bar and formed a liveried association in hopes of regaining political power. The rebels rode "in a warlike manner and arrayed with armed force, to the disturbance of the king's and the people's peace," threatening all who opposed them with murder and mayhem. The appeal to the king's peace and the formulaic vocabulary of violence successfully gained the officeholders royal justice in the form of indictments against the insurgents.[8]

Over the following eighteen months, the Crown heard a series of charges and counter-charges that obscured more than illuminated the situation. In February 1382, for example, both Quixley and Gisburne appeared in Chancery where the former was ordered to repay sums of money extorted from citizens in 1380, and to promise that no citizen would suffer further harm.[9] In the end, the Crown terminated its fruitless investigations and instead offered York a general pardon: since it forgave "all insurrections, treasons, seditions, murders, felonies, forestalments, etc., and all forfeitures for transport of wools…without payment of custom or subsidy," its cost of one thousand marks may have been worth the blanket coverage it offered.[10] Beyond temporary imprisonment of the rebels and the monetary fines, the Crown attempted no further punishment of citizens or even a precise determination of culpability.

Had the uprisings in Norwich and York occurred at any other time, such local events might not have been of great interest to the royal government. On their own, these two cases (to which can be added the uprisings in Beverley and Scarborough) provide clear examples of powerful interrelationships. Ruling officials in the towns were forcibly reminded of their obligation to rule responsibly over all urban subjects, especially those craftsmen whose economic and political aspirations had not been totally fulfilled in post-plague society and who were not reticent in their complaints or litigation. The officials balanced that obligation with loyalty to the Crown, obedience which had assured them their liberties and their royally-sanctioned ability to suppress dissension. These urban cases of unrest share with the insurgents of the south the desire more to arrest the misuse of power structures than to introduce new measures and systems. Both examples reveal a frightening willingness among the disadvantaged to turn to violent expressions of grievances. They illuminate how quickly royal attention could be gained when disturbances were described in terms of threats to the realm, threats that no longer seemed remote after 1381.

Archbishop Scrope and the First Lancastrian

In 1405, a northern rising against Henry IV brought the king to his leading provincial city harshly to punish its rebels and extirpate the treasonous influence of one of its leaders. The monarchy's action was swift and sharp, penalizing an entire borough to save a struggling dynasty. Archbishop of York Richard Scrope was the unlikely fomenter of rebellion in this case, and the exact nature of his role in the uprising cannot be fully known. Described by one historian as "an obscure and colourless figure," Scrope was a younger son of a minor northern noble family, who had gained a scholarly education and received some small favors from the king since 1399.[11] Even during the years immediately preceding the rebellion, it is hard to find evidence of deep-seated resentment on his part against the king. Nevertheless, it remains true that Scrope organized town merchants and workers so effectively against the young Lancastrian government that the monarch felt forced to respond with actions that denied civic liberties to those in rebellion against the source of those privileges.

The manifesto Scrope published at York provided reasons for the archbishop's resistance and for the citizens' call to arms. It contained complaints that the Church and clergy had been wronged, particularly by the financial burdens of a strapped government. Tax demands and purveyance had also hurt the laity, and merchants in particular suffered from excessive customs duties and forced loans. Given what we know of economic problems in the north early in the fifteenth century, this argument alone illuminates the citizens' participation in the movement.[12] Both Scrope and the citizen-army lacked military skills, so that it seems likely that the archbishop raised the force not for independent action but for coordination with that of the earl of Northumberland. Intent upon avenging his family's defeat two years earlier, the earl could find useful Scrope's contribution of "a spurious air of religious mission," even more than the rebel forces bringing with them less training than spiritual enthusiasm.[13]

Disturbed by reports of insurrection, Chancery issued writs to the mayor of York and the sheriffs of the northern counties "to stop the malice of those who are daily trying to cause trouble in the realm."[14] Unfortunately for Scrope, the writs were soon followed by royal forces. Unable to join his allies, Northumberland fled the realm and left Scrope to continue on alone. Seditious sermons in York Minster were followed by a three-day wait with his troops outside the city, eventually to be met not by the earl but by the king's forces. The eloquent archbishop attempted to talk his way out of his predicament, presenting the manifesto as a loyal subject's suggestions for reform, but the king at least was not persuaded. The citizen army disbanded and on Henry's orders its members were allowed "safely [to] return to their homes without fear of arrest and sue for pardons by fine or otherwise." The king seized the goods of the major conspirators, and in response to the treasonous act that had been narrowly averted he deprived York of its freedom and liberties.[15]

The king executed Archbishop Scrope in June, after which the government of the city was placed in the hands of two Crown-appointed keepers. Henry totally rejected investigation and government by civic officials for several months, until he allowed Mayor William Frost to join the keepers. The joint accounts made by the three men at the Exchequer reveal that, in respect to what the city owed the Crown, the loss of civic liberties left York in a somewhat worse financial position than before the seizure. The royal keepers and Frost together soon petitioned for allowances totaling almost £300, for they had been unable to account for numerous rents from tenements and messuages.[16] York's financial problems may have been one reason why in August Henry freed the citizens and their successors from toll, pavage, pontage and stallage throughout England: "notwithstanding that for particular causes those liberties among other things are seized into the king's hand...the king's will is to show them special favor, that seizure notwithstanding."[17] Henry did not forget his own purse: over the next few years, rebellious citizens paid a few marks apiece to the hanaper in return for pardons, while the officers made more substantial payments.[18] Restoration of their liberties cost the citizens a further £200. To be certain that he had not forgotten any source of funding and to re-establish a civic official's major task, Henry reminded Mayor Frost that this was an appropriate time to inquire into sums of money due the king and concealed by sheriffs, escheators, and aulnagers.[19]

Crown reaction to the Scrope revolt took the form it did for several reasons. For one, Scrope's continued influence in the city of York makes clear why the king acted as swiftly and as harshly as he did. Even at the height of Henry V's popularity, a cult grew up around the martyred prelate. Veneration of Scrope centered at his tomb in the Minster: it began immediately after his execution and was probably encouraged by the vicars choral who transported the archbishop's body from the field in which he was executed.[20] Moreover, Henry IV, fresh from overcoming rebellious Percies, acted harshly when faced with what he assumed could grow into another attack on his right to rule. The punishment did not quite fit the crime, as the entire city had not armed to fight with Scrope, but from Henry's perspective a sympathetic borough and a well-liked prelate could have proven a dangerous combination. Avoiding for as long as possible the use of civic officials, the king pronounced sentence and appointed his own rulers to keep the city for the Crown. But poverty and a need for support won out over vengeance and caution. The first Lancastrian not only had to return to more time-honored and balanced methods of peacekeeping, but he was forced to make monetary concessions to secure the profits of free trade his budget demanded.

Norwich 1433–50

The complexities of Norwich's electoral privileges and the city's jurisdiction debate with neighboring religious houses have been studied already in this work.[21] It remains to examine the situation from the perspective of violence, royal reactions to internal disorder, and the role that local nobles played in settling disputes. The result may bring us no closer to the truth of what actually happened in Norwich during Henry VI's reign, but it should illuminate the importance of these events far beyond the issue of whether or not the streets ran red with blood.

The worst problems began on 1 May 1433, when outgoing mayor Thomas Wetherby, "a man of grete goodes and grete pryde" who had first served as mayor in 1427 and later as parliamentary representative, intervened in the election of a new mayor.[22] This action reveals two important, and inevitably fatal, attributes of the man. Flaunting the accepted procedure of royal charters, Wetherby attempted to substitute his own candidate for the duly selected individual, a violation of the corporate nature of politics citizens believed necessary for civic harmony. Moreover, this former mayor and relative newcomer to city politics represented a group of middle-aged citizens and officers who recognized and defended the rights of various religious houses to physical and legal control of areas inside and outside of Norwich walls. A younger group of citizens, some of whom presently held office, disagreed with this position, denying a 1429 indenture giving the cathedral priory some rights within the city, and believing that the honor of the city depended upon the full exercise of its rights in all of the disputed areas. The composition of civic records preserving accounts of these events was in their hands, so our view of Wetherby and the violence is colored by their philosophy. Intent on having their way, they had recently dismissed the city's recorder, Sir John Heydon, from office for having favored the priory over the city. Their objections to Wetherby's electoral actions, however, involved all parties in a series of conciliatory overtures. Several commons first approached Wetherby himself to negotiate for peace, then sought the intervention of the bishop of Norwich. But the general atmosphere of hostility prompted Wetherby himself to petition the royal chancellor for help. The royal government thereupon constituted a commission to inquire into the events and instruct the civic assembly to levy punishments. Although his friends and associates accepted the panel's fines, Wetherby himself refused even to appear, resulting in heavy financial penalties and his removal from all civic office.[23]

Over the following three years, Wetherby worked quietly to place men of his faction in civic office and to create an alternate written version of events that favored his own actions. Norwich officers reached out for assistance naturally enough to the earl of Suffolk, particularly to ask his help against the abbot of St. Benet's, Holm, who had challenged their exercise of judicial rights in the suburbs. Suffolk duly became involved, bringing with him his royal household associates Sir Thomas Tuddenham and Sir John Heydon, all of whom rapidly revealed they favored Wetherby more than the younger party.[24]

At the same time, the royal government had become concerned enough about Norwich events to send serjeant-at-law William Goddard to investigate; much of what we know about the 1433 events comes from his report four years later. Goddard upheld the actions of the city's officers, chastised Wetherby, and advised arbitration. Wetherby urged Suffolk to view the case, a choice of umpires even his enemies could not have disputed. Norwich was soon to discover the earl's true feelings, when he overturned the Goddard findings and ordered Wetherby and friends restored to power as the best way to restore civic harmony. More important, he announced that the young king had heard of Norwich's dissension and had sent him to investigate on his behalf. Since 1433, Suffolk had acted as steward of the household and was working closely with the council to maintain county-level peace and lawfulness beyond the capacities of the king. His intervention was the proper action of a local lord and carried additionally the weight of royal command. But it was not to the liking of the civic officials, who rapidly appealed for help to the duke of Gloucester.[25]

Alerted to the possibility of violence at the upcoming 1 May elections, the privy council ordered Wetherby to appear and sent trusted councilors to view events and impose order. This response alone is more important than the nature of the disturbance that occurred. The riot and the justices' certification that describes attacks between Wetherby's opponents and his own friends have been called "legal fabrication[s], constructed to serve the interests of one of two groups competing for power in the city government...."[26] The magnitude of the disturbance matters less in this context than the intervention of royal government and its clear anticipation of trouble. Obviously, peaceful internal means of negotiation and mediation had failed and the Crown had no choice but to intervene directly. By July, the privy council had taken away Norwich's liberties and exiled Wetherby and his chief opponent from the city. London alderman John Welles became keeper of Norwich, and two sheriffs were appointed to see that the king received all profits due him.[27]

Suspension of liberties proved to be less helpful in restoring peace than first realized. The king found Welles' wardenship expensive, so that the council suggested the substitution of a "neutral" mayor. The possibility of a large fine was also raised by the royal council, whose members thought the citizens would be best punished if all trade except cloth was prohibited from passing through Norwich.[28] Accordingly, John Cambridge became mayor in late November, having previously served as mayor in 1430. At the same time, civic officials received a mandate under privy seal prohibiting unlawful assemblies and the "stirring up of strife between greater and lesser men of Norwich," one way to describe Wetherby and his younger opponents.[29] Early in the new year (1438), the citizens began making trips to London to petition for restoration of the franchises, which was finally accomplished on 6 March.[30]

The 1 May disturbances have been linked to the 1433 events by the figure of John Heydon, still protesting his dismissal from office for having disclosed evidence to the prior.[31] Giving credence to this interpretation are the renewed hostilities occurring in 1438 between the city and a newly-selected prior eager to charge urban officials with suburban encroachments. While the prior began a series of legal actions on those points, Wetherby offered him encouragement while persuading the abbots of St. Benet's, Wendling and Walsingham to join in with their own issues against the citizens.[32] Acting either out of spite or genuine concern, the prior cited a statute of Edward III and exercised his right to intervene in a badly-governed city by calling for a commission of oyer and terminer. Meeting first at Thetford in July 1441 then moving to Norwich, the commission heard evidence about the New Mills, priory jurisdiction, and the city's illegal arrests in the suburbs and surrounding hamlets.[33] Once again, the issue came to arbitration, delivered by the earl of Suffolk in June 1442. His award favored the religious houses and demanded the destruction of the mills, a document the citizens refused to sign. For the remainder of the year, they played for time by asking him to clarify ambiguous points, and expressed their frustration by engaging in fisticuffs with priory servants.[34] At a civic assembly called on 25 January 1443 to discuss the problem, those opposed to the award removed the common seal from the hall. The situation rapidly deteriorated into a four-day siege of the priory, the destruction of the prior's prison, and the aiming of ordnance at him. The proceedings may not have fulfilled the technical legal definition of riot, but it did not fail to upset the royal council. When the duke of Norfolk and earl of Oxford arrived to control the situation, Norwich sealed its own fate when it closed the gates to them, as though in time of war.[35]

A new commission of oyer and terminer seized Norwich liberties for the second time in six years and levied heavy corporate fines. The mayor eagerly traveled to Westminster to explain the situation, only to find himself imprisoned in the Fleet for six weeks. In his absence, Wetherby took charge at home, sealed Suffolk's award, and ordered the destruction of the New Mills. A new commission headed by justices Yelverton and Paston declared that the city had no right to jurisdiction within the disputed suburbs or in areas surrounding the priory and its palace.[36] The city fell quiet, no doubt helped by the death of Wetherby in 1445. Fears of riot were replaced by apprehension about finances. As soon as the franchise was forfeit, the privy council expressed concern about the economic loss the king might suffer. Councilors ordered a search among the pipe rolls to determine how well the fee farm and other rents had been paid when the liberties were first seized in 1437–38. The search revealed that no losses had occurred at that time, and the council hoped the same situation would again prevail. By July, the government began taking steps to collect more than £1500 in fines owed by individual rioters.[37]

But Norwich finances were about as secure as the king's peace in the city. The fine proved unpayable, and the government had to accept the reduced figure of 1000 marks.[38] A month after the liberties were seized, Norwich did not pay the balance of its fee farm due at Easter term and continued to miss payments for over four years.[39] Once the king took control of a borough, all charges and profits should have fallen directly into Crown hands, but apparently this was not the case in Norwich. Civic officials claimed that citizens left town and trade fell off; they calculated their losses at £20,000, a sum in the realm of fiction but nonetheless indicative of their observation of financial decline.[40] The problem was not settled until Easter 1452, when the Crown discharged Norwich from the accumulated fee farm payments and ordered it to answer for only a small amount of profits and issues. It was no coincidence that such mercy was extended at the end of a four-year process during which Norwich amalgamated city government with the guild of St. George, adding to the former the guild's arbitral mechanisms and moral clout.[41]

Norwich's jurisdiction disputes had not yet ended, but the worst period of disorder and Crown intervention was over. Suffolk's murder in 1450 and his evolution into an all-purpose scapegoat gave the citizens courage to write a new version of these events, one in which Suffolk, Tuddenham, and Heydon played malevolently dominant roles aided and abetted within city government by the late Thomas Wetherby.[42] This version of events stresses the violence of the encounters and may indeed exaggerate the damage. What cannot be manipulated as easily was the royal government's response. Seizure of liberties for a combined period of over five years, to the detriment of royal as well as urban finances, constituted extreme measures. Royal commissions had attempted to deal with the roots of the unrest, examining the jurisdiction claims and affirming the rights of the city's neighbors established in writing a generation earlier. Suffolk's failed interventions must have confounded the privy council: the man who was holding royal government together in these decades could make no impact on urban subjects determined to increase their legal control and expand their identity as a borough. Removal of the same privileges they wished to extend was the harsh and punitive response of a royal government anxious to keep control even at the expense of a borough's changing concept of itself and its rights.

The Wars of the Roses

The battles of the Wars of the Roses from the mid-1450s to 1497 involved England in no more than four hundred days of active warfare and preparation, for which towns' military contributions were slight.[43] But much of the tension, not to mention the dynastic disputes, involved the same local nobility who acted as urban patrons, had inflicted acts of violence upon town subjects, and recruited them for their own uses. Henry VI understood the relations between national threats and urban discord when in March 1457 he drew civic officials' attention to the riots and insurrections that troubled his entire realm, then proceeded to name York as a major center for unlawful assemblies, "gret slaughters, murders of oure peple, and other mischeves…." He ordered the mayor to proclaim that such riots were unlawful and that the display of defensive weapons or noblemen's livery would result in the forfeiture of York's liberties.[44] Clearly, the same nobles who provided welcome if temporary employment and livery brought a less beneficial legacy to urban peacekeeping. Even the mere proximity of nobles to a town during these years could instigate discord, as was the case in Nottingham in 1459 when citizens and soldiers exploded into a fierce dispute over the character of Northumberland and Westmorland's men, discord serious enough to end in borough court.[45]

Prelude to the Wars

Although such isolated incidents could be multiplied, Henry had good reason for directing his concern to the northern capital. York's economic troubles and the intervention of a member of a local noble family intent on disorderly behavior drew the city officers into conflict with the royal government and with their own delegated role as peacekeepers. York's particular nemesis mid-century was Thomas Percy, second son of the earl of Northumberland, created Lord Egremont November 1447. Without the responsibilities or resources of a noble eldest son, Egremont passed the time in ways that could not have made

Yorkshire residents feel secure. Early in 1447, he and his friends went on a disorderly spree that resulted in their imprisonment in York.[46] The Scottish wars distracted him for a few years during which he also cared for his family's estates in Cumberland, where he certainly defended the Percy right to influence there against encroachments of the Neville family. When enmity between his family and the Nevilles heated up in 1453, he turned his attention to Yorkshire. The time was ripe for violent intervention: the Percies had not been able to recover lost lands or receive as much preferential treatment at court and Exchequer as had the Nevilles, kin of Henry VI. Moreover, the general economic climate of northeast England in the 1450s exacerbated Percy dissatisfaction.[47]

For military support, Egremont turned to the city of York, whose declining cloth industry left many craftsmen unemployed and willing to accept Percy livery. Ignoring Henry VI's orders to "do us service of war" in Gascony, Egremont recruited York craftsmen and others to attack several Neville partisans and retainers, and generally wreak havoc and violence throughout the northeast. Matters came to a head in August 1453, when Egremont's forces ambushed several members of a Neville wedding party making their way from Lincolnshire to Sheriff Hutton north of York. Percy may have had close to one thousand men under his command, and for months afterward, bands of partisans of both families moved all over the northeast attacking their enemies' tenants and property. The royal government, its king in a state of mental collapse, protested helplessly and ineffectually.[48]

As the result of indictments stemming from a full-scale inquiry into the assault, it is known that over 15% of Egremont's forces had come from the city of York. The city's stake in the proceedings as well as its desire to avoid becoming involved in violence bestowed a responsibility upon urban officers for helping to keep the peace between the two greatest families in the county.[49] In October, Neville and Percy forces gathered at Topcliffe outside York, while the mayor's agent tried to discover their intentions. The city's offer of arbitration remained the most constructive suggestion made by local or central government thus far, and indeed bloodshed was averted at Topcliffe by the discreet mediation of a party led by the archbishop of York.

Deliberately causing harm to York may not have been Egremont's chief concern, but he was not going to let the city's desire for peace get in his way. Complicating matters by the end of 1453 was the support given the Nevilles by Richard duke of York, already Salisbury's brother-in-law and soon to become Protector of the Realm. The Percies began looking for allies of equal strength. By spring 1454, Egremont had returned to York to gain military assistance; he distributed liveries in the city, and renewed his reputation for bellicosity by beating up Salisbury's supporters within York.[50] Henry Holand duke of Exeter joined him at that time, and in May forces of both men entered York. They held the mayor and recorder prisoner in the chapter house and later demanded the chief magistrate relinquish the keys to Bootham Bar, although to the citizens' relief Egremont and Exeter thereafter spent more of their time north of the city.[51]

In an effort to underline his concern for order, the duke of York held a commission of oyer and terminer, assisted by the earl of Warwick and York's mayor. They recommended imprisonment for Exeter and Egremont, although fewer than half of their followers including the York craftsmen were punished for fear of creating a hardened core of anti-Yorkist/Neville feeling.[52] York citizens and officials were spared further suffering, for they were already the victims of the magnates' choice of venue for their private battles and the paralysis of royal government in stopping them. Although no residents appear to have lost their lives in the confrontations, the period preceding the first battle of St. Albans was a time of tension and uncertainty. In an atmosphere already fraught with economic uncertainties, society appeared to be creating conditions whereby lawlessness could be pursued without correction, the royal government consistently failed to foster balanced relations in the counties, and the peace and order necessary for prosperous urban life was constantly under threat.

Such an environment of unrest took shape even in boroughs with no obvious economic strains, such as fifteenth-century Exeter. Throughout the 1440s, the earl of Devon watched the rise of his local rival, William Bonville, with a suspicion that would shortly take active expression. After Bonville and Courtenay were both granted stewardship of the duchy of Cornwall, mutual hatred increased and could not be vanquished even by arbitration offered by the royal council and overseen by the king himself.[53] At Courtenay's instigation, violence broke out throughout the West Country, and Bonville retainers and friends found themselves victims of armed attacks. Between 1444 and 1451, lawlessness decreased as Bonville was occupied overseas as seneschal of Gascony. The combination of his return and Devon's alliance with the duke of York renewed hostilities by the late summer of 1451. When York embarked upon shows of force against the court faction that denied him influence, Courtenay was right behind him, using the opportunity to strike at his own enemies. With a force of men exaggerated to the number of five thousand, Devon and his associate Lord Cobham pursued Bonville, attacked the latter's tenants throughout the west, and eventually besieged Taunton Castle in which Bonville had taken refuge. York moved quickly to end the siege, eager to give the appearance of upholding law and order in the realm. His influence, however, assured that Courtenay suffered no immediate punishment for his actions.[54]

Exeter itself had not yet been touched except by rumor of local disorder, but the situation was soon to change. In April 1454, the earl of Devon's sons and several hundred armed men entered the city and attacked Bonville, busy collecting a loan to the Crown from the citizens.[55] Although the earl himself was under bond to keep the peace, his henchmen were not intimidated: on 20 June one of them led a group of armed men into the city, seized the gates and attacked the mayor and citizens for two days.[56] In retaliation for Bonville's sympathy with the court faction, the earl's son and over a hundred tenants attacked the home of Exeter recorder and Bonville counselor Nicholas Radford, murdering him in cold blood in October 1455. A few days later, they moved to the earl's manor of Exe Island, from which vantage point they impeded the arrival of justices coming to the assizes, and later entered Exeter itself. The earl's men occupied the city until 21 December, using the opportunity to attack the homes of Bonville tenants and remove Radford's treasure (gold and silver plate valued at £600) from the cathedral, where the clergy had been protecting it.[57]

The earl was not content to use the city as a mere resting place and source of plunder. Courtenay wanted more active support than the civic officials were willing to grant him. He was particularly concerned that they refuse entry to William Bonville. Bonville was expected to join his friend and ally Sir Philip Courtenay in a defense of Powderham Castle south of the city, which Devon was besieging because of that alliance. Exeter's mayor affirmed that he and his councilors were the king's tenants and could not keep any lord out of their city. The earl accepted their attitude without further opposition and returned to the siege. He saved his enmity for Bonville, defeating the latter in a brief battle at Clyst Heath a few miles outside of Exeter on 15 December. When the earl returned in victory that night to Exeter, the city blazed with torches and rewarded him and his men with gifts of wine.[58]

On the night of his victory, Devon had no way of knowing how his actions, including those against a major cathedral city, sent shock waves through the royal government. In mid-November, the commons in parliament described the "great and grievous riots" instigated by the earl, attributing to him eight hundred horsemen and four thousand footmen in typical numerical exaggeration. But parliament had reason to inflate the severity of the disorder, for the members demanded a protector to quell the violence, and York was the man they had in mind.[59] On 19 November, York became protector for the second time; on 3 December, he dismissed Courtenay from the local commission of the peace, and two days later ordered west country nobles to join him in suppressing the earl's "full unfitting governaunce and mysreule."[60] With even his supporter York turned against him, Courtenay had little choice but to surrender to the protector and endure a two-month imprisonment in the Tower, incarceration that lasted only as long as York's protectorate.[61]

Despite a March 1456 proclamation ordering the disbanding of west country assemblies, violence recurred once the earl was again at large.[62] His son again impeded judicial sessions in Exeter and then occupied the city with his forces on 8 April, forcing the justices of the peace to leave. There were no further incidents of violence in Exeter until a commission of oyer and terminer arrived in August to investigate the disturbances of the previous spring. Although parliament had asked that both Bonville and Courtenay be imprisoned for their roles in the disorder, the jury was packed with Bonville supporters who neither punished their ally nor concocted a list of the earl's offenses that bore any semblance of reality. Exeter jurors were unwilling to punish nobles they had patronized for years and who retained useful ties to the central administration. The royal government sought balance by restoring Courtenay to the commission of the peace, and pardoned him and his sons. A significant factor was the marriage of Devon's heir to Queen Margaret's niece; certainly civic officials spared no expense in wooing the couple with expensive presents. City and county knew no more unrest from either party up to Courtenay's death in 1458 and Bonville's three years later.[63]

The Yorkist Regime

Before Henry's reign ended, borough officials took concrete action to curb internal dissent inspired by and exacerbating national discord. As Hoker explained Exeter's situation, the mayor and counsell seeing the trobles and civill warres to encrease dayly more and that the state was very daungerose, dyd for the better safty and preservation of the citie dyd [sic] apoynt a contynual guarde and watche of a competent nomber of men well harnessed and apoynted to kepe the gates both day and night.[64]

Strangers were also asked to leave Exeter, and no one carrying a weapon was permitted entry. Likewise, Norwich officials ordered extra guards for the gates throughout the 1460s and at times locked all but a few even in the daytime.[65] In 1461, Exeter among other boroughs received orders from Chancery to arrest "seditious vagabonds" in the city and suburbs, reflecting a suspicion of poverty and homelessness that did not wait for the Tudors to initiate.[66] Norwich officials acted quickly to instill respect for the new king: when in 1462, a city tailor donned a white rose badge, said to be a presumptuous act of disrespect against the monarch, he was condemned to ten weeks' imprisonment until ordered released by the royal justices.[67] Early in Edward's reign, when risings occurred in favor of Henry VI, the mayors of Exeter, Dartmouth and Totnes joined to arrest the instigators.[68] As late as 1468–69, local records note payment for night vigils against unknown threats to Exeter's civic peace.[69]

By March 1470, those threats had definite identities, when Exeter experienced a return to the kind of violence it had known when the Courtenays were at full power. At that time, the duke of Clarence and the earl of Warwick retreated to the west country in rebellion against Edward IV.[70] They hoped to raise some of Clarence's retainers to return to battle, but events did not favor them. Although they were able to rejoin Clarence's wife, sent to Exeter for shelter, they found the city under a siege directed by Sir Hugh Courtenay.[71] To Exeter's relief, Clarence and Warwick embarked for Calais, having decided that the Courtenay disturbance was too local and the citizens too volatile for the situation to be turned to their advantage. Hard on their heels was Edward IV, who received a warm welcome from Exeter but not the quarry he desired.[72]

Edward himself was soon forced to leave the country, but despite changes in kings boroughs like Exeter intended to survive and profit. Day and night watches commenced in the city, the gates were guarded, and messengers brought back news from the surrounding countryside, for in "troublesome tymes" the mayor and council were unsure of the outcome of events. But these were men who, for the sake of their city, gave "good contenans and interteynement to both parties," Lancastrian and Yorkist, so that when Henry VI was briefly restored to power the city receiver presented Queen Margaret and her son with a £20 gift to retain Lancastrian good will.[73]

Yet Exeter and its liberties survived the end of the Readeption as well, and at least some credit should be given to patronage of Yorkists like prodigal royal brother Clarence and the king's sister Anne duchess of Exeter.[74] All of the boroughs went to great lengths to prove their loyalty to the restored king. In 1471, Norwich voluntarily sent a tailor and his friends to the Tower at city expense after hearing reports of speech threatening Edward. In a Star Chamber case the same year, Nottingham's officers relinquished the right to punish rioters within the town when Edward intervened and demanded they appear before him and his council better to ensure their punishment.[75] Fortunately for English towns, their timely actions to preserve the peace combined with well-chosen patrons and extension of hospitality prevented many other such losses of urban privileges during these years. Officers and kings alike were quick to discern that national upheaval encouraged local discord, and the former took steps to prove their devotion to the peace and order too often neglected by the king himself.

Pretenders and the First Tudor

During Henry VII's reign, boroughs had to contend not only with continued internal disorder, but also with the violence spread by pretenders to the throne and their noble adherents. In June 1487, Henry was in Norwich when he heard of Lambert Simnel's arrival in England, and Nottingham was one of the first urban centers he called upon in gathering troops.[76] York suffered much more directly from this early pretender. Asserting that he was the duke of Clarence's son and the Yorkist heir to the throne, Simnel had been crowned Edward VI in Dublin in May, and within a few weeks landed in Lancashire with Irish and Burgundian troops in search of English support. The earl of Lincoln, former head of the Council of the North and Richard III's nephew, joined Lord Francis Lovell in writing to York for permission for the party to enter and rest, but the city council maintained its loyalty to Henry.[77] By early June, York streets filled with armed men, said to have numbered six thousand. When they left town to join the king in Nottinghamshire, John Lord Scrope of Bolton and his cousin Thomas Lord Scrope of Masham attacked the city in the hope of reviving the Middleham-based patronage they had enjoyed while Richard III was alive.[78] They did little physical damage, but succeeded in distracting the earl of Northumberland from marching towards the king. Even without Percy, Henry defeated Simnel's forces at Stoke, and soon after ordered celebrations to be held in York Minster, thus reclaiming his leading northern city.

The earl of Northumberland's fortunes continued to be tied to those of the city. Henry VII's taxation policies and the nature of his rule of northeastern England provoked some serious incidents of lawlessness in York. Taking over where Richard III had left off, Henry refused to allow local magnates or even the Council of the North to exercise quasi-regal power.[79] Although resistance to this change of policy was minimal, suppressed resentment was incited by tax levies that smacked (at least to northerners) of royal greed. Accustomed to being excused from subsidies by the region's good lord Richard III, the north smarted under the first Tudor's demands for a heavy subsidy earmarked for a campaign in Brittany.[80] In April 1489, a new installment of the tax fell due before the former amount was completely collected. Marked refusal to contribute, as well as news of a rebel gathering, prompted the earl of Northumberland to investigate the stubbornness of his own tenants. He was killed for his pains on 28 April, in an uprising of seven hundred rebels near Thirsk.[81]

News of Percy's murder reached York's council the same day, precipitating the mayor to command all aldermen and councilors to stay within the city.[82] The several hundred rebels who pressed on with their grievances in early May found leaders in Sir John Egremont and Robert Chamber. With the assistance of York alderman and Ricardian partisan Thomas Wrangwish, Egremont and his followers stormed the city, entered through Wrangwish's ward damaging Fishergate Bar in the process, and took possession of the city. York had been in confusion all month: Lord Clifford had asked for admittance with one hundred of his men, and although the officers agreed to his entry, the commons of York bitterly refused. The sheriff of Yorkshire was likewise excluded, on the grounds that the city was being kept for the king by the officers alone. This tension lasted for about two weeks, at the end of which time Mayor John Harper consented to Egremont's request for twenty men with horses to ride with him to Richmondshire,

forsomuch as [Egremont] had reule and his people here, that to denye hym they thoght he and his people wold rob the cite, and if he wold pay ther costes in avoding such iuperdies unto the tyme thai myght be better providet that to graunt hym.

However, the rebellion collapsed after these plans were made, in the face of the substantial force the king had raised from amongst the realm's most powerful lords and gentlemen.[83]

Between 29 May and 4 June 1489, a commission of oyer and terminer sat in York's Guildhall and the Castle, headed by the earl of Oxford.[84] Its jurors included various aldermen and city merchants, and one of its first indictments was made against former mayor Thomas Wrangwish. He was charged with having falsely and heinously aroused and procured three men from the Acomb suburb, with other rebels, to help Egremont and Chamber. It was alleged that he had sent several city yeomen and weavers with the Acomb men to join Egremont in battle against the king, and received payment for his assistance. The file also contains a second charge against Wrangwish as warden of Walmgate ward, admitting that there was not enough money to repair Walmgate and Fishergate Bars nor enough men to post in their defense. Nevertheless, Wrangwish was charged with negligence for allowing the rebels to burn the defenses and enter at those points.[85]

Royal justice was applied firmly, but on relatively few of the insurgents. The serious nature of the charge of treason may have stayed the jurors' hands: only five rebels were condemned to death, and not all of them were hanged. When summoned early in 1490, John Egremont did not appear before the justices and could not be found by the sheriff.[86] This was not surprising, for Egremont had fled to the Yorkist court of Margaret of Burgundy, although his accomplice Chamber was captured and executed at York with several of his supporters.[87] Although Thomas Wrangwish was accused of treason and sentenced to hang, he was pardoned late in the year and died in 1490.[88]

The rising and a civic official's part in it prompted Henry to take firmer measures with the city. In March 1491, he wrote to deplore the felonies and riots committed within its walls, "and but letill or no coreccon doon therin."[89] He was especially disturbed by the fact that three city craftsmen who had been condemned as traitors were still free within York despite a sentence of outlawry and an order of arrest direct from the king. Henry then gave the earl of Surrey, head of the Council of the North, the responsibility of checking on the mayor's execution of justice and reporting any lapses, an extension of the Council's duties which Henry had previously been loath to condone. These actions stirred

Mayor William White to direct a letter to Henry, reminding the king that royal letters establishing commissions of the peace allowed the mayor and aldermen, and no one else, to sit in judgment several times a year.[90] White asserted that for the past thirteen years, York had been free of riot and murder, preferring not to remind the king of recent disturbances. Nevertheless, the mayor regretted that economic problems made the pursuit of justice difficult and admitted that peace would come about with as much difficulty as wall repair and the purchase of guns, "as it is evydently and opynly knawen that this your seid Citie is in gret decaye, ruyne and povertie, as knaweth the blessed Trenite...."[91] As always, civic officials under pressure rooted problems of obedience to the Crown in financial difficulties.

Henry VII's impatience with civic peacekeeping stemmed at least in part from the new threat to the throne constituted from 1491 by Perkin Warbeck, a pretender who quickly realized the value of urban alliances. York seemed to have learned some lessons from the previous decade, refusing to be drawn away from obedience to the monarch. As early as 1493, while Perkin's efforts at gaining support still were concentrated on European rulers, the city of York received word about him but made no move to encourage him. Warbeck's later alliance with York's traditional enemy the Scots did nothing to endear the pretender's cause to civic officials.[92]

Of all boroughs, Exeter suffered the most from Warbeck's actions. Early in September 1497, he and a small group of men landed in Cornwall and began collecting forces for an attack on Exeter, the leading borough of the west. The city had recently suffered a siege led mostly by Cornishmen marching to London to demonstrate their distress over the taxes and loans raised to fight Warbeck.[93] Henry VII, advised of the pretender's landing by an efficient system of posts throughout the country, expressed immediate concern for the fate of this vulnerable city. On the evening of 16 September, he wrote to the Courtenay earl of Devon, a Tudor supporter at least since 1483 when he left England to join Henry in exile.[94] The king approved of the military measures Courtenay had already taken and urged him to join forces with the lord chamberlain's army in order to trap Warbeck. By use of a system of placards spread all over the west and in the ports, a reward of one thousand marks was offered for Perkin's capture. In the letter, Henry showed two principal concerns: that Perkin should be taken alive, and that the city of Exeter should not fall into the pretender's hands.

Courtenay was the natural choice for champion of the west country, given his family's relations with the city for over two hundred years.

The rebel forces attacked Exeter the next day, before the king's letter could reach its intended recipient. When the earl refused to surrender the city, Perkin laid siege, setting fire to the gates. The rebels were repelled until the following day, when they entered Exeter much to the surprise of the earl, who was wounded as he came out of his lodgings. By late morning of 18 September, the citizens had defeated the rebels, who retreating northwards. Courtenay wrote the king that only part of Henry's objectives had been achieved, for although Exeter was saved for the king, Perkin had escaped.[95]

Captured by royal forces later in the month, Perkin returned in chains to Exeter where Henry began judicial proceedings against the rebels. Shrewder than Henry VI, the Tudor monarch fully realized the malevolent influence local nobles and gentry could have on the king's peace. Henry was particularly harsh on the magnates and gentlemen of Devonshire, whom he blamed for allowing the rebellion to go so far as to threaten Exeter.[96] From the cathedral treasurer's house, Henry daily viewed the common rebels, forced to beg for mercy beneath his windows. Some were pardoned, many more were fined, and execution was reserved for those deemed to be dangerous leaders. Before leaving the city in November, Henry praised the citizens for their steadfast resistance to rebellion, and gave them a state sword and cap of maintenance to augment civic pride and recognize their obedience to the Crown.[97]

The pretenders' claims are easy to dismiss now, but Henry VII never failed to take them seriously or to lower his expectations of borough loyalty to the Tudor line. Not only did he expect urban officials to suppress treasonous talk and illegal retaining, but also to rise to the physical threat brought to towns by the pretenders' invasions. Violence then became the approved means of response, sanctioned by the royal government and used in its behalf to preserve the true ruler. Military engagement and the penal processes that followed gave violence an essential public role in medieval society, one intended to identify the king as the sole individual rightfully able to wield such a tool. Subjects who learned the wrong lesson, and who adopted violent means themselves, could expect to court punishment for themselves and their communities.

Violence—both its threat and its reality—brought boroughs to Crown attention throughout the later Middle Ages. It was the kind of attention few towns really wanted, particularly when it resulted in loss of civic liberties. Urban officials could blame economic problems, inadequate support from the royal government, or the malign influence of local magnates, but such excuses could not veil the truth of their failure to keep the king's peace to the king's satisfaction. Suffering disorder of any magnitude thrust towns into a passive position, their officers made helpless in their duty to maintain order, and their residents turned from profitable activities to take up the position of victims at best and combatants at worst.

The case studies in this chapter reveal how easily placid urban relations could degenerate into factionalism, oppression, and bloodshed. Throughout the period, towns continued to assess power structures within local government, balancing elite entitlement against broad participation in civic affairs, knowing all the time that failure would only encourage the disenfranchised to turn to violence. Even when the balance had been achieved, divergent interpretations of urban policy could fracture the empowered into discord, for not all who had influence in a town agreed on its direction of growth and its relations with other institutions.

Even more disturbing than internal social disruption were the unnatural relations forced upon towns by local magnates, particularly during periods of weak or recovering monarchical power. Nobles hailed as "good lords" and relied upon to promote town needs within royal and bureaucratic circles turned into bitter enemies of urban peacekeeping as they brought their quarrels within city walls. The individuals sought as guides through the changes of dynasty and claims of pretenders that mark the second half of the fifteenth century could as frequently place urban subjects at odds with the Crown.

This bleak picture is ameliorated less by assertions that violence had little impact than by studies of the actions town governments took to counter its corrosive effect. Civic officials initiated watches and vigils in times of disorder, standing ready to augment military resources that may have been less than impressive. They extended and organized offers of arbitration, often with the participation of local clergy, to keep relations with feuding magnates in balance. They expanded offers of urban patronage to a wider variety of elites, gambling that the familial and governmental connections of at least some of their good lords and ladies would guide them through the dynastic changes of the fifteenth century. And they showed willingness to cooperate with the judicial investigations of the royal government and with the public displays of justice choreographed by the Crown, not least to support the accepted and legally-sanctioned use of violence in medieval society. By such actions, towns sought to identify themselves as the partners of kings, the friends of justice, the local representatives of order and process, and the models for harmonious and prosperous living guaranteed by the blessings of peace.

NOTES

1   The study by Philippa C. Maddern, *Violence and Social Order: East Anglia 1422–1442* (Oxford: Clarendon Press, 1992), is the best example of this re-evaluation of the nature of crime and violence. A masterful examination of complex problems, it nevertheless underestimates the impact of disorder and the threat of violence within an urban context. Richard W. Kaeuper in *War, Justice and Public Order: England and France in the Later Middle Ages* (Oxford: Clarendon Press, 1988), provides valuable insights into the problems arising from a royal government that promised too much in terms of justice. For study of these themes in the reign of a specific monarch, see Edward Powell, *Kingship, Law and Society: Criminal Justice in the Reign of Henry V* (Oxford: Clarendon Press, 1989).

2   R. B. Dobson, ed., *The Peasants' Revolt of 1381* (London: Macmillan, 1970), pp. 256–61; Richard Hart, "A Translation of Thomas of Walsingham's Account of Littester's Rebellion in 1381," *Norfolk Archaeology* 5 (1859): 348–53.

3   *Rot. Parl.*, 3:96–97; Miller, *VCH*, pp. 81–82.

4   R. B. Dobson, "The Risings in York, Beverley and Scarborough, 1380–1381," in *The English Rising of 1381*, ed. R. H. Hilton and T. H. Aston (Cambridge and New York: Cambridge University Press, 1984), p. 120. His court connections alone would have alienated many subjects given the atmosphere of the 1370s.

5   *CCR, 1377–81*, pp. 420, 421, 486–87. A few of the rioters were released the following January, but many waited over a year before being taken into the York mayor's custody.

6   *Ibid.*, pp. 523–25.

7   *York Mem. Bk.*, 1:40; 2:69–70. The monetary fine was £40. In September 1382, royal justices investigating Gisburne's misdeeds heard similar arguments from the mayor's attorney that citizens could not be impleaded outside town walls for offenses committed within York itself: Dobson, "Risings in York, Beverley, and Scarborough," p. 119.

8   Dobson, *Peasants' Revolt*, pp. 288–89; *CCR, 1381–85*, pp. 31, 32, 115; *CPR, 1381–85*, pp. 35, 81, 137, 187, 201; P.R.O., C.47/86/31/830.

9   *CCR, 1381–85*, p. 31; *CPR, 1381–85*, p. 137; P.R.O., E.372/231, mem. 8v; KB.27/482, rex 11.

10 *CPR, 1381–85*, p. 187; *Rot. Parl.*, 3:135–36.
11 Peter McNiven, "The Betrayal of Archbishop Scrope," *The Bulletin of the John Rylands Library* 54 (1971): 177 (quote). The archbishop headed commissions, lent the king money, and received toll payments for passage "across his water at Hullbrigge": *CPR, 1399–1401*, pp. 85, 356, 520; *1401–1405*, pp. 50, 129, 441.
12 McNiven, "Betrayal of Archbishop Scrope," pp. 181–84. See also James Raine, ed., *Historians of the Church of York and Its Archbishops*, 3 vols., Rolls Series, vol. 71 (London, 1879, 1886, 1894), 2:294–311; R. L. Storey, "Clergy and the Common Law," *Medieval Legal Records: Edited in Memory of C. A. F. Meekings*, ed. R. F. Hunnisett and J. B. Post (London: Her Majesty's Stationery Office, 1978), pp. 342–44. For the economic context, see A. J. Pollard, *North-eastern England during the Wars of the Roses: Lay Society, War, and Politics 1450–1500* (Oxford: Clarendon Press, 1990), pp. 43–52, 71–73.
13 McNiven, "Betrayal of Archbishop Scrope," pp. 186–200 (quote p. 192).
14 P.R.O., C.81/1541/20.
15 P.R.O., C.81/1358/42; *CPR, 1405–1408*, pp. 58, 66; *CFR, 1399–1405*, p. 310.
16 P.R.O., SC.6/1088/16. Frost had served Henry IV loyally for several years, raising loans and inspecting Crown property, receiving in 1404 a royal grant of wine for life: Jennifer I. Kermode, *Medieval Merchants: York, Beverley and Hull in the Later Middle Ages* (Cambridge: Cambridge University Press, 1998), p. 50.
17 *CFR, 1399–1405*, p. 310; *CCR, 1402–1405*, p. 405. Henry's generosity continued into the spring of 1406, when he granted murage and pontage for the citizens' benefit: *CPR, 1405–1408*, pp. 166, 171.
18 *CPR, 1405–1408*, p. 76. Henry IV's consort Joan was set to profit from fines consequent upon York's seizure of liberties, but the sheriffs gained exemption from the payment: *York Mem. Bk.*, 2:38.
19 *CPR, 1405–1408*, pp. 153–54, 183.
20 Certain canons may also have been involved in Scrope's uprising, given their haste to obtain royal confirmation of their grants and the examples of resignation from prebends: Storey, "Clergy and Common Law," pp. 394–95. Miracles were said to have taken place at the tomb, and pilgrims made contributions in hope of special favors. York's serjeants-at-arms received orders from the Crown to prevent worship at the tomb, but when they obeyed royal command they were dismissed by the mayor. Wills dated as late as 1458 record bequests of Scrope's personal belongings, preserved as sacred relics, as well as gifts of money to the keeper of the tomb: *York Mem. Bk.*, 1:236–38; John McKenna, "Popular Canonization as Political Propaganda: The Cult of Archbishop Scrope," *Speculum* 45 (1970): 608–13; James Raine, ed., *Testamenta Eboracensia, Volume II*, Surtees Society, vol. 30 (London and Durham, 1855), pp. 231–33.
21 See above, pp. 260–64.
22 *Norwich Records*, 1:348; William Blake, "Thomas Wetherby," *Norfolk Archaeology* 32 (1961): 60; Winifred I. Haward, "Economic Aspects of the Wars of the Roses in East Anglia," *English Historical Review* 41 (1926): 175–76. Wetherby served on royal commissions, invested in county property, and married his daughter Elizabeth to Norwich counselor and M.P. John Jenney: James Gairdner, ed., *The Paston Letters*, 6 vols. (London: Chatto and Windus, 1904; New York: AMS Press, 1965), 3:39.

[23] *Norwich Records*, 1:330–35, 345 (Heydon's dismissal); Maddern, *Violence and Social Order*, pp. 183–85. His associates' fines were waived upon the men's humble submission, indicating that recognition of the transgression of civic peace was the panel's true object rather than vindictive punishment: Ben R. McRee, "Peacemaking and its Limits in Late Medieval Norwich," *English Historical Review* 109 (1994): 858.

[24] *Norwich Records*, 1:329–30, 348; 2:68.

[25] John Watts, *Henry VI and the Politics of Kingship* (Cambridge: Cambridge University Press, 1996), pp. 157 note 132 (stewardship beginning July 1433), 176–78.

[26] Maddern, *Violence and Social Order*, p. 176. As certified to the king eighteen days later, Norwich's elections were interrupted by a group of eight citizens led by Wetherby's chief opponent Robert Toppes, a former mayor who had served in office in 1435. Toppes and his fellows were joined by members of one of the city's guilds, the Bacherie, and later by a crowd of two thousand in the marketplace. A small group of craftsmen then attacked Wetherby's friend Grey, stopped the sheriff from arresting one of the insurgents, and plucked a dagger from the sheriff's belt, "seying that thei shuld suffre no man to be arested that day there for no maner of cause, and also seyng trew don that grotbelly to the ground, namyng the [justice of the peace Thomas Ingham] grotbelly." Toppes' servant then attacked Wetherby personally, and a group of 59 craftsmen (ranging from goldsmiths to weavers) began their assault. They refused to let anyone enter the Guildhall to vote in the elections except those of their own opinion, so frightening their opponents that the latter offered no resistance: P.R.O., KB.9/229/1, mem.106. See also KB.29/71, mem.2v. Other historians who accepted the traditional view of these events as marked by horrendous violence are William Hudson and John C. Tingey, editors of the Norwich records (*Norwich Records*, 1:lxxxiii–xciii); and R. L. Storey, *The End of the House of Lancaster* (London: Barrie and Rockliff, 1966; Gloucester: Alan Sutton Publishing, 1986), pp. 217–25.

[27] Nicholas H. Nicolas, ed., *Proceedings and Ordinances of the Privy Council of England*, 7 vols. (London: Record Commission, 1834–37), 5:34, 45; *CPR, 1436–41*, pp. 76, 89.

[28] Nicolas, *Privy Council*, 5:76–78. Cloth was exempted so Henry could receive its profits.

[29] *CPR, 1436–41*, p. 146; *Norwich Records*, 1:283; N.R.O., 16-d, Assembly Book I, f.7.

[30] *Norwich Records*, 1:283; P.R.O., E.28/63, f.34; *CPR, 1436–41*, p. 357.

[31] Maddern, *Violence and Social Order*, pp. 190–92.

[32] NNRO, 9-c; 16-d, f.4r (levy of 6d. on each citizen to cover the city's cost in defense); Maddern, *Violence and Social Order*, pp. 193–94. The abbot of St. Benet's, Holm, complained about damage done his area by the city's New Mills: see above, pp. 219–20. The abbot of Wendling had an issue with the city over a rented quay. The abbot of Walsingham's complaint was not recorded.

[33] *Norwich Records*, 1:lxxxviii (discussion of the statute 28 Edward III, c.9), 325–28.

[34] N.R.O., 9-c (award); 8-a, no.10, presentments 1440 (attacks).

[35] *Norwich Records*, 1:340–41 (an account written in 1482 can be found *ibid.*, 1:348–51); P.R.O., KB.9/84/1. Maddern, *Violence and Social Order*, p. 198 denies that it

was a riot. See the more balanced comments in McRee, "Peacemaking and its Limits," 865.

[36] *Norwich Records*, 1:328 (East Dereham commission of 23 September), 351–55 (arrest and fine).

[37] Nicolas, *Privy Council*, 5:242–43, 306–307. The council was so sure of the collective fine of 3000 marks that the sum was immediately allocated for the victualing of the "bastile of Dieppe."

[38] P.R.O., E.28/71, f.49; E.28/72, ff.23, 38, 53.

[39] Partly to blame was the destruction of the New Mills, used by local bakers and other citizens, and contributing £26 *per annum* to the fee farm: see above, p. 220.

[40] *Norwich Records*, 1:347; P.R.O., KB.9/272; Storey, *House of Lancaster*, pp. 224–25.

[41] *Norwich Records*, 1:342–43; McRee, "Peacemaking and its Limits," 865; Ben R. McRee, "Religious Gilds and Civic Order: The Case of Norwich in the Late Middle Ages," *Speculum* 67 (1992): 90–92.

[42] *Norwich Records*, 1:344–47.

[43] Anthony Goodman, *The Wars of the Roses* (London: Routledge and Kegan Paul, 1981), pp. 221–22, 227–28. See above, p. 198.

[44] *York Mem. Bk.*, 2:200–201; P.R.O., E.28/70/2/92; E.28/71/1/41. The city council acted on the letter by establishing a fine of £5 for those so endangering urban franchises.

[45] *Nott. Records*, 2:368–69; Goodman, *Wars of the Roses*, pp. 203–4. See above, p. 198. Nottingham also suffered from such upheaval during the 1480s when Henry Willoughby and Edward Grey Lord Lisle violently pursued a private feud during the sessions: *Report on the Manuscripts of Lord Middleton*, Historical Manuscripts Commission (London: His Majesty's Stationery Office, 1911), pp. 118–20.

[46] *CPR, 1446–52*, pp. 41–42.

[47] Landed income fell 10–15% by 1440 after years of agrarian crisis, a fact of greater moment to the Percies because of their diminished land resources: Pollard, *North-eastern England during the Wars of the Roses*, pp. 71–72; *idem*, "The North-Eastern Economy and the Agrarian Crisis of 1438–40," *Northern History* 25 (1989): 104–105.

[48] Ralph A. Griffiths, "Local Rivalries and National Politics: The Percies, the Nevilles, and the Duke of Exeter, 1452–1455," *Speculum* 43 (1968): 594–99, 602–603; Pollard, *North-eastern England during the Wars of the Roses*, pp. 248, 253–54, 255–57; Watts, *Henry VI and the Politics of Kingship*, pp. 300–3.

[49] Two months after the initial attack, the recorder of York and three city counselors visited the earl of Salisbury with messages from the mayor, who offered to arbitrate in the quarrels of the Nevilles and Egremont: Dobson, *Chamberlains' Accounts*, p. 77.

[50] P.R.O., KB.9/148/7; *Rot. Parl.*, 5:394–96.

[51] P.R.O., KB.9/148/1, mem. 15; KB.9/149/1, mem. 39. For Holand's reasons for disliking the Nevilles, see Ralph A. Griffiths, *The Reign of Henry VI* (Berkeley and Los Angeles: University of California Press, 1981), pp. 719–25; S. J. Payling, "The Ampthill Dispute: A Study in Aristocratic Lawlessness and the Breakdown of Lancastrian Government," *English Historical Review* 104 (1989): 884–85, 888.

52 Storey, *House of Lancaster*, pp. 144–49; Griffiths, "Local Rivalries," 615–20; Nicolas, *Proceedings of the Privy Council*, 6:189–90. For the indictments of the commission, see P.R.O., KB.29/89. Egremont remained at large, gathered more forces, and suffered capture at Stamford Bridge October 1454. He died amidst the royal army at the battle of Northampton 10 July 1460.

53 Nicolas, *Proceedings of the Privy Council*, 5:158–61, 165, 173–75. For the appointments, see *CPR, 1436–41*, pp. 133 (Bonville, 1437), 532 (Devon, 1441).

54 Storey, *House of Lancaster*, pp. 90–92; G. L. Harriss and M. A. Harriss, eds., "John Benet's Chronicle," in *Camden Miscellany XXIV*, Camden Society, 4th series, vol. 9 (London, 1972), pp. 167–68, 205–206.

55 *CCR, 1447–54*, p. 512; P.R.O., E.28/85; Martin Cherry, "The Crown and the Political Community in Devonshire 1377–1461," (Ph.D. diss., University College of Swansea, University of Wales, 1981), pp. 291–92. The earl himself, until recently a royal council member, had been ordered to keep the peace under penalty of £1000; after the April attack, the bond rose to £2666 13s. 4d.

56 P.R.O., KB.9/275, mem. 137.

57 Gairdner, ed., *The Paston Letters*, 3:48–50; Mrs. G. H. Radford (Lady Radford), "The Fight at Clyst in 1455," *Transactions of the Devonshire Association* 44 (1912): 255–57; idem, "Nicholas Radford," *Transactions of the Devonshire Association* 35 (1903): 252–53, 256, 264, 270; J. G. Bellamy, *Crime and Public Order in England in the Later Middle Ages* (London: Routledge and Kegan Paul, 1973), pp. 55–57; J. R. Lander, "Henry VI and the duke of York's second protectorate, 1455–6," in *Crown and Nobility 1450–1509* (London: Edward Arnold, 1976), pp. 85–86.

58 Radford, "Fight at Clyst," 260–62; D.R.O., Receivers' Roll, 34–35 Henry VI; Book 51, f.310v.

59 *Rot. Parl.*, 5:285–86; P. A. Johnson, *Duke Richard of York 1411–1460* (Oxford: Clarendon Press, 1988), pp. 168–69.

60 Nicolas, *Proceedings of the Privy Council*, 6:267–68.

61 Storey, *House of Lancaster*, p. 173; Lander, "Second Protectorate," pp. 87–90.

62 *CPR, 1452–61*, p. 304.

63 Storey, *House of Lancaster*, pp. 173–74. See above, p. 109.

64 D.R.O., Book 51, f.313v, *sub* 1460–61.

65 *History of the City and County of Norwich, from the Earliest Accounts to the Present Times* (Norwich: John Crouse, 1768), p. 138.

66 *CPR, 1461–67*, pp. 35, 101, 232 (for the years 1461 and 1463).

67 N.R.O., 16-d, Assembly Book I, f.54.

68 *CPR, 1461–67*, pp. 33 (June), 102 (July).

69 D.R.O., Receivers' Roll, 8–9 Edward IV; Book 51, f.317.

70 Details of the following can be found in Michael A. Hicks, *False, Fleeting, Perjur'd Clarence* (Gloucester: Alan Sutton Publishing, 1980), pp. 71–72; D.R.O., Book 51, ff.316r–v; Book 55, f.40.

71 The knight's aims were personal, directed against Lords FitzWarin and Dynham who had come to the city to arrest Hugh on the king's orders. Since 22 March, Hugh had stopped traffic entering the city and prevented markets from being held and food distributed. Hugh demanded the keys to the gates, threatening ruin to all within. FitzWarin and Dynham put added pressure on the civic officials, and the townspeople complained about the lack of food. The mayor, however, withstood all

the importuning and raised the siege with the help of cathedral canons who acted as arbitrators. As Hoker recalled, "great were the trobles to the whole citie, but yn greater perplexitie stode the mayor and his brethren and being as it were assayled mony wayes could not fynde one way how to be safed and releaved": D.R.O., Book 51, f.316.

72   See above, p. 81.

73   D.R.O., Book 51, f.317.

74   See above, pp. 109, 110.

75   N.R.O., 16-d, Assembly Bk. I, f.90; *Nott. Records*, 2:384–87. Edward also took the opportunity to scold local noble Henry Lord Grey of Codnor for retaining Nottingham residents. Grey, however, denied that the rioters were his men.

76   Michael Van Cleave Alexander, *The First of the Tudors: A Study of Henry VII and His Reign* (Totowa, New Jersey: Rowman and Littlefield, 1980), pp. 56–57. Norwich excused itself from providing soldiers with a gift of £40: see above, p. 201.

77   York officials in fact sent the letter to the earl of Northumberland, with copies to the king: *York House Books*, pp. 570–71. Henry and Percy were already aware of a threat: two months earlier, the officials forwarded to them the confession of a man who accused Lincoln of plotting rebellion: *ibid.*, pp. 540–43. At that time, Percy advised no more than caution, but later took the threat seriously. York's own, flattering account of the Simnel invasion and the measures it took can be found *ibid.*, pp. 571–73, 577. The most recent discussion and analysis of the Simnel threat is Michael Bennett, *Lambert Simnel and the Battle of Stoke* (New York: St. Martin's Press, 1987), but still valuable is Robert Davies, "Original Documents relating to Lambert Symnell's Rebellion in the Second Year of King Henry VII," in *Memoirs Illustrative of the History and Antiquities of the County and City of York* (London: Architectural Institute of Great Britain and Ireland, 1848), pp. 1–32.

78   Lorraine C. Attreed, "An Indenture between Richard Duke of Gloucester and the Scrope Family of Masham and Upsall, Yorkshire," *Speculum* 58 (1983): 1018–25.

79   Pollard, *North-eastern England during the Wars of the Roses*, pp. 392, 404.

80   A. K. McHardy, "Clerical Taxation in Fifteenth-Century England: The Clergy as Agents of the Crown," in *The Church, Politics, and Patronage in the Fifteenth Century*, ed. Barrie Dobson (Gloucester: Alan Sutton Publishing, 1984), pp. 181, 188.

81   Michael A. Hicks, "Dynastic Change and Northern Society: The Career of the Fourth Earl of Northumberland, 1470–89," *Northern History* 14 (1978): 78–79; *idem*, "The Yorkshire Rebellion of 1489 Reconsidered," *Northern History* 22 (1986): 40–44, 61–62; James Gairdner, *Henry the Seventh* (London: Macmillan and Co., 1899), pp. 72–73. Percy's death has been the subject of much speculation, and some historians have followed Francis Bacon's lead in interpreting it as just punishment meted out by Ricardian sympathizers resentful over the earl's perceived lack of military assistance at Bosworth: Francis Bacon, *The History of King Henry VII*, vol. 6 of *The Works of Francis Bacon*, edited by James Spedding *et al.* (London: Longmans, 1858), pp. 88–89.

82   For what follows, see *York House Books*, pp. 647, 649–51 (quote at p. 651).

83   Michael J. Bennett, "Henry VII and the Northern Rising of 1489," *English Historical Review* 105 (1990): 44–45. Bennett argues that the power of the force

raised "testifies as much to the weakness as to the strength of the Tudor regime": *ibid.*, pp. 48–49.

[84]   P.R.O., KB.9/381; *CPR,1485–94*, p. 285. For discussion of the indictment file, see Hicks, "Yorkshire Rebellion," 42–43.

[85]   P.R.O., KB.9/381, mm. 3, 6, 38; Hicks, "Dynastic Change," 78–79.

[86]   P.R.O., KB.9/382; KB.27/914, Hilary 1490. The case was postponed until Easter term, when Egremont still did not appear: KB.27/915. His case was adjourned until 1491, as were the trials of some of his supporters.

[87]   Bacon, *Henry VII*, p. 89; Gairdner, *Henry VII*, pp. 72–73; Francis Drake, *Eboracum* (London: W. Bowyer, 1736), p. 306; Rachel R. Reid, *King's Council in the North* (London: Longmans, 1921; Totowa, N.J.: Rowman and Littlefield, 1975), p. 76. All assert that Chamber's first name was John (following the author of the *Great Chronicle of London*, and Polydore Vergil), but the indictments list him as Robert.

[88]   P.R.O., KB.29/120.

[89]   *York Civic Records*, 2:65. Henry had written a similar letter to Coventry in 1490: Mary D. Harris, ed. *The Coventry Leet Book*, 2 vols., Early English Text Society, o.s., vols. 134–35, 138 & 146 (London, 1907, 1913), 1:538–39.

[90]   *York Civic Records*, 2:69.

[91]   *Ibid.*, 2:70. For difficulties in paying for measures of defense, see above pp. 185–86.

[92]   *Rot. Parl.*, 6:503–505. One York merchant was attainted for plotting on Warbeck's behalf with former Exeter customer John Tayllour: see above, p. 248. A similar case emerged in Nottingham, when town officers tried to determine whether a citizen had sworn to help the Scots invade the north on Warbeck's behalf, only to decide that the accusation arose from a vindictive personal quarrel: *Nott. Records*, 3:401, and above, p. 210 note 89.

[93]   Ian Arthurson, "The Rising of 1497: A Revolt of the Peasantry?" in *People, Politics and Community in the Later Middle Ages*, ed. Joel Rosenthal and Colin Richmond (Gloucester: Alan Sutton Publishing, 1987), p. 10. For fuller discussion and analysis of the rising and its consequences, see Ian Arthurson, *The Perkin Warbeck Conspiracy 1491–1499* (Stroud: Alan Sutton Publishing Ltd., 1994), pp. 162–68, 181–83.

[94]   Lorraine C. Attreed, "A New Source for Perkin Warbeck's Invasion of 1497," *Mediaeval Studies* 48 (1986): 519–21; Arthurson, *Perkin Warbeck Conspiracy*, pp. 184–88.

[95]   Attreed, "New Source," 518. This second letter is printed in Henry Ellis, ed., *Original Letters Illustrative of English History*, 3 vols. (London: Harding, Triphook, and Lepard, 1824), 1:36–37.

[96]   D.R.O., Book 51, f.328v.

[97]   *Ibid.*, f.329v; Arthurson, "Rising of 1497," p. 14. For analysis of the process as a judicial spectacle, see above, pp. 79–80. Other towns were not as lucky: Somerset merchants had been more active in Perkin's favor and were heavily fined for their disloyalty, especially the civic officials of Wells. Royal records indicate that Henry assessed fines of over £14,000 even before an act of attainder was passed in 1504: Ellis, *Original Letters*, 1:38–39; C. G. Bayne and William H. Dunham, Jr., eds., *Select Cases in the Council of Henry VII*, Selden Society, vol. 75 (London, 1956), p. clxxiv.

PART FIVE

CONCLUSION

No king of the fourteenth or fifteenth centuries spared us the trouble of conjecture by articulating a clear policy statement on the role of towns in the English realm. The closest we come to such an account can be found in Henry VII's threatening admonition to York's authorities after riots had fractured the peace and respect for law essential to both town and Crown. By 1495, the commons' riots over suburban lands controlled by various religious houses had prompted the king to demand the personal presence of the mayor and other officers at Greenwich. They were joined there by the earl of Surrey in his role as head of the Council of the North, a body to which they disliked turning even when unable to keep the peace themselves.

The king began by praising the city of York for its long history of honor and prosperity, a direct result of the wise and prudent rule of past officers. In that golden age, the authorities had executed laws that were both their own and the king's, and they ruled the city as though the king were present in his own person. If they could not return to that happy state, Henry would be forced to impose officers of his own choosing, much as that distressed the local rulers, for he could not allow the city to deteriorate either legally or economically. He then dismissed them with the admonition to keep the peace and the king's laws, and to turn to Surrey and the Council of the North if they needed help. If they followed such advice, the king in turn promised to be "good and graciouse lord to you and to all the other my citicins and inhabitauntes ther in there reasonable desires...."[1]

York's scolding epitomizes a number of themes in Crown-town relations, but it is far from a perfect summation of the relationship. Its most interesting element is the concept of the legal fiction of the king's presence, made a reality by the respectful governing of the officers according to the monarch's laws. Those laws belonged both to the king and to his urban subjects, and their correct execution brought forth conditions of honor and prosperity fruitful to all parties. As we have seen throughout the period, attaching a financial element to a plea for help or obedience increased its chances of being taken seriously by king and citizen alike. Henry's low tolerance of opposition also raises the possibility that he would indeed have acted upon his threat to impose officers of his own choosing. After all, he had not been shy in nominating swordbearers and recorders, and this threat is used by Tudor historians as evidence of the interventionist and authoritarian nature of the "new monarchy."[2]

But it is unlikely that Henry would have risked that much ill-will in a leading borough, particularly at a time when he needed a loyal showing of unity against pretenders to his throne. Nevertheless, the censure neatly summarizes the strengths and weaknesses of the basic relationship: urban subjects had to determine how to govern themselves successfully and independently, because if they failed to maintain peace and order the source of their privileges would repossess their liberties and deny them autonomy. Many of England's towns had struggled since at least the eleventh century to attain a considerable degree of independence in judicial, financial, and administrative affairs. But the fact remained that the very nature of their endowments thrust them into a permanent state of adolescence, yearning for freedom and chafing at restrictions yet dependent upon a stronger progenitorial figure for protection and especially for financing.

The extended time period over which this study takes place allows us to track certain evolutionary tendencies in the relationship between borough and king. There is, however, little indication that any unprecedented growth of royal power can be discerned through the lens of urban policy. Although the concept of a "new monarchy" has been largely discredited, and Yorkist and early Tudor reigns searched in vain for practical or theoretical innovations, there remains the impression that Edward IV and Henry VII must have been achieving something new and effective in public policy regarding towns.[3] Contributing to that impression, and to a great extent forming it, is the nature of the sources. As stark financial accounts and local court records are augmented by council minutes and complemented by gentry letter collections, we gain more explicit and detailed narratives but not necessarily proof of changing policies. Moreover, the salient elements of the "new monarchy"—reliance upon household government, regional and specialist councils and chamber finance rather than established departments of state—touched very little upon the essential ways most boroughs continued to relate to the Crown. Nor is there strong evidence that later kings had a tighter hold over their towns than earlier ones. Richard II's concept of towns was in keeping with his understanding of government in general, as the means to insure his sovereign rule, revealed most starkly by his punishment of London and favoring of York. There is nothing in his philosophy of power, much less in his actions towards towns and their liberties, that would have prevented him from threatening a lawless borough just as Henry VII did a century later. Henry VI, a king not particularly noted for his assertive rule, punished Norwich harshly by removing its liberties twice during his reign, action more in keeping with thirteenth-century, or even sixteenth-century monarchs of far greater force.

The changes we can successfully track occurred on more subtle levels than the mere progression of royal successions. Changes in the economy following the earliest bouts of the Black Death are far more rewarding to measure, although there is no need to impose Marxist models on urban behavior. Whether towns thought they were on the brink of economic disaster or managing their debts quite well, their economic outlook is a vital element but it did not determine the full spectrum of their relations with the royal government. At the very least, however, the study of four very different towns inhibits broad generalizations about financial health. Local industry, international trade patterns, competition from London, internal guild restrictions, beneficent or malicious neighbors, and recovery from debt combined in differing proportions to provide towns with unique foundations from which to exercise and augment their privileges. York and Norwich both served as regional administrative and ecclesiastical centers, active in the wool and cloth trades and supplying manufactured goods to the countryside in return for its provisions. Yet the former suffered decline in population and prosperity after the first quarter of the fifteenth century while the latter enjoyed growth and rising status, all because of their differing responses to these factors and others. Providing some shading to this stark contrast are the examples of Exeter and Nottingham. The southwestern port was on the verge of greatness, enabled in no small way by careful financial management and a balanced spectrum of noble patrons and legal advisors. Slightly smaller in size and prospects, Nottingham had no such brilliant future to anticipate, but its very lack of extreme poverty, violence, and decay provides the note of moderation needed in a comparative study.

As the last two examples indicate, not all towns experienced poverty and decay during the post-plague decades. However, most of them employed the vocabulary of economic complaint to spice their requests and sober their excuses. Every borough had to meet internal expenses to maintain the fabric and personnel of urban government, but all had debts to the Crown as well. Of these four towns, only York had serious and sincere problems meeting local and royal demands. Yet all four recognized the power of pleas of poverty, employing them consistently to remind the king that urban financial health was intimately connected to the realm's well-being.

By the second quarter of the fifteenth century, towns used descriptions of hardship whether real or fictional not only to reduce tax and loan demands, but to excuse themselves from military contributions, to extract fairs and trade concessions, and explain why the peace was imperfectly kept. Such excuses had moderate success but never released boroughs from all of their responsibilities. Unlike their Iberian counterparts, English townsmen did not constitute the best-trained military force, but kings relied upon their contributions of men and materiel not least for the sense of connection they forged to national campaigns. Yet it was not the battles in France that were blamed by contemporaries for draining local resources and diminishing loyalty for the monarch, but the frequent mustering for dynastic battles after the mid-fifteenth century and their attendant raids against the Scots. Valiant attempts by all four of the towns to meet royal military demands did not go unnoticed by kings, whose appreciation of their contributions allowed them to accept pleas of poverty with greater goodwill. Boroughs' crafty connection of local conditions to policies of the realm also brought them some trade advantages. Fairs, highway construction, and toll exemptions cost kings little to grant and increased the revenue useful for royal budgets. No amount of complaint, however, persuaded monarchs to allow local desires to interfere with national patterns of commerce or relations with foreign merchants essential to the realm's balance of trade.

In every town's experience there were some areas in which financial solvency, or a pretense at such, was essential. Even during the later Middle Ages, boroughs still craved administrative privileges most securely attained by royal charter. Not all were headed by mayors; some desired county status or a more formal corporate nature, while all valued the simple confirmation of older charters by a new monarch. None of these gifts was likely to be granted to a town truly destitute, decayed, and abandoned by its population. In granting officers and rights of self-government, the monarch delegated royal power to local authorities he had to be able to trust absolutely. He could not have been unaware that chartered rights required intelligent civic leaders to apply them fairly to real problems and human subjects. Like every other member of society, the king relied chiefly upon a town's social leaders, the political elite of the realm, to rule. Such men of wealth and mercantile experience applied their sharp business skills to the task of steering a town into peace and prosperity, creating a collegial relationship profitable to both borough and Crown.[4] How successfully they executed this duty could be checked during a royal visit, when urban subjects had the chance to display the fruits of flourishing self-government while educating the source of their privileges in what remained to be granted. Even towns knowing real hardship found the funds necessary to provide the pageants, feasts, and gifts necessary for welcoming visiting royalty. Likewise, budgets were stretched to cover the offerings extended to nobles, gentry, and civil servants identified as useful patrons with court connections able to promote the welfare of a generous town.

Keeping the king's peace and upholding laws that were both local and national provided civic authorities with their greatest challenges, as York's authorities in particular learned to their distress. Urban subjects quickly discerned the economic element in peacekeeping as well, excusing their lapses by citing the financial problems that denied them equipment or which agitated destitute inhabitants beyond control. But pleas of poverty made their least impact in the realm of justice. A monarch could manage without urban revenue, at least for a limited time, given the small proportion it contributed to the realm's wealth. He could not tolerate lapses in peacekeeping because the maintenance of laws granted by the king formed an essential part of royal strength and national unity. As has been carefully studied for the realm as a whole, medieval subjects held increasingly high expectations of justice and especially the royal courts as the fifteenth century progressed. These ideals may not by themselves have decreased incidents of violence or inequity in medieval society, but they did make subjects and especially town officers sensitive to their presence and intolerant of their practice. The five case studies examined in this work fully reveal the apprehension of boroughs victimized by violence and the alacrity with which the

Crown responded to those threats. Royal removal of urban privileges, from York after Archbishop Scrope's rebellion and twice from Norwich during bitter factionalism, constituted the harshest punishment by reminding a town of the distress and power of the source of their liberties.

But keeping the king's peace involved more than police duties of watch and ward. Although urban subjects had access to courts and mediation within their boroughs, and their civic officials gained the powers of justices of the peace, nothing deterred them from seeking settlement in royal courts or through the intervention of royal servants. Equity and prerogative courts heard urban cases brought by those who genuinely sought impartial justice there as well as by those intent on harassing their opponents. Far more complex were those cases relinquished to arbitration, often arranged and sometimes personally executed by the lord chancellor himself. Financial stresses emerge in many urban disputes with neighboring institutions over land claims, particularly when suburbs were kept from townspeople desperate for pasture. But the arbitration cases have greater import, for they forced civic authorities to contemplate the very nature of the town. They pursued these cases, often over several decades, in the conviction that constitutional privileges ought to be exercised over the widest possible physical extent of a town, and that the peace and prosperity of an entity held for both the king and his people depended upon that full exercise. Navigating royal courts, identifying helpful patrons, searching archives, and articulating demands acquainted provincial townsmen with more sophisticated techniques of rule than they often experienced at home. Those activities accelerated a town's progress out of dependent adolescence into a more mature understanding of borough needs and nature.

To a great extent, identity lies in the eye of the beholder. To monarchs of the later Middle Ages, their royal boroughs were centers battered by plague mortality, which truthfully or not claimed that they could not make the same financial contributions to the realm as they had in previous centuries. Crown policy towards these centers balanced their needs against the ways in which they could be encouraged to help themselves, and against the needs of the realm as a whole. Yet the boroughs remained vital links to the provinces, exhibiting loyalty and obedience that provided valuable models for behavior within the entire realm. As Henry VII reminded York, they implemented royal laws to make real the presence of the king within the town, a presence more paternal and overbearing than many of them appreciated. Henry bridled when he discerned that civic authorities did not fully share his understanding of the role of a town. But townspeople naturally had their own concept of urban identity.

Our emphasis in this study has been on the officeholding class, because those men had the most direct relations with the royal government. We have seen that through the acquisition of chartered liberties and the exercise of their delegated powers, most particularly in legal matters, those officers gained crucial experience. The rulers of towns both big and small, prosperous or failing, all struggled to break free of a relationship that by its nature made them dependent. They sought to strike a balance between subservience to the Crown and the considered employment of its services. If they could not change the fact that they acquired freedoms, financing, and privileges through royal grace, they could make sure that they received all the advantages they deserved and which would bring about the greatest benefits for the town. If their own honor and prosperity increased as a result, that hardly made them unfit to govern. As Henry explained to York, kings expected their civic authorities to rule "wisely, poliktikly and accordyng to due justice to the encrece and prosperite of my said citie." The execution of that directive forged a new role for towns in late medieval society, one that accepted the responsibilities that come with privilege and the independence that is the gift of maturity.

NOTES

1   Y.C.A., B7, f.129 (*York Civic Records*, 2:116, omits this penultimate line).
2   S. J. Gunn, *Early Tudor Government, 1485–1558* (New York: St. Martin's Press, 1995), p. 59; John Watts, "'A New Ffundacion of is Crowne': Monarchy in the Age of Henry VII," in *The Reign of Henry VII: Proceedings of the 1993 Harlaxton Symposium*, ed. Benjamin Thompson (Stamford: Paul Watkins, 1995), pp. 31–53.
3   For general discussion of the origins and profit of such a line of inquiry, see A. J. Pollard, *The Wars of the Roses* (New York: St. Martin's Press, 1988), pp. 95–104; J. R. Lander, *The Limitations of English Monarchy in the Later Middle Ages* (Toronto: University of Toronto Press, 1989), pp. 53–55; and Christine Carpenter, *The Wars of the Roses: Politics and the Constitution in England, c.1437–1509* (Cambridge: Cambridge University Press, 1997), ch. 11 *passim*, and bibliographic essay pp. 278–80.

4   G. L. Harriss, "Political Society and the Growth of Government in Late Medieval England," *Past and Present* 138 (Feb. 1993): 56–57.

BIBLIOGRAPHY

A. Archival Sources

British Library, London
Additional MS. 46354, Sir Thomas Wriothesley's Book of Arms

Dean and Chapter Archives, Exeter
Documents relating to jurisdiction dispute with city:
Piece numbers 503, 2093, 2114–2119, 2291, 2335, 2337, 2361, 2849/2, 2883, 2884, 2890, 2892, 2899, 2977, 3498, 3679, 4720, 3550 (Chapter Act Book 1382–1434).

Devon Record Office, Exeter
Act Book I, 1508–1538; Act Book II, 1509–1560
Book 51, Hoker's Annals: The Commonplace Book of John Vowell alias Hoker
Book 55, Freemen's Book
City Charters
D 267, 282, 283, Document Collection, Thomas Calwodeley bequest, 1496
Letters 1 (29 June *tempore* Henry VII); 2 (23 June 1508); 312 (1537)
Mayor's Court Roll, 1458–59
Miscellaneous Rolls 2, 3, 6, 82
Receivers' Rolls/Accounts, 1 Richard II–1 Henry VIII

Norfolk Record Office, Norwich
7a-g, Treasurers' and Chamberlains' Accounts, and miscellaneous accounts
7-I, Subsidy returns and assessments, 1350s–1570s
8-a-10, Presentments to Norwich justices of the peace, 1440–41
8-a-11, Plea of fresh force, 1459
8-c-2, Exemplification of London charters, 1377–78
8-c-3 & 4, Petitions concerning Sir Thomas Erpingham, 1414
8-c-5, Ordinances for city government, 1415
8-c-6, Inspeximus of Henry VI of constitutions of and restrictions on the mayor, aldermen and citizens made for their good and quiet government, 1424
8-c-7, Charter 33 Edward I, extracted from Plea Rolls 1306
8-c-8, Draft petition to Edward IV, 1461
8-c-9, Abstract of Edward IV's second charter, 1462
8-c-11, Arbitration of corporations of Norwich and London 1516, concerning imposition of bailage
8-c-13, Notes on lands held by prior of Norwich and on disputes with corporation, sixteenth century

9-a-2, List of rights claimed by cathedral priory, n.d.

9-a-4, Statement of rights of the prior, n.d.

9-a-5, Statement of contents of charters Richard I, Henry III, Edward I, concerning rights of city and priory

9-b-1, Exemplification of composition between priory and citizens concerning disputed lands, 1306

9-b-5&6, Pleas in dispute between city and prioress of Carrow, 1416

9-b-7, Inquisition at Cringleford concerning city encroachments in suburbs, 1417

9-c-1, Documents relating to Wetherby dispute, 1433–34

9-c-2, Complaint of city officials against Thomas Tudenham and others, 1434–35

9-c-4, Presentment of city against Tudenham and others

9-c-5, Royal inspeximus exemplifying proceedings against Wetherby, 1437

9-c-6, Complaints of mayor against prior and convent, 1440s

9-c-7, Commission of enquiry into encroachment on liberty of prior and transcript of pleas presented in King's Bench 1441–42

9-c-8, Articles and replies between mayor and commonalty, the bishop of Norwich, the abbot of St. Benet, the prior of the cathedral church, and the abbot of Wendling, concerning the New Mills etc., 1438–40

9-c-9, Miscellaneous documents concerning disputes of 1440s

9-c-10, Letters from duke of Norfolk to city concerning Wetherby

9-c-11, Fragmentary transcript of pleas in King's Bench concerning encroachment on liberty of prior, 1442

9-c-12, Petition to bishop of earl of Suffolk to intercede with Henry VI for restitution of city liberties, 1442

9-c-13, Drafts of letters, etc. relating to disputes, 1442

9-c-14, Award of earl of Suffolk concerning disputes between city and ecclesiastical bodies, 1442

9-c-15, List of articles in disputes between city and ecclesiastical bodies, 1442; drafts of petition to earl of Suffolk for "reformation" of his award 1442–43

9-c-16, List of matters in dispute between city and prior, n.d.

9-c-17, Indenture made between John abbot of St. Benet, and mayor and commonalty to abide by arbitration, 1443

9-d-1, Draft agreement of mayor and commonalty to submit to arbitration of earl of Suffolk in disputes with ecclesiastical bodies, 1441

9-d-3, Copy of letters patent concerning disputes between city and priory, 1444

9-d-4, Certificate of lieutenant of Fleet prison, London, 1482

9-d-5, Letter from Sir John Clifton to mayor and commonalty urging them to behave, 1446

9-d-6, Acknowledgment by Sir John Clifton of payment to him by city, 1446

9-d-7, City petition to marquis of Suffolk to plead for return of liberties, c.1447

9-d-8&9, Copies of petition by city to be excused arrears of fee farm payment, 1447

9-d-10, Form of letters patent concerning excuse from fee farm

9-d-11, Letter patent restoring liberties of city, 1447

9-d-14, Copy of order to remit fee farm, 1454

9-d-15, Drafts of documents concerning agreement between city and prior to abide by arbitration, n.d.

9-d-16, Indenture of agreement between city and prior to abide by arbitration, 1450
9-d-17, Copies of definition of bounds of the liberties of the cathedral church, n.d.
9-e, Disputes between mayor and prior over jurisdiction, 1474–1505
9-f, Disputes between mayor and prior over jurisdiction, 1511–23
9-g, Disputes between mayor and prior over jurisdiction, 1524
9-h, Agreements and quitclaims of mayor and prior concerning property jurisdiction, 1524 to *tempore* Philip and Mary
16-a, Proceedings of Mayor's Court, 1440–1456
16-c, Assembly Minute Books: I, 1492–1510; II, 1510–50
16-d, Proceedings of the Municipal Assembly: Book I, 1434–91; Book II, 1491–1553
17-a, *Liber Albus*, c.1426
17-b, Book of Pleas, c.1454; Domesday Book, c.1396
17-c, Old Free Book, 1317–1549
17-d, Apprenticeship Indenture Book 1548–61 (contains Chamberlains' accounts 1448-58)
18-a, Chamberlains' Account Book: I (1384–1448), II (1470–90), III (1479–87), IV (1493–98)
21-f, 9-58, (Box II) Notes of John Kirkpatrick, antiquary (d.1728)
26-f, Royal letters patent

Nottinghamshire Record Office, Nottingham
CA380A, Sheriffs' bond, 1488
CA4770, Greaves' notes
CA4771, Gregory's notes on "The Red Book"
CA4217–CA4219, CA4441, CA4517C, CA4562A, CA5536, Retford tolls case
CA4472B, CA4535, CA4536, CA4548, CA4732, CA3966B–C/1–11, Freedom from tolls
CA4477, CA4518, Leen Bridge
CA4527, CA4529, CA4530, CA4532, Corner Wong
CA4549, CA4551, Recognizances of debt, sixteenth century
CA7416, Mayors' Accounts, 1470–71
CA7423, Mayors'/Chamberlains' Account c.1500
CA7452, Contributions to Special Expenses 1459–71
CA7644a-b, Patent letter enrollment, 1445

Public Record Office, London
Chancery (C.):
 1 Early Chancery Proceedings
 47 Miscellanea of the Chancery
 61 Gascon Rolls
 81 Chancery Warrants, First Series
 82 Chancery Warrants, Second Series
 241 Chancery Miscellanea Rolls
 260 Chancery Miscellanea Rolls

Common Pleas (CP.):
40   Common Plea Rolls

Exchequer (E.):
28   Council and Privy Seal
30   Diplomatic Documents
101 Accounts Various
122 Particular Customs Accounts
159 King's Remembrancer Memoranda Rolls
179 Lay Subsidy Rolls
199 Sheriffs' Accounts
356 General Customs Accounts
357 Escheators' Accounts
364 Foreign Accounts
368 Lord Treasurers' Remembrancer Memoranda Rolls
372 Pipe Rolls
401 Receipt Rolls
403 Issue Rolls
404 Warrants for Issue

Justices Itinerant (JI.):
1   Justices Itinerant Assize Rolls

King's Bench (KB.):
9   Ancient Indictments
27   *Coram Rege* Rolls
29   Controlment Rolls

Privy Seal Office (PSO.):
1,2 Privy Seal Office, Richard II to Henry VII

Special Collections (SC.):
1   Ancient Correspondence
6   Ministers' Accounts
8   Ancient Petitions

Star Chamber (STAC.):
1   Star Chamber, Henry VII

Record Office, House of Lords, London
2 & 3 Edward VI, no. 49, An act for the enlarging of the liberties of the city of Exeter.

York City Archives, York
B.7–9, House Books, volumes 7–9
C.5:1, 5:2, 5:3, Chamberlains' Accounts, 1501–2, 1506–7, 1508–9
D.1, Freemen's Register I, 1272–1671

Robert H. Skaife, "Civic Officials of York" (3 MS. volumes, held in the City Library)

B. Printed Sources
1. Primary Sources

Attreed, Lorraine C., ed. *The York House Books, 1461–1490.* 2 vols. Gloucester, England, and Wolfeboro, N.H.: Alan Sutton Publishing, for the Yorkist History Trust, 1991.

Baildon, William P., ed. *Select Cases in Chancery 1364–1471.* Selden Society, vol. 10. London, 1896.

Baker, J. H., ed. *The Reports of Sir John Spelman.* 2 vols. Selden Society, vol. 94. London, 1977.

Ballard, Adolphus, ed. *British Borough Charters 1042–1216.* Cambridge: Cambridge University Press, 1913.

Bateson, Mary, ed. *Borough Customs.* 2 vols. Selden Society, vols. 18, 21. London, 1904, 1906.

Bayne, C. G., and William H. Dunham, Jr., eds. *Select Cases in the Council of Henry VII.* Selden Society, vol. 75. London, 1956.

Bede. *Ecclesiastical History of the English People.* Translated by Leo Sherlay-Price. Rev. ed. Harmondsworth: Penguin Books, 1990.

Bickley, Francis B., ed. *The Little Red Book of Bristol.* 2 vols. Bristol: W. C. Hemmons, 1900–1901.

Bruce, J., ed. *Historie of the Arrivall of Edward IV in England.* Camden Society, o.s. 1. London, 1838.

Calendar of the Charter Rolls preserved in the Public Record Office. Vol. 3, 1300–1326; Vol. 4, 1327–1341; Vol. 5, 1341–1417; Vol. 6, 1427–1516. London: His Majesty's Stationery Office [HMSO], 1908, 1912, 1916, 1927.

Calendar of the Close Rolls preserved in the Public Record Office, 1377–1509. London: HMSO, 1914–63.

Calendar of the Fine Rolls preserved in the Public Record Office, 1377–1509. London: HMSO, 1926–62.

Calendar of Inquisitions Post Mortem, Henry VII. Vol. 1, 1485–96; Vol. 2, 1497–1504; Vol. 3, 1504–9. London, HMSO, 1898, 1915, 1955.

Calendar of the Patent Rolls preserved in the Public Record Office, 1377–1509. London: HMSO, 1895–1916.

Calendar of State Papers, Milan, Volume I: 1385–1618. Edited by Allen B. Hines. London: His Majesty's Stationery Office, 1912.

Calendar of State Papers, Spanish, Vol. IV, Part 2, 1531–1533. Edited by Pascual de Gayangos. London: Her Majesty's Stationery Office, 1882. Reprint. Nendeln: Kraus Reprint, 1969.

Calendar of State Papers, Venetian, 1202–1509. Edited by Rawdon Brown. London: Her Majesty's Stationery Office, 1864. Reprint. Nendeln: Kraus Reprint, 1970.

Campbell, William, ed. *Materials for a History of the Reign of Henry VII.* 2 vols. Rolls Series, vol. 60. London, 1873, 1877.

Cokayne, G. E., *et al.*, eds. *The Complete Peerage of England, Scotland, Ireland, and the United Kingdom.* 12 vols. in 13. London: St. Catherine Press, 1910–59.

Davies, Robert, ed. *York Records: Extracts from the Municipal Records of the City of York*. London: J. B. Nichols and Son, 1843. Reprint. Dursley, England: Gloucester Reprints, 1976.

Davis, Norman, ed. *Paston Letters and Papers of the Fifteenth Century*. 2 vols. Oxford: Clarendon Press, 1971, 1976.

Dobson, R. B., ed. *The Peasants' Revolt of 1381*. 2d ed. 1970; London: Macmillan, 1983.

———. *York City Chamberlains' Account Rolls 1396–1500*. Surtees Society, vol. 192. Gateshead, 1980.

Douglas, David C., and George W. Greenaway, eds. *English Historical Documents II, 1042–1189*. New York: Oxford University Press, 1968.

Dunham, Jr., William Huse, ed. *The Fane Fragment of the 1461 Lords' Journal*. New Haven: Yale University Press, 1935.

Dunstan, G. R., ed. *The Register of Edmund Lacy, Bishop of Exeter, 1420–1455, Registrum Commune*. 5 vols. Vol. 1: Devon and Cornwall Record Society, vol. 60 (Torquay, 1963). Vol. 2: Canterbury and York Society, vol. 61, and Devon and Cornwall Record Society, vol. 61 (Torquay, 1966). Vol. 3: Devon and Cornwall Record Society, vol. 62 (Torquay, 1967). Vol. 4: Devon and Cornwall Record Society, vol. 63 (Torquay, 1971). Vol. 5: Devon and Cornwall Record Society, n.s. 18 (Torquay, 1972).

Ellis, Henry, ed. *Original Letters Illustrative of English History*. 3 vols. London: Harding, Triphook, and Lepard, 1824.

———. *Three Books of Polydore Vergil's English History*. Camden Society, vol. 29. London, 1844.

Feudal Aids. 6 vols. London, 1899–1920.

Flower, C. T., ed. *Public Works in Mediaeval Law, Volume 2*. Selden Society, vol. 40. London, 1925.

Gairdner, James, ed. *The Paston Letters*. 6 vols. London: Chatto and Windus, 1904. Reprint. New York: AMS Press, 1965.

Gardiner, Dorothy M., ed. *A Calendar of Early Chancery Proceedings relating to West Country Shipping 1388–1493*. Devon and Cornwall Record Society, n.s. 21. Torquay, 1976.

Glasscock, Robin E. ed. *The Lay Subsidy of 1334*. British Academy Records of Social and Economic History, n.s. 2. London: Oxford University Press, 1975.

Hamilton, N. E. S. A., ed. *William of Malmesbury's De Gestis Pontificum Anglorum*. Rolls Series, vol. 52. London, 1870.

Hammond, Peter W., ed. *The Complete Peerage, Volume 14, Addenda and Corrigenda*. Stroud: Sutton Publishing, 1998.

Harris, Mary D., ed. *The Coventry Leet Book*. 2 vols. Early English Text Society, o.s. 134–35, 138 & 146. London, 1907, 1913.

Harriss, G. L., and M. A. Harriss, eds. "John Benet's Chronicle." In *Camden Miscellany XXIV*. Camden Society, 4th series, vol. 9. London, 1972.

Horrox, Rosemary, and P. W. Hammond, eds. *British Library Harleian MS. 433*. 4 vols. London and Upminster: Alan Sutton Publishing for the Richard III Society, 1979–83.

The Household Books of John Howard, Duke of Norfolk, 1462–1471, 1481–1483. Introduction by Anne Crawford. Stroud: Alan Sutton Publishing, 1992.

Hudson, William, ed. *Leet Jurisdiction in the City of Norwich during the XIIIth and XIVth Centuries.* Selden Society, vol. 5. London, 1892.

———, and John C. Tingey, eds. *The Records of the City of Norwich.* 2 vols. London and Norwich: Jarrold and Sons Ltd., 1906, 1910.

Hughes, Paul L., and James F. Larken, eds. *Tudor Royal Proclamations: 1. The Early Tudors, 1485–1553.* New Haven and London: Yale University Press, 1964.

Kirby, J. L., ed. *Calendar of Signet Letters of Henry IV and Henry V.* London: Her Majesty's Stationery Office, 1978.

Kowaleski, Maryanne, ed. *The Local Port Customs Accounts of the City of Exeter 1266–1321.* Devon and Cornwall Record Society, n.s. 36. Exeter, 1993.

Leach, A. F., ed. *Beverley Town Documents.* Selden Society, vol. 14. London, 1900.

Leadam, I. S., ed. *Select Cases before the King's Council in the Star Chamber, Volume I: 1477–1509.* Selden Society, vol. 16. London, 1903.

———. *Select Cases in the Court of Requests 1497–1569.* Selden Society, vol. 12. London, 1898.

Leland, John, ed. *De Rebus Britannicis Collectanea.* 2d ed. 6 vols. London: Gvl. and Jo. Richardson, 1770.

Luders, A., et al., eds. *Statutes of the Realm.* 11 vols. London: Dawsons of Pall Mall for the Record Commission, 1810–28.

Moore, Stuart A., ed. *Letters and Papers of John Shillingford, Mayor of Exeter 1447–50.* Camden Society, n.s. 2. London, 1871.

Neilson, Nellie, ed. *Year Books of Edward IV: 10 Edward IV and 49 Henry VI, 1470.* Selden Society, vol. 47. London, 1930.

Nicolas, Nicholas H., ed. *Proceedings and Ordinances of the Privy Council of England.* 7 vols. London: Record Commission, 1834–37.

———, ed. *Testamenta Vetusta.* 2 vols. London: Nichols and Son, 1826.

Oppenheim, M., ed. *Naval Accounts and Inventories of the Reign of Henry VII, 1485–88, and 1495–97.* Navy Records Society, vol. 8. London, 1896.

Percy, Joyce W., ed. *York Memorandum Book, Volume III.* Surtees Society, vol. 186. Gateshead, 1973.

Potter, K. R., ed. *Gesta Stephani.* Rev. ed. Oxford: Clarendon Press, 1976.

Pronay, Nicholas, and John Cox, eds. *The Crowland Chronicle Continuations 1459–1486.* London: Alan Sutton Publishing for the Yorkist History Trust, 1986.

Raine, Angelo, ed. *York Civic Records, Volumes 2, 3, 4, 5.* Yorkshire Archaeological Society Record Series, vols. 103, 106, 108, 110. Leeds, 1941, 1942, 1945, 1946.

Raine, James, ed. *Historians of the Church of York and Its Archbishops.* 3 vols. Rolls Series, vol. 71. London, 1879, 1886, 1894.

———. *Testamenta Eboracensia.* 4 vols. Surtees Society, vols. 4, 30, 45, 53. London and Durham, 1836, 1855, 1865, 1869.

———. *A Volume of English Miscellanies Illustrating the History and Language of the Northern Counties of England.* Surtees Society, vol. 85. Durham, 1890.

Report on the Manuscripts of Lord Middleton. Historical Manuscripts Commission. London: His Majesty's Stationery Office, 1911.

Rowe, Margery M., and John M. Draisey, eds. *The Receivers' Accounts of the City of Exeter 1304–1353*. Devon and Cornwall Record Society, n.s. 32. Exeter, 1989.

Rowe, Margery M., ed. *Tudor Exeter: Tax Assessments, 1489–1595*. Devon and Cornwall Record Society, n.s. 22. Torquay, 1977.

Rymer, Thomas, ed. *Foedera, Conventiones, Letterae...*. 10 vols. 3d ed. The Hague: John Neaulme, 1739–45.

Sachse, William L., ed. *Minutes of the Norwich Court of Mayoralty*. Norfolk Record Society, vol. 15. Norwich, 1942.

Sayles, G. O., ed. *Select Cases in the Court of King's Bench: Volume 7, Under Richard II, Henry IV, and Henry V*. Selden Society, vol. 88. London, 1971.

Sellers, Maud, ed. *York Memorandum Book: Part I (1376–1419), Part II (1388–1493)*. Surtees Society, vols. 120, 125. London and Durham, 1912, 1915.

Skaife, R. H., ed. *The Register of the Guild of Corpus Christi in the City of York*. Surtees Society, vol. 57. Durham, 1872.

Smith, Lucy Toulmin, ed. *York Plays*. Oxford: Oxford University Press, 1885. Reprint. London: Russell and Russell, 1963.

Smith, Toulmin, ed. *English Gilds*. Early English Text Society, o.s. 40. London, 1870. Reprint. London: Oxford University Press, 1963.

Sneyd, Charlotte A., ed. and trans. *A Relation or rather a True Account of the Isle of England about 1500*. Camden Society, o.s. 37. London, 1847.

Stephen, Leslie, et al., eds. *Dictionary of National Biography*. 22 vols. 1917; reprint, London: Oxford University Press, 1921–22.

Stevenson, W. H., ed. *Records of the Borough of Nottingham*. 5 vols. London: Bernard Quaritch, 1882–1900.

———. *Royal Charters Granted to the Burgesses of Nottingham*. London and Nottingham: Bernard Quaritch, 1890.

Strachey, John, ed. *Rotuli Parliamentorum*. 6 vols. London, 1767–77.

Stubbs, William, ed. *William of Malmesbury's De Gestis Regum Anglorum*. 2 vols. Rolls Series, vol. 90. London, 1887, 1889.

Tawney, R. H., and Eileen Power, eds. *Tudor Economic Documents*. 3 vols. New York: Longmans, Green and Company, 1924.

Thomas, A. H., ed. *Calendar of Select Pleas and Memoranda of the City of London, 1381–1412*. Cambridge: Cambridge University Press, 1932.

———, and I. D. Thornley, eds. *The Great Chronicle of London*. London: G. W. Jones, 1938. Reprint. Gloucester: Alan Sutton Publishing, 1983.

Warkworth, John. *A Chronicle of the First Thirteen Years of the Reign of King Edward the Fourth*. Ed. James O. Halliwell. Camden Society, o.s. 10. London, 1839.

Weinbaum, Martin, ed. *British Borough Charters, 1307–1660*. Cambridge: Cambridge University Press, 1943.

Wylie, J. H., ed. *Report on the Records of the City of Exeter*. The Historical Manuscripts Commission, vol. 199. London: His Majesty's Stationery Office, 1916.

2. Secondary Sources

Abrams, Philip, and E. A. Wrigley, eds. *Towns in Societies: Essays in Economic History and Historical Sociology*. Cambridge: Cambridge University Press, 1978.

Alexander, J. J. "The Early Boroughs of Devon." *Transactions of the Devonshire Association* 58 (1926): 275–87.

―――. "Exeter Members of Parliament, Part II: 1377–1537." *Transactions of the Devonshire Association* 60 (1928): 183–214.

―――. "Leading Civic Officials of Exeter 1330–1537." *Transactions of the Devonshire Association* 70 (1938): 405–21.

Alexander, Michael Van Cleave. *The First of the Tudors: A Study of Henry VII and His Reign.* Totowa, New Jersey: Rowman and Littlefield, 1980.

Allmand, Christopher. *Henry V.* Berkeley and Los Angeles: University of California Press, 1992.

―――. "Taxation in Medieval England: The Example of Murage." In *Villes, bonnes villes, cités et capitales*, edited by Monique Bourin, 223–30. Caen: Paradigme, 1993.

Alsop, J. D. "The Exchequer in Late Medieval Government, c.1485–1530." In *Aspects of Late Medieval Government and Society: Essays Presented to J. R. Lander*, edited by J. G. Rowe, 179–212. Toronto: University of Toronto Press, 1986.

Anglo, Sidney. "The 'British History' in Early Tudor Propaganda." *Bulletin of the John Rylands Library* 44 (1961): 17–48.

―――. *Spectacle, Pageantry, and Early Tudor Policy.* Oxford: Clarendon Press, 1969.

Archer, Rowena E., ed. *Crown, Government and People in the Fifteenth Century.* New York: St. Martin's Press, 1995.

―――. "'How ladies...who live on their manors ought to manage their households and estates': Women as Landholders and Administrators in the Later Middle Ages." In *Woman Is a Worthy Wight: Women in English Society c.1200–1500*, edited by P. J. P. Goldberg, 149–81. Stroud: Alan Sutton Publishing Ltd., 1992.

―――. "Rich Old Ladies: The Problem of Late Medieval Dowagers." In *Property and Politics: Essays in Later Medieval English History*, edited by Tony Pollard, 15–35. New York: St. Martin's Press, 1984.

―――, and Simon Walker, eds. *Rulers and the Ruled in Late Medieval England: Essays Presented to Gerald Harriss.* London and Rio Grande: Hambledon Press, 1995.

Arthurson, Ian. *The Perkin Warbeck Conspiracy 1491–1499.* Stroud: Alan Sutton Publishing Ltd., 1994.

Aston, Margaret. "A Kent Approver of 1440." *Bulletin of the Institute of Historical Research* 36 (1963): 82–90.

Atherton, Ian, *et al.*, ed. *Norwich Cathedral: Church, City and Diocese, 1096–1996.* London and Rio Grande: The Hambledon Press, 1996.

Attreed, Lorraine C. "Arbitration and the Growth of Urban Liberties in Late Medieval England." *Journal of British Studies* 31 (1992): 205–35.

―――. "England's Official Rose: Tudor Concepts of the Middle Ages." In *Hermeneutics and Medieval Culture*, edited by Patrick Gallacher and Helen Damico, 85–95. Albany: State University of New York Press, 1989.

―――. "An Indenture between Richard Duke of Gloucester and the Scrope Family of Masham and Upsall, Yorkshire." *Speculum* 58 (1983): 1018–25.

―――. "The King's Interest—York's Fee Farm and the Central Government, 1480–1492." *Northern History* 17 (1981): 24–43.

―――. "Medieval Bureaucracy in Fifteenth-Century York." *York Historian* 6 (1985):

24–31.

———. "A New Source for Perkin Warbeck's Invasion of 1497." *Mediaeval Studies* 48 (1986): 514–21.

———. "The Politics of Welcome—Ceremonies and Constitutional Development in Later Medieval English Towns." In *City and Spectacle in Medieval Europe*, edited by Barbara Hanawalt and Kathryn L. Reyerson, 205–35. Minneapolis: University of Minneapolis Press, 1993.

———. "Poverty, Payments, and Fiscal Policies in English Provincial Towns." In *Portraits of Medieval Living: Essays in Memory of David Herlihy*, edited by Samuel K. Cohn Jr. and Steven A. Epstein, 325–48. Ann Arbor: University of Michigan Press, 1996.

———. "Preparation for Death in Sixteenth-Century Northern England." *Sixteenth-Century Journal* 13 (1982): 37–66.

Ault, W. O. *Private Jurisdiction in England*. New Haven: Yale University Press, 1923.

Avery, Margaret E. "The History of the Equitable Jurisdiction of Chancery before 1460." *Bulletin of the Institute of Historical Research* 42 (1969): 129–44.

Bacon, Francis. *The History of the Reign of King Henry VII*. Vol. 6 of *The Works of Francis Bacon*. Edited by James Spedding *et al.* London: Longmans, 1861.

Barbour, Willard Titus. *The History of Contract in Early English Equity*. Vol. 4 of the Oxford Studies in Social and Legal History. Edited by Paul Vinogradoff. Oxford: Clarendon Press, 1914.

Barlow, Frank, ed. *Exeter and Its Region*. Exeter: University of Exeter Press, 1969.

———, ed. *Leofric of Exeter: Essays in Commemoration of the Foundation of Exeter Cathedral Library in AD1072*. Exeter: University of Exeter Press, 1972.

Bartlett, J. N. "The Expansion and Decline of York in the Later Middle Ages." *Economic History Review*, 2d series, 12 (1959): 17–33.

Bartlett, N., ed. "Lay Poll Tax Returns for the City of York in 1381." *Transactions of the East Riding Antiquarian Society* 30 (1953): n.p.

Beckett, John, ed. *A Centenary History of Nottingham*. Manchester and New York: Manchester University Press, 1997.

Bennett, H. S. *The Pastons and Their England*. 2d ed. 1932. Reprint. Cambridge: Cambridge University Press, 1979.

Bennett, Josephine W. "The Mediaeval Loveday." *Speculum* 33 (1958): 351–70.

Bennett, Michael. "Henry VII and the Northern Rising of 1489." *English Historical Review* 105 (1990): 34–59.

———. *Lambert Simnel and the Battle of Stoke*. New York: St. Martin's Press, 1987.

Benson, George. *Later Medieval York: The City and County of the City of York from 1100 to 1603*. York: Coultas and Volans, 1919.

———. *York from the Reformation to the Year 1925*. York: Cooper and Swann, 1925.

Benson, J. "Nicholas Radford." *Devon and Cornwall Notes and Queries* 25 (1952): 95–96.

Benton, John F., ed. *Town Origins: The Evidence from Medieval England*. Boston: D. C. Heath and Co., 1968.

Bhanji, S. "The Involvement of Exeter and the Exe Estuary in Piracy." *Transactions of the Devonshire Association* 130 (1998): 23–49.

Bidwell, P. T. *Roman Exeter: Fortress and Town*. Exeter: Exeter Museum Service, 1980.
Bird, Ruth. *The Turbulent London of Richard II*. London: Longmans, Green and Company, 1949.
Blake, William. "Thomas Wetherby." *Norfolk Archaeology* 32 (1961): 60–72.
Blatcher, Marjorie. *The Court of King's Bench 1450–1550: A Study in Self-Help*. London: Athlone Press, 1978.
Blomefield, Francis. *A Topographical History of the County of Norfolk*. 2d ed. 11 vols. London: William Miller, 1805–10.
Bolton, J. L. *The Medieval English Economy 1150–1500*. London: J. M. Dent and Sons, 1980.
Bond, Shelagh, and Norman Evans. "The Process of Granting Charters to English Boroughs." *English Historical Review* 91 (1976): 102–20.
Bridbury, A. R. "Dr. Rigby's Comment: A Reply." *Economic History Review*, 2d series, 39 (1986): 417–22.
———. *England and the Salt Trade in the Later Middle Ages*. Oxford: Oxford University Press, 1955.
———. "English Provincial Towns in the Later Middle Ages." *Economic History Review*, 2d series, 34 (1981): 1–24.
———. *Medieval English Clothmaking: An Economic Survey*. London: Heinemann Educational Books, Ltd., 1982.
Britnell, Richard. "The Black Death in English Towns." *Urban History* 21 (1994): 196–210.
———. *The Commercialisation of English Society 1000–1500*. Cambridge: Cambridge University Press, 1993.
Brooks, F. W. *York and the Council of the North*. St. Anthony's Hall Publication 5. York, 1954.
Broome, D. M. "Exchequer Migrations to York." In *Essays in Medieval History Presented to Thomas Frederick Tout*, edited by F. M. Powicke and A. G. Little, 291–300. Manchester: R. and R. Clarke for the subscribers, 1925.
Bryson, Emrys. *Portrait of Nottingham*. London: Robert Hale Publishing, 1978.
Bryson, W. H. *The Equity Side of the Exchequer*. London: Cambridge University Press, 1975.
Burrow, Ian. "The Town Defences of Exeter." *Transactions of the Devonshire Association* 109 (1977): 13–40.
Burwash, Dorothy. *English Merchant Shipping 1460–1540*. Toronto: University of Toronto Press, 1947.
Butcher, A. F. "Rent, Population, and Economic Change in Late-Medieval Newcastle." *Northern History* 14 (1978): 67–77.

Cam, Helen M. "The King's Government, as Administered by the Greater Abbots of East Anglia." *Proceedings of the Cambridge Antiquarian Society* 29 (1928), 25–49.
Campbell, Bruce M. S., ed. *Before the Black Death: Studies in the "Crisis" of the Early Fourteenth Century*. Manchester and New York: Manchester University Press, 1991.
Carpenter, Christine. "Law, Justice and Landowners in Late Medieval England." *Law and History Review* 1 (1983): 205–37.

————. *Locality and Polity: A Study of Warwickshire Landed Society, 1401–1499.* Cambridge: Cambridge University Press, 1992.

————. *The Wars of the Roses: Politics and the Constitution in England, c.1437–1509.* Cambridge: Cambridge University Press, 1997.

Carter, A. "The Anglo-Saxon Origins of Norwich: The Problems and Approaches." *Anglo-Saxon England* 7 (1978): 175–203.

Carus-Wilson, E. M. "The Aulnage Accounts: A Criticism." *Economic History Review* 2 (1929): 114–23.

————, and Olive Coleman. *England's Export Trade 1275–1547.* Oxford: Clarendon Press, 1963.

————. *The Expansion of Exeter at the Close of the Middle Ages.* Exeter: University of Exeter Press, 1963.

————. *Medieval Merchant Venturers.* 2d ed. London: Methuen and Co., 1967.

————. "The Overseas Trade of Late Medieval Coventry." *Économies et Sociétés au Moyen Ages: Mélanges offerts à Edouard Perroy.* Paris: Publications de la Sorbonne, 1973.

Cherry, Martin. "The Courtenay Earls of Devon: The Formation and Disintegration of a Late Medieval Aristocratic Affinity." *Southern History* 1 (1979): 71–97.

————. "The Liveried Personnel of Edward Courtenay, Earl of Devon, 1384–5, Parts I–V." *Devon and Cornwall Notes and Queries* 35 (1983–85): 151–59, 189–93, 219–25, 258–63, 302–10.

Chevalier, Bernard. *Les Bonnes Villes de France du XIVe au XVIe siècle.* Paris: Aubier Montaigne, 1982.

Cheyette, Fredric L. "*Suum Cuique Tribuere.*" *French Historical Studies* 6 (1970): 287–99.

Childs, W. R. "England's Icelandic Trade in the Fifteenth Century: The Role of the Port of Hull." *Northern Seas Yearbook* 5 (1995): 11–31.

Chope, R. Pearse. "The Last of the Dynhams." *Transactions of the Devonshire Association* 50 (1918): 431–92.

Chrimes, S. B. *Henry VII.* Berkeley and Los Angeles: University of California Press, 1972.

Clanchy, M. T. "The Franchise of Return of Writs." *Transactions of the Royal Historical Society,* 5th series, 17 (1967): 59–79.

————. "Law and Love in the Middle Ages." In *Disputes and Settlements: Law and Human Relations in the West,* edited by John Bossy, 47–67. Cambridge: Cambridge University Press, 1983.

Clark, Peter, and Paul Slack, eds. *Crisis and Order in English Towns 1500–1700.* Toronto: University of Toronto Press, 1972.

Clayton, Dorothy J., Richard G. Davies, and Peter McNiven, eds. *Trade, Devotion and Governance: Papers in Later Medieval History.* Stroud: Alan Sutton Publishing Ltd., 1994.

Cobb, Henry S. "Local Port Customs Accounts prior to 1550." *Journal of the Society of Archivists* 1 (1958): 213–24.

Conway, Agnes. *Henry VII's Relations with Scotland and Ireland 1485–1498.* Cambridge: Cambridge University Press, 1932. Reprint. New York: Octagon Books, 1972.

Cooper, T. P. "The Medieval Highways, Streets, Open Ditches and Sanitary Conditions of the City of York." *Yorkshire Archaeological Journal* 22 (1912–13): 270–86.

Cozens-Hardy, B., and Ernest A. Kent, eds. *The Mayors of Norwich*. Norwich: Jarrold and Sons, 1938.

Cross, Claire. "From the Reformation to the Restoration." In *A History of York Minster*, edited by G. E. Aylmer and Reginald Cant, 193–232. Oxford: Clarendon Press, 1977.

Curtis, Muriel E. "A Note on the Dating of an Exeter Charter." *English Historical Review* 45 (1930): 290–91.

———. *Some Disputes between the City and the Cathedral Authorities of Exeter*. History of Exeter Research Group, Monograph 5. Manchester: Manchester University Press, 1932.

Darby, H. C., and R. Welldon Finn, eds. *The Domesday Geography of South-West England*. Cambridge, 1967.

Darnton, Robert. *The Great Cat Massacre and Other Episodes in French Cultural History*. New York: Basic Books, 1984.

Davies, Robert. "Margaret Tudor at York." *Yorkshire Archaeological Journal* 7 (1882): 305–29.

———. "Original Documents relating to Lambert Symnell's Rebellion in the Second Year of King Henry VII." *Memoirs Illustrative of the History and Antiquities of the County and City of York*. London: Architectural Institute of Great Britain and Ireland, 1848.

De La Garde, Philip C. "On the Antiquity and Invention of the Lock Canal of Exeter." *Archaeologia* 28 (1839): 7–26.

Deering, Charles. *Nottinghamia Vetus et Nova*. Nottingham: G. Ayscough and T. Willington, 1751.

Dietz, Frederick C. *English Government Finance 1485–1558*. University of Illinois Studies in the Social Sciences, vol. 9. Urbana: University of Illinois Press, 1920.

Dobson, R. B. "Cathedral Chapters and Cathedral Cities: York, Durham, and Carlisle in the Fifteenth Century." *Northern History* 19 (1983): 15–44.

———, ed. *The Church, Politics and Patronage in the Fifteenth Century*. Gloucester: Alan Sutton Publishing, 1984.

———. *Durham Priory 1400–50*. Cambridge: Cambridge University Press, 1973.

———. "The Later Middle Ages 1215–1500." In *A History of York Minster*, edited by G. E. Aylmer and Reginald Cant, 44–109. Oxford: Clarendon Press, 1977.

———. "The Residentiary Canons of York in the Fifteenth Century." *Journal of Ecclesiastical History* 30 (1979): 145–73.

———. "Richard III and the Church of York." In *Kings and Nobles in the Later Middle Ages*, edited by R. A. Griffiths and J. W. Sherborne, 130–54. New York: St. Martin's Press, 1986.

———. "The Risings in York, Beverley and Scarborough, 1380–1381." In *The English Rising of 1381*, edited by R. H. Hilton and T. H. Aston, 112–42. Cambridge and New York: Cambridge University Press, 1984.

———. "Urban Decline in Late Medieval England." *Transactions of the Royal Historical Society*, 5th series, 27 (1977 for 1976): 1–22.

————. "Yorkshire Towns in the Late Fourteenth Century." *Publications of the Thoresby Society* 59 (1983): 1–21.

Drake, Francis. *Eboracum*. London: W. Bowyer, 1736.

Druery, J. H. "The Erpingham House, St. Martin's at Palace, Norwich." *Norfolk Archaeology* 6 (1864): 143–48.

Du Boulay, F. R. H., and Caroline Barron, eds. *The Reign of Richard II: Essays in Honour of May McKisack*. London: Athlone Press, 1971.

Dunlop, David. "King Edward's War: The Anglo-Scottish Conflict of 1480–84." Photocopy provided by author.

————. "The 'Masked Comedian': Perkin Warbeck's Adventures in Scotland and England from 1495 to 1497." *Scottish Historical Review* 70 (1991): 97–128.

Dyer, Alan D. *Decline and Growth in English Towns, 1400–1640*. Cambridge: Cambridge University Press, 1995.

Edwards, Goronwy. *The Second Century of the English Parliament*. Oxford: Clarendon Press, 1979.

Edwards, K. C., ed. *Nottingham and Its Region*. Nottingham: Nottingham Local Executive Committee of the British Association, 1966.

Edwards, Rhoda. *The Itinerary of King Richard III 1483–1485*. London: Alan Sutton Publishing for the Richard III Society, 1983.

Epstein, S. R. "Regional Fairs, Institutional Innovation, and Economic Growth in Late Medieval Europe." *Economic History Review*, 2d series, 47 (1994): 459–82.

Everitt, Alan, ed. *Perspectives in English Urban History*. London: Macmillan, 1973.

First Report of the Royal Commission on Historical Manuscripts. London: Her Majesty's Stationery Office, 1874. Reprint. Nendeln: Kraus Reprint, 1979.

Flenley, Ralph. "London and Foreign Merchants in the Reign of Henry VI." *English Historical Review* 25 (1910): 644–55.

Fortescue, Thomas (Lord Clermont), ed. *A History of the Family of Fortescue in All Its Branches*. 2d ed. London: Ellis and White, 1880.

Foss, Edward. *The Judges of England*. 9 vols. London: Longman, Brown, Green, and Longmans, 1848–64.

Fox, Aileen. *Roman Exeter (Isca Dumnoniorum): Excavations in the War-Damaged Areas 1945–1947*. History of Exeter Research Group, Monograph 8. Manchester: Manchester University Press, 1952.

Freeman, Edward A. *Exeter*. London: Longmans, Green and Co., 1890.

Friedrichs, Christopher R. "Urban Politics and Urban Social Structure in Seventeenth-Century Germany." *European History Quarterly* 22 (1992): 187–216.

Fudge, John D. *Cargoes, Embargoes, and Emissaries: The Commercial and Political Interaction of England and the German Hanse 1450–1510*. Toronto and London: University of Toronto Press, 1995.

Gairdner, James. *Henry the Seventh*. London: Macmillan and Co., 1899.

————. *History of the Life and Reign of Richard III*. Cambridge: Cambridge University Press, 1898.

Geertz, Clifford. "Centers, Kings, and Charisma: Reflections on the Symbolics of

Power." In *Local Knowledge: Further Essays in Interpretive Anthropology*, 121–46. New York: Basic Books, 1983.

Gillett, Edward, and Kenneth A. MacMahon. *A History of Hull*. 2d ed. Hull: Hull University Press, 1989.

Gillingham, John. *The Wars of the Roses*. Baton Rouge: Louisiana State University Press, 1981.

Giuseppi, M. S. "Alien Merchants in England in the Fifteenth Century." *Transactions of the Royal Historical Society*, 2d series, 9 (1895): 75–98.

Goldberg, P. J. P. "Mortality and Economic Change in the Diocese of York, 1390–1514." *Northern History* 24 (1988): 38–55.

———. "Urban Identity and the Poll Taxes of 1377, 1379, and 1381." *Economic History Review*, 2d series, 43 (1990): 194–216.

Goodman, Anthony. *The New Monarchy: England, 1471–1534*. Oxford: Basil Blackwell, 1988.

———. *The Wars of the Roses*. London: Routledge and Kegan Paul, 1981.

Granger, James. *Old Nottingham: Its Streets, People, etc*. Nottingham: Nottingham Daily Express Office, 1902.

Gray, Duncan. *Nottingham Through 500 Years*. 2d ed. Nottingham: Derry and Sons, 1960.

Green, Alice S. *Town Life in the Fifteenth Century*. 2 vols. London and New York: Macmillan and Co., 1894.

Green, Thomas A. *Verdict According to Conscience: Perspectives on the English Criminal Trial Jury, 1200–1800*. Chicago: University of Chicago Press, 1985.

Griffiths, Ralph A. "Local Rivalries and National Politics: The Percies, the Nevilles, and the Duke of Exeter, 1452–1455." *Speculum* 43 (1968): 589–632.

———, ed. *Patronage, the Crown and the Provinces in Later Medieval England*. Gloucester: Alan Sutton Publishing, 1981.

———. *The Reign of Henry VI*. Berkeley and Los Angeles: University of California Press, 1981.

———. "The Trial of Eleanor Cobham." *Bulletin of the John Rylands Library* 51 (1968–69): 381–99.

Grummitt, David. "Henry VII, Chamber Finance and the New Monarchy." *Historical Research* 72 (1999): 229–43.

Gunn, S. J. "The Courtiers of Henry VII." *English Historical Review* 108 (1993): 23–49.

———. *Early Tudor Government, 1485–1558*. New York: St. Martin's Press, 1995.

———. "Sir Thomas Lovell (c.1449–1524): A New Man in a New Monarchy?" In *The End of the Middle Ages? England in the Fifteenth and Sixteenth Centuries*, edited by John L. Watts, 117–53. Stroud: Sutton Publishing, 1998.

Guy, J. A. *The Court of Star Chamber and its records to the reign of Elizabeth I*. Public Record Office Handbooks No. 21. London: Her Majesty's Stationery Office, 1985.

Hadwin, J. F. "From Dissonance to Harmony in the Late Medieval Town." *Economic History Review*, 2d series, 39 (1986): 423–26.

———. "The Medieval Lay Subsidies and Economic History." *Economic History Review*, 2d series, 36 (1983): 200–17.

Hall, Richard. *The Viking Dig*. London: Bodley Head, 1986.

Hammond, P. W., and Anne F. Sutton. *Richard III: The Road to Bosworth Field.* London: Constable and Co., 1985.

Hampton, William E. *Memorials of the Wars of the Roses.* Upminster: Richard III Society, 1979.

Hanawalt, Barbara A., and Kathryn L. Reyerson, eds. *City and Spectacle in Medieval Europe.* Minneapolis and London: University of Minnesota Press, 1994.

Harding, Alan. *The Law Courts of Medieval England.* Historical Problems: Studies and Documents, no. 18. London: Allen and Unwin, 1973.

———. *Law-Making and Law-Makers in British History.* London: Royal Historical Society, 1980.

Hare, J. N. "The Wiltshire Risings of 1450." *Southern History* 4 (1982): 13–31.

Harris, Mary D. "Laurence Saunders, Citizen of Coventry." *English Historical Review* 9 (1894): 633–51.

Harrison, D. F. "Bridges and Economic Development, 1300–1800." *Economic History Review,* 2d series, 45 (1992): 240–61.

Harrison, Frederick. *Life in a Medieval College: The Story of the Vicars-Choral of York Minster.* London: John Murray, 1952.

Harriss, G. L. "Aids, Loans and Benevolences." *Historical Journal* 6 (1963): 1–19.

———. "Fictitious Loans." *Economic History Review,* 2d series, 8 (1956): 87–99.

———. "Political Society and the Growth of Government in Late Medieval England," *Past and Present* 138 (1993): 28–57.

———. "Preference at the Medieval Exchequer." *Bulletin of the Institute of Historical Research* 30 (1957): 17–40.

Harrod, Henry. "Queen Elizabeth Woodville's Visit to Norwich in 1469." *Norfolk Archaeology* 5 (1859): 32–37.

Hart, Richard. "A Translation of Thomas of Walsingham's Account of Littester's Rebellion in 1381." *Norfolk Archaeology* 5 (1859): 348–53.

Haskett, Timothy S. "The Medieval English Court of Chancery." *Law and History Review* 14 (1996): 245–313.

Hastings, Margaret. *The Court of Common Pleas in Fifteenth-Century England.* Ithaca, N.Y.: Cornell University Press, 1947.

Hatcher, John. "The great slump of the mid-fifteenth century." In *Progress and Problems in Medieval England: Essays in Honour of Edward Miller,* edited by Richard Britnell and John Hatcher, 237–72. Cambridge: Cambridge University Press, 1996.

Haward, Winifred I. "Economic Aspects of the Wars of the Roses in East Anglia." *English Historical Review* 41 (1926): 170–89.

———. "Gilbert Debenham: A Medieval Rascal in Real Life." *History* 13 (1929): 300–14.

Heath, P. "North Sea Fishing in the Fifteenth Century: The Scarborough Fleet." *Northern History* 3 (1968): 53–69.

Heaton, Herbert. *The Yorkshire Woollen and Worsted Industries.* 2d ed. Oxford: Clarendon Press, 1965.

Henderson, Christopher. "Exeter (*Isca Dumnoniorum*)." In *Fortress into City,* edited by Graham Webster, 91–119. London: Batsford, 1988.

Hewitt, H. J. *The Organization of War Under Edward III.* Manchester and New York: Manchester University Press, 1966.

Hicks, Michael A. "Dynastic Change and Northern Society: The Career of the Fourth Earl of Northumberland, 1470–89." *Northern History* 14 (1978): 78–107.

―――. *False, Fleeting, Perjur'd Clarence.* Gloucester: Alan Sutton Publishing, 1980.

―――, ed. *Profit, Piety and the Professions in Later Medieval England.* Gloucester: Alan Sutton, 1990.

―――. "Restraint, Mediation and Private Justice: George, Duke of Clarence as 'Good Lord'." *Journal of Legal History* 4 (1983): 56–71.

―――. "The Yorkshire Rebellion of 1489 Reconsidered." *Northern History* 22 (1986): 39–62.

Highfield, J. R. L., and Robin Jeffs, eds. *The Crown and Local Communities in England and France in the Fifteenth Century.* Gloucester: Alan Sutton Publishing, 1981.

Hill, J. W. F. *Medieval Lincoln.* Cambridge: Cambridge University Press, 1948.

History of the City and County of Norwich, from the Earliest Accounts to the Present Times. Norwich: John Crouse, 1768.

Hoker, John (alias Vowell). *The Description of the Citie of Excester.* 3 vols. Edited by W. J. Harte, J. W. Schopp, H. Tapley-Soper. Devon and Cornwall Record Society. Exeter, 1919, 1947.

Holmes, G. A. *The Estates of the Higher Nobility in Fourteenth-Century England.* Cambridge: Cambridge University Press, 1957.

Horrox, Rosemary, ed. *Richard III and the North.* Hull: University of Hull Centre for Regional and Local History, 1986.

―――. *Richard III: A Study of Service.* Cambridge: Cambridge University Press, 1989.

―――. "The Urban Gentry in the Fifteenth Century." In *Towns and Townspeople in the Fifteenth Century*, edited by John A. F. Thomson, 22–44. Gloucester: Alan Sutton Publishing, 1988.

Hoskins, W. G., and H. P. R. Finberg. *Devonshire Studies.* London: Cape, 1952.

―――. "English Provincial Towns in the Early Sixteenth-Century." *Transactions of the Royal Historical Society*, 5th series, 6 (1956): 1–19.

―――. *Two Thousand Years in Exeter.* Exeter: James Townsend and Sons Ltd., 1960.

Houghton, K. N. "Theory and Practice in Borough Elections to Parliament during the Later Fifteenth Century." *Bulletin of the Institute of Historical Research* 39 (1966): 130–40.

Howard, D. and C. A. Pratt. "The Evolution of Norwich." *Geography* 26 (1941): 125–30.

Howlett, Richard. "Norwich Artillery in the Fourteenth Century." *Norfolk Archaeology* 16 (1905): 46–75.

Hudson, William. "Norwich Militia in the Fourteenth Century." *Norfolk Archaeology* 14 (1901): 263–320.

―――. "Traces of the Early Development of Municipal Organization in the City of Norwich." *Archaeological Journal* 46 (1889): 293–330.

―――. *Wards of the City of Norwich.* London: Jarrold and Sons, 1891.

Hunnisett, R. F. *The Medieval Coroner.* Cambridge: Cambridge University Press, 1961.

Hunnisett, R. F., and J. B. Post, eds. *Medieval Legal Records: Edited in Memory of C. A. F. Meekings.* London: Her Majesty's Stationery Office, 1978.

Hunt, R. W., *et al.*, eds. *Studies in Medieval History Presented to Frederick Maurice Powicke.* Oxford: Clarendon Press, 1948.

Ives, E. W. "Andrew Dymmock and the Papers of Antony, Earl Rivers, 1482–3." *Bulletin of the Institute of Historical Research* 41 (1968): 216–29.
———. *The Common Lawyers of Pre-Reformation England.* Cambridge: Cambridge University Press, 1983.
———, and A. H. Manchester, eds. *Law, Litigants and the Legal Profession.* London: The Royal Historical Society, 1983.

Jackson, A. M. "Medieval Exeter, the Exe, and the Earldom of Devon." *Transactions of the Devonshire Association* 104 (1972): 57–79.
Jacob, E. F. *The Fifteenth Century, 1399–1485.* Oxford: Oxford University Press, 1961.
Jalland, Patricia. "The 'Revolution' in Northern Borough Representation in Mid-Fifteenth-Century England." *Northern History* 11 (1976 for 1975): 27–51.
James, Mervyn. "Ritual, Drama, and Social Body in the Late Medieval English Town." *Past and Present* 98 (1983): 3–29.
———. "A Tudor magnate and the Tudor state: Henry fifth earl of Northumberland." In *Society, Politics and Culture: Studies in Early Modern England,* 48–90. Past and Present Publications. Cambridge: Cambridge University Press, 1986.
Jefferies, Peggy. "The Medieval Use as Family Law and Custom." *Southern History* 1 (1979): 45–69.
Jenkins, Alexander. *The History and Description of the City of Exeter and Its Environs.* Exeter: P. Hedgeland; London: Scatcherd and Letterman, 1806.
John, Trevor. "Sir Thomas Erpingham, East Anglian Society, and the Dynastic Revolution of 1399." *Norfolk Archaeology* 35 (1970): 96–108.
Johnson, P. A. *Duke Richard of York 1411–1460.* Oxford: Clarendon Press, 1988.
Johnston, Alexandra F. "The Plays of the Religious Guilds of York: The Creed Play and the Pater Noster Play." *Speculum* 50 (1975): 55–90.

Kaeuper, Richard W. *War, Justice and Public Order: England and France in the Later Middle Ages.* Oxford: Clarendon Press, 1988.
Kaye, Walter J. "Yorkshiremen Who Declined to Take Up Their Knighthood." *Yorkshire Archaeological Journal* 31 (1932–34): 360–65.
Keen, Maurice. *England in the Later Middle Ages.* London: Methuen and Co., Ltd., 1973.
Kelly, Henry A. *Divine Providence in the England of Shakespeare's Histories.* Cambridge, Mass.: Harvard University Press, 1970.
Kendall, Paul Murray. *Richard the Third.* New York: W. W. Norton and Co., 1955.
Kermode, Jennifer I. *Medieval Merchants: York, Beverley and Hull in the Later Middle Ages.* Cambridge: Cambridge University Press, 1998.
———. "Urban Decline? The Flight from Office in Late Medieval York." *Economic History Review,* 2d series, 35 (1982): 179–98.
Ketton-Cremer, R. W. *Felbrigg: The Story of a House.* London: Boydell Press, 1962.
Kingsford, Charles L. *Prejudice and Promise in XVth Century England.* Oxford: Oxford University Press, 1925.
Kipling, Gordon. *Enter the King: Theatre, Liturgy, and Ritual in the Medieval Civic Triumph.* Oxford: Clarendon Press, 1998.

Kowaleski, Maryanne. *Local Markets and Regional Trade in Medieval Exeter.* Cambridge and New York: Cambridge University Press, 1995.

Lander, J. R. *Crown and Nobility 1450–1509.* London: Edward Arnold, 1976.
———. *The Limitations of English Monarchy in the Later Middle Ages.* Toronto: University of Toronto Press, 1989.
Leggett, Jennifer I. "The 1377 Poll Tax Return for the City of York." *Yorkshire Archaeological Journal* 43 (1971): 128–46.
Lehmberg, Stanford E. *The Reformation of Cathedrals: Cathedrals in English Society, 1485–1603.* Princeton: Princeton University Press, 1988.
———. "Star Chamber: 1485–1509." *Huntington Library Quarterly* 24 (May 1961): 189–214.
Lepine, David N. "The Courtenays and Exeter Cathedral in the Later Middle Ages." *Transactions of the Devonshire Association* 24 (1992): 41–58.
Lloyd, T. H. *Alien Merchants in England in the High Middle Ages.* New York: St. Martin's Press, 1982.
Loach, Jennifer and Robert Tittler, eds. *The Mid-Tudor Polity c.1540–1560.* London: Macmillan Press Ltd., 1980.
Lobel, Mary D., ed. *Historic Towns Volume I.* London: Lovell Johns, 1969.
———. *Historic Towns Atlas Volume II.* London: Scolar Press, 1975.
———. *The British Atlas of Historic Towns Volume III: The City of London from Prehistoric Times to c.1520.* Oxford: Oxford University Press, 1989.
Lyon, Bryce. *A Constitutional and Legal History of Medieval England.* 2d ed. New York: Norton and Co., 1980.

MacCaffrey, Wallace T. *Exeter 1540–1640: The Growth of an English County Town.* 2d ed. London and Cambridge, Mass.: Harvard University Press, 1975.
MacDougall, Hugh A. *Racial Myth in English History.* Hanover, New Hampshire: University of New England Press, 1982.
Macdougall, Norman. *James III: A Political Study.* Edinburgh: J. Donald, 1982.
Mace, Frances A. "Devonshire Ports in the Fourteenth and Fifteenth Centuries." *Transactions of the Royal Historical Society,* 4th series, 8 (1925): 98–126.
MacFarlane, Alan. *A Guide to English Historical Records.* Cambridge: Cambridge University Press, 1983.
Mackie, J. D. *The Earlier Tudors, 1485–1558.* Oxford: Clarendon Press, 1952.
Mackie, R. L. *King James IV of Scotland.* Edinburgh and London: Oliver and Boyd, 1958.
Maddern, Philippa C. *Violence and Social Order: East Anglia 1422–1442.* Oxford: Clarendon Press, 1992.
Maddicott, J. R. "Trade, industry and the wealth of King Alfred." *Past and Present* 123 (1989): 3–51.
Madox, Thomas. *Firma Burgi.* London: W. Bowyer, 1726.
Malden, A. R. "An Official Account of the Battle of Agincourt." *Ancestor* 11 (1904): 26–31.
Marcus, G. J. "The First English Voyages to Iceland." *Mariner's Mirror* 42 (1956): 314–25.

Masschaele, James. "Transport Costs in Medieval England." *Economic History Review*, 2d series, 46 (1993): 266–79.

McFarlane, K. B. "At the Deathbed of Cardinal Beaufort." In *Studies in Medieval History presented to F. M. Powicke*, edited by R. W. Hunt, W. A. Pantin, R. W. Southern, 405–28. Oxford: Clarendon Press, 1948.

———. *England in the Fifteenth Century*. London: Hambledon Press, 1981.

McGee, C. E. "Politics and Platitudes: Sources of Civic Pageantry, 1486." *Renaissance Studies* 3 (1989): 29–34.

McIntosh, Marjorie K. "Local Change and Community Control in England, 1465–1500." *Huntington Library Quarterly* 49 (1986): 219–42.

McKenna, J. W. "Popular Canonization as Political Propaganda: The Cult of Archbishop Scrope." *Speculum* 45 (1970): 608–23.

McKisack, May. *The Fourteenth Century, 1307–1399*. Oxford: Oxford University Press, 1959.

———. *The Parliamentary Representation of the English Boroughs during the Middle Ages*. Oxford: Clarendon Press, 1932.

McRee, Ben R. "Peacemaking and its Limits in Late Medieval Norwich." *English Historical Review* 109 (1994): 831–66.

———. "Religious Gilds and Civic Order: The Case of Norwich in the Late Middle Ages." *Speculum* 67 (1992): 69–97.

McNiven, Peter. "The Betrayal of Archbishop Scrope." *The Bulletin of the John Rylands Library* 54 (1971): 173–213.

———. "Prince Henry and the English Political Crisis of 1412." *History* 65 (1980): 1–16.

Meagher, John C. "The First Progress of Henry VII." *Renaissance Drama*, n.s. 1 (1968): 45–73.

Merewether, Henry A., and A. J. Stephens. *The History of the Boroughs and Municipal Corporations of the United Kingdom*. 3 vols. London: Stevens and Sons, 1835.

Michalove, Sharon D., and A. Compton Reeves, eds. *Estrangement, Enterprise and Education in Fifteenth-Century England*. Stroud: Sutton Publishing, 1998.

Milner, John D. "Sir Simon Felbrigg, K.G.: The Lancastrian Revolution and Personal Fortune." *Norfolk Archaeology* 37 (1978): 84–91.

Mollat, Michel. *The Poor in the Middle Ages*. Translated by Arthur Goldhammer. New Haven and London: Yale University Press, 1986.

Moreton, C. E. *The Townshends and Their World: Gentry, Law, and Land in Norfolk c. 1450–1551*. Oxford: Clarendon Press, 1992.

Morgan, Philip. *War and Society in Medieval Cheshire 1277–1403*. Chetham Society, 3d series, vol. 34. London, 1987.

Morris, William A., and J. R. Strayer, eds. *Fiscal Administration*. Vol. 2, *The English Government at Work, 1327–1336*. Cambridge, Mass.: The Mediaeval Academy of America, 1947.

Myers, A. R. *The Household of Edward IV*. Manchester: Manchester University Press, 1959.

Newhall, Richard A. *The English Conquest of Normandy, 1416–1424*. New Haven: Yale University Press, 1924.

Nightingale, Pamela. *A Medieval Mercantile Community: The Grocers' Company and the Politics and Trade of London 1000–1485.* New Haven and London: Yale University Press, 1995.

Ormrod, W. M. "The Crown and the English Economy 1290–1348." In *Before the Black Death: Studies in the "Crisis" of the Early Fourteenth Century,* edited by Bruce M. S. Campbell, 149–83. Manchester and New York: Manchester University Press, 1991.

Otway-Ruthven, A. J. *The King's Secretary and the Signet Office in the XV Century.* Cambridge: Cambridge University Press, 1939.

Owen, L. V. D. "The Borough of Nottingham 1284–1485." *Transactions of the Thoroton Society* 50 (1946): 25–35.

Page, William, ed. *The Victoria History of the County of Norfolk.* 2 vols. London: Archibald Constable and Co., Ltd., 1901, 1906. Reprint. London: William Dawson and Sons Ltd., 1975.

———. *The Victoria History of the County of Nottingham.* 2 vols. London: Archibald Constable and Co., Ltd., 1906. Reprint. London: Dawsons of Pall Mall, 1970.

Palais, H. "England's First Attempt to Break the Commercial Monopoly of the Hanseatic League, 1377–1380." *American Historical Review* 64 (1959): 852–65.

Palliser, David M. "A Crisis in English Towns? The Case of York, 1460–1640." *Northern History* 14 (1978): 108–25.

———. "Town Defences in Medieval England and Wales." In *The Medieval Military Revolution: State, Society, and Military Change in Medieval and Early Modern Europe,* edited by Andrew Ayton and J. L. Price, 105–20. London and New York: Tauris Academic Studies, 1995.

———. *Tudor York.* Oxford: Oxford University Press, 1979.

———. "Urban Decay Revisited." In *Towns and Townspeople in the Fifteenth Century,* edited by John A. F. Thomson, 1–21. Gloucester: Alan Sutton Publishing, 1988.

———. "Urban Society." In *Fifteenth-Century Attitudes: Perceptions of Society in Late Medieval England,* edited by Rosemary Horrox, 132–49. Cambridge: Cambridge University Press, 1994.

Parry, H. Lloyd. "The Exeter Swords and Hat of Maintenance." *Transactions of the Devonshire Association* 64 (1932): 421–54.

———. "The Fee Farm of Exeter." *Transactions of the Devonshire Association* 81 (1949): 197–99.

Patterson, Catherine F. *Urban Patronage in Early Modern England: Corporate Boroughs, the Landed Elite, and the Crown, 1580–1640.* Stanford: Stanford University Press, 1999.

Payling, S. J. "The Ampthill Dispute: A Study in Aristocratic Lawlessness and the Breakdown of Lancastrian Government." *English Historical Review* 104 (1989): 881–907.

———. "Law and Arbitration in Nottinghamshire 1399–1461." In *People, Politics and Community in the Later Middle Ages,* edited by Joel Rosenthal and Colin Richmond, 140–60. Gloucester, England and New York: Alan Sutton Publishing and St. Martin's Press, 1987.

————. *Political Society in Lancastrian England: The Greater Gentry of Nottinghamshire*. Oxford: Clarendon Press, 1991.

Phythian-Adams, Charles. "Ceremony and the Citizen: The Communal Year at Coventry 1450–1550." In *Crisis and Order in English Towns 1500–1700*, edited by Peter Clark and Paul Sack, 57–85. Toronto: University of Toronto Press, 1972.

————. *Desolation of a City: Coventry and the Urban Crisis of the Late Middle Ages*. Cambridge: Cambridge University Press, 1979.

————. "Urban Decay in Late Medieval England." In *Towns in Societies*, edited by Philip Abrams and E. A. Wrigley, 159–85. Cambridge: Cambridge University Press, 1978.

Platt, Colin. *Medieval Southampton*. London: Routledge and Kegan Paul, 1973.

Pollard, A. F. *The Reign of Henry VII from Contemporary Sources*. 3 vols. London: Longmans, Green, 1913.

Pollard, A. J., ed. *Property and Politics: Essays in Later Medieval English History*. Gloucester: Alan Sutton Publishing, 1984.

————. "The North-Eastern Economy and the Agrarian Crisis of 1438–40." *Northern History* 25 (1989): 88–105.

————. *North-eastern England during the Wars of the Roses: Lay Society, War, and Politics, 1450–1500*. Oxford: Clarendon Press, 1990.

————. *The Wars of the Roses*. New York: St. Martin's Press, 1988.

Pollock, Frederick, and F. W. Maitland. *The History of English Law*. 2 vols. 2d ed. Cambridge: Cambridge University Press, 1905.

Polwhele, Richard. *The History of Devonshire*. 3 vols. London: Trewmen and Son, 1793–1806. Reprint. Dorking: Kohler and Coombes, 1977.

Post, J. B. "Courts, Councils, and Arbitrators in the Ladbroke Manor Dispute, 1382–1400." In *Medieval Legal Records*, edited by R. F. Hunnisett and J. B. Post, 290–339. London: Her Majesty's Stationery Office, 1978.

————. "Equitable Resorts before 1450." In *Law, Litigants and the Legal Profession*, edited by E. W. Ives and A. H. Manchester, 68–79. London: The Royal Historical Society, 1983.

Pounds, N. J. G. *An Economic History of Medieval Europe*. New York: Longman, 1974.

Powell, Edward. "Arbitration and the Law in England in the Late Middle Ages." *Transactions of the Royal Historical Society*, 5th ser., 33 (1983): 49–67.

————. *Kingship, Law and Society: Criminal Justice in the Reign of Henry V*. Oxford: Clarendon Press, 1989.

————. "Settlement of Disputes by Arbitration in Fifteenth-Century England." *Law and History Review* 2 (1984): 21–43.

Power, Eileen, and M. M. Postan, eds. *Studies in English Trade in the Fifteenth Century*. London: G. Routledge and Sons, Ltd., 1933.

Powers, James F. *A Society Organized for War: The Iberian Municipal Militias in the Central Middle Ages, 1000–1284*. Berkeley and Los Angeles: University of California Press, 1988.

Powicke, Michael. *Military Obligation in Medieval England*. Oxford: Clarendon Press, 1962.

Prestwich, Michael. *Armies and Warfare in the Middle Ages: The English Experience*. New Haven and London: Yale University Press, 1996.

————, ed. *York Civic Ordinances, 1301.* St. Anthony's Hall Publication, Borthwick Paper no. 49. York, 1976.

Prince, A. E. "The Strength of English Armies in the Reign of Edward III." *English Historical Review* 46 (1931): 353–57.

Pronay, Nicholas. "The Chancellor, the Chancery, and the Council at the End of the Fifteenth Century." In *British Government and Administration: Studies Presented to S. B. Chrimes,* edited by H. Hearder and H. R. Loyn, 87–103. Cardiff: University of Wales Press, 1974.

Pugh, Ralph B. *Imprisonment in Medieval England.* Cambridge: Cambridge University Press, 1968.

Pugh, T. B., and C. D. Ross. "The English Baronage and the Income Tax of 1436." *Bulletin of the Institute of Historical Research* 26 (1953): 1–28.

Radford, Cecily. "An Unrecorded Royal Visit to Exeter." *Transactions of the Devonshire Association* 63 (1931): 255–63.

Radford, Mrs. G. H. (Emma Louise, Lady Radford). "The Fight at Clyst in 1455." *Transactions of the Devonshire Association* 44 (1912): 253–65.

————. "Nicholas Radford." *Transactions of the Devonshire Association* 35 (1903): 251–78.

Raine, Angelo. *Medieval York.* London: John Murray, 1955.

Ramsay, G. D. *English Overseas Trade during the Centuries of Emergence.* London: Macmillan, 1957.

Ramsay, James F. *Lancaster and York.* 2 vols. Oxford: Clarendon Press, 1892.

Ramsey, Peter. "Overseas Trade in the Reign of Henry VII: The Evidence of Customs Accounts." *Economic History Review,* 2d series, 6 (1953–54): 173–82.

Rawcliffe, Carole, and Susan Flower. "English Noblemen and Their Advisers: Consultation and Collaboration in the Later Middle Ages." *Journal of British Studies* 25 (1986): 157–77.

————. "The Great Lord as Peacekeeper: Arbitration by English Noblemen and Their Councils in the Later Middle Ages." In *Law and Social Change in British History,* edited by J. A. Guy and H. G. Beale, 34–54. London: The Royal Historical Society, 1984.

————. "'That Kindliness Should be Cherished More, and Discord Driven Out': The Settlement of Commercial Disputes by Arbitration in Later Medieval England." In *Enterprise and Individuals in Fifteenth-Century England,* edited by Jennifer Kermode, 99–117. Gloucester: Alan Sutton Publishing, 1991.

Rees Jones, Sarah, ed. *The Government of Medieval York: Essays in Commemoration of the 1396 Royal Charter.* Borthwick Studies in History 3. York, 1997.

Reid, Rachel R. *King's Council in the North.* London: Longmans, Green and Company, 1921. Reprint. Totowa, N.J.: Rowman and Littlefield, 1975.

Reynolds, Susan. "Decline and Decay in Late Medieval Towns." *Urban History Yearbook 1980,* 76–78.

————. "The Forged Charters of Barnstaple." *English Historical Review* 84 (1969): 699–720.

————. *Ideas and Solidarities of the Medieval Laity: England and Western Europe* Aldershot: Variorum Press, 1995.

————. An Introduction to the History of English Medieval Towns. Oxford: Oxford University Press, 1977.

————. "Medieval Urban History and the History of Political Thought." Urban History Yearbook 1986, 14–23.

Richardson, H. G. The Medieval Fairs and Markets of York. St. Anthony's Hall Publication 20. York, 1961.

Richardson, W. C. Tudor Chamber Administration, 1485–1547. Baton Rouge: Louisiana State University Press, 1952.

Richmond, Colin. "English Naval Power in the Fifteenth Century." History 52 (1967): 1–15.

————. "Fauconberg's Kentish Rising of May 1471." English Historical Review 85 (1970): 673–92.

————. The Paston Family in the Fifteenth Century: Fastolf's Will. Cambridge: Cambridge University Press, 1996.

————. The Paston Family in the Fifteenth Century: The First Phase. Cambridge: Cambridge University Press, 1990.

Rigby, Stephen H. "English Provincial Towns in the Later Middle Ages." Economic History Review, 2d series, 34 (1981): 1–24.

————. "Late Medieval Urban Prosperity: The Evidence of the Lay Subsidies." Economic History Review, 2d series, 39 (1986): 411–16.

————. "Urban Decline in the Later Middle Ages: The Reliability of the Non-statistical Evidence." Urban History Yearbook 1984, 45–54.

Robbins, Edgar C. "The Cursed Norfolk Justice: A Defence of Sir William Yelverton (c.1400–1477)." Norfolk Archaeology 26 (1936): 1–51.

Roberts, S. Order and Dispute. Harmondsworth: Penguin, 1979.

Rosenthal, Joel. "Feuds and Private Peace-making: A Fifteenth-Century Example." Nottingham Mediaeval Studies 14 (1970): 84–90.

————, and Colin Richmond, eds. People, Politics and Community in the Later Middle Ages. Gloucester: Alan Sutton Publishing, 1987.

Roskell, J. S. The Commons in the Parliament of 1422. Manchester: Manchester University Press, 1954.

————, Linda Clark, and Carole Rawcliffe, eds. The History of Parliament: The House of Commons, 1386–1421. 4 vols. Stroud: Alan Sutton Publishing for the History of Parliament Trust, 1992.

Ross, Charles D. Edward IV. London: Eyre Methuen, 1974.

————, ed. Patronage, Pedigree and Power in Late Medieval England. Gloucester: Alan Sutton, 1979.

————. Richard III. London: Eyre Methuen, 1981.

Rosser, Gervase. Medieval Westminster 1200–1540. Oxford: Clarendon Press, 1989.

Rowney, Ian. "Arbitration in Gentry Disputes of the Later Middle Ages." History 67 (1982): 367–76.

Rubin, Miri. Charity and Community in Medieval Cambridge. Cambridge: Cambridge University Press, 1987.

————. Corpus Christi: The Eucharist in Late Medieval Culture. Cambridge: Cambridge University Press, 1991.

Rublack, Hans-Christoph. "Political and Social Norms in Urban Communities in the Holy Roman Empire." In *Religion, Politics and Social Protest: Three Studies on Early Modern Germany*, edited by Kaspar von Greyerz, 24–60. London: George Allen & Unwin, 1984.

Russell, Conrad. "English Land Sales, 1540–1640: A Comment on the Evidence." *Economic History Review*, 2d series, 25 (1972): 117–21.

Russell, Josiah C. *British Medieval Population*. Albuquerque: University of New Mexico Press, 1948.

Russo, Daniel G. *Town Origins and Development in Early England, c.400–950 A.D.* Westport and London: Greenwood Press, 1998.

Rutledge, Elizabeth. "Immigration and Population Growth in Early Fourteenth-Century Norwich: Evidence from the Tithing Roll." *Urban History Yearbook 1988*, 15–30.

Saul, Anthony. "English Towns in the Late Middle Ages: The Case of Great Yarmouth." *Journal of Medieval History* 8 (1982): 75–88.

Saul, Nigel. *Richard II*. New Haven and London: Yale University Press, 1997.

Sayer, Michael. "Norfolk Involvement in Dynastic Conflict 1469–71 and 1483–87." *Norfolk Archaeology* 36 (1977): 305–26.

Sayles, G. O. "Medieval Judges as Legal Consultants." *Law Quarterly Review* 56 (1940): 247–54.

Scofield, Cora L. *The Life and Reign of Edward the Fourth*. 2 vols. London: Longmans, Green and Company, 1923.

Sellers, Maude. "The City of York in the Sixteenth Century." *English Historical Review* 9 (1894): 275–304.

Shaw, David Gary. *The Creation of Community: The City of Wells in the Middle Ages*. Oxford: Clarendon Press, 1993.

Sheils, W. J., and Diana Wood, eds. *Voluntary Religion*. Studies in Church History, vol. 23. Oxford: Basil Blackwell, 1986.

Sherburne, J. W. "English Barges and Balingers of the Late Fourteenth Century." *Mariner's Mirror* 63 (1977): 109–14.

Slavin, Arthur J., ed. *Tudor Men and Institutions*. Baton Rouge: Louisiana State University Press, 1972.

Steel, Anthony. *Receipt of the Exchequer, 1377–1485*. Cambridge: Cambridge University Press, 1954.

Stenton, F. M. *Anglo-Saxon England*. 3d ed. Oxford and New York: Oxford University Press, 1989.

Stephens, W. B. "The Origins and Nature of the Exeter Town Customs Duties." *Devon and Cornwall Notes and Queries* 28 (1961): 246–50.

Storey, R. L. *The End of the House of Lancaster*. London: Barrie and Rockliff, 1966. Reprint. Gloucester: Alan Sutton Publishing, 1986.

Swanson, Heather. *Medieval Artisans: An Urban Class in Late Medieval England*. Oxford and New York: Basil Blackwell, 1989.

Thomas, Keith. *The Perception of the Past in Early Modern England*. The Creighton Trust Lecture. London: University of London, 1983.

Thompson, Benjamin, ed. *The Reign of Henry VII: Proceedings of the 1993 Harlaxton Symposium*. Stamford: Paul Watkins, 1995.

Thomson, John A. F. "The Courtenay Family in the Yorkist Period." *Bulletin of the Institute of Historical Research* 45 (1972): 230–46.

———. "John de la Pole, Duke of Suffolk." *Speculum* 54 (1979): 528–42.

———, ed. *Towns and Townspeople in the Fifteenth Century*. Gloucester: Alan Sutton Publishing, 1988.

———. *The Transformation of Medieval England 1370–1529*. London: Longmans, 1983.

Thrupp, Sylvia L. "A Survey of the Alien Population of England in 1440." *Speculum* 32 (1957): 262–73.

Tillot, P. M., ed. *The Victoria History of the Counties of England: A History of Yorkshire, The City of York*. London: Oxford University Press, 1961.

Tilsley, David. "Arbitration in Gentry Disputes: The Case of Bucklow Hundred in Cheshire, 1400–1465." In *Courts, Counties and the Capital in the Later Middle Ages*, edited by Diana E. S. Dunn, 53–70. New York: St. Martin's Press, 1996.

Tingey, John C. "The Grants of Murage to Norwich, Yarmouth, and Lynn." *Norfolk Archaeology* 18 (1913): 129–48.

Tittler, Robert. *Architecture and Power: The Town Hall and the English Urban Community c.1500–1640*. Oxford: Clarendon Press, 1991.

———. "The Incorporation of Boroughs, 1540–1558." *History* 62 (1977): 24–42.

———. *The Reformation and the Towns in England: Politics and Political Culture, c.1540–1640*. Oxford: Clarendon Press, 1998.

Tout, Thomas F. *Chapters in the Administrative History of Mediaeval England*. 6 vols. Manchester: Manchester University Press, 1920–33.

Turner, Hilary L. *Town Defences in England and Wales*. London: John Baker Ltd., 1971.

Virgoe, Roger. "The Divorce of Sir Thomas Tuddenham." *Norfolk Archaeology* 35 (1969): 406–18.

———. "A Norwich Taxation List of 1451." *Norfolk Archaeology* 40 (1989): 145–54.

———. "The Parliamentary Subsidy of 1450." *Bulletin of the Institute of Historical Research* 55 (1982): 124–38.

———. "The Recovery of the Howards in East Anglia, 1485–1529." In *Wealth and Power in Tudor England: Essays Presented to S. T. Bindoff*, edited by E. W. Ives, R. J. Knecht, and J. J. Scarisbrick, 1–20. London: Athlone Press, 1978.

Walker, Simon. *The Lancastrian Affinity 1361–1399*. Oxford: Clarendon Press, 1990.

Watts, John. *Henry VI and the Politics of Kingship*. Cambridge: Cambridge University Press, 1996.

Wedgwood, Josiah C. *History of Parliament: Biographies of the Members of the Commons House 1439–1509*. London: His Majesty's Stationery Office, 1936.

Weinbaum, Martin. *The Incorporation of Boroughs*. Manchester: Manchester University Press, 1937.

White, Eileen. *The York Mystery Play*. York: Ebor Press, 1984.

White, Stephen D. "'Pactum...Legum Vincit et Amor Judicium': The Settlement of Disputes by Compromise in Eleventh-Century Western France." *American Journal of Legal History* 22 (1978): 281–303.

Wilkinson, Bertie. *The Mediaeval Council of Exeter.* History of Exeter Research Group, Monograph 4. Manchester: Manchester University Press, 1931.

Willard, J. F. "The Scotch Raids and the Fourteenth-century Taxation of Northern England." *University of Colorado Studies* 5 (1908): 237–42.

———, and William A. Morris, eds. *Central and Prerogative Administration.* Vol. 1, *The English Government at Work 1327–1336.* Cambridge, Mass.: Mediaeval Academy of America, 1940.

———, William A. Morris, and W. H. Dunham, Jr., eds. *Local Administration.* Vol. 3, *The English Government at Work 1327–1336.* Cambridge, Mass.: Mediaeval Academy of America, 1950.

Williams, Neville. *Contraband Cargoes: Seven Centuries of Smuggling.* London: Longmans, 1959.

Wolffe, Bertram. *Henry VI.* London: Eyre Methuen, 1980.

———. *The Royal Demesne in English History.* London: George Allen and Unwin Ltd., 1971.

Wylie, J. H. *The History of England under Henry IV.* 4 vols. London: Longmans, 1884–98. Reprint. New York: AMS Press, 1969.

———. *The Reign of Henry V.* 3 vols. Cambridge: Cambridge University Press, 1914–29.

Youings, Joyce A. *Early Tudor Exeter: The Founders of the County of the City.* Exeter: University of Exeter Press, 1974.

———. *Tuckers Hall Exeter.* Exeter: University of Exeter Press, 1968.

Young, Charles R. *The English Borough and Royal Administration, 1130–1307.* Durham, N.C.: Duke University Press, 1961.

C. Dissertations

Allen, Bruce H. "The Administrative and Social Structure of the Norwich Merchant Class, 1485–1660." Ph.D. diss., Harvard University, 1951.

Barron, Caroline. "The Government of London and Its Relations with the Crown, 1400–1450." Ph.D. diss., University of London, 1970.

Cherry, Martin. "The Crown and the Political Community in Devonshire 1377–1461." Ph.D. diss., University College of Swansea, University of Wales, 1981.

Garrett-Goodyear, R. Harold. "Revival of Quo Warranto and Early Tudor Policy towards Local Governors, 1485–1540." Ph.D. diss., Harvard University, 1973.

Palliser, David. "Some Aspects of the Social and Economic History of York in the Sixteenth Century." D.Phil thesis, University of Oxford, 1968.

Schofield, R. S. "Parliamentary Lay Taxation 1485–1547." Ph.D. diss., University of Cambridge, 1963.

Wright, A. P. M. "The Relations between the King's Government and the English Cities and Boroughs in the Fifteenth Century." D.Phil. thesis, University of Oxford, 1965.

INDEX

S

St. Benet's, Holm, 117, 118, 219, 290, 292, 308n.32
St. Leger, Thomas, 81, 110
St. Mary's Abbey, York, 52, 120, 135n.106, 216, 256, 278n.64; abbot of, 123, 250, 256–59, 275n.30; liberty of, 256, 278n.67
Salisbury, earl of. *See* Neville family
Savage, Emma, 246
Savage, Sir John, 122, 147–48, 173n.30
Savage, Robert, 246
Savage, William, 246
Scales, 223. *See also* Weights and measures
Scales, Thomas de Scales, Lord, 118
Scarborough, 61n.2, 286
Scotland and the Scots: campaigns against, 14, 183, 202, 312n.92; king of, 79, 193, 196–97, 209n.73; prejudice against, 193, 209n.70; trade with, 233; troops for, 7, 27n.10, 82, 84, 144, 192–97, 209n.72; truces with, 197
Scrope, John, Lord of Bolton, 110, 201, 300
Scrope, Lords of Masham: Henry, 65n.42; Thomas, 201, 300
Scrope, Richard, Archbishop of York, 9, 79, 287–89, 307n.20, 318
Serjeants, royal, 39, 229
Serjeants-at-law, 53, 73, 106, 290
Sheriff Hutton, 123, 295
Sheriffs, urban, 24, 38, 40, 41, 42, 45, 65n.47, 146, 148, 217, 262, 264
Shillingford, John, 125, 217, 236n.40, 248, 265, 281n.106
Ships and shipping, 183, 191, 204n.10, 214. *See also* Barges; Pirates
Shrewsbury, George Talbot, earl of, 122
Simnel, Lambert, 184, 201, 300–301, 311n.77
Spain, monarchs of, 201, 212n.114

Spectacles, civic, 6, 72, 317; Henry VII and York, 84–90; of judicial punishment, 78–80, 304; planning and pageant planners, 77, 78, 86, 94n.33; Richard III and York, 81–84. *See also* Visits, royal
Sponer, John, 48
Stafford, Lord Henry, 111
Stafford, Humphrey, earl of Devonshire, 110
Stafford, John, Lord Chancellor, 125, 238n.54, 265–66
Star Chamber, council in, 8, 49, 52, 223, 226, 300; use of, 247, 249–51, 259, 263, 274n.27
Suffolk, duchesses of, dukes of, earls of. *See* Pole family
Surrey, earl of. *See* Howard family
Swordbearers, 54–55, 76
Swords, civic, 39, 41, 73; of Exeter, 77, 92n.10, 304; of Norwich, 92n.10

T

Tanghall, 136n.108
Tapton, Alice, 49
Taxes and tax collection, 197, 301. *See also* Lay subsidies
Tayllour, John, 60, 251, 275n.35, 312n.92
Thetford, 16
Thomas, Keith, 88
Thrisk, John, 51
Tolls: freedom from, 225–26, 288; for murage, 185; scavage, 226–27, 250; on trade, 13, 14, 16, 18, 20, 25, 26, 84, 143, 147
Tong, John, 48
Topsham, 105
Toppes, Robert, 59, 308n.26
Town, defined, 4
Trade and commerce, profits of, 8, 145–46, 214, 233–34. *See also* Customs; Fairs and markets;

Merchants; Tolls; Weights and
measures; Weirs
Trent, river, 25, 214–15
Trial by battle, 79
Tuddenham, Sir Thomas, 115, 116,
117, 132n.70, 279n.87, 290, 293
Tunstall, Sir Richard, 123

V

Vavasour, John, 53
Vere family, earls of Oxford: John de,
12th earl (d.1462), 292; John de,
13th earl (d.1513), 117, 119,
210n.90, 302
Vicars choral. *See* York Minster
Violence, 9, 18, 260, 262, 274n.28,
283–84, 294, 305–306; during
elections, 251–52, 259, 285, 291;
in Exeter, 296–300, 303–304; in
Norwich, 289, 291–92, 308n.26;
in Nottingham, 294, 300;
prosecution of, 249; in York, 284–
89; 295–96, 300–303. *See also*
Great Revolt (1381)
Visits, royal, 5–6, 71, 77; to Exeter,
77–79, 81, 299; gifts for, 76,
96n.62, 144; to Norwich, 16, 19,
74–77, 80, 220–21; to
Nottingham, 25, 79, 121, 255;
preparations for, 74–75, 83, 86; to
York, 76–84, 86–90
Vowell, John. *See* Hoker

W

Walls and gates: defensive purposes,
184–86; murage grants, 185,
206n.25, 307n.17. *See also*
Defenses
Wapentake. *See* Ainsty
Warbeck, Perkin, 184, 196–97, 201,
300, 303–304

Wars of the Roses, 7, 9, 71, 80–81,
181, 294–304; troops and
supplies, 197–201
Warwick, earls of: Richard Neville
(d.1471), 81, 121, 183, 186, 299;
Thomas Beauchamp (d.1401),
105, 112
Weights and measures, 222–23,
237n.43. *See also* Scales
Weinbaum, Martin, 38
Weirs, fishweirs, 22–23, 120, 214–17
Welles, John, 291
Wensum, river, 214
Westmorland, Ralph Neville, earl of,
120
Wetherby, Thomas, 219, 289–93,
307n.22, 308n.26
White, William, 303
William of Malmesbury, 22
Willoughby, Henry, 122, 309n.45
Willoughby de Broke, Robert, Lord,
111
Wilton, Henry, 57
Wine, 23, 137, 170, 191, 239n.76
Winter, John, 112–13
Wolsey, Thomas, Cardinal, 37, 248,
251, 264, 275n.33
Woodville family: Anthony, Earl
Rivers, 118, 209n.73, 220;
Elizabeth, queen of England, 77,
93n.32, 172n.16
Wool, 15, 25; and wool staple, 17, 25,
252
Worcester, 86, 88, 89
Wrangwish, Thomas, 54, 73. 301–302
Writs, quashing of, 115, 131n.60, 262,
279n.83

Y

Yelverton, William, 115, 116, 292
York, archbishop of, 14, 52, 55, 217,
255, 259, 277n.56; arbitration of,
257, 295